Michael Volpe

Bullied To Death: Chris Mackney's Kafkaesque Divorce

Written by Michael Volpe
Edited by Michelle MacDonald
Cover Photo Design Janice Wolk Grenadier
Published by FAMILYcourt.com, INC

Foreword	2
Introduction	4
Chapter 1: The Suicide of Chris Mackney	5
Chapter 2: Christopher Hines Machnij	31
Chapter 3: The Murder of Sam Degelia, Jr.	36
Chapter 4: The Marriage	60
Chapter 5: The Divorce	64
Chapter 6: Dr. Samenow and His Bogus Evaluation	87
Chapter 7: Techniques for Devious People in Family Court	106
Chapter 8: The Child Support Hustle	138
Chapter 9: The Unheard Epidemic	146
Chapter 10: Legal Abuse Syndrome	164
Chapter 11: Family Court Corruption and the Media	176
Chapter 12: Would a Guardian Ad Litem Have Saved Chris Mackney?	197
Chapter 13: Conclusion	208
Acknowledgements	228
Appendix	**230**
Good Men Did Nothing	231
Samenow's Evaluation	296
Chris Mackney's Complaint to ACFEI	328
Email from Chris Mackney to Kyle Bartol, November 20, 2013	335
Email Exchange between Chris Mackney and "Mitch Jefferson" July 2013	339
Dr. William Zuckerman's Psychological Evaluation of Chris Mackney	352
Exit Letter from Robert Surovell to Jim Cottrell and Kyle Bartol	371
Marc Randazza letter to Rachelle Hill	374

Foreword

"I am at once taunted and threatened with poverty. That I can bear. I can school myself to worse than that: but my two children are taken away from me by legal procedure. That is, and always will remain to me, a source of infinite distress, of infinite pain, of grief without end or limit. That the law should decide and take upon itself to decide that I am one unfit to be with my own children is something quite horrible to me. The disgrace of prison is nothing compared with it. I envy the other men who tread the yard along with me. I am sure that their children wait for them, look for their coming, will be sweet to them."

Oscar Wilde from *DeProfundis*

Attorney Michelle MacDonald, FAMILYcourt.com, INC

The book you hold in your hands by investigative reporter Michael Volpe is by far the most significant of the thousands of true court stories that comprise my thirty years of family law practice. Dina Mackney's father, Pete Scamardo, pays known hit man -Woody Harrelson's dad- to kill his business partner and childhood friend. Afterwards, he visits and comforts the grieving widow.

But why is the 1968 murder of Sam Degelia, Jr. important to Chris Mackney's 21st century divorce story?

After the murder, Scamardo gets prosecuted, found guilty, but gets no jail time. He leaves Texas for Virginia, where nobody knows about the murder. He starts a small business putting siding on homes and becomes a multimillionaire, touted in business magazines.

His daughter, Dina, an infant when her dad had his friend murdered, lives off her dad's money when she meets Chris "Machnij". They marry shortly after and Chris works for his father-in-law, and starts seeing behind the façade.

In Michael Volpe's riveting book, you learn the power to sue is the power to punish, delay and devastate. As the divorce unfolds, Chris Mackney confronts his wife about the murder, and the next day she hires a divorce lawyer who advertises "he's not the type to settle so have your wallet open."

Then, Chris Mackney's father-in-law repeats history by arranging hired guns -lawyers, custody evaluators, judges and others - to destroy the father of his grandchildren, who ends up dead.

Michael Volpe

But even Chris Mackney's death doesn't stop the legal bullying. Dina's lawyer gets a Judge to name her executor of his estate, ignoring Chris Mackney's last request to leave his only possession- besides the gun he used, and the car he did it in - a laptop computer, to his brother, so that TWO murders, and a father's existence, are erased from cyberspace.

But what these bullies didn't count on is investigative reporter, Michael Volpe, who knew that Chris Mackney had painstakingly recorded every detail of his ordeal on that laptop, as a husband and father hunted and marked for certain death because his wife wanted to divorce him. Michael Volpe has the data that proves family court is corrupt and their dad was bullied to death, preserved in his epic book.

I say epic because on September 11, 2013, around the time Michael Volpe began to research the corruption you'll read about here, Chris Mackney was in jail in Virginia, and I had just filed a federal civil rights lawsuit against a Judge on behalf of a bullied mother. The next day, I was arrested, tortured and jailed for taking a picture of a deputy during a break in a child custody trial, another story Michael Volpe exposed. It's business as usual in family court.

While Michael Volpe, author of *Prosecutors Gone Wild* and *The Definitive Dossier of PTSD in Whistleblowers* had begun probing child protection and corrupt custody evaluators, he was busy with Obamacare stories. Michael Volpe's mind was on another topic that captured the world's attention. But once he turned his attention to research for this book, after interviews with hundreds of people, he figured out that litigants like Chris Mackney and attorneys, like me, who represent hundreds like him, are experiencing Kafkaesque divorce processes, with lots of Machiavellians, and gas-lighting: all words you'll come to understand very well by the time you finish this book.

And when the children act out, it's not because of the trauma they experience when their mom and dad divorce. As Michael Volpe points out, the adversarial court process destroys families and its' engineers take no responsibility.

Poverty stricken, and told if he leaves the state and never sees his kids again, he'll be left alone, the SWAT team extradites him back, to spend months in jail until he's acquitted by a jury. Suicidal, with no money to pay millionaires, Chris Mackney's threatened some more. Here Michael Volpe exposes the Debtors' Prison that is our child support enforcement system.

Chris Mackney's murder was deliberate. The thought of going back to jail pushed him over the edge, It wasn't just the judges the court system aiding and abetting every step of the way. Michael Volpe's book reveals that nearly everybody's hands are bloody in this.

Michael Volpe's book will undoubtedly change the way you view family and family court. When you've completed *Bullied to Death*, you will have a new perspective on what's possible as you bear witness to the hideous display of inhumanity to each other that has evolved. Chris Mackney was determined to survive against literally impossible odds in order to tell his story, to be the agent for ushering a new consciousness.

Bullied to Death: Chris Mackney's Kafkaesque Divorce

Michael Volpe couldn't write this story in time to save Chris Mackney's life. But his book will spare millions, and bring awareness to the masses. This book sprung from his tenaciousness and, perhaps, guilt. Nearly every day, people are bullied in family court. The emotional and financial destruction that is family court can take away your home, money, kids, job, dignity and ultimately the will to live. How many of these stories are covered?

I have come to know Michael Volpe very, very well over the past few months- in fact we communicate on a daily basis. He has been telling Chris' story to audiences numbering in the thousands. Chris Mackney wrote he was being bullied to death, and Michael Volpe felt compelled to reconstruct his blog - Good Men Did Nothing, and get his message to the world.

Michael Volpe weaves dozens of other true family court stories of bear minimum survival. The very first moment I heard him tell Chris Mackney's story, I knew that he'd nailed it, something that will be evident when you finish this book. It's a message of survival in that countless others bullied to death by the legal -not justice- system will go on living to tell about it.

Michael Volpe didn't seek FAMILYcourt.com, INC out for assistance in having this book published. We did the seeking. I told him I would support his project in every way possible: not only would I edit the book and write the forward, but I'd also do everything in my power to bring Chris Mackney's saga to the public eye. And all of this was done because of the feeling I had when I first heard him on the radio in the first few moments.

Chris Mackney's story will touch you deeply. How could this happen? Where does such animosity come from? Chris Mackney was not left to tell this mind-blowing story.

Because of Michael Volpe, it was not "until death do us part" for Chris Mackney. I am honored to play a role in bringing Chris Mackney's and other family court stories to the attention of the world.

Attorney Michelle MacDonald, FAMILYcourt.com, INC.

Introduction

"The love that my daughter and I shared was truly special. She is such a sweet, kind and gentle spirit. I am so sorry that I will not be there to see her grow into a beautiful woman. It absolutely crushed me to not be in her life over the last three years… My son was just entering kindergarten when I lost access to him. He is gregarious, outgoing and a great athlete. He is smart and fearless. He could have just as much fun by himself as he could with other kids. Even the older boys in our neighborhood wanted to play with him. It absolutely breaks my heart that I will not be able to help him grow into a man."

Chris Mackney from his suicide note

…

Michael Volpe

At about 7PM on February 4, 2014 I received this email from an editor at a news website about Chris Mackney's story: "I did my best, but my managers have declined your story entirely."

Prior to receiving the email, I presumed they were about to publish his story into article, but my best chance for such an article was suddenly dashed. For much of the previous week I'd rewritten this article until I thought I finally found a version which worked. Seven hours earlier this editor sent me what I thought was the final copy for publication.

I've had stories denied by editors but none edited and approved by an editor only to be denied by some nameless manager from above. This was a whole new phenomenon.

From the moment I received the final copy until the denial, I thought my involvement in Chris Mackney's story ended. I was content to publish this article and move on to the next story, but this email gave me an epiphany; the media doesn't want to hear about family court abuse. I set out to prove these nameless and faceless managers wrong.

Bullied to Death: Chris Mackney's Kafkaesque Divorce was born.

Chapter 1: The Suicide of Chris Mackney

"The only difference between a suicide and a martyrdom really is the amount of press coverage."

Chuck Palahniuk, author of the book *Fight Club*

…

The Last Days of Chris Mackney

Christmas Eve 2013 was a festive time for all except Chris Mackney who had suicide on his mind and less than one hundred twenty hours to live. While his children eagerly anticipated the arrival of Santa, he was spending the holiday alone, the fourth straight Christmas where a court order forbade him from having any contact with them. He spent the evening composing his suicide note, and published it on the World Wide Web for the world to see, uploading the note as a blog post- *Bullied to Death* -on his website, *Good Men Did Nothing*, which chronicled his nightmarish divorce and first went online that November 20th. The name chosen for the site is from the famous quote by Irish author and philosopher Edmund Burke, "all that is necessary for evil to triumph is for good men to do nothing."

"The pain from the emotional abuse, psychological abuse, parental alienation and legal abuse has been unbearable. My children and I were abused and when we spoke out and no one did anything. No one. Not the attorneys, doctors or Judges." Mackney began his 3,449 word suicide note. "They all recognized the patterns of behavior and the source of conflict and turned a blind eye and then blocked me from bringing in a third party or Guardian Ad Litem to identify the abuse. At any point throughout this case, if the Court had ruled in my favor on any of my motions, the outcome would have been different. At any point, if my ex-wife had shown ANY kind of act of good faith, the outcome would have been different. The facts are that not one of my motions was ever granted by the Court and my ex-wife never once acted in good faith."

Mackney was living in one room in the basement of an old church, with electricity but no heat while it was being renovated into condominiums by a company owned by friend, Terry Hindermann. While the room had few amenities the rental rate - nothing- was all Mackney could afford, and he told almost no one where he was living. While Mackney's ex-wife lived in a spacious million dollar home they once shared, he lived with a space heater, television set, and air mattress: a bed was too expensive.

The suicide note sat idle and unnoticed by anyone, including me, for five more days. I'm Michael Volpe, an investigative journalist who first spoke with Mackney in late October 2013 for a project on family court abuse. I spent November putting Mackney off to work on other projects I deemed more important at the time, namely stories related to the failed rollout of the Affordable Care Act. I took his story more seriously in December and at the end of the month was nearly ready to present an article on his story, known as "pitching" in journalism, to an editor. Still, my timeframe and Mackney's for writing his story were far apart, and I believe he died viewing me as a good man who did nothing, a thought which has brought me great sadness and motivation.

The suicide note wasn't the last post Mackney wrote for his website. Later that evening, Mackney published a post entitled *Emotional Invalidation- My Concern for My Children which Was Completely Ignored.* He also wrote the post *No Presents from Dad*, with these two paragraphs being the last thing he wrote on the blog on Christmas Day.

My wife has not let me see or speak to my children in over 3 years. She has blocked all communication and the court has blocked all access to their teachers and doctors, despite the fact that there has been no abuse.

My children get no presents from dad this year. Merry Christmas James and Ruby. It's in your best interest that you get no presents from your father.

(Ruby and James are pseudonyms for Mackney's two children: the birth names of my favorite actress and actor; long and complex quotes will be in italics.)

"Now, the only additional protection granted to my ex-wife was the ability to put me in jail for contacting my children by sending them a letter or sending them a birthday or Christmas card." Mackney said explaining the title of his blog.

(Photo inside Mackney's room in the final two months of his life courtesy of Terry Hindermann)

Mackney's ex-wife, Dina, claimed a protective order was necessary because she feared Chris Mackney, but didn't fear her father, who once ordered the murder of his friend.

Chris Mackney also left a comment on the website Marilynstowe.co.uk, behind an article entitled *High Court judge warns of damaging feuds between parents*, on Christmas Day. The article featured Judge Mary Parker warning parents about manipulating kids in custody battles.

"Parents who obstruct the relationship with either mother or father are inflicting untold damage on their children and it's about time the professionals truly understood this." Parker said. "I regard parental manipulation of children, of which I distressingly see an enormous amount, as exceptionally harmful."

"Bravo to Judge Parker! More Judges need to start speaking out like this." Mackney responded in the comments section. "My case is as bad as it gets because the judges involved refused to acknowledge patterns of alienation and abuse. The more people who call it abuse the sooner the abuse will end."

Mackney last communicated with me on December 26, 2013, sending an email showing how he got the run around when he approached places like the American Psychological Association (APA), the Virginia Board of Psychology and the American College of Forensic Examiners International (ACFEI) to hold the psychiatrist in his case, Dr. Stanton Samenow, accountable.

I also wanted to point out that when I contacted the ACFEI about Dr. Samenow they said they would investigate complaints about its members. Then when I got into the details of the complaint, they claimed that they could not investigate complaints. They said that if the State Board of Psychology would find him unethical, then his membership with the ACFEI would come into question. The problem is that the State BOP does not investigate 'ethical' complaints. They are only responsible for the laws in which they are empowered to govern, which are strictly licensing related. The Licensing laws that the BOP enforces do not have anything to do with ethics or Standards of Practice; they made that clear when they denied my complaint.

The Board of Psychology will tell you to file a complaint for ethics or standards of practice with the APA or ACFEI and the APA and ACFEI will tell you file a complaint with the BOP.

When I challenged the ACFEI to hold Dr. Samenow accountable I got the runaround from their lawyer.

"Good stuff, I'll check it out." I responded nonchalantly; Chris Mackney had less than seventy two hours left to live.

During the last days of his life, Mackney had an on and off text message conversation with his friend Jill Peterson Mitchell, the ex-wife of Dina Mackney's longtime boyfriend, Bryan Mitchell. Bryan Mitchell and Dina Mackney went out for several years including living together but

Michael Volpe

broke up in the beginning of 2015. In the text messages, which carried on from December 23-28, Mackney talked about pain, sadness, and suicide; here are the relevant texts, with their date and times.

I don't have money, or a place to live, and I can't even focus to work. I need relief and can't get it. 8.59PM Eastern Time (ET) on December 23, 2013

They won't stop. 8:41PM ET on December 23, 2013

They'll come after me. 8:44PM ET December 23, 2013

There is no escape. 8:44PM Eastern Time December 23, 2013

Child support enforcement....Will garnish....Trust me, Virginia will. I pissed off too many people. 8:47-8:50PM ET December 23, 2013

It's too late. I really can't do it anymore. I wish I was stronger. 8:54PM ET December 23, 2013

I'm surprised I hung on as long as I did. 8:55 PM ET December 23, 2013

I'm just tired of fighting. My memory sucks from PTSD. 9:25PM ET December 23, 2013

I just want the pain to end. It hurts too much, all the time. I was a good dad, and they knew that; it's so sick. 9:29 PM ET December 23, 2013

Talked to suicide lady...no help. 3:47PM ET December 24, 2013

They (suicide hotline) can't do shit. 11:12 PM ET December 24, 2013

Bought the shotgun shells today. Check out the videos for the movie, Divorce Corp on YouTube. December 26, 2013 6:00PM ET

I told him (Bryan Mitchell) I would do it (commit suicide) if Dina did not lower my child support or some other act of good faith. December 26 6:04PM ET

They have made my life unlivable. 7:35PM ET December 26, 2013

Please just accept it; I have. 7:40PM ET December 26, 2013

I'm tired of living like this and being abused. 7:46PM ET December 26, 2013

It's only going to get worse. I've kicked the hornet's nest. 7:48PM ET December 26, 2013

I choose not to live as a slave to them. 8:16PM ET December 26, 2013

Hours before his suicide, Officer Hakaan Karaali of the Washington D.C. Metropolitan Police Department (DCMPD) checked on Mackney's welfare, after a tip from the Fairfax County Police following reports he might be suicidal.

R-1(unidentified Fairfax police officer) reports that C-1(Chris Mackney) has been going thru a long custody battle with his ex-wife over their children in common. C-1 lost the custody battle and started to act erratically and started sending emails to everyone that was involved with the court process, that he was going to hurt himself.

R-1 also stated that for the last four days prior to this report date, C-1 actually stated that he was going to commit suicide. R-1 of Fairfax County Police Department asked MPD to check on the welfare of C-l at the possible location that they tracked thru C-1's cellphone.

Officer Karaali didn't find Mackney at the church, filed an incident report, and nothing more.

Machiavellianism

Mackney created a final blog post on the day of his suicide, linking to an article on the website *Illimitable Men* entitled *Utilizing the Dark Triad- Psychopathy* published on that site a day prior covering themes which repeated themselves in his story. Mackney was convinced that his former wife's father Pete Scamardo —who literally got away with murder – exhibited the clinical characteristics of a psychopath, and attributed much of his torment to him: "All psychopaths are Machiavellians, but not all Machiavellians are psychopaths. You can learn some of the traits psychopaths use by utilizing stoicism to emulate psychopathic traits," according to the blog post. "Not all proficiently Machiavellian individuals are psychopathic, but almost all psychopaths are Machiavellian."

The story Mackney linked to in his final blog post takes its name, *The Dark Triad*, from a paper which popularized the term by Delroy Paulhus and Kevin Williams. Here's part of the paper.

"The three members –Machiavellianism, narcissism and subclinical psychopathy – often show differential correlates but share a common core of callous manipulation."

Machiavellianism is defined as "the employment of cunning and duplicity in statecraft or in general conduct," according to the *Oxford English Dictionary*, and Scamardo is an especially Machiavellian person who spent the days immediately following the murder ingratiating himself with his victim's family, including the victim's widow, calling routinely, bringing food, and even being part of a search party for the man he had murdered.

"One has to remark that men ought either to be well treated or crushed, because they can avenge themselves of lighter injuries, of more serious ones they cannot; therefore the injury that is to be done to a man ought to be of such a kind that one does not stand in fear of revenge." Niccolo Machiavelli, the man for whom the term is named, wrote in *The Prince* about the ruthlessness of Machiavellians.

Mackney spent the last five and a half years being victimized by the family court system at the behest of Scamardo, which saw Mackney lose four jobs, jailed four times, and forced to move out of Virginia and back to Virginia over the last year of his life.

Michael Volpe

Chris Mackney's Kafkaesque Divorce

The stew of this Machiavellian individual in bed with several corrupt courts -namely family court- created Chris Mackney's Kafkaesque divorce.

"Someone must have been telling lies about Josef K., he knew he had done nothing wrong but, one morning, he was arrested," began Franz Kafka's *The Trial*.

Here's Frederick Karl, a Kafka biographer from *The New York Times*.

What's Kafkaesque, it is when you enter a surreal world in which all your control patterns, all your plans, the whole way in which you have configured your own behavior, begins to fall to pieces, when you find yourself against a force that does not lend itself to the way you perceive the world.

You don't give up; you don't lie down and die. What you do is struggle against this with all of your equipment, with whatever you have. But of course you don't stand a chance. That's Kafkaesque.

"I could fill a book with all the lies and mysterious rulings of the court," Mackney said in his suicide note summing up his Kafkaesque divorce.

As one example, the court downplayed and ignored Scamardo's murder calling Mackney "obsessed" with it and a court order forbade him from speaking about it referring to facts as allegations.

Family courts throughout the world can be quite Kafkaesque; here's a story from Britain from *The Daily Telegraph* published on December 15, 2014.

A father who was banned from his own street, cut off from his children for five months, with no opportunity to defend himself, and then arrested for text messaging his son, was treated like a character from a Kafka novel, a senior judge has admitted.

…

His ordeal began in June when he came home from work "as normal" to find that a Deputy District Judge had imposed the strict non-molestation order at the request of his wife of 20 years during a five-minute hearing.

…

Although the order was originally intended only for a few days, it remained in place for five months because backlogs in the court system meant he could not even get a date for a hearing to challenge it until September.

During that time he was arrested and charged with a technical breach involving the fact he had not left immediately on the night he first learnt of the order and later text-messaged his son – something which was not even forbidden.

Mr R, who is described as having a "responsible" job, was then brought before magistrates and allowed to plead guilty to the charge, without having had legal advice.

Here's a story out of Canada about a woman who tried to keep her child away from her molesting ex.

"It was like one professional described it: 'Kafkaesque' is the best term that comes to mind. It's as if the people involved were just twisting everything," the mother said.

Jack Hittrich, the mother's lawyer, says the Ministry of Children and Family Development was negligent, reckless, and acted in bad faith.

"When mom was frantically trying to convince the ministry that the sexual abuse allegations were real, they basically labelled her as crazy. And the more she protested, the more she was labelled as being crazy," he said. "It's a horrific nightmare."

Crazy is what victims of a Kafkaesque family court nightmare are often called.

Chris Mackney's Last Day

Chris Mackney made his last public statement on his Facebook page linking back to the suicide note. "I'm sorry. I wish I was stronger," he wrote at 2:43 AM ET on December 29, 2013.

Several friends responded with messages like Kevin Ogleby at 3:29PM ET the same day: "Chris, let's talk about this. There is a way out," but Mackney's suicide was a *fait accompli*.

That day, Chris Mackney got into his car, drove to East Potomac Park in Washington D.C., and in his parked car put a rifle underneath his chin, pulled the trigger, and blew his head off; he had to be identified by fingerprints. In the car, he left a note instructing authorities to hand over his laptop which he left in the passenger seat to his brother, Jeff.

The Bible refers to suicide as the unpardonable sin, but it could have been worse. Mourad Samaan of California killed his daughter Madeline before killing himself in 2011 shortly after being served with a court order giving his ex-wife sole custody.

Brian Benedict, a military veteran murdered his ex-wife on the campus of the University of California Irvine on September 9, 2009 after a judge doubled his child support to $920 per month even though he'd recently gone from making $80,000 yearly working for Northrop Grumman to making $26,000 yearly as a research assistant during graduate school. Benedict was convicted of first degree murder on August 7, 2014 and will spend the rest of his life in prison.

It could also have ended better. Mackney's good friend Rich Ware repeatedly told him to sneak across the border and start over in Mexico because "it's better than putting a rifle underneath your chin."

He couldn't leave the country legally by this point because past due child support forbade him from getting a passport.

The Aftermath

On New Year's Eve, Dina Mackney informed friends and family of Mackney's suicide in a group email; in the email she blamed the suicide on an unspecified mental illness. Her contention that Mackney had some sort of unspecified mental illness was one she repeated many times throughout the divorce.

"Dear Friends, I cannot imagine why Chris is including you on this type of email again, again and again; however, you must realize by now that **Chris has lost touch with reality (emphasis mine).**" Dina Mackney said in a separate email to friends. "I sincerely hope that Chris gets the mental health help he needs and that he stops involving you soon."

Those sentiments were echoed by Mackney's children; shortly after his suicide, they told Jill Peterson Mitchell's children that it didn't matter that he was dead "because he was crazy anyway," according to her recollection.

The next order of business was the laptop with hundreds of documents related to the marriage, the divorce, and the murder involving Pete Scamardo saved on it.

Days after the suicide, Jeff was contacted by the DCMPD to pick it up in person at the police station. Jeff was informed that Dina already stopped by the station to secure the laptop but was told Jeff was next of kin. Dina made at least one more unsuccessful attempt to secure the laptop. Because Jeff lived in California, he sent a letter authorizing Mike Harris, an old friend of Chris Mackney's who lived in the Virginia area, to retrieve the laptop for him.

While the logistics of Mackney's dying wish were unfolding, Dina Mackney's attorneys apparently with the help of the Washington DC Office of Attorney General (DCOAG) and a Virginia judge made Dina executor of Mackney's estate (amounting to his car and laptop) as the mother of his children because he died without a will. She used that authorization to secure the laptop. The whereabouts of the laptop remain unknown to Mackney's relatives and friends. Ted Gest, spokesperson for the DCOAG, said, "The property was released to the wife under a valid court order."

While Dina Mackney may have been made executor of his estate, nothing is valid. When I asked Mr. Gest to explain why Chris Mackney's dying wish was ignored by DC authorities he said, "We do not as a matter of policy discuss our legal advice to D.C. government agencies -it is given confidentially."

As the church lady might say, "How convenient!"

I asked the DCMPD for an explanation, sending Gwendolyn Crump, the Director of their Office of Communications, an early draft of this portion of the book by email on September 24, 2014. Six days later, I received this response, "The executor of the decedent's estate (Dina) may contact us."

"That statement makes you sound corrupt, if that's a problem shouldn't the people expect the DCMPD to be the one to reach out, can you deny you've just made a revealing admission?" I told Crump in an email hours later.

The next day, I called for comment; she refused to speak to me, saying all further communications would be by email. When an updated version of the book was emailed simultaneously to Crump, Dina Mackney, and Pete Scamardo, none responded and Ms. Crump subsequently told me she'd say nothing more on this matter.

The DCMPD has refused to answer any questions for this book, making "The executor of the decedent's estate may contact us," their only official statement.

Dina Mackney and her father failed to respond to more than thirty email requests each for comment. Dina Mackney has noticed me, blocking my twitter account from viewing hers, depriving me the titillation of tweets promoting her jewelry company, Dina Mackney Designs.

The "grieving widow" was just getting started. As Chris Mackney's family was preparing his funeral, Dina's legal team threatened them with legal action if Mackney's blog, *Good Men Did Nothing,* wasn't removed from the internet, which it was on January 24, 2014.

Before *Good Men Did Nothing* disappeared, several people, including me, copied his blog and saved it on our computers. I've also recovered many, though not all, of the documents stored on Mackney's computer and they formed the basis of much of this book.

As a fiduciary for their children, Dina Mackney is not allowed to destroy the laptop but obligated to turn it over to James and Ruby when they turn 18: though I'm certain Hell won't be frozen over when they are of age.

The Suicide Note Resurfaces

Mackney's note first resurfaced on Henry Makow's website, *Save the Males*, in February 2014 after I passed it anonymously (until now) to him. Makow dutifully protected my anonymity throughout the process.

Makow lives in Canada. When he was eleven, he had a syndicated column in about fifty newspapers and made millions in the 1980s with his board game Scruples: "a board game based on ethical dilemmas" according to its Wikipedia page.

It's etched into popular culture psyche after being the subject of two bits on the *Tonight Show with Johnny Carson* as well as the centerpiece of the plot in the first season episode of the hit show *Everybody Loves Raymond* entitled *The Game*.

Makow is now a college professor, author, and conspiracy theorist with thousands of followers believing in the dominance of the Illuminati.

"The West is controlled by Masonic Jewish banking interests (the Illuminati)...**Family law makes marriage dangerous for men, disempowers them and encourages single mothers to raise children alone without fathers (emphasis mine)**...It breaks up the family, a long time (Illuminati and Communist) goal. Divide and conquer along gender lines."

The note had a nice response on Makow's site and popped up on about fifteen websites throughout the months of February, March and April of 2014, including the forum of the men's rights group, A Voice for Men (AVFM).

The Copyright Notice

With no more news about his suicide to report, Chris Mackney was fading into obscurity until Dina Mackney set off a chain of events which turned him into a martyr. With the assistance of Rachelle E Hill of the Virginia law firm, Bean, Kinney and Korman, Dina Mackney successfully argued in an Arlington County, Virginia court of Judge James Almand in March 2014 that as executor of his estate she should have copyright over all his work, including the suicide note, not for exclusive commercial use, but to destroy and eliminate from cyberspace.

ORDERED AND DECREED that Petitioner shall have the legal authority to take any reasonable action necessary to access, remove and destroy any web postings, to require that websites be taken down and/or otherwise dispose of intangible property including but not limited to information that the deceased has posted online on any website or social media account.

...

And to wind down and remove any website posts or other online activity by the decedent at such time and in such direction as the Administrator may deem appropriate, it being the intent that this Order shall apply to any online activity by the decedent during his lifetime.

Almand's order included a plethora of documents which Mackney turned into web pages using Google Docs and other platforms which turn PDFs and Word documents into web pages. Even the photo which graced Mackney's Facebook page was deemed Dina Mackney's property and set for destruction. Many of these documents were hyperlinks which he'd created inside his suicide note and other posts in his blog. These documents included email correspondences, court orders, court transcripts, and other documentation which he used to build his case that he was bullied to death. These hyperlinks have since been removed from the internet as a result of the copyright purge though I've restored many of them as new hyperlinks and Ms. Hill has not used this order to challenge their continued existence in cyberspace.

Dina Mackney took control of the laptop, bullied his family into removing *Good Men Did Nothing*, and got a copyright notice for the sole purpose of removing anything he ever wrote from cyberspace. Dina Mackney wasn't merely attempting to remove Chris Mackney from cyber existence; she was trying to remove any evidence of their divorce, now sealed by the court, from public view.

"Will you log into my email and blog?" Mackney asked in a text message at 9:37PM ET to Jill Peterson Mitchell on December 27, 2013.

"Will you do it? Dina will try to get it deleted…I give you the log-ins and it will look like the site is still active…Otherwise Dina will get them shut down," Mackney said in a prescient manner minutes later.

"Not if you kill yourself, I reject that option for you." Jill Peterson Mitchell finally responded fatefully soon after.

In April 2014, armed with this copyright, Dina Mackney's attorneys began bullying websites into removing the suicide note.

Please be advised that this firm represents Dina Mackney, individually, as Administrator of the Estate of Christopher Hines Machnij a/k/a Christopher Hines Mackney (the "Estate") and as mother of minor children James and Ruby Mackney, both under age 13 (hereinafter, the "Minor Children").

We hereby provide notice of copyright infringement pursuant to the terms of the Digital Millennium Copyright Act (the "Act") and privacy violations (including the divulgence of information pertaining to Minor Children) regarding the unauthorized publication of information subject to doctor-patient confidentiality. Enclosed are the offending materials, showing unauthorized use of the Estate's copyrighted material and publication of an extremely sensitive matter.

Several websites, including Scribd complied with the judge's order immediately and removed the note. Every document relating to this case which Chris Mackney downloaded using Google Docs was removed from the internet soon after.

The people Chris Mackney blamed for bullying him to death were bullying him in death. Had Ms. Hill been successful, a handful of professional related pages would be all to immortalize Chris Mackney in cyberspace.

The order was so expansive it included sites where Chris Mackney left comments in their comment sections like on Marilyn Stowe's site. In such cases, the website has an explicit right to carry all comments in perpetuity; thus a copyright notice, especially one ordered months after publication, is worthless. Since Marilyn Stowe is based in England, the court order is even less effective.

The court order included the websites Wikipedia and MurderPedia. Both of these would presumably cover Pete Scamardo's involvement in a murder and those details will be discussed fully in an upcoming chapter.

The folks at MurderPedia didn't respond to my email but Jay Walsh, the press representative for Wikipedia said they hadn't received a takedown notice and one is worthless because all work on that site is "immediately placed under a creative commons license," meaning no one can claim copyright.

What was Dina trying to accomplish? Here's what one prescient commenter said on the site Tech Dirt.

"They're simply throwing everything at the wall in the hope that something will 'stick', where 'stick' does NOT mean stand up in court, but simply work to win *voluntary* compliance with the request. That's all they're hoping for, as that's all they're legally entitled to. The sites may well comply not because they're not sure they'd win in court, but because they simply don't care enough about the content posted by this one user to pay even one lawyer to fight it."

Ms. Hill failed to return numerous emails from me about her legal bullying campaign.

"I remember on Memorial Day 2008, when I went to pick up my children for lunch at their grandparents' house, Pete Scamardo came outside to confront me." Mackney said in the suicide note. "I looked at him and said 'Pete, you are nothing but a bully.' He responded 'That's right, and I love it!' He said this in front of Dina, his wife and my children. When I got in the car to take my children to lunch, my son asked me, 'Dad, what's a bully?'"

Like in a school playground, if you stand up to a bully, show them you aren't afraid, they're afraid. Someone did that on April 23, 2014.

The Mackney...er Streisand Effect

That day AVFM received a takedown notice but turned the tables and published the order to remove the suicide note into a blog post.

Does a wife who may have driven a husband to suicide with the assistance of our corrupt family court system, then have a legal right to claim copyright — of his suicide note?

According to attorney Rachelle E. Hill, of Bean, Kinney and Korman, and a judge, that is precisely the claim. Their lawyer has written the offices of A Voice for Men to demand that we remove a post from the forums containing the note.

It is not going to happen.

Bullied to Death: Chris Mackney's Kafkaesque Divorce

AVFM then posted part of Mackney's suicide note, expressing their contempt with the order. I contacted the website later that evening for the first time but not before; the decision to challenge the takedown notice was theirs alone.

The post went viral, and within a week Mackney's suicide note was on hundreds of new websites, with more than a dozen people reading it aloud on You Tube; the internet branded Dina Mackney psychopathic and evil. Today, the search term "Chris Mackney suicide (note)" consumes more than thirty pages on a Google search.

This phenomenon is known as The Streisand Effect, after a lawsuit filed by Barbara Streisand which demanded internet tycoon turned environmentalist Kenneth Adelman take down photos he published on his website of a California coastline because they included her estate. Initially, the photos were viewed six times, twice by Streisand's lawyers, but after news of the lawsuit spread, the photos were viewed hundreds of thousands of times. The lawsuit was eventually dismissed, and Streisand was even forced to pay Adelman's legal fees. Frivolous lawsuits which attempt to suppress information but only draw media attention exponentially increasing the number of people who view it are now referred to as The Streisand Effect.

In 2014, Mike Masnick, who coined The Streisand Effect wrote two stories about Mackney's suicide and the copyright notice. I was the anonymous source for his follow-up published on May 2, 2014; he became the first to report that the copyright order didn't merely copyright the suicide note but hundreds of documents.

As the suicide note went viral, extremists advocated for violence against Dina Mackney and many posted personal information about her: (known by the slang term doxing) including her email, home address, and work details. Some even ordered pizzas and other food to her home. This comment posted on May 2, 2014, on the web forum, *Digitally Imported*, is typical of the venom: "Sorry to say this, but, if I were him, I would have killed his ex first before committing suicide. I hope something bad happens to her."

Another extremist spammed this comment in dozens of websites.

Chris Mackney committed suicide on December 29, 2013 because his ex wife was using the divorce courts in America to torture him and kidnap his children from him. He wrote a 4 page suicide note before killing himself.

MAKE THIS VIRAL! THIS IS THE MOST IMPORTANT ISSUE EVER TO HIT THE MRA/MANOSPHERE WORLD. THIS IS WHY YOU NEVER GET MARRIED IN AMERICA!!!!!!!!!

LATEST UPDATE: The ex-wife is such a psychopath that she is trying to copyright her ex-husband's suicide note, in order to prevent it from being circulated on the internet. She is using her lawyers to threaten legal action against websites that published Chris's suicide letter.

Michael Volpe

The most thoughtful response came from a poet calling himself forty-two with the poem *Who Really Killed Chris Mackney*.

Who really killed Chris Mackney
look into the shadows and you will see
the sharks that prowl within the courts
and the judges, their main cohorts
that feed upon the bones of men
and repeat the process again and again
Chris Mackney did not kill himself
he was murdered by destroying his mental health
by torture you could not conceive
with no justice possible, to receive
the judges and lawyers in the system
they are the people that did kill him
the police that would take him off to jail
when to pay child support he did fail
you can not pay what you have not got
a simple fact the system forgot
those that delivered impossible demands
they all have blood upon their hands
Who really killed Chris Mackney
look in the shadows and you will see
the lawyers that stripped away his pride
that way his fate they did decide
he cried out but no one could hear
and locked him in a prison, we call fear
Chris rose four times from the dust
found employment to earn a crust
yet each time he was struck back down
becoming homeless in his home town
the man that proudly sold real estate
the system caused a humiliating fate
they took away his last will to live
when access to children they would not give
when the system made him feel so small
he then chose not to live at all
so all that refused to see the pain to see
you are the ones that killed Chris Mackney
the ex wife that laid down all the rules
the lawyers and judges that danced like fools
the people that said they all knew best
they all laid Chris down to rest
no guardian for his children you would provide
you all caused Chris Mackney's suicide
look around at what you have done
realise no victory has been won
then you try to clean the internet

in hope that everyone will forget
but there are millions just like he
saying there but for the grace of god goes me
we have nothing you can take
so this protest we shall make
Chris's story will be heard
in written and a spoken word
until this society never can say he is irrelevant, he's just a man

By May, the internet was abuzz with the story. One post on the website Imgur copying the suicide note had nearly 180,000 hits within a month. A You Tube video of men's rights activist Victor Zen reading the note had over 14,000 hits in a week, and *The Raw Story* article had 2,298 comments.

Dina Mackney's social media accounts went silent between ten days to two weeks after the note went viral. As she remained cyber silent, each of those pages was on the receiving end of numerous nasty messages like this one from the twitter handle *Cheese Man*, "Warning-the owner of this business is a psychopath who caused the death of her husband."

During that period she was the subject of a peculiar puff piece in a trade website named *Dandizette Magazine* on April 30, 2014 where reporter Tracy Bozarth asked hard hitting questions like "What is your signature? Do you have a style or stone that is a part in all your collections?" and "In addition to beautiful stone jewelry you have incorporated Italian glass pieces into your collection. Can you tell us more about that?"

I sent an email on the curious timing of this piece to the site but no response. Dina Mackney eventually came back on-line and her presence on the internet increased dramatically. If that's to create search engine optimization (SEO), that's largely failed: most online searches incorporating her name have numerous links related to the story on the first page.

The story reached the mainstream when acting on my tip *The Washington Post* blogger and well-known first amendment expert Eugene Volokh, of the eponymous *Volokh Conspiracy* wrote a blog post on May 15, 2014. He concluded people had a right to post Chris Mackney's writing arguing the note had no commercial value, was being published with no commercial intent and because Mackney initially published it online his implicit intent was to have it read far and wide.

Marc Randazza, also a well-known first amendment lawyer, represented AVFM in their dispute with Dina Mackney and sent a letter to Hill on May 1, 2014: "She (Dina) is attempting to take the dying words of this man as her own property, despite no intention by him to grant her any such right. Then, she is attempting to use that right in order to erase his expression from any further public existence."

After Randazza sent his letter to Hill, AVFM never heard from Hill and the note and all subsequent blog posts (including an early version of the murder chapter they published on my behalf on July 18, 2014) on this story remained on their website. The suicide note, other parts of Mackney's blog, and documents related to his divorce, continue being released on the internet by me and others.

Besides releasing the early draft of the murder chapter on AVFM, I've also released an expose of Samenow, and done interviews with Marti Oakley, Kenneth Boxberger, Laurie Roth, and several others about Mackney's story. In response to all this, the Scamardo family and their legal team have remained silent, putting to rest any questions about the validity of their absurd copyright claim, their motives in this story, and their status as bullies.

I hope this book will lead to coining The Mackney Effect to describe situations where people who aren't famous (with The Streisand Effect reserved to the already famous) becoming notorious after attempting in a frivolous manner to use the legal system to block the publication of material they don't like.

Feminists, the MRM, and the Gender wars

The so-called Men's Rights Movement (MRM) or Men's Rights Activists (MRAs) turned Chris Mackney's suicide into a cause célèbre following the lead of AVFM. Paul Elam, who heads AVFM, told me the MRM is a counterculture answer to feminism.

Those in the MRM who picked up Mackney's story used it as ammunition in their ongoing ideological war with feminists. Greg Becker, a member of Men Go Their Own Way (MGTOW), a sub-category of the MRM, said this on You Tube, "The law, feminism and society; it's the unholy trinity with feminism as the godhead spearheading those other two entities. It's because of the money it generates. This guy (Mackney) was not bigger than the money it generated."

In its most extreme form, the MRM advocates for misogyny and violence against women. The MRM's extreme elements are led by Peter Andrew Nolan, who runs the site *Crimes against Fathers*. Nolan is a victim of family court abuse in Australia living in Europe. He regularly advocates violence saying to me on Facebook, "If men cared about men someone else would have killed Dina Mackney and do Chris the favor. I have long told men that if they cared about each other they would watch each other's backs."

Nolan justified his call for murder by suggesting there is a war against men in family courts, and this is a legitimate response to war.

His website published some of the most extreme and inflammatory statements against Dina Mackney calling her a "man hating bitch" and published Dina Mackney's office address, Twitter handle, Facebook page, Linked In page, and other personal information.

This behavior is not new for Nolan who in 2013 revealed the name of a female Ohio University student who he believed filed a false sexual assault claim: publishing her name, phone number, street address, and email. The disclosure forced the student to drop out of school that semester, and it turned out Nolan targeted the wrong individual; it's also far from clear that the sexual assault allegation was false.

In a Buzzfeed article on the controversy, Nolan was unapologetic saying that even if the woman "goes out tomorrow and buys a gun and blows her head off that's not a problem for me. I'm prepared to say that in the public. Now the reason I'm prepared to say that in public is because I'm reflecting back the exact same attitude that it would be if it were a man."

Other extreme elements of the MRM claimed that Mackney's case was evidence that men in America should stop marrying and breeding.

People like Nolan likely did more harm than good in spreading Mackney's story. "They discredited themselves," Jill Peterson Mitchell told me of their rhetoric.

The more mainstream elements of the MRM center on the aforementioned AVFM run by Paul Elam, who I've worked with on this story. Elam has been criticized for writing a blog post in 2010 which some say made light of rape, and even encouraged others to commit the act. Elam has repeatedly countered that the post was a piece of "provocative satire." In June 2014, Elam and AVFM hosted the first International Conference on Men's Issues. Local feminists protested the conference so aggressively it needed to be moved from the Double Tree Hotel in Detroit to a Veteran of Foreign War facility in the suburbs. Despite the controversy, or possibly because of it, the conference was covered by most mainstream media, with stories appearing on Fox News Channel, *USA Today*, CNN, MSNBC, *Salon*, and others. AVFM condemned Nolan as an extremist in a blog post in May 2014. Nolan has countered that he's not an MRA but starting an alternative to fight on behalf of men.

I've found Elam, like Henry Makow, to be honest and professional, while Nolan is frightening. Furthermore, though I believe Makow and Elam have a specific agenda toward this story, they want the whole truth told; they both detailed the 1960s murder for hire by Scamardo though this did little to advance their agenda.

Not everyone has the same respect for these men. The so-called Manosphere, a loose collection of blogs and other MRM websites, was blamed by Mark Potok of the Southern Poverty Law Center for the shooting massacre perpetrated by Elliot Rodger at University of California at Santa Barbara in May 2014 because these websites often become a forum for men to release frustrations on the female race. This was a dubious and inflammatory charge; Rodger had a long history of mental illness and three of his six victims were male but shows how the MRM has been demonized.

Attached to an ideology viewed as extreme and misogynistic Mackney's story took a credibility hit as this poster on Imgur noted. "The association with MRAs and AVFM has seriously undermined my ability to believe this guy's story."

Michael Volpe

Chris Mackney and the Gender Wars

(A Father's rights group using Mackney's image to advance their cause)

For about a month, his story also became a focal point for the ongoing gender war. When the far left website, *The Raw Story*, picked up the saga on May 2, 2014, the comments section turned into a screaming match between feminists and the MRM with each side calling the other extremists.

In fact, the personal and passionate nature of the arguments between feminists and the MRM on *The Raw Story*, as with many of the debates between these two groups, mirror arguments between passionate liberals and conservatives. Liberals and conservatives often believe all the ills of our world can be attributed to their political enemies, and feminists and the MRM believe the same thing about each other: that's the simplified version of their debate.

Extend that same perspective to Chris Mackney. If his story is a cause célèbre to the MRM, then by extension, he is a villain to feminists. In *The Raw Story* article a feminist using the handle Sharon Armstrong, possibly a pseudonym, repeatedly defended Dina Mackney, attacked Chris Mackney, and at one point referred to Marc Randazza as "woman hating." MRAs blistered Ms. Armstrong suggesting she was stupid and a man hater. (Armstrong's comments have since been removed by *The Raw Story*)

The zenith of this ideological battle occurred when Janet Bloomfield, a female MRA, read Mackney's suicide note on You Tube changing all the sex identifying words to female, in an attempt to show society they respond differently to a woman's suicide.

Chris Mackney never involved himself in gender politics. Some called him a family court reformer but that's strictly because he started *Good Men Did Nothing*. Chris Mackney no more believed in the illuminati than I believe in the illuminati though some, like Sharon Armstrong, have falsely associated him with that movement because his note first went up on Makow's site.

Both feminists and the MRM believe the family court system is corrupt and biased, but disagree on which gender is on the receiving end of the bias; Chris Mackney had no time for such philosophical debates: he wanted an end to his family court nightmare.

Mackney reached out to Donna Andersen, author of the *Lovefraud* series, along with the corresponding website about her marriage and subsequent divorce with a psychopath. Andersen told me that while she found Mackney's story plausible, she had no time to investigate him to make sure it was real.

Hera McLeod Is Mackney's Muse

Hera McLeod is a former contestant on *The Amazing Race* where she partnered with her father, a retired Central Intelligence Agency (CIA) spy. She has a successful six figure career but also runs a site called *Cappuccino Queen*, detailing her family court nightmare. Prior to that, she commented on Andersen's website. Months after meeting Joaquin Rams on the on-line dating website, Match.com, she fell in love and got pregnant. Then, after her sister came home with the shocking accusation that Rams raped her, McLeod's family did a background check and found he was suspected in two murders, an ex-girlfriend and his mother. Rams will go on trial in January 2016 for murder after their son drowned during an unsupervised visit allowed by family court over her vociferous objection. Since being arrested for this murder, he's also been charged in the murder of his ex-girlfriend, and remains suspected of murdering his mother.

On May 21, 2014, after speaking with me, she published an article on Mackney's suicide saying his story had been twisted by people with an agenda. "Upon googling Chris' name to find out the details of his death, I noticed many websites that have attempted to exploit and twist his story in an attempt to make it appear as though it was something that it was not."

In the same post, McLeod noted Chris reached out to her, arguing he was no gender ideologue.

The very fact that Chris had asked to work with me shows that he was not a man trying to tie himself with an anti-women's movement or speak out against mothers. From what I knew of Chris through our conversations, he was a man who was trying to survive the horrible legal abuse he was enduring. He was trying to find a way to get back into his children's lives. He was trying to navigate a broken system.

Initial Contact:

12/31/2012 – "My name is Chris Mackney. I post on your site as madmacks…my case is so bad it's incredible. I want to call for an investigation because there is so much corruption. The pattern is so clear and they pretend it's not there. I wanted to see if we might work together to expose the court's failures in our cases."

Chris Mackney didn't merely read Hera's blog and comment. Hera was Mackney's muse; here's from the aptly titled blog post *Cappuccino Queen*.

She had only been blogging a few months and was very selective and discerning about her posts, so I looked forward to them. Then in October 2012, I read the unthinkable. The Cappuccino Queen's son, Prince, was murdered by his father. He was only 15 months old. After her son was drowned by her ex-husband, she chose to come forward and speak out publicly about the people responsible for her son's death. The Court knew her ex-husband was a psychopath, as the result of a Court ordered evaluation and it did nothing. For psychopaths it's about control and domination. They will use children to hurt the person they are targeting. Yet, the Court took no preventative measures to protect her child.

In both our cases, our children were taken to hurt us, because we knew the truth.

Cappuccino Queen's story and her courage gave me the inspiration to create this blog and speak truth to power and speak out about abuse. Thank you for your strength, Hera.

The Suicide Note Leads to Gas-lighting

Days after publishing the suicide note, Henry Makow received this email from someone claiming to be Liza Mulaney.

I found your post because my daughter brought it to my attention when she googled her friend. It is unimaginable that you would further harm these kids and make their life more difficult. This is their personal tragedy, not fodder for some crusade of yours. They are kids and should be allowed to grieve in private and lead a normal life - i (sic) think this post should be taken down as it is inappropriate.

Second, you clearly don't vet your stories. We know this family and the situation well and I can guarantee that this note is the most ridiculous projection I have ever read. This man did not have his kids taken from him. He refused his own visitation when he had it and then terrorized and stalked when he didn't. He was mentally ill and his behavior with the kids became quickly dangerous. He was given many chances to be reunited with (the) kids and was given the key to do so but he chose not to take that path. I would like to think that he didn't do so because he was mentally ill but maybe he just had his own agenda - I don't know. What I do know is that he abused that family, not the other way around. Furthermore, what kind of man pays zero in child support to the point that this mother had to work 24/7 just to support the kids? He is just such a man - never paid a penny - so I don't know why he says he was broke - go get a job like everybody else for goodness sakes. There was no conspiracy here, just a man who didn't care enough to do the right thing. So if you want to "save the males" you should choose fitting men who actually do have a noble crusade because this man did not.

(This is a photo from Google Maps of the home where Dina Mackney lives; worth seven figures the home does not jive with the image of a woman struggling to feed her kids made by Liza Mulaney.)

Mental illness, deadbeat dad, and blaming Mackney for all the marital problems; this is called gas-lighting, "a form of mental abuse where information is twisted/spun, selectively omitted to favor the abuser or false information is presented with the intent of making victims doubt their own memory, perception, or sanity."

In layman's terms, gas-lighting is when you drive someone crazy and then claim they're crazy.

The so-called Liza Mulaney didn't respond to my email for comment and is almost certainly a pseudonym. According to White Pages, there's no one in the USA with that name, and a Google search for Liza Mulaney comes up empty as well.

I sent Dina Mackney an email asking if she was Mulaney.

Michael Volpe

Ms. Mulaney wasn't the only one using this technique as the suicide note made its way around the internet. In the comments' section of the *Volokh Conspiracy*, the pseudonyms Balins and Lavidaafim made comments with many of the same themes. (The comments are printed exactly as written including spelling Mackney's first and last name with lower letters which Dina Mackney also tends to do)

"It is shocking to see the commentary of those who know nothing of this situation and who simply accept the words of an obviously disturbed chris mackney (sic) as the truth. the (sic) mother, like any other respectable divorced person, would never involve kids in details of the divorce, disagreements and intimate issues, let alone do so in such a public way. Doesn't that tell us that this chris mackney (sic) is a little crazy? doesn't (sic) it strike anyone as incredibly disturbing that this guy would rant in public and blame someone else for his own suicide when they have minor kids?" Laviidafam said in a comment published at 10:16 AM ET on May 26, 2014. "It doesn't surprise me at all that she wants this suicide note and any other denigrating information taken down in any possible way. She is the sole guardian who is raising two grieving kids - aren't any of you parents? Does the exploitation on the internet know no boundaries?"

"I have no horse in this race - I am just a guy who has his own issues with his ex and custody/financial settlement as apparently mackney (sic) did but I cannot fathom the absurdity of posting a nasty suicide note for his kids to see and have as his legacy," Laviidafim said but also said, "it is widely known that the father didn't pay any child support for years and in fact left $0 in his estate to his kids."

Here's what the so-called Balins said in a comment posted at 3:49PM on May 26, 2014.

Very interesting set of legal issues concerning copyright and fair use and good analysis. It is really unfortunate that it is all cloaked in such a deeply personal set of issues involving a broken marriage and the deteriorating mental condition of one parent, who unfortunately abandoned his children in the most cowardly way and the desperate actions of another who sought to protect them by hiding the evidence of the deterioration of the fathers (sic) state of mind and his self-inflicted death in any way possible. If it were me, I think I would do what I could to remove such a public disclosure concerning my kids - allowing the children to mourn privately in this private matter. With that said, the legal argument advanced by Volokh here seems to bear up.

I tend to agree with Laviidafam in that the internet is no place to create historical record of a mental breakdown that culminates in a violent suicide, even if you might have the right to do so. Doing so is evidence in and of itself that the individual was not well. The kids deserve better than to have their horror serve as fodder for any of us and the responsibility for delivering perpetual pain on the kids rests squarely on the legacy of the deceased. You don't have to be affiliated with or even know either party to know that is true....you just need to understand what it is to be a living parent taking care of your own kids. I know I'm going home tonight and giving mine a hug!

Balins first commented about five hours after another commenter suggested Laviidafam was Dina Mackney.

A similar comment was made by a woman named Joanne Ver Ploeg on *Cappuccino Queen's* Facebook page after her story on May 21, 2014.

"I will not give details, but you should know Chris was a deeply troubled person long before the divorce. He brought on a lot of the issues himself." Ver Ploeg said in the post. "Do not assume that I believe the courts acted with due process - I am well aware how broken the system really is. But a man that refuses to seek help and then takes his life to prove a point? The point he made is that he left his children fatherless."

Ver Ploeg quickly removed her comment after I called it gas-lighting and didn't respond when I contacted her through Facebook.

These thoughts were echoed by the so-called Mitch Jefferson, in a set of emails in July 2013 to Chris Mackney.

"You demonstrate your instability with every flailing e-mail. The people you are e-mailing know that you are a deadbeat Dad who is lawless and mentally unstable. You prove it with every ridiculous outbound e-mail you send. The system treats you the way it does because of your lawlessness - your reckless actions are a threat to society and that is why society is pursuing you. The state has a clear interest in making sure deadbeat Dads like you are made to pay their financial obligations," said the so-called Mitch Jefferson in one such email.

According to Jill Peterson Mitchell, who examined the email chain, Mitch Jefferson is really her ex-husband Bryan Jefferson Mitchell. She said this wasn't only because the pseudonym was an anagram of his name but because the so-called Mitch Jefferson knew several extremely personal details of the story, including the exact amount of Chris Mackney's child support, which he constantly referred to as equaling $47 per day, per child: translating to $2,816 per month. (It actually translates to $2820 per month but Jefferson was rounding up)

Bryan Mitchell is the former Chairman and Chief Executive Officer (CEO) of MCG Capital, and was forced to step down as Chairman in disgrace in 2002 after he falsely claimed in a Securities and Exchange Commission (SEC) filing he'd graduated from Syracuse University, when he'd only taken classes there. According to *The New York Times*, MCG Capital stock, which trades on the NASDAQ under the symbol MCGC, fell nearly 40% from $8.40 to $5.06 the day the news was announced. Mitchell resigned as CEO in 2006 after he failed to pay back interest on loans he took from the company and is no longer affiliated with MCGC.

Jill Peterson Mitchell refers to the tandem of her ex-husband and Dina as a match made in hell and believes her ex-husband exhibits many of the same traits as Dina Mackney.

Emails to Bryan Mitchell and Mitch Jefferson were left unreturned.

Ironically, in an email from October 24, 2014 to his ex-wife, Mitchell justified being behind on divorce related bills.

"I am a hired consultant and as I've said before, I do not earn enough to pay for 100% of (their daughter's) $30,000+ annual college costs on top of paying for all of the debts from our marriage you saddled me with and all of your and the boys' expenses plus my own costs. I have said this from the outset and you disregarded this fact and did not have a single consultation with me despite my efforts with both of you when you decided on where she would go to college." Mitchell said. "The difference between my actions and his are night and day – from 2010 until his suicide he never paid a penny of child or spousal support to his ex to support his kids and since 2010 I have paid over $400,000 to you and I have paid alimony and child support in full every single month. I am willing to pay everything that I can and have demonstrated that time and again but I cannot pay what I don't have."

Virginia issued a bench warrant for Mitchell in June 2015 for $21,111.13 in child support arrearages.

Dina Facilitates Bryan Mitchell's Gas-lighting

Jill Peterson Mitchell told me her ex-husband is proficient at gas-lighting. She said when gas-lighting: he turns off their kid's cell phones and then complains she doesn't call them or send them a text at an appropriate time, cancels times he's supposed to spend with their children and then accuses her of trying to keep him away from their children, and once attacked her telling police she was making up being attacked to alienate their children from him. This is called Parental Alienation Syndrome which I'll describe in more detail later in the book.

"Ms. Mitchell stated she wanted to speak to her children about going to lunch the following day and that upon her arrival her ex-husband, Mr. Bryan Mitchell, argued with her that she could not see her children and proceeded to push her from the front porch to the ground. She stated that Mr. Mitchell then 'manhandled' her and forced her back into her vehicle before slapping her on her right cheek." The police report stated. "Ms. Mitchell had a small amount of dirt streak on her right pant leg and some slight redness on her right cheek."

Bryan Mitchell claimed his ex-wife arrived unannounced at his home during his custody time and a verbal argument occurred as a result, but nothing physical occurred. The police report stated there wasn't enough probable cause for an arrest, but Jill Peterson Mitchell disputes this characterization saying the police who arrived on scene asked her to come to the police station to help fill out an arrest warrant. Mitchell said she declined because it was past midnight, but did show up two days later, when a new police officer claimed there wasn't enough evidence for probable cause.

Bryan Mitchell was helped by his girlfriend, Dina Mackney, who said in the police report: "Ms. Mackney advised that Ms. Mitchell had recently taken Mr. Mitchell to court for more child support."

Jill Mitchell told me the charge isn't true, and the only divorce related matter she'd taken up recently was to codify a new children visitation arrangement. Making the charge took chutzpah, Dina Mackney spent over $1 million in legal fees during her divorce while insisting throughout that Chris pay more than $2,800 monthly for child support: refusing his repeated requests to reduce it to a level he could afford.

(Bryan Mitchell from a separate driving while impaired (DWI) arrest in Minnesota in April 2015.)

What is the DCMPD Hiding?

On April 18, 2014, I made a Freedom of Information Act (FOIA) request with DCMPD for a copy of Chris Mackney's suicide note because by law if I received the suicide note through FOIA that would trump the copyright notice.

The DCMPD denied my FOIA request on May 20, 2014 citing the privacy rights of his ex-wife and their children though Dina's actions caused millions to read the note.

By that point it was academic; no one took the copyright notice seriously any more, a point I made when receiving this denial.

Whether or not this note should be made public depends on its accuracy. If these are simply the writings of a mentally ill individual then the note should remain private. If the suicide note is accurate and Mackney was bullied to death by a corrupt judicial system, then this is NOT a matter of privacy but evidence of corruption, unethical behavior, and possibly acts of criminality which led to Chris's suicide. That's why one of the questions I asked Ms. Crump was, "What if any investigation was done into his suicide? What can be shared from that investigation?"

I've since received a copy of the police report from his suicide and the answer is: very little and nothing of substance. The suicide note is included in the blog which is reprinted in full in the appendix of the book.

Chapter 2: Christopher Hines Machnij

(A very young Chris Machnij)

Christopher Hines Machnij was born on November 17, 1968, in Boston, Massachusetts, the middle of three sons to Caroline and Greg Machnij. Mackney changed his name from Machnij in 2002 upon the insistence of his wife Dina, who liked Dina Mackney Designs more than Dina Machnij Designs for her new jewelry business. I believe Dina Designs sounds better than both and avoids the need for a name change but I digress. While several of his friends found the name change peculiar, none made an issue at the time. For continuity I will refer to him by the name he had at the particular period I'm describing.

Machnij had an older brother Greg Jr., born in 1966, and a younger brother Jeff, born in 1973. Greg is unmarried and lives in California, while Jeff got married for the first time in 2010 and recently started a family, living out west.

His Early Years

Machnij spent his early years moving around following his father who was in the hotel business. He moved to North Carolina and then New Mexico where he attended kindergarten. He moved to St. Louis for three years before attending fourth and fifth grade in Hawaii then back to St. Louis where he lived through his high school graduation.

His College Years

(Mackney, third from the left, at a fraternity event)

In September 1986, Machnij enrolled in Southern Methodist University (SMU) in Dallas, Texas, where he joined the Phi Gamma Delta (Fijis) fraternity. His fraternity brothers described him as one of the guys, outgoing, sociable, and a ladies' man. Many of the friendships he formed at SMU he maintained until his life ended. One way in which the blond haired Machnij stood out was in his 6'5" frame, making him the tallest person in most rooms. Fraternity brothers Rich Ware and Mike Harris agreed to have their names used while several others spoke on background and off the record.

At SMU, Machnij was an average student getting B's and C's and didn't put much effort into academics. He graduated in 1990 with a degree in economics.

Machnij in the Big Apple

After graduation, he moved to New York City, where a year later he was joined by a fraternity brother who got Machnij an interview with Bloomberg Financial Markets, a profitable subsidiary of Bloomberg LP which sells software providing investment professionals with analytics for managing investment portfolios. Machnij then spent about a year and a half living and working in Princeton, New Jersey, where Bloomberg had their training center. For the next two and a half years, Machnij moved to New York City and lived in an apartment two floors below a friend from SMU.

Mark Duda is currently a musician "with a day job" who worked with Machnij at Bloomberg. They roomed together during training in Princeton and both, along with Duda's brother

Andrew, became good friends during Machnij's days in New York. Duda also described Machnij as outgoing, sociable, a ladies' man, and a happy individual with lots of friends.

(Machnij, standing second from the left in the back, at a fraternity brother's wedding in Florida shortly after graduation)

After about four years at Bloomberg, Machnij was offered a deal filed under, "it seemed like a good idea at the time."

He was making approximately $150,000 yearly when offered an opportunity with a lower base salary but significantly higher potential commissions with a regional competitor of Bloomberg's.

The job turned into a debacle; the company struggled financially and eventually went out of business. About the time he met Dina Scamardo, in the summer of 1998, he was in a dead end job.

Chris and Dina Meet

"He remembers having been attracted to her physical looks, the fact that she had a sweet personality and that she had an MBA degree. " Mackney told an evaluator of his initial impressions of Dina.

(Chris Mackney sitting in the front with Dina standing to his right at a posh ski resort during better times)

But on their first date Dina exhibited red flags: "I often tell the story of how she berated the waitress on our first date for a problem that originated in the kitchen and was not the fault of the server. I remember how embarrassed I was but I blew it off to a 'strong personality.'"

(A photo of Mackney coaching little league, second from right, from his Facebook page)

Though such an incident normally means no second date, they began dating.

Dina Scamardo was part of a very exclusive and chic crowd of trust fund babies. She was always immaculately well dressed, going out to dinner at the most expensive restaurants, and then to the hottest night clubs. Mark Duda remembers her using a car service and Dina and Chris spent several weekends vacationing in the Hamptons. On the surface, Machnij and his working class upbringing scored a woman out of his league.

Chris Mackney's Dad Dies

As Chris and Dina's relationship blossomed, tragedy struck. A drunk driver lost control of his car, jumped a curb and killed Machnij's father, who was working in the front yard of his home in November 1998.

"There was considerable difficulty for his mother to adjust to the death of his father, a death that took place when the elder Mr. Machnij was hit by a car," according to a divorce evaluation. "Mr. Mackney remembers having had difficulties himself dealing with the loss, though, at the time, he was already nearly 30. His mother, however, had been quite dependent on his father, and had difficulty putting her life in order after he died."

The tragedy brought Chris and Dina closer. "He remembered that a few months later, perhaps around Thanksgiving, his father had been killed, and he was impressed, too, with the fact that his wife responded in a sympathetic way."

His mother died in 2009 at the age of sixty-three.

(Chris Machnij during college with his mom)

Chris and Dina Fall in Love

Rich Ware said he believed his dad's death caused Machnij to re-examine his life and decide it was the time to marry and start a family.

Dina had similar feelings, "Ms. Mackney knew Chris Mackney for two years before they married. She said that, even though she had doubts, she was 'ready to get married and have a family.'" Dr. Samenow's report stated.

Mark Duda was surprised by how quickly Machnij's relationship progressed with Dina Scamardo. He said that while Dina was an attractive woman Chris dated many women far more attractive and several relationships lasted longer before Machnij and Scamardo got engaged. He described Dina as quiet, with her own set of friends. Once the two became an item, he saw Chris far less, and rarely with Dina.

When Chris came around, Duda said, "It was usually unannounced."

He'd go to a friend's apartment or one of the bars they frequented, hoping someone would be there, as though he stopped by in the middle of appointments with his new girlfriend.

About a year after meeting, Chris and Dina got engaged.

Career Change; Life Change

He also made a career decision which unwittingly planted the seeds of his destruction. He turned down a sales position with the software company BAE Systems in New York with a $125,000 yearly base salary plus a commission structure to work as a commercial real estate salesman for his soon to be father-in-law at Scamardo's real estate company, Centennial Development Corporation (CDC) in Virginia. The career move also meant a move to Virginia, living less than an hour away from his soon to be in-laws.

Chris Machnij was a well-adjusted individual with no signs of mental problems as he was about to marry Dina Scamardo. In interviews with more than twenty of his friends and business colleagues, none agreed with assessments from Dina Mackney, Joanne Ver Ploeg, Liza Mulaney, Laviidafam, Mitch Jefferson, and Balins, that Chris Machnij had any long standing mental health issues.

On the other hand, the patriarch of the Scamardo family is a murderer.

Chapter 3: The Murder of Sam Degelia, Jr.

"You think that your laws correct evil - they only increase it. There is but one way to end evil - by rendering good for evil to all men without distinction."

Leo Tolstoy

"Pete Scamardo took away fathers from six children under ten years old,"

Rich Ware

Sam Carmelo Degelia, Jr.'s Last Day

Michael Volpe

Sam Carmelo Degelia, Jr. woke on a beautiful summer Saturday morning expecting to spend time with his family and conduct business; it was July 6, 1968. Born and raised in Texas, the thirty year old grain dealer was a product of his environment: comfortable in a ten gallon hat, cowboy boots and jeans. He was married to Ginger, a blond beauty with a pleasant smile, with four children under ten years old. He lived in Hearne, Texas, a small town with about four thousand residents in Robertson County in central Texas but was on business for a week in Edinburg, Texas, a border town on the southern tip of Texas on the Rio Grande Valley in Hidalgo County with a well-earned reputation for lawlessness and corruption.

Degelia, Jr. owned Commodity Trading Corporation (CTC) with his friend and business partner, Pete Scamardo, and was in the area buying and selling grains. Two days prior, his cousin Peter Trentacost, his wife, his maid Alene Norfleet, and four children came down to stay with him at an apartment he rented when in the area. An early riser Sam Degelia, Jr. was off to do errands while his family was still asleep; he had less than twelve hours to live.

Degelia, Jr. came back to the apartment from running errands at about noon and cooked lunch: steak, corn, hamburger patties, hot rolls, and creamed potatoes. He and his family ate their last meal together as a happy family. At 2:30 PM everyone went down to the local bowling alley and then to the pool at the apartment at 4PM. At around 5:10PM, Degelia, Jr. received a phone call from a man he'd never met proposing to get together for a grain deal. About ten minutes later, Degelia, Jr. was dressed and told his wife he was going to McAllen, Texas, a town about ten miles south of Edinburg known today as a popular entry point for illegal immigrants from Mexico and Central America. On his way out, he left $6-7 for the family's dinner.

"He told me he was going to see a man about a grain deal and I said ok," Ginger Degelia said of the last words between her and her husband: Sam Degelia, Jr. had less than ninety minutes to live.

The Murderers' Day

Meanwhile, Charles Voyde Harrelson and Jerry O'Brien Watkins woke up that day in Houston. They met at the airport at about 8AM, and took an early flight on Trans Texas Airway to McAllen, Texas. They first met three weeks prior at Lucky Pierre's, a private club in Houston, becoming friends over hours of gin rummy. Harrelson initially introduced himself to Watkins as Charles Stoughtenborough, one of several aliases he used, and that is the name Watkins knew him by. A previous trip to the Rio Grande Valley area, on June 21, 1968, turned into an adventure, so Harrelson invited Watkins to join him for another trip to the Valley, leaving and coming back the same day with Harrelson picking up all expenses.

Besides that the trip was sketchy. "The only thing he said about the reason he was coming was that he had some business to attend to," Watkins would later say of what Harrelson said about the trip beforehand.

They arrived in McAllen at about 10AM, rented a car at approximately 10:45AM, and headed to Brownsville, Texas, where Watkins hoped to meet up with a man named Albert Hastings for a business deal.

In the car, Harrelson told Watkins he was in the area to, "strum a guy's head," or give someone a beating.

Harrelson then took out a twelve gauge sawed off shotgun setting off an argument; Watkins wanted Harrelson to lose the shotgun which Harrelson refused.

In Brownsville, they couldn't find Hastings and after a couple hours headed toward McAllen, Texas. On the highway, Watkins, still concerned about Harrelson's shotgun, noticed an exit toward Mexico and headed south of the border hoping to get rid of his weapon there.

In Mexico, they continued to argue over the shotgun; Harrelson finally relented about an hour later breaking it into pieces and throwing it out the car shortly before crossing the border back into the USA. They arrived in the McAllen area sometime in the afternoon and planned to have lunch at the Holiday Inn where they were staying. On their way to the hotel, they drove down a lonely road about a mile and a half outside the McAllen city limits where they spotted a shack.

"This is where I'm going to bring him to strum him up." Harrelson told Watkins. "I can leave him tied up and we will be on the plane and gone before he can get loose."

The two had lunch at the Holiday Inn at about 2:30PM and then drinks at the hotel's private club at approximately 4PM. Harrelson had a scotch and water, while Watkins' stomach was giving him trouble so he had two Alka-Seltzers. After a few minutes, Watkins' stomach still wasn't feeling better so, "I figured I could not feel any worse so I ordered a double vodka," according to a statement he gave to the Texas Rangers.

Over the next two hours, Harrelson excused himself several times though Watkins wasn't sure if he was going to the bathroom or making phone calls. At about 5PM, Mrs. Wayne Sparks, whose husband was a business associate of Sam Degelia, Jr., received a call from an unidentified male. Though the individual mispronounced Degelia, when asking to reach Sam Degelia, Jr. in Edinburg, she still gave him the number of Sam's Edinburg apartment.

At about 5:10PM, Harrelson called Sam Degelia, Jr. and asked to meet to discuss a grain deal. After a few minutes, the two agreed to meet in a McAllen diner.

Sam's Last Minutes

At approximately 6:15PM that evening, Jimmie Horn, Sam Degelia, Jr.'s bookkeeper, was walking into Luby's Cafeteria in McAllen, Texas when Horn noticed his boss waiting in the parking lot in his car. Horn got into Degelia's car and asked him to join him for dinner.

(Photo of Sam Degelia, Jr. shortly before his death courtesy of the Degelia family)

"They talked a few minutes." A Texas Rangers report revealed. "Degelia told Jimmie that he was to meet a man but that he didn't know what he looked like or what kind of a car he was driving but said that they might do some business with this person when they returned to Hearne."

A few minutes later, Charles Voyde Harrelson and Jerry O'Brien Watkins picked up Sam Degelia, Jr.; he had less than a half hour to live.

For the first few minutes, the car ride appeared normal, with the three men discussing a supposed grain deal.

"Let's go to Reynosa (Mexico) and have a drink," Harrelson suggested.

"Sam made some remark to the effect that people were going to think that he lived over there or did all of his business over there as every time someone came to buy grain they went to Reynosa for a drink," Watkins said in the same Texas Rangers report and then described the last minutes of Sam's life.

At this time, I was driving, Charles was sitting up front and Sam was riding in the back seat. The car which we had rented was a Ford Galaxie Four-Door Sedan. When we reached this same road which we had previously turned off on, Charles told me to take this road, that this was a short cut. When we had gone a short distance on this short cut, Charles pulled a 25-Caliber Automatic Pistol from his right coat pocket and pointed it over the back of the front seat at Sam. Charles told him, "sit back, sit back god damn you!" because Sam had been leaning forward while they were discussing prices of grains, shipping costs and things like that. When Charles did this, Sam suddenly sat back, threw his hands back and said, "What's the matter; my god; what's the matter!" Then Charles told him to get down on the floor board and told him not to do anything foolish. Sam tried to get on the floor board, but there was not enough room behind the seat. Charles told me to move the seat forward. At that time, Charles was leaning over the back of the front seat and apparently holding the pistol against Sam. I moved the seat forward. Charles took a piece of nylon fiber rope about a quarter of an inch in thickness and about 3 and a half inches long out of his right hand coat pocket and proceeded to tie Sam's hands behind his back. Prior to this, Charles had shifted his pistol to his left hand. This piece of rope which he took from his pocket already had a loop made in it about a foot from the end. During all of this time, Charles was talking to Sam telling him not to do anything stupid, that he did not want to have to hurt him or shoot him but that he was just going to have to teach him to keep his nose out of other people's business. I drove onto the shack which we had previously visited, drove past it, turned around and came back. When I got back to the shack, Charles told me to stop right there which I did.

He told Sam to get out of the car, but real careful and not to do anything silly. Charles then opened his door and got out, opened the rear door on the right side and by holding on to the piece of rope helped Sam get out. Charles continued to caution Sam about doing anything foolish. Charles closed both doors which he had opened and left with Sam heading toward the shack. At that time, Sam was walking ahead of Charles and Charles was holding onto the piece of rope and following close behind him. I stayed in the car with the air conditioner on. They went to the shack. Right after they entered the shack I took a cigarette out to light it when I heard a noise like a small caliber pistol being fired coming from the direction of the shack. This startled me and I dropped my lighter. By the time I picked it up, I heard another pop similar to the first.

The Aftermath

In the abandoned shack, Harrelson shot Sam Degelia, Jr. twice in the back of the head and left his body to rot in the farm, treating him no better than a wild animal.

"This is not the only son of a bitch I've had to ring the bell on." Harrelson yelled at Watkins as they drove away. "Don't you give me any argument or any problems or I'll do it to you too!"

Five minutes after the murder, Harrelson broke up the gun and threw it out the window as they drove along the same road. They returned to the airport and barely made the 7:20PM flight back to Houston where they were two of four passengers. Watkins pretended to sleep to avoid talking to Harrelson while Harrelson hit on twenty year old stewardess Victoria De La Pez.

"Chuck asked me for a date and I said no." De La Pez told the Texas Rangers. "He then kept asking for a drink and a refill. Later I got up and checked on my other passengers. Before I got up, Chuck attempted to kiss me on the cheek, and I pushed him away. He tried this several times and that is when I got up and check on my other passengers."

Sam Degelia, Jr.'s body rotted in this shack for five days before John Pawlik, a farmer working in the area, discovered it. What no one except Harrelson yet knew was that Pete Scamardo paid him to kill Sam Degelia, Jr. Watkins eventually got a deal and his statements were made as a cooperating witness.

Pete Scamardo and Sam Degelia, Jr. Were Lifelong Friends

"They (Scamardo and Degelia, Jr.) were both altar boys together," Sam Degelia, Jr.'s sister, Cindy Wallace, said.

They'd been friends since they were little. They went to Texas A&M together and were business partners at the time of his murder.

A relative of Sam Degelia Jr., who wished to remain anonymous, described Scamardo as a "nice, quiet, and gentle person...not a bully at all."

Wallace is seventeen years younger than her brother and said she had limited recollections of the details of the murder, but her family was close with Scamardo's in-laws, the DeStefano's, and she was particularly close to Scamardo's sister-in-law, Debbie DeStefano; until the murder that is.

Immediately after the murder, Scamardo was keeping up appearances. When people in Hearne organized a search party, he was a volunteer.

"Ginger called me Monday 7-8-68. She told me he had been missing since Saturday. This is the first time I had heard of Sam being gone." Scamardo told Tolliver Dawson of the Texas Rangers. "Fred Moss, Fred C. Ferrer and I left Hearne at 11:30AM and drove to Edinburg in Fred Moss's car. We arrived in Edinburg at about 7PM. We returned to Hearne on Wednesday 7-10-68."

Cindy Wallace remembers seeing Scamardo at her brother's funeral days later offering condolences to the relatives and friends of the man he had murdered: acting as though he'd done nothing wrong.

Scamardo was even one of the pallbearers who carried the casket.

Ginger Degelia made Scamardo a pallbearer because they'd been business partners, but also because shortly after the murder Scamardo, ever the Machiavellian, helped search for her husband and called regularly to make sure the family was doing all right. She's regretted that decision ever since.

Charles Harrelson: drunk, degenerate gambler, wife beater, and famous father

Harrelson and Watkins were two shady individuals with long criminal records. According to a February 27, 1970, story by the *Associated Press*, Watkins was "a former convict who had been released from a federal prison in El Paso, Texas in 1963" who "at one point was interested in selling machine guns to someone in Mexico."

Harrelson was also a career criminal, degenerate gambler, drug addict, and contract killer suspected in twenty murders with a Jekyll and Hyde personality. Sandra Sue Attaway, his former girlfriend, was quickly swept of her feet by his legendary charm, but months into the relationship he became physically abusive and pressured her into helping him commit several crimes including another murder.

Harrelson is now known mostly for being the estranged father of Woodrow (Woody) Tracy Harrelson, born July 23, 1961, who first achieved fame as Woody Boyd on the 1980's hit television show *Cheers*, and in movies like: *White Men Can't Jump*, *Indecent Proposal*, *Natural Born Killers*, and *No Country for Old Men*, based on a book which borrowed from Charles

Harrelson's alleged deeds. When Harrelson played a psychopathic killer in *Natural Born Killers*, it was reported the director, Oliver Stone, encouraged Woody repeatedly to act like his father.

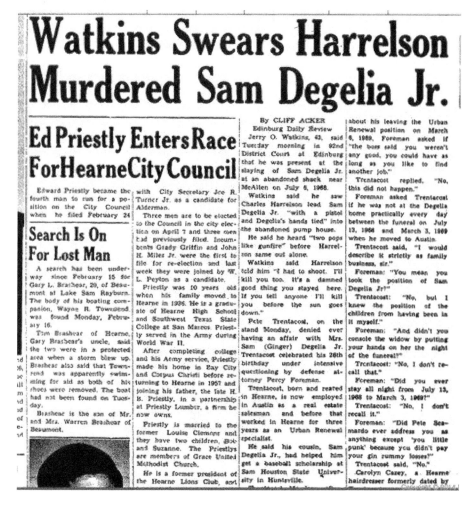

(Screenshot of a newspaper article from Harrelson's trial from newspaper.com)

Woody Harrelson said in interviews that his father disappeared from his life in 1968, and they didn't communicate again until 1981. Charles Harrelson had a knack for creating single mothers; Woody was raised almost entirely by his mother, Diane nee Oswald, who divorced Charles in 1964.

Charles Harrelson and Sandra Sue Attaway's Life of Crime

At the time of the murder, Charles Harrelson was shacking up with the aforementioned Sandra Sue Attaway, an attractive 24 year old twice married, twice divorced, woman with few skills who left her young son with her mother to move to Houston in 1967. She first met Harrelson on August 3, 1967 in Houston and by September 3, 1967, was so enamored they took off to Las Vegas, where Harrelson quickly lost the $5,000 he started with and high tailed it to Des Moines, Iowa, where he claimed to have work available.

Attaway described an existence like this which continued for about a year, where Harrelson would swoop into some area, run up debts, or otherwise get in trouble, and rush, with Attaway at his side, to another town.

"I was not allowed to have any girl friends or go anywhere without him. I was beginning to find out what bad things he had done such as collecting bad debts for a booking organization," Attaway said to the Brazoria County Sheriff's Office on November 13, 1968. "I asked him if he hurt people when he did this and he said, 'Of course.' I had no doubt that he would because he had hurt me too."

(Like father like son, mugshots of Charles and Woody Harrelson in their 20s)

The Berg Murder

Over time Attaway tried and failed multiple times to extricate herself from Harrelson but by April 1968, she was helping him commit a murder for hire. He told her that a carpet dealer named Allen Berg cheated an associate, Frank DiMaria, out of $7,000, and Harrelson was tasked, for $2,000, with collecting the purported debt. Here's what Attaway said happened.

Michael Volpe

On a Tuesday night, he came into the apartment and said he wanted me to make a phone call and he would tell me exactly what to say and that I was to repeat what Allen said so that he could hear what was being said. He told me to talk the boy into meeting me somewhere which was done and he was to meet me at the Brass Jug Club.

He had already bought the red Cadillac 1967 convertible with a white top at a used car lot on Post Oak Freeway from a man named Martin and we went in it. I drove and he told me how to go. We drove around the club and saw the boy going into the club and drove around the block and stopped by the boy's Cadillac as he walked back across the street. Chuck jumped out and forced Allen to enter our car by use of a gun and a shove.

Attaway lured Berg to the car with the promise of oral sex.

Attaway said they drove to a secluded area unfamiliar to her where she got the car stuck in the mud. Harrelson forced Berg into the trunk then removed the car from the mud.

Attaway said they kept driving with Harrelson noticeably nervous when "he said to stop right where we were."

Harrelson forced Berg out of the trunk while Attaway waited in the driver's seat, assuming Harrelson would rough Berg up. Instead, she heard a shot.

"I jumped out of the car and looked behind the car. Allen was laying on the ground on his face." Attaway said.

Berg wasn't dead, and Harrelson later used a rope to suffocate Berg after he noticed him still alive as he was digging a hole for his body.

This murder for hire was recently documented by Berg's brother, David Berg, in the book, *Run, Brother, Run* released in 2013. In the book, Berg said the motive for the murder was payback. DiMaria worked briefly for Berg, running his carpet business in San Antonio, until Berg accused him of stealing. Berg's father spent the next year telling every banker in Texas not to loan money to "the thief who stole us blind."

"Leonard (the investigator hired by the Berg's) had told Dad that Frank DiMaria was behind Alan's death and that the motivation was spite: he wanted to destroy Dad. He had paid someone else to commit the murder: Charles Harrelson, a thirty-one year old contract killer whom the Texas Rangers suspected of having murdered a dozen men or more."

Wallace said shortly after her brother's murder, Allen Berg's mother called her mom.

Heroin Trafficking Leads to Murder

"Meanwhile, I had met a man from Hearne, Texas named Pete Scamardo who was introduced as an old friend of Chuck's from Huntsville and Chuck told me, not in Pete's presence, that Pete had some business they were discussing. About the same time that Allen was killed

Chuck came home with some white powder packaged in a prophylactic which he told me was heroin and that Pete had brought it back from Mexico and considered himself completely unsuspicious because he was a businessman and had never been in any trouble." Attaway said. "Chuck was to try and sell the stuff for Pete as Chuck had more contacts. …Then, Chuck told me that there was no place in Houston that he could find to sell the heroin and that he had gotten the name of a contact from Frank DiMaria so we went to K.C."

Watkins said he only met Scamardo once recalling this cryptic and uncomfortable encounter at Lucky Pierre's.

"He (Harrelson) introduced him (Scamardo) by some name which I do not recall and said he was in the insurance business. They were sitting at a table and when I walked over they quit talking, and after the introduction, they remained silent."

Things didn't go as planned in Kansas City. After a tip from a confidential informant, Kansas City Police stopped Harrelson on June 3, 1968. Harrelson managed to dump the heroin in a sewer before they searched his car, but the heroin was lost. Harrelson was detained for possessing a sawed off shotgun in violation of their statute for altering firearms but made bail shortly after his arrest.

"Sometime around June or July (1968) Chuck told me that he had to pay Pete Scamardo a favor owed him and that he and Jerry (Watkins) were going to fly to the Valley and kill a man for Pete so that he could collect some insurance on a business partnership on a policy they had on each other." Attaway said.

By summer 1968, Scamardo was facing financial difficulties, and since Harrelson now owed for the heroin he lost, Scamardo came up with a plan. He would pay Harrelson $2,000 to kill Sam Degelia, Jr., because as business partners he'd collect $100,000 in life insurance.

"$50,000 of that went directly to a bank to pay off their business loan, and $50,000 Scamardo would pocket by stiffing their other creditors." Berg stated in *Run, Brother, Run*. "For his part, Harrelson would receive $2, 000."

"Isn't it hell when your buddy kills you to collect the insurance?" Harrelson told Watkins days after the murder.

But there may have been another motive for Scamardo to kill Sam Degelia, Jr., who told several people in the months prior to the murder he was thinking of dissolving their partnership because Scamardo wasn't pulling his weight.

The Investigation

The murder of Sam Degelia, Jr. didn't end Scamardo's financial troubles; on September 13, 1968, Scamardo, along with his attorney Owen Stidham, went to see a local polygraph examiner, Bob Musser. According to an *Associated Press* story Scamardo was visiting Musser's office because he was trying to borrow more money to clean up debts in his business and couldn't get a loan. Scamardo approached Sam Degelia, Sr., the father of the man he had murdered, for a loan, and Degelia, Sr., suspecting he killed his son, refused to lend him any money until he was cleared of his son's murder.

If Scamardo thought visiting Musser would clear his name, he was in for a rude awakening. After a series of questions, Musser suspected Scamardo was the killer and testified at Scamardo's trial, "I told him it sounded like he had a very good motive for having Degelia killed."

"You're right," Musser recalled Scamardo saying, "I had Sam shot."

Scamardo's lawyers attempted to keep this testimony out of the trial, arguing it was hearsay evidence, but the judge allowed it.

By fall 1968, evidence against Scamardo was mounting. Besides Musser, the Texas Rangers, which led the investigation, also interviewed Attaway and in October and November, they developed two pieces of physical evidence which sealed their case.

On October 10, 1968, the Texas Rangers produced a report detailing a check written by Pete Scamardo in the amount of $200 to Charles Stoughtenborough.

On November 20, 1968, Harrelson was arrested in Atlanta, where he was staying in rooming house under another alias, Terry Southern, and had Scamardo's 1969 light green Oldsmobile in his possession. True to Machiavellian form, Scamardo reported that car stolen five days earlier.

But on November 14, 1968, three long-time residents of Hearne saw Scamardo driving on State Highway 21 just west of the Brazos River Bridge. He and a light blue Ford pulled rapidly off the highway and stopped. Scamardo then got out of his 1969 Oldsmobile, got into a light blue Ford and drove off in the Ford shortly thereafter. Records showed days earlier Harrelson rented a 1969 light blue Ford Tudor from a Hertz in Reno, Nevada. The Tudor was found in a Hearne ditch abandoned on November 20, 1968.

Finally, on November 29, 1968, Tolliver Dawson identified two more money orders written to Charles Stoughtenborough. One, from September 30, 1968, was sent by Pete Scamardo, and the other was sent on November 10, 1968, by Bennie Johnson, an alias used by Scamardo.

Armed with this evidence, Scamardo was arrested on December 7, 1968, and charged with Sam Degelia, Jr.'s murder. He was released three days later after posting a $50,000 bond.

Harrelson was already incarcerated in nearby Brazoria County awaiting trial for Allen Berg's murder. Watkins was arrested with Scamardo, but he cut a deal and that day and provided his first formal written statement in the presence of one of his attorneys detailing everything.

"He (Harrelson) told me that Pete would not tell them (the police) anything because he had told Pete that he had a partner and that if Pete ever said anything; he would be dead before the sun went down." Watkins said in his initial statement of Harrelson's Machiavellian nature; Scamardo didn't rat out Harrelson and later testified for the defense.

Scamardo's Ruthless Defense Attorney

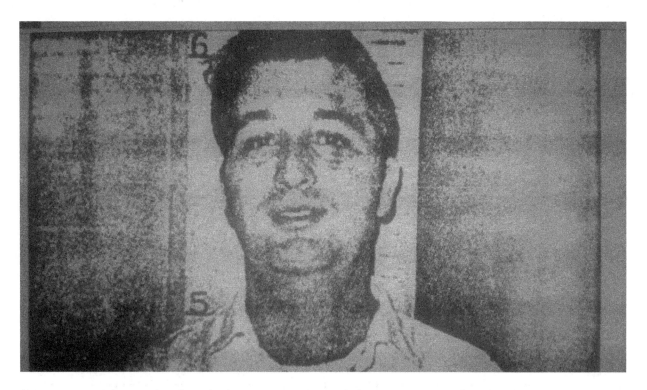

(Pete Scamardo's mugshot from his arrest in the murder of Sam Degelia, Jr. from the Texas Ranger investigative file)

Both Scamardo and Harrelson retained Percy Foreman, considered among the greatest lawyers in the history of the USA, losing 53 out of more than 1,500 murder trials. His clients include James Earl Ray, Martin Luther King Jr.'s killer and socialite Candy Mossler. Where did Harrelson and Scamardo come up with Foreman's sizable legal bills? That question remains unanswered. Foreman also represented Harrelson and DiMaria in their trials for the Berg murder.

Foreman was worth every penny. In Harrelson's first trial for Degelia, Jr.'s murder, Foreman put on nightclub singer Louise Scott Gannon who claimed she was having dinner with Harrelson at the time of the murder. The trial ended in a hung jury: 11 for conviction, one for acquittal.

In *Run, Brother, Run* David Berg said this stunt was standard operating procedure for Foremen.

"He reached into his stable of 'reserve witnesses,' as he called them: former clients and others who repaid his favors by swearing to have been with his defendant at the time of the crime. It wasn't just opposing prosecutors who knew that Foreman operated this way: his colleagues and even attentive laymen understood that he would do anything, no matter how dishonest, to win at trial."

Foreman died in 1988.

The Sensational Trial

As a result, Scamardo was tried without the benefit of Harrelson's conviction. The sensational trial included testimony by Musser and Attaway, who detailed how Harrelson lost Scamardo's drugs and how this led Scamardo to manipulate Harrelson into killing Degelia, Jr.

The defense put on 26 witnesses and introduced 81 items into evidence and the prosecution called 62 witnesses and introduced 80 items into evidence.

Foreman put the victim and his family on trial, a strategy aided by the thorough investigation of the Texas Rangers which uncovered unpleasant aspects of Degelia, Jr.'s life. Here's what a confidential informant told the Texas Rangers.

"Informant states that the deceased and a Reuben Amos (Degelia's uncle), formerly owned the Fodsco Food Locker Plant in Hearne, Texas. The food locker plant was won nearly completely through gambling operations in the Bryan/Hearne area. This plant is reportedly worth nearly $200,000 and the deceased and Reuben Amos obtained ownership of it for $56,000 cash and the remainder was in lieu of gambling debts on what was due the deceased and Reuben Amos."

"In several instances when we needed money we would loan money to each other writing checks on out of town banks. By the time the checks cleared the out of town banks we would have the money to cover the check when it bounced back. This is called kiting checks." Scamardo said. "I gave Sam a check for $2,000 before he went to the valley. I did not have the money to cover this check and Sam knew it. This was to repay Sam for $2,000 he loaned me a few days before this. This check was on the University National Bank in College Station (Texas). I first gave Sam a check for $2,000 on the Hearne bank and 2 or 3 days later Sam asked if I had the money yet. I told him I did not. Then I wrote the check on the College Station bank. I told him to tear up the first check but I do not know if he did or not."

The most explosive charge was this assertion by Scamardo.

"He (Scamardo) confessed to me that he and Sam Degelia, Jr. had been involved in smuggling heroin from Mexico." Texas Ranger Tolliver Dawson wrote in his report on August 29, 1968.

"The information as follows was related to me by my husband the evening of May 19, 1968. On May 17 around 2PM he received a phone call from Pete Thomas Scamardo. He was to get

$2,000 (small bills) and meet Scamardo in Bryan (a town which borders Hearne) in an hour. He did and returned home. Early May 18 he left for McAllen, Texas. He was to check into the Holiday Inn and meet Scamardo. That night they rented a car and crossed the border. Sam returned to the hotel while Pete Thomas Scamardo made contact with someone and received heroin. Pete Thomas Scamardo then went to Houston and Sam left early Sunday morning May 19 and returned home. He told me this because he felt bad about doing it and he said he would never have anything to do with it again." Ginger Degelia said in a Texas Rangers report.

Mrs. Degelia said her words were twisted. While Scamardo asked to borrow the money, he didn't give a reason. As business partners and friends, borrowing and loaning money to each other was fairly common, so Sam did as asked. Then, Scamardo asked Sam to accompany him to Mexico, a place Sam went all the time. It wasn't until the two of them were in Mexico that Scamardo gave the whole story. In fact, Scamardo asked Sam to accompany him on the drug buy but he refused and stayed in the hotel.

"That's when he decided he was through with him (Scamardo)," Ginger Degelia told me.

"My husband was no angel," she told me, but added he was a good father and husband, who deserved much better. Ginger Degelia has since remarried and now goes by Ginger Elich.

Ironically, Sam Degelia, Jr. unwittingly helped set in motion his murder because this was the heroin Scamardo gave Harrelson to sell.

At trial, Foreman aggressively used his favorite tactic, innuendo.

"I will prove that at least 20 to 30 people had a reasonable motive to kill Sam Degelia," Foreman said in his opening statement. "I have at least 20 hypotheses of possibilities of assassinations of Sam Degelia by people who didn't even know Pete Thomas Scamardo."

During his closing argument, he referred to Musser as "a certified liar", and suggested Mrs. Degelia had been unfaithful and Sam was possibly killed by a jealous husband.

"(Mrs. Degelia) may not have been as careful with her morals as a schoolgirl as she should have been." Foreman said. "There would have been more men in her life than Sandra Sue Attaway if she had not married Sam Degelia, Jr."

"The defense contended that Mrs. Degelia and Pete Anthony Trentacost, a cousin of the victim, had engineered the killing because of a love affair." according to a *United Press International (UPI)* article on the trial.

"Did you know that from the summer of 1967 to this good hour, right now, February 19, 1970, that Pete Trentacost has not dated another girl but you?" Foreman asked Mrs. Degelia during her cross-examination.

"No, I did not know that." Mrs. Degelia responded. "We spend a lot of time together if you want to make something of that. He has done that since he was 12."

"Foreman also talked about a Louisiana man who may have killed Degelia because Degelia may have been having an affair with the Louisiana man's wife." The same *UPI* article said. "Foreman wasn't definitive- he was just probing in his usual style."

He also suggested the Degelia family had criminal ties and the murder could have been committed by the criminal element.

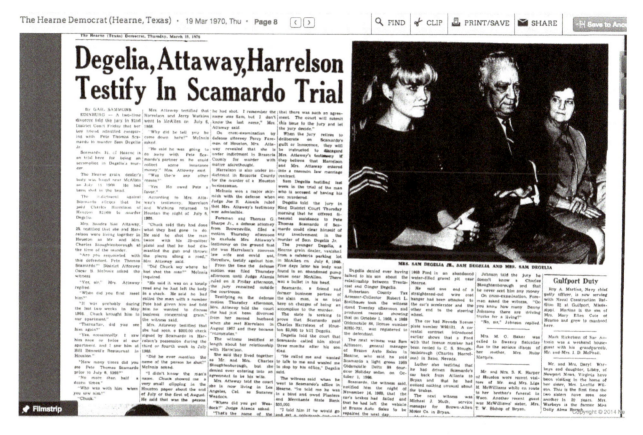

(Screenshot from a Hearne Democrat article on the trial also courtesy of newspapers.com Ginger Degelia is pictured far left with her husband's parents)

"I don't have to prove anything; I didn't say I was going to prove it." Foreman retorted to the judge who admonished him for these outlandish theories. "I said I was going to prove a reasonable hypothesis. If I said I was going to prove someone killed someone, I'd be as stupid as the lawyer who said he'd prove Dr. Sam Sheppard (the inspiration for the hit television series and movie, *The Fugitive*) killed his wife."

One day during the trial, Scamardo showed his true colors to Ginger. As she was leaving the courthouse and walking to her car, something got her attention. When she turned around, she saw a car pull up, driven by Scamardo's sister; Pete's arm was hanging out of the passenger side and when she looked at them, he laughed in her face as they sped away!

Scamardo Convicted But...

Despite Foreman's best efforts, a jury of six men and six women deliberated for about twelve hours and convicted Scamardo of accomplice to commit murder.

"But I didn't do it, I didn't!" Scamardo screamed after the verdict was read.

Though District Attorney Oscar McInnis asked for the death penalty, these same six good men and women did not vanquish evil. After deliberating for an hour and twenty-two minutes during the sentencing phase, the jury sentenced Scamardo to seven years' probation and no jail time.

Berg said this amounted to getting away with murder In *Run, Brother, Run*.

On March 31, 1970, Hidalgo County veteran DA, Oscar McInnis obtained a conviction against Scamardo for being an accomplice to murder-an astonishing victory for any prosecutor facing Foreman. But Foreman never stayed down for too long: during the punishment phase, Foreman introduced evidence of Scamardo's otherwise clean record and his devotion to church and family- and convinced the jury to probate every day of his seven year sentence.

Probation for murder! Thank you Percy.

The Degelia family believes this happened because the jury was corrupted.

"He (Foreman) made sure that trial was in Edinburg for a reason," Ginger told me.

This hypothesis is propped up by Hidalgo County's long history of corruption, which includes the 1979 conviction of Oscar McInnis in a kidnapping plot as well as the 1994 conviction of Hidalgo County Sheriff, Brig Marmolejo, for taking bribes from drug dealers.

In a December 1994 *Texas Monthly* story on Marmolejo's conviction, a lawyer in the area said, "There's more corruption in South Texas than Brig Marmolejo and Brig's not necessarily the most corrupt among them."

Titillating Tidbits about Foreman

"Foreman himself has been charged with several crimes, from using foul language in the presence of a minor girl to subornation of perjury (knowingly putting on false testimony)." David Berg said in *Run, Brother, Run*. "Representing himself, he won them all, only burnishing his unbeatable image."

Berg quoted the lifelong bachelor Foreman as once telling him the best thing about being a lawyer was "all the broads" and suggested Foreman kept DiMaria in prison more than a week after DiMaria's initial arrested for his brother's murder to have sex with DiMaria's wife.

David Berg has been long-time practicing attorney in the same area.

Harrelson Tried Again

Harrelson was tried again in 1972 in Brownsville, Texas. Texas Ranger Tolliver Dawson was in the courtroom with an arrest warrant for Gannon so she fled to Aruba making Scamardo a key witness for the defense.

"I know how it feels to have been falsely accused and falsely convicted and I am here because I don't want to see this happen to anyone else." Scamardo testified at Harrelson's second trial.

"Or, stated another way, he agreed to testify because he was scared shitless that if he didn't, Harrelson would get out of jail and kill him, too," Berg retorted in *Run, Brother, Run*.

Scamardo's Perjury at Harrelson's Trial

When testifying, Scamardo explained away a series of personal checks written to Harrelson by claiming Harrelson was his debt collector. David Berg detailed how McInnis destroyed this narrative on cross-examination in *Run, Brother, Run*.

"As a matter of fact, you didn't get any bad checks in your business to amount to anything, did you?"

"Yes sir, we got a number of checks that did not clear the bank."

"All right sir. Then can you give me a list of the people that he collected bad checks from you and Sam?"

"No sir, I cannot at this time."

"Well, can you name just one person that he ever collected a check for, for you or Sam?"

"I don't recall at this time, no sir."

"So out of forty-five checks over the past three years, you can't tell the jury just a name of one of those people so that we can get him down here and see whether or not this man collected a check from him?"

"I'm sure I could check and find out."

"Well, think about it a little right now. Can you give us one right now?"

"No, sir, not that I can recall."

Another bone of contention during Scamardo's testimony was the size of the insurance policy, with Scamardo saying it wasn't enough to clean up debts, giving him no motive to kill Sam. In a case of life imitating art, the policy had a double indemnity rider if Sam's death was accidental. Here's more from *Run, Brother, Run*.

"Come on, Mr. Scamardo. You thought that you had $50,000 total insurance on the life of Sam Degelia, Jr., and $100,000 in case of accidental death; is that right?"

"No, sir, that is not correct?"

"In fact, did you not, on the eighth day of July 1968, before Sam's body was found on the eleventh day of July, make the statement to Tol Dawson, a Texas Ranger, and in the presence of Chief of Police A.C. Gonzalez, Edinburg, Texas, at the police station here in Edinburg, before you left to go back to Hearne, that in the event Sam turned up dead that you had two $25,000 policies on his life?"

"No, sir, I don't recall making such a statement."

But the two law enforcement officers did- and instead of putting them on the stand during the state's case in chief, the wily district attorney had waited, allowed Foreman to elicit Scamardo's lie about the amount of insurance proceeds he thought he'd receive, before putting Ranger Dawson and Chief Gonzalez on the stand in rebuttal, to quote Scamardo saying he had expected to receive $100,000. Foreman knew that when those two very credible men testified, the intricate web of lies that he and Scamardo had created would collapse. The King of the Sandbag had been sandbagged, and, judging from his next step, Foreman knew it. He called Charles Harrelson to the stand.

McInnis tried numerous times to revoke Scamardo's probation for things like perjury and an appellate court judge on January 14, 1974 found Scamardo perjured himself during Harrelson's trial but determined it was not material to the case, and declined to revoke his probation.

Harrelson Finally Convicted

With Foreman's strategy destroyed, Harrelson was found guilty and sentenced to 15 years in prison.

"Congratulations, you are as hard as nails," Harrelson, always the charmer, told McInnis after verdict was read while shaking his hand.

With time off for good behavior, he was free in five years. He and DiMaria were found not guilty of Berg's murder.

Harrelson was convicted of the 1979 killing of Sam Wood, a federal judge, in 1981 and died in prison in 2007. Wood was the only federal judge murdered in the twentieth century. He also once claimed to have murdered John F. Kennedy before retracting his statement. In the last years of Charles Harrelson's life, Woody Harrelson financed an unsuccessful legal campaign to set him free.

Pete Scamardo left Hearne for Virginia and settled in that area the rest of his life. He's never apologized or explained his actions to any of the Degelia family; no one in the Scamardo or DeStefano family apologized to the Degelia's for this murder.

The Murder Traumatizes Hearne, Texas

Wallace said she was shielded from details of the murder in her youth. For instance, she had no idea her father suspected immediately Scamardo was the killer, but as she got older, she figured out the murder divided the town akin to the Hatfield and McCoy's.

While many in the town sided with the Degelia family, the DeStefano family was also prominent and each citizen took one side or the other. She said no one in her family has spoken to anyone in the DeStefano or Scamardo family since Scamardo first became a suspect in her brother's murder.

As she grew up she felt she had a relatively normal childhood, but looking back the murder turned her into a victim. She now remembers many times when she would be in town and hearing whispers of other town folks speaking in the distance discussing details of her brother's murder.

In her early twenties Cindy Wallace became obsessed with what she would say if she got the chance to confront Pete Scamardo. One day that chance came. Scamardo's father-in-law died when she was in her early twenties and Scamardo made one of his few return visits for the funeral. Leaving church one Sunday, she came eye to eye with her brother's killer. The moment turned into paralysis by hyper analysis and she froze saying nothing; she's regretted that moment ever since.

Scamardo's Media Makeover

In Virginia, Pete Scamardo reinvented himself as a real estate developer and investor. In 1975, he started CDC and took advantage of the real estate boom near Tyson's Corner Center, a mega mall first built in 1968 in unincorporated Fairfax County between McLean and Vienna, Virginia, boasting of having more visitors yearly than Disney World. Scamardo became a multimillionaire, possibly worth as much as $100 million. Scamardo owns a home in McLean, Virginia and a farm in Upperville, Virginia, one of the wealthiest cities in the country.

In a 1981 newsletter for Reston, Virginia he was featured as a prominent builder in a profile entitled *Pete Scamardo: An Important Role in Reston's Growth.*

"With 1.35 million sq. ft. of office/R & D (Research and Development) space either under construction, or in the planning process, CDC is a dominant presence in the bustling Reston development scene today." The newsletter ignored the murder in favor of painting Scamardo as a consummate entrepreneur. "Pete Scamardo began his development career working with a relative in Texas. He came to the Washington area in 1970 as an assistant to the home building general manager of Boise Cascade. He then managed projects in Prince George's County and later Fairfax County."

He was one of several builders featured in *The Washington Post* article in 1985 on the real estate boom in Reston.

When Centennial Development Corp. President Pete Scamardo looks down from the top of his new six-story Executive III office building near Dulles Toll Road, the Reston he sees around him is vastly different from the Reston of 1978.

(Photo of Scamardo from the Reston newsletter)

That was the year Scamardo, then an adventuresome, budding developer, made his decision to develop his first office building in Reston. In those days, the major commercial space was concentrated at Reston's own International Center and in the U.S. Geological Survey buildings.

Now, Centennial, the largest single developer of commercial space in Reston, has more than 750,000 square feet of office space in Reston, and another 500,000 is planned for construction in the next 18 months. The 21-year-old new town itself has blossomed into a major office market.

Michael Volpe

Scamardo popped up occasionally in the real estate section of *The Washington Post* adding his thoughts to articles about growth and specific projects cementing his image as a successful builder.

Scamardo's transformation was complete when *The Washington Post* did a profile of him on August 23, 1999.

Fifteen years ago, Pete T. Scamardo was shingling roofs and putting up aluminum siding in Northern Virginia. His small contracting company had two full-time employees.

By the mid-1980s, his real estate interests were valued at more than $80 million, according to sources, and his enterprise, the Centennial Cos., was on its way to becoming one of the half-dozen largest commercial developers in the Washington metropolitan area.

None of *The Washington Post* pieces mentioned the murder, and the paper has never done an exposé of Scamardo's past. None of the authors responded to my email for comment.

Another article from the website *Bis Now* which said Scamardo has developed "more than one million SF (square feet) of office condos in the region," also failed to mention the murder. The site and author, Stacy Pfarr, didn't respond to an email for comment.

The charity, Charity Works, featured Scamardo's wife, Andrea, as one especially dedicated individual in their August 2003 issue: "Andy Scamardo is our 'Steel Magnolia'- you wouldn't believe how tough and hardworking this quiet Texas lady can be. Her organizational skills, quiet charm and wonderful laugh are legendary and served her well in co-chairing the 2002 extravaganza. This was not a gala, but a huge production- everything had to be contracted for separately, and on the day of the Gala, had to arrive on time and in the proper sequence. At midnight, when the guests left, Andy rolled up her evening gown and coordinated removing all the equipment. At 3:30 in the morning, we found Andy, broom in hand, sweeping the National Building Museum to insure that was in perfect shape."

That charity and Mrs. Scamardo didn't respond to an email for comment.

A March 24, 1970 story from the *Associated Press* presented a different Andrea Scamardo. The story suggested she lied during her testimony in her husband's trial.

Sam Degelia Sr., the victim's father, was put on the stand to dispute testimony given Monday by Andrea Scamardo, the defendant's wife. Degelia testified that he did not have a brother named Ben Degelia.

Mrs. Scamardo said that Harrelson, the alleged triggerman, was a cousin-in-law of the victim. She said this relationship existed because Glenda Watson, a niece of Harrelson, married Anthony Reina, a nephew of Ben Degelia.

Despite the serene image presented by these articles, Scamardo has been involved in numerous lawsuits. He was featured in the *Washington Times* in May 1991 about an $80 million lawsuit filed against him by Chevy Chase Bank. That story also failed to mention his role in the murder of Sam Degelia, Jr.

Since the 1970s, Scamardo has been a defendant or plaintiff in more than one hundred lawsuits in Fairfax County, Virginia.

Chris Mackney also accused Scamardo of doing an end run around Virginia laws and using his daughter, Dina Mackney, as a front to get a horse racing license which he, a felon, couldn't get.

"I wanted to bring to your attention the fact that my wife and her father were involved in a felony conspiracy," Chris Mackney said in an email, "during the course of the marriage when Mr. Scamardo used his daughter to obtain a Virginia horse racing license."

I sent an email to Kimberley Mackey, the administrator for the Virginia Racing Commission but that email was left unreturned.

Mackney's claim about the horse racing license raises another question, *how did Pete Scamardo, a convicted felon, get a real estate license?*

(Scamardo, far right, pictured in the article from *Bis Now*)

I posed that question in an email to Amanda Pearson, the media relations person for the Virginia Department of Housing and Community Development, but she didn't respond.

Dina Mackney also received favorable press. She is often featured in *Washington Life Magazine* at swanky events. In a September 2007 issue she said this was her most embarrassing moment: "Trying to dance with my 6-foot-5 husband in six inch platform heels while nine months pregnant."

On September 27, 2010, the *Washington Post* did a profile of her entitled *Jewelry designer makes inroads with upscale retailers*: "From her basement studio in Vienna, Dina Mackney started designing semiprecious gemstone necklaces and rings eight years ago, following an encounter with a local boutique owner who was taken with a piece she created for herself. Mackney has since caught the attention of the likes of Nordstrom and Saks Jandel, where her collections are sold. And starting this month, the venerable luxury retailer Neiman Marcus will carry Dina Mackney Designs at select stores."

None of the retailers who carry Mackney's gems responded to my emails for comment for this book. Danielle Douglass, who wrote *The Washington Post* profile, also didn't respond to an email.

The Washington Post has never written about the salacious details of her divorce.

Chris Mackney and the Murder of Sam Degelia, Jr.

Among the web pages removed as a result of the copyright notice was a Google Drive which Mackney created containing about fifteen articles about the murder. These articles were removed even though others wrote each of them, while Mackney organized the articles into one electronic drive.

Before they were removed from the internet, I downloaded most of the articles and they were incorporated into the research for this chapter. Mackney also received the Texas Ranger investigation of the murder of Sam Degelia, Jr. through a FOIA request, and this remains active on the internet because the document was specifically marked "no copyrighted material."

Cindy Wallace told me she corresponded with Mackney for more than a year during his divorce. He initially asked her, "Is there any chance he didn't do it?"

Everyone in the Degelia family told me they have no doubt Pete Scamardo hired Charles Harrelson to kill Sam Degelia, Jr.

Cindy Wallace told me she found Chris Mackney intelligent, well-spoken, but also traumatized. She stopped communicating with him because she felt talking about the pain the murder caused her family only added to his trauma.

Cindy Wallace's life has come full circle; she works with crime victims and continues to live in Hearne. Much of the Degelia family and Ginger Elich also live in the area.

Chapter 4: The Marriage

"By all means, marry. If you get a good wife, you'll become happy; if you get a bad one, you'll become a philosopher."

Socrates

The Idyllic Wedding

Chris and Dina Machnij held their wedding reception on Pete Scamardo's farm on June 3, 2000. In Upperville, Virginia the farm is at least 250 acres, according to Mackney's friends who have seen it. It's been called amazing, and Mike Harris called it "idyllic." The entertainment was provided by Chris Machnij's new brother-in-law, Warren Haynes, formerly of The Allman Brothers Band, who also played with the Grateful Dead and is currently leader of his own band, Gov't Mule. Haynes is married to Dina's sister, Stefani Scamardo, who is Gov't Mule's manager along with a disk jockey with Sirius XM radio. I sent her an email but she didn't respond.

Harris moved to Virginia after college and didn't see Chris Machnij regularly until he also moved to Virginia. He said when he saw the bride on her wedding day, the farm and his father-in-law's wealth Harris thought Chris struck the proverbial lottery in the marriage. Harris and his family socialized routinely with the Machnij's and later Mackney's. He said everything appeared fine in the marriage and once said in court he considered both good parents.

The Troubled Marriage

The idyllic wedding was followed immediately by turmoil when Dina attacked Chris while driving in a rental car in Maui on their honeymoon.

"She attacked me in the car, as I was driving. I pulled the car over to the side and told her that this was the first time any woman had ever physically attacked me and that it was unacceptable. I told her that if I had done that to her I would go to jail." Chris Mackney said in his complaint to the American Psychological Association.

About a year into the marriage, Chris and Dina moved into a spacious Mclean, Virginia home with about 5,000 square feet costing roughly $500,000. At this point, Dina's business hadn't started and Chris wasn't making nearly enough to afford the home on his own, so payments were augmented by Dina's father.

The newly married Chris Machnij was working for his father-in-law, living near his father-in-law, and in a home financed in part by his father-in-law, all Machiavellian.

Machnij worked for Scamardo for about five years, and it was a source of infinite stress, of infinite frustration, of pressure without end or limit. Scamardo rejected every deal Chris brought him. The reasons are numerous and complicated but at least one has to do with a dark family secret; Pete Scamardo was a murderer and convicted felon. The entire Scamardo family, including Dina, hid this secret from Chris during their courtship and the duration of their marriage. As a convicted felon, Scamardo was limited in the deals he could do directly. Instead, he used fronts, people with clean records who signed their names on Scamardo's behalf. If these fronts didn't like the deal Chris proposed, Scamardo rejected it without giving Chris the real reason.

(Chris Machnij from 2002)

While Scamardo was helping pay his mortgage, he made sure Machnij couldn't make enough to afford the home on his own. Chris Machnij found himself trapped. He was unable to sustain the lifestyle his new wife had grown accustomed to and his new father-in-law was making sure he couldn't advance professionally to be able to provide that lifestyle, also quite Machiavellian.

Stress from work and home caused the free spirited Chris Machnij to experience unprecedented turmoil and seek professional help.

"Mr. Mackney stated that prior to his marriage he and his wife had done some marital counseling as a result of the fact that they did not communicate well. Indeed, he remembers that they fought and found it difficult to compromise." A psychological evaluation attached to

Mackney's divorce stated. "They had, he asserted, 'poor conflict resolution' skills. That period of marital counseling lasted for a couple of months. They continued to do some couples' therapy, however, when they moved to the Washington, DC area to be near his wife's family. That work dealt with the result of the stresses within their marriage and the stresses they experienced at work. He remembers having been in psychotherapy between 2003 and 2004."

The Name Change

In 2002, they changed their name to Mackney so that Dina could start her jewelry business called Dina Mackney Designs and had their first child, daughter Ruby. By 2003, the marriage appeared heading for an end. They lived apart for several months but got back together and had their second child, James, in 2004.

The Car Accident

On New Year's Day 2003, Dina and Chris Mackney were involved in an auto collision with a truck which left Dina with memory loss and severe pain which she described in a deposition.

"I had a lot of headaches from the accident, but, you know, the more concerning thing is my issues I had with- you know, not remembering things and using the wrong words for identifying objects...I was on a lot of pain medication, and I couldn't get out of bed. I had to use the bedpan. So, the treatment was medication. I believe they did tests, you know, MRI's and CAT scans, but I don't- it was very confusing. I don't know when or what. They eventually fit me for a custom brace...I think he (her doctor) had taken another one because he was concerned about some of the problems I was having, and he also thought there could be some minor- not minor- some other bleeding around the brain, so he reassessed it and referred me to another doctor for that particular part of my accident, the head injury."

Her doctor had her see a specialist for the memory loss.

"Dr. Cooney referred me to Dr. Spector because I had been seeing Dr. Cooney for my vertebrae injuries after I returned to the DC area, and we were also talking about a lot of issues that I realized I was having trouble with memory and retrieving words and just other issues. He calls them cognitive issues."

The injuries resulted in a settlement for several hundred thousand dollars in 2007.

Chris said the pressure in the marriage intensified after the accident. His wife became forgetful; her clients occasionally called his cell phone looking for her after she forgot to call them back or make appointments. He also said his wife would forget messages he gave her and then start arguments claiming he never told her, a form of gas-lighting.

The Marriage from 2005 On

Michael Volpe

Sometime during 2004-2005, Chris Mackney began visiting internet chat rooms and created an online dating account which led to at least one affair. Mackney insisted to friends he only cheated on Dina with one individual; she insisted it was many more; I don't know who was telling the truth. Mackney described Dina as cold and distant and this was the reason, though not the excuse for his cheating. "She wouldn't kiss me when I came home from work," he said.

When his wife caught him cheating he began to see a psychiatrist named Dr. Colleen Blanchfield. Here's part of a psychological evaluation.

In 2005 he began seeing a psychiatrist, Dr. Colleen Blanchfield, and he continues to see her, primarily for the administration of medicines, including both Welbutrin and Effexor. He remembers having considered going off those medications in 2008, but was convinced to remain on them because of the stress of the marital situation.

He also raised the discussion of a feeling of personal inadequacy that led him to become involved in internet chat rooms with women, an effort, he explained, to reach out, trying to validate himself. It was when his wife found out that she insisted that he see a therapist.

Dr. Blanchfield's office declined to make her available for an interview.

The Marriage Crumbles

Mackney left CDC some time in 2005 and moved first to CB Richard Ellis and then to Trammell Crow in 2007, two heavyweights in commercial real estate.

Unlike working for his father-in-law, Mackney consistently closed deals from 2005-2007 and made six figures each year. In 2007, largely on the strength of closing a $50 million deal he made more than $250,000, but things at home weren't any better, with near non-stop arguing and emotional turmoil for the last three years of their marriage.

The Fight That Ends It All: January 19, 2008

The marriage disintegrated on January 19, 2008; a verbal argument turned physical, the police were called, Dina gas-lighted and her dad hid evidence. Here's part of Mackney's blog post.

I encountered the Fairfax County legal system first on January 19th, 2008. This was the day the straw broke the camel's back in my relationship with my ex-wife and her family. I called the police after my ex-wife had assaulted me in front of our children, James and Ruby. I did nothing to threaten or anger her, as I just woke up and she was already angry and hiding my car keys, preventing me from escaping her wrath. I had seen it before and knew exactly that leaving is the only way to avoid the conflict. She knew that I knew that I would leave and deliberately blocked me from leaving.

When I called the police, they found me locked in my son's room, with my children. I had a shirt ripped from my body and scratches and marks all over my back and neck, where she attacked me from behind. My children witnessed the entire situation. Now, Dina had to talk first, which is how she controls the situation and manages 'impressions'. She tried to justify hitting me from behind, as I tried to escape the situation, she had prevented me from escaping, by saying that I turned over a tray of her beads. Her judgment is in denial of facts or an awareness of how her behavior harms others.

After speaking with my ex-wife, I open the door for the police officers, who witness the evidence of assault. Now, if I had been the one to rip her shirt and leave marks on her neck and back, I would have gone to jail, no questions asked, do not collect $200. In this situation, the Police officer decided to leave both the parties and the children in the house together.

After I called the Police, I also called my ex-wife's parents. I wanted them to see how differently Dina was acting and that I had never harmed her. Her parents were there at the time the police arrived and before they spoke to me. When the police officer left and did nothing, after witnessing domestic violence, I was shocked. As I walked out the door, to the gym, in a replacement shirt, I deliberately left the shirt that Dina ripped off me on the kitchen counter. When I came back 90 minutes later the evidence of an assault had vanished. Of course, I asked her about it. She denied any knowledge of the shirt, having no clue of its whereabouts. My reaction to being lied to and 'gas-lighted' was to respond in kind, in an effort to have the shirt returned. I sat down at the computer and threatened to delete her Jewelry business files from the computer. That seemed to do the trick. She then called her father, who had taken the evidence of the assault, and had him drive it back to the house.

Though still living together following this incident, divorce was imminent.

Chapter 5: The Divorce

"A parent has a fundamental right to make decisions concerning the upbringing, education, and care of the parent's child."

Virginia statute on parental rights

The Restraining Order

The divorce officially started in May 2008; before that the jockeying began. Chris hired Sean Kelly as his divorce attorney while Dina hired Mark Carlin of Ain & Bank, considered one of the premiere divorce firms in the area.

Using the old adage "possession is nine tenth of the law" Dina pressured Chris into leaving their family home thereby possessing two key items: home and kids.

In April 2008, Carlin sent Chris a letter demanding child support, alimony, half his retirement, and that he leave the home. Here's part of the letter.

Dina continues to seek an amicable resolution of the matters between you.

Toward that end, and subject to full financial disclosure by you, Dina proposes that she retain the home; her business; all other assets in her sole name; and one half of the value of all your retirement, savings/investment, and other accounts as of December 31, 2007. The contents of the home will be divided fairly between you. Child support will be paid to Dina in accordance with the Virginia child support guidelines. Dina will be seeking spousal support, but we are not in a position to make any proposal until we receive your financial disclosure...Once we receive all of your financials, we can promptly move toward a final separation agreement.

There are pressing substantive matters that require your immediate attention. You need to address the enormous tension in the household. A major contributor to that tension is your failure to contribute economically to the ongoing needs of your family. I understand that your contributions are limited to paying relatively small household bills and that you have failed to consistently make even those modest payments. As a result, cable and telephone services were cut off and a discontinuance notice of gas service was received.

...

The tension in the household can be reduced if you move from (the home). The property is in Dina's sole name, and she pays the entire mortgage. She asks that you remove your belongings by Friday April 18.

Initially, Chris wouldn't leave the home, "fearful that he would be seen as abandoning the children. Further, he could not afford such a move, and, as a result, he did not comply with the request," according to a psychological evaluation.

When pressure alone didn't work, Dina Mackney did what millions of people- mostly women- do in American divorces: she got a restraining order.

Chris Mackney had no criminal record, no history of domestic violence, and there were no photos or other physical evidence suggesting he was an abuser. Still, on May 23, 2008, Dina Mackney filed a motion for protection against Chris Mackney, arguing she feared for her life and needed him removed from the house. She documented three incidents including her version of the fight from January 19, 2008.

"This began from an argument about his continuing to text and on-line date with other women on the internet. He then took (while I was sleeping) my studio (jewelry) keys. He wouldn't give them back so I took his. An argument ensued and ended with physical pushing and his throwing and destroying thousands of dollars of jewelry around my studio. He threw trays at me and all around the room."

Dina's Innuendos: The Drug Issue

Question number twelve of the protective order asked: "Does the respondent have a drug or alcohol problem. If so, please describe the kind and frequency of drug abuse?"

Dina Mackney replied, "He may have a drug problem," and nothing else.

Dina Mackney was asked a two part question and didn't answer the second part, requiring specificity: a glaring red flag.

This was not the only time that Dina Mackney accused her ex-husband of having a drug addiction, she made a similar accusation in Samenow's report, and that made Mark Duda especially angry.

"It is character assassination," Duda said. During the years he saw Mackney regularly, Mackney went out, he drank, and smoked marijuana on occasion, but it was socially and rarely drank to get drunk. His drinking, Duda told me, was no worse than the average single successful person and suggesting Chris Mackney had a drug or alcohol problem means nearly all successful people in their twenties and thirties have drug problems.

While Mackney did smoke marijuana on a few occasions, he stopped before they got married and only smoked when hanging out with Dina's sister and her rock star husband Warren Haynes: once every few months. Rich Ware told me Mackney picked it up again toward the end of his life as a method of self-medication, but that was long after these accusations were made.

Furthermore, during the marriage after Dina complained that he'd gotten too inebriated on one occasion, Chris stopped drinking entirely.

Nevertheless, the protective order was granted the same day it was filed and twelve days later there was a "settlement agreement" permanently removing Chris Mackney from his home. Mackney could not afford an apartment; he moved in temporarily with Rich Ware and released Sean Kelly as his attorney.

Chris Mackney Discovers the Murder

On June 23, 2008, Chris Mackney, while searching for Pete Scamardo's middle name (Thomas) on the internet found an article about Sam Degelia, Jr's. murder with a reference to Scamardo. He fired off an email to his wife that day with the subject: *Do I need to be worried?*

In 1974, Charles Harrelson was convicted in the July 1968 killing of Hearne grain dealer Sam Degelia Jr., who was shot in the head south of McAllen. Pete Scamardo, Degelia's business partner, was convicted of paying Harrelson $2,000 to kill Degelia so he could collect insurance money, according to a September 1970 article that appeared in The Monitor.

http://www.themonitor.com/onset?id=1032&template=article.html

Dina didn't deny knowing about the murder when she responded dismissively.

I already know about this and you have no idea about the details and at this point it is none of your business. D

But Dina fired Ain & Bank the VERY NEXT DAY and immediately hired Cottrell, Fletcher, Schinstock, Bartol, & Cottrell led by Jim Cottrell who boasts, "He's not the type to settle so have your wallets open."

A few weeks later, Dina tried to entrap Chris into blackmailing her. She called him and secretly recording the phone conversation asking: "What will it take for you to stop talking about my father?"

Mackney responded that he didn't want money but his share of the equity in the house (there was about $500,000 in total equity)

"That recorded conversation was taken to the police as evidence of blackmail but the police did not see it that way," according to a psychological evaluation describing the incident.

Because the article Mackney read only mentioned Scamardo in passing, he initially didn't make too much of the murder but this incident piqued his interest; he soon made a FOIA request for the Texas Ranger investigative file into Degelia's murder which he received in October 2008. Once he understood the seedy details of the murder, things clicked: the Scamardo's were all psychopaths and he became obsessed with the murder and psychopathy.

Chris Mackney believed the switch to Cottrell and most legal strategies going forward were devised not by Dina but her father. The first line item on Cottrell's bill was a fifteen minute phone call to Pete Scamardo, suggesting Cottrell thought the same thing.

Dina Gets Horny: Emails Chris

Dina then sent Chris an email inviting him to a hotel for sex on July 7, 2008.

Mackney turned the email into a hyperlink but that hyperlink was destroyed as part of the copyright purge and is one of the few documents I couldn't retrieve. Jill Peterson Mitchell saw a copy of the email and Rich Ware remembers that day.

Rich Ware, with whom Mackney was still staying, remembered the two of them exchanging text messages that day and Dina showed up in her car outside Ware's residence.

"I told him not to get sucked back in," Ware told me and Mackney thought better of the sexual encounter.

Fathers' divorce attorney David Pisarra, when he had me on his podcast, noted this is often a ploy by the woman to then say the order was violated or to draw a man into the room and suggest he attacked her. While that's speculative in Dina Mackney's case- since it never materialized- Pisarra is right in the larger sense.

It was during this period Dr. Guy Van Syckle was appointed as parenting coordinator, a nebulous title with broad powers to intervene and direct a divorce. He wasn't entirely one sided saying at one hearing that Chris Mackney was "under tremendous stress" as a result of the divorce but generally sided with Dina. Van Syckle didn't respond to my email for comment.

Dina's Innuendos: Chris Owns a Gun

For years, Chris Mackney legally owned a shotgun without incident. Still, in her protective order, Dina made Mackney's free exercise of the 2nd amendment an issue: "Chris has become increasingly irrational and physical especially since we began talking about divorce. I simply cannot feel ok in a house when a heated argument inevitably becomes physical. He keeps a gun in the house and (I) don't want my kids or myself exposed to continued hostility which I feel could harm me."

That wasn't the only time in her application that guns became an issue: "Chris and I got into another argument in which he got generally enraged and sounding angry. He had just shown his gun to me and I was afraid. I called the police."

The police declined to file a report or charges. Chris Mackney reached out to the National Rifle Association (NRA) for help, but the NRA ignored him.

In October 2008, Dina escalated the accusations, claiming during a hearing for a subsequent protective order Chris pointed a handgun at her.

"He cocked the gun once at me in a fight and aimed it. He pulled it out from the mattress. I hid it." Dina said in Dr. Samenow's report.

But Chris owned a shotgun not a handgun, a contradiction he pointed out at this hearing, and it would be quite difficult to hide a shotgun in a mattress. The timing of this allegation is inexplicable. In May, she filed a restraining order against Chris, he moved out in June, she asked him to a hotel for sex in July, and in October she accused him of pointing a handgun at her. When did this purported incident occur and why wait until this hearing to first mention it?

Dina Mackney subsequently claimed this incident occurred in 2005, but this would mean it occurred during their marriage. She conveniently waited until a protective order hearing to first reveal it and somehow forgot about it when she first filed for a protective order. None of these contradictions and discrepancies became an issue and Dina was granted protective orders repeatedly, including this one.

Chris Mackney hired Robert Surovell as his new divorce attorney soon after to reach a settlement as soon as possible, a doomed strategy since Cottrell was paid NOT TO SETTLE.

Cottrell's Legal Bullying Strategy...

Rich Ware told me in Cottrell Pete Scamardo found someone like Percy Foreman: 1) both are known and respected in their fields 2) both think the best defense is a good offense and 3) both have no problem putting the victims on trial to advance their client's interests.

Cottrell's aggressive style is summarized in a court filing for another divorce: "the plaintiff and defendant engaged in extensive litigation, including numerous discovery disputes, pendent lite matters, a plea in bar, motions for declaratory judgment, sanctions motions, the filings of amended complaints and counterclaims, and other matters. Multiple hearings, including several evidentiary hearings, have been conducted to resolve pending disputes."

"This sort of thing happens rather often in custody situation, the person who controls the money is able to prevail irrespective of the facts," Dr. Michael Stone, a noted forensic psychologist said, "because they hire attorneys who are vigorous quality and also to go and make one motion and counter motion in order to exhaust the resources of the other party."

"It was orchestrated by attorneys who were paid not to settle and insisted on litigating every single issue without discussion." Mackney said in his suicide note. "It was all done to increase the stress and pressure. I saw behind the mask and the facade and I needed to be eliminated, just like Sam Degelia needed to be eliminated for discovering Pete Scamardo was trafficking heroin. The plan was to have attorneys negatively interpret anything I say or do and then litigate every issue. I needed to be portrayed as the source of conflict, so the legal and financial pressure could be applied."

One example of the legal bullying is this email to Cottrell on October 30, 2008.

I have no money for an attorney to challenge you in court; I do not wish to fight Mrs. Mackney or her family.

You have subpoenaed work for information that I have expressed numerous times, I will voluntarily provide. This is harassment and unnecessary. Mrs. Mackney is not acting in good faith.

What does Mrs. Mackney want to end this madness? I truly believe she is acting in the best interest of her father and not her children.

...Financed by Pete Scamardo

Over the next five years, Dina Mackney spent over $1 million in legal fees, an amount affordable only to her father. Chris Mackney was in court for 54 hearings and dealt with exponentially more written motions, letters, affidavits, and other legal documents.

On May 13, 2009, Dina Mackney claimed in a deposition her parents hadn't been paying her legal expenses until recently.

"Are your parents paying your legal expenses?" Surovell asked her.

"No. I paid for much of the legal expenses. They have helped me recently because I have run out of money." Dina responded.

Her attorneys failed to provide copies of their invoices to Surovell for this hearing despite a subpoena.

"I'll take the blame for that, Rob. That was inadvertent. She provided it. We have — it's not that she's not paying us." Cottrell interjected.

By the time Mackney received the invoices the case had largely been decided but they showed Pete Scamardo made seven payments over the first year of Cottrell's services with the first payment on June 25, 2008: the day after Cottrell was hired. Dina Mackney was never held accountable for her faulty testimony.

DATE	AMOUNT	CHECK #
June 25th, 2008	$15,000	5976
Nov. 18th, 2008	$4,811	6531
Feb. 4th 2009	$15,000	6136
Feb. 24th 2009	$12,205	6153
March 18th, 2009	$9,719	6167
April 9th, 2009	$909	6180
April 10th, 2009	$15,000	6181

TOTAL $72,643.95

(A part of a blog post showing checks paid from CDC to Cottrell for Dina Mackney's representation)

In an email on November 14, 2008, Mackney first suggested to Surovell that he was being bullied to death, "Did Mr. Cottrell give you any indication that there may be a settlement available or do you see them taking this to court? These people are going to bully me until eternity."

Legal Bully Cottrell Refuses to Settle

Dina's initial settlement demands- as described in a November 16, 2008, email Surovell sent to Chris Mackney- were: 1) sole custody to Dina with visitation for Chris 2) full marital assets to Dina and 3) $6,000 monthly in child support payment. Surovell assured Mackney there would be a more equitable agreement.

On December 10, 2008, Surovell made his initial settlement offer.

"In fact, this is a walk away deal. All that we ask for is $120,000 out of the house and a reasonable custodial access schedule. We retain the services of Dr. Van Syckle, who I am confident can manage the Mackneys into a reasonable manner of sharing that responsibility." Surovell said in the letter. "In candor, if Chris spends the kind of time that he proposes to spend with the children, it will be not only to the benefit of the children and Chris, but to Dina's as well. The children now spend a fair amount of time with daycare providers and I'm sure they would do just as well with doting parents."

Jim Cottrell ignored the settlement offer and demanded more information twelve days later.

Before we can adequately respond to Mr. Mackney's proposal we need to have more complete information on Mr. Mackney's income and resources. Specifically, we have discussed and Mr. Mackney has discussed with his wife that he has been expecting to close a substantial sale this month. We need verification regarding that sale and how much Mr. Mackney is going to receive in compensation.

Regarding Mr. Mackney's proposal for child custody and visitation, Ms. Mackney does not agree with your proposal, however she would agree to an order with the following terms:

Ms. Mackney shall have sole legal custody of their children. She will keep Mr. Mackney informed regarding the children's school and health. At this time, Mr. Mackney is simply not prepared or qualified to share in legal custody...Mr. Mackney's malicious conduct has to stop."

Along with the letter, Cottrell filed an Affidavit and Petition For Rule to Show Cause in which he spelled out the so-called malicious acts: one nasty email, allegedly "verbally assaulting" (yelling really loudly) at his wife in front of their children, and making "outrageous and malicious statements about the wife and her family" (calling his father-in-law a murderer and saying Dina suffered a traumatic brain jury).

For the next six months, this was the dynamic: Surovell attempted to settle with a man paid not to settle until Chris Mackney ran out of money.

Dina Frustrates Chris's Parental Time

"Further creating tension for him was the fact that in that month (June 2008) his wife began restricting his visits with his children, a plan he now sees as deliberately aimed at creating frustration for him," according to a psychological evaluation.

"My wife has once again waited until the last minute and has ruined all my holiday plans for me and my children. This has happened over Halloween, Thanksgiving, and now Christmas." Mackney emailed Surovell.

Chris Mackney then filed a formal complaint with the Juvenile and Domestic Relations (JDR) Court of Fairfax County on October 7, 2008: "Over the last several weeks, my wife has denied me visitation with my children. Additionally, she has not facilitated communication with my children. I have left voicemails for my children which are not returned and dozens of emails and voicemails to see and speak to my children."

Cottrell moved this complaint to family court where it died.

In the complaint Mackney made what Cottrell considered disparaging remarks. "I am also very concerned about the mental health of my wife and her family. My wife had a severe head injury and has consistently shown bad faith and poor judgment since our decision to divorce. Her father is a convicted murderer and admitted drug trafficker and her sister is a habitual and long term drug user. Both of whom are left unsupervised with the children."

Though Dina played up her head injury in their lawsuit, she denied it had any lasting effect during the divorce, arguing the accusation disparaged her.

Over time Cottrell secured court orders forbidding Mackney from disparaging his ex-wife and her family, repeating allegations about Pete Scamardo, and eventually even orders to stop emailing his ex-wife.

On October 21, 2008, things boiled over; Chris Mackney picked up Ruby unannounced after school.

"The Potomac School just called in a panic," Dina emailed Chris urgently later that day. "You cannot just snatch a kid out without telling anyone or without signing her out."

"The bus radioed to the lower school that Ruby was not on the bus and yet Ruby's teacher said she left to get on the bus as usual."

"I was not aware of the protocol," Chris Mackney responded about ninety minutes later, "because you have not bothered to share any of Ruby's information with me."

Samenow's Bait and Switch

A father's rights group first recommended Dr. Stanton Samenow to Chris Mackney to do a psychological evaluation; Dina quickly made the idea hers because unbeknownst to Chris Mackney Samenow and Cottrell's law firm had a longstanding working relationship. Mackney and Samenow first spoke on October 20, 2008; on January 23, 2009, Chris and Dina Mackney settled on a temporary arrangement called a Pendente lite, meaning "awaiting the litigation" in Latin; Dr. Samenow was introduced into the divorce as part of this Pendente lite which also set visitation times.

Initially, Chris Mackney had standard non-custodial time: alternate weekends after school on Friday until Sunday at 5PM and every Wednesday after school until 6:45PM. Chris Mackney's parenting times were still frustrated by Dina's interference. Furthermore, a disastrous commercial real estate market along with crippling divorce costs caused Chris financial hardship forcing him to cancel other dates because he couldn't afford them.

Dr. Stanton Samenow is the author of several books including *Inside the Criminal Mind*, *The Myth of out of Character Crime*, and *In the Best Interest of the Child*. He's testified as an expert in criminal and civil trials thousands of times, most notably as an expert for the prosecution in the trial of Lee Boyd Malvo, the protégé of the Beltway Sniper, John Muhammad. He received mainstream attention when his 1977 study *The Criminal Personality* written with Dr. Samuel Yochelson was referenced in the penultimate episode of *The Sopranos* entitled *Blue Comet*. When Dr. Melfi's mentor and therapist Dr. Elliot Kupferberg played by Peter Bogdanovich realized that Tony Soprano was a sociopath, he confronted Dr. Melfi at a dinner party full of psychologists.

"So I googled any new stuff on sociopathic personalities. Apparently, the talking cure actually helps them become better criminals." Dr. Kupferberg said in the episode. "It was fascinating. The study was by Yochelson and Samenow. Studies turn around every few years. This other, I think it was Robert Hare, suggested that sociopaths actually quite glibly engage on key issues, like mother, family. I seem to remember that from residency."

It was this study- Dr. Melfi obsessively read the study later in the episode- which convinced Dr. Melfi to dump Tony Soprano.

The *Toronto Star* praised Samenow's work when reviewing the episode.

"The seminal mid-'70s work, conducted by Americans Stanton Samenow and the late Samuel Yochelson, suggested that criminals who undergo therapy actually learned to better manipulate others and that they are more likely to reoffend than those who do not go through therapy."

In his evaluation, Dr. Samenow said the Pendente lite tasked him with "performing a psychological evaluation and assessment of the parties and the minor children in order to make recommendations to the Court and the parties regarding what custodial arrangements would best suit the parties and the children."

This is psychological sleight of hand; he claimed to a psychological evaluation while describing a custody evaluation. A custody and psychological evaluation are distinct, and exactly as they sound; a psychological evaluation measures the psychological profile of the parents, and a custody evaluation provides a report on the best custody arrangement. In a psychological evaluation interviewing the children is not allowed and the evaluator is not allowed to make custody recommendations.

Mackney wanted Dr. Samenow to do a psychological evaluation because he believed Dina was a psychopath and a psychological evaluation would reveal it; a custody evaluation was a different matter. Dr. Samenow was tasked with doing a psychological evaluation but wound up doing a custody evaluation. In a subsequent hearing, Jim Cottrell said they were "the same thing", and they were "the same thing" in the same way an oil change is the same thing as a tune up. Chris Mackney made several complaints- the APA, ACFEI, the Virginia Board of Psychology, and others- that this amounted to fraud, but none of these bodies did anything.

Mackney's Spiral Continues

In March 2009, at a pre-trial custody hearing, Mackney's child support was set at $2,813 per month, based on his 2007 income of about $250,000. It would be bumped up by three dollars soon after and kept there the remainder of his life, long after his income could not support that amount. Mackney made next to nothing starting in the fall 2009.

"I honestly need some relief Mr. Bartol. I cannot pay the $2816 per month. I have not been able to pay it because I no longer work at the #1 real estate services company in the world and the real estate market is not as robust as it was in 2007." Mackney said in an email to Cottrell's law partner, Kyle Bartol, in January 2013, one of several desperate emails begging to reduce his child support.

In June 2009, Robert Surovell quit in frustration; he cited an inability to reach a deal, Cottrell's lack of cooperation, and because Chris could no longer afford to pay him.

This tragic case isn't getting any better. When I got into this case I sent you a proposal. It was a reasonable proposal. I've never received a response to it. Instead I have had motion after motion after motion trying to drag whatever you can out of Chris Mackney - his gun, his participation in a second experience with a mental health professional, money which he doesn't have, cessation of his drumbeat about his father-in-law's criminal background...Now you're trying to get him fired. That's exactly what is going to happen if you keep screwing around with his employer...You even asked for alimony for a wife who has been supported by her parents all the way through the age of forty-two. I mean no disrespect toward Dina. She is actually an interesting and industrious woman who has had remarkable success with her creativity designing and selling jewelry, but we all know that Chris has never supported her.

...

Now, my casual discovery that Mr. Scamardo's company seems to have had his daughter on the payroll in earlier years at a time when she wasn't rendering any services for them, appearing to deduct what would have otherwise been gifts and not deductible, raises some interesting questions which depositions and further discovery might elaborate.

Surovell was prescient on one point; Cottrell's legal bullying cost Mackney at least one job, CB Richard Ellis. Mackney was fired after Cottrell demanded the company be held in contempt for not producing Mackney's supervisor for a deposition.

Surovell didn't respond to an email for comment.

After letting Surovell go, Mackney was out of money and for most of the remainder of his life navigated the divorce pro se: representing himself.

When this happened Rich Ware advised him to withdraw entirely from the divorce, move to a country with no extradition treaty for back due child support if necessary. Terry Hindermann offered Mackney similar advice but he told me Mackney's competitive nature kept him fighting.

Samenow's Evaluation Bullies Chris

On August 3, 2009, Samenow delivered his custody evaluation blaming Chris Mackney for nearly everything. Samenow accused Chris Mackney of being "narcissistic", a "pathological liar", suggested that Dina feared his temper, referred to her "alleged" head injury, downplayed the murder calling it "the incident from the 1960's" which was "irrelevant" to custody.

Initially, Samenow and Van Syckle lobbied for supervised visitation for Mackney before settling on sole custody to Dina with Chris seeing his children about 5% of the time: four hours every other Wednesday and 10:00AM-7:30PM every other Saturday, and never over-night.

Samenow's son, Jason, is currently a weather editor for *The Washington Post*; when I suggested this might be why the paper passed on Chris's story, the paper's court reporter, Tom Jackman, said: "What does the guy who writes weather stories have to do with any of this? We aren't asking him if it's ok to cover anything on the news side. And he has zero influence on that. Dr. Samenow is who he is and you're taking him on. Have at it. If The Post wanted to take him on, we would. The weather guy would not get a say."

Chris Mackney Calls Pete Scamardo a Psychopath

"I have given you facts that if viewed with an open mind would lead a psychological professional to certainly CONSIDER THE POSSIBILITY that he could be a psychopath." Mackney said to Dr. Samenow in an email from December 9, 2009. "I also gave you the name John Sobecki to speak to about Mr. Scamardo's behavior. You did not contact him and you did not mention him in the report."

(Sobecki is a business colleague of Scamardo's; Samenow declined to interview him for the evaluation.)

Dr. Samenow immediately forwarded the email to Dina Mackney's attorneys and the pressure continued to ratchet up. This so-called independent expert routinely shared emails Chris sent him with Dina's side but never shared anything Dina sent him with Chris.

Chris Mackney's Custodial Rights Are Terminated

In September 2009, following his mother's death, Chris Mackney inherited approximately $156,000 and hired attorney James Watson to help prepare for a hearing in November 2009. Watson didn't respond to my email and I'm not sure how long he represented Mackney but it was short; Mackney was out of money again by the spring 2010.

With Samenow's report as leverage, Dina Mackney argued for sole custody and all marital assets at the hearing which Watson advised Mackney to accept, but Dina Mackney wanted even more.

At that hearing, Dina Mackney argued to cut off all contact between Chris Mackney and his children, despite no evidence to justify such drastic action.

Judge Bellows called the request "extraordinary" but found Chris Mackney violated a previous court order to stop sending harassing emails, suspended all visitations for three months, and invited a third shrink into the proceedings by requiring Mackney to receive a psychological evaluation.

This new evaluation, done by Dr. William Zuckerman, cost Mackney thousands more he didn't really have. In addition to interviewing Mackney and Samenow, Dr. Zuckerman also interviewed Dr. Colleen Blanchfield and Dr. Guy Van Syckle producing an objective report concluding Mackney was a frustrated litigant and a danger to no one: "At the same time, his narrative was consistent with the sense of him feeling overwhelmed, overmatched, not in control, and frustrated, along with some suggestive of depressive qualities...he presented material in a clear and organized fashion, reflecting no serious cognitive psychopathology."

Dr. Zuckerman then testified that there was no reason Chris Mackney shouldn't see his kids and Samenow, the so-called independent expert, testified for Dina Mackney. On direct examination, Samenow regurgitated Dina Mackney's version of events of the infamous fight from January 19, 2008; during his cross-examination, Mackney produced his ripped shirt and Samenow admitted Mackney had shown him this shirt in their sessions, unable to explain how the ripped shirt squared with his testimony on direct examination. Chris Mackney had a victory, albeit a short lived one.

"So after 6 months of being kept from my children by Judge Bellows, I was to have overnights again with my children for the first time in over a year, over Easter weekend," Mackney said in a blog post, but Dina Mackney filed a motion to stop overnight visits.

During this time, Mackney had moved into an apartment and was ordered to fax over a copy of the lease and a receipt for first payment to Dina's lawyers. Mackney didn't write down the instructions and only faxed a copy of the lease. On April 1, Chris Mackney's Kafkaesque nightmare climaxed when this was used as the reason to remove overnight visits.

"Judge Bellows was told that I was going from memory and that the fax of the lease communicated all the information requested." Mackney said in a blog post of what happened next. "When I objected to the fact that he was taking away visitation because I failed to send a copy of the receipt, which had nothing to do with my children, I became very frustrated and upset. So then Judge Bellows then took away all visitation, simply because I forgot to send a copy of a receipt in a fax."

In June 2010, Judge Bellows made it permanent by issuing a final order forbidding Chris Mackney from ever seeing or speaking on the phone with his children which he never did for the rest of his life.

James Mackney Isn't Invited Back to School

Though Dina insisted that Chris was the source of every problem, the children exhibited behavioral problems with her as their sole parent. On February 6, 2012, Dina Mackney sent a letter to the Head of the Potomac Elementary Lower School begging the school to reconsider its decision not to invite James back the following year.

I was looking forward to recounting to you what I think is an excellent example of how the Potomac School and a family had productively worked together to identify, secure professional perspective and guidance and move to resolve a challenging issue for my son James Mackney. I have worked closely with his counselor David Beigel, his teacher Ms. Smith and you as the new Head of the Lower School throughout the fall of 2011 to identify the cause and address James's periodic disruptive behavior. Importantly, it was made clear to me through these discussions that James's academic competencies and progress were not in question; instead, it was his periodic uncontrollability and its associated classroom disruptions that was the issue. It is through our mutual efforts and productive dialogue that it was determined that the root cause of his behavioral issues could well be attributed to excessive restlessness, impulse control challenges and inattention.

As we moved through the early fall, we determined that James should be assessed for ADHD and after working through considerable scheduling challenges associated with accelerating that process, the professional assessment was completed in December by a highly regarded expert in the field. Confirming suspicions, Dr. Catherine McCarthy determined that James did in fact have ADHD and that his medical condition was fully treatable through medication and constructive behavior modification techniques.

...

It was with great disappointment that I learned that James was not asked to re-enroll when his sister Ruby was extended the opportunity.

Attention Deficit Hyperactivity Disorder (ADHD), what Dina blamed for James' behavior, has become a chic term to explain away many problems exhibited by children and adults. While ADHD is an accepted mental disorder, several heavyweights have suggested the disorder is bogus.

Leon Rosenberg, considered "the father of ADHD", admitted months before his death in 2011 to the German newspaper *Der Spiegel* that "ADHD is a prime example of a fictitious disease."

Dr. Robert Spitzer, who coined the terms Attention Deficit Disorder (ADD) and ADHD, said in 2007 that as many as 30% of youngsters are misdiagnosed with ADHD and ADD.

"ADHD is fraud intended to justify starting children on a life of drug addiction," said Dr. Edward C. Hamlyn, a founding member of the Royal College of General Practitioners.

Dina Mackney started James on Ritalin; the drug's side effects include: nervousness, agitation, anxiety, insomnia, stomach pain, loss of appetite, weight loss, nausea, vomiting, dizziness, palpitations, headaches, vision problems, increased heart rate, increased blood pressure, sweating, skin rash, psychosis, numbness, tingling, and cold feeling in hands and feet.

This was not the only example of James' behavioral problems; Ms. Birnie Shea, a teacher at Country Day School –James Mackney's previous school- said in May, 2009, after a child bumped into him James pushed the youngster back hard enough to cause injury.

Because Mackney was allowed no access to his children he wasn't aware of this crisis. I found no evidence that anyone- in school, in a psychiatrist's office, or in family court- linked James' behavioral problems to being deprived a father.

Dina Continues Bullying Chris Who Makes Bonehead Moves

Meanwhile, Dina Mackney was taking further steps to keep Chris out of his kids' lives. In October 2012, Dina Mackney applied for another order of protection. There wasn't much more she could stop Chris from doing since he was already not allowed to see his children or speak to them on the phone. Now, he could go to jail for any contact with Dina Mackney or her family, even a birthday or Christmas card to his children would land him in the slammer.

"When I cross examined her she could not state a single threat or act of violence. She then claimed that I pointed a shotgun at her over 7 years ago. This was a complete lie. She had forgotten that she had testified in 2008 that I pointed a 'handgun' at her, which was also a total lie," Mackney stated in a blog post about the hearing for this protective order which was granted as usual.

For seven hours Jason Hughes tortured Natalie Allman, slitting her throat and beating her up in front of their twin boys. Hughes is now in jail however by court order Allman must update him at least three times a year or face jail: Jason Hughes has more parental rights than Chris Mackney.

Terry Hindermann estimated Mackney sent about twenty-five emails to Dina Mackney and others in violations of court orders, referring to them as "boneheaded moves." On one occasion, Hindermann recalled, Chris was caught watching his son at the bus stop by his ex-wife; he had gone more than one hundred days without having any contact with his children.

Mackney acknowledged these mistakes in his suicide note: "In hindsight, I recognize that my reactions to being bullied, abused and denied access to my children gave my ex-wife's attorney the ammunition they were looking for her to bring me into Court."

In part because of these "bonehead moves", Mackney estimated he owed about $200,000 in fees and sanctions- including some of his ex-wife's legal bills- and was about $125,000 behind on child support at the time of his death.

Chris Goes to Jail Whenever Dina Wants

The strategy to destroy Chris Mackney was multi-pronged: first he was removed from his home, then his funds were drained, and after that his custodial rights were removed. Many parents are victimized this way; most don't take their own lives. Ulf Carlsson, whose story has been told in the documentary *Divorce Corp* said all of these things happened to him. He was flat broke, without any access to his property, and isolated from his daughter as his divorce unfolded.

"Fuck you," were his daughter's last words to him. "I don't need a father in my life."

He developed Post Traumatic Stress Disorder (PTSD) and thought about suicide several times, but never followed through. Carlsson's story has many startling similarities to Mackney's, but there's one main difference; he never went to jail.

Prior to his divorce, Mackney was never in trouble with the law. During the divorce, Mackney went to jail four times upon his wife's requests, three times for contempt of family court, and once criminally charged with attempted extortion.

Those who think divorce and other civil proceedings work like a criminal court when someone is jailed- including rules of evidence, discovery, a jury trial and testimony- have rose colored glasses. Civil detentions include almost none of that and give judges enormous leeway with proceedings lasting a few minutes resulting in jail time up to six months.

Janice Wolk Grenadier's case is similar to Mackney's. She alleges as part of a divorce she was defrauded out of $20 million. She said her former mother-in-law, a powerful attorney in Virginia, was the Machiavellian figure controlling her divorce.

On October 22, 2014, Grenadier was summoned to court to answer for charges she refused to pay $8,100 in legal fees the court deemed she owed, not for her own representation, but to her ex-husband's lawyers. At that hearing, the attorney claimed she lived in a $700,000 home and had enough money to pay the fees. When Grenadier attempted to interject, she told me, the judge shut her down, and minutes after the proceedings started she was jailed to compel her to pay the fees.

Though she lived in a $700,000 home, she was months behind on the mortgage and destitute from the divorce.

Grenadier spent the next twenty two days in jail- fourteen in solitary confinement- on hunger strike. When she was released the judge said to her, "Ms. Grenadier, you've won; I'm releasing you."

He then turned to the other attorneys and said, "I'm sorry I can't get your legal fees for you. You're going to have to get a judgment." (Like everyone else who's owed money)

That's what happened to Chris Mackney; over the last three years of his life he was incarcerated four times: three times civilly and once criminally all at the behest of his ex-wife. The shortest stint was ten days, the longest six months. The civil violations included: failure to pay past due bills, repeating allegations about Pete Scamardo, and failing to abide by a parenting plan during a time he wasn't allowed to be a parent. Like Grenadier, Mackney was jailed after hearings lasting minutes, afforded less civil rights than suspected rapists and murderers, but spent about as much time in prison as free over the last two years of his life.

While in prison in March 2012, for past due bills, the court ruled him indigent, and assigned him attorney Robert Worster. Fairfax County jailed Mackney to coerce payment while ruling him too poor to afford a lawyer which Worster said was "basically debtor's prison" and got Mackney released.

Worster summarized Mackney's legal troubles.

On October 7, 2011, Mr. Mackney was sentenced to 10 days of incarceration for criminal contempt and also held in civil contempt for failing to abide by the Final Custody Order entered on July 26, 2010. He was remanded to the Fairfax County Regional Detention Center until he purged himself of civil contempt by paying Ms. Mackney $31,000 in sanctions; and Submitting a plan to the Court describing how he will abide by the Final Custody Order.

On March 16, 2012, the Court found Mackney to be indigent and appointed Robert Worster to represent him (without pay). Later, the Court also appointed Mr. Mark Bodner as his Guardian ad litem (without pay).

Mr. Mackney was released on July 30, 2012 and Mr. Worster and Mr. Bodner's representation of Mr. Mackney ceased.

Here's part of a blog post in which Mackney explained being jailed for exercising the first amendment: "Judge Randy Bellows ordered that I could not 'repeat allegations' about Pete Scamardo, so I thought posting facts about the murder of Sam Degelia on the Charles Harrelson Wikipedia page, anonymously, would not be in violation of his order not to 'repeat allegations'. My ex-wife paid her attorney to have me held in contempt of Court for repeating allegations. Naturally, Judge Bellows found me guilty and sentenced me to jail, for contempt of Court, even though everything I posted was a fact that I got off the internet and reposted on the internet, anonymously, until today. In fact, everything I posted is still there and adheres to the Wikipedia standards for posting 'verifiable' information, from a public source."

The reference to Scamardo is still on Harrelson's page and currently says, "Pete Scamardo was also tried in the case, found guilty of being an accomplice to the murder, and sentenced to seven years' probation."

A GAL for Suicidal Mackney

For three months in 2012, a Guardian ad Litem (GAL) was appointed for Chris Mackney and that is peculiar. GALs are, "adults who are legally responsible for protecting the well-being and interests of their ward, who is usually a minor. A guardian ad litem is a unique type of guardian in a relationship that has been created by a court order only for the duration of a legal action. Courts appoint these special representatives for infants, minors, and mentally incompetent persons, all of whom generally need help protecting their rights in court," according to the website *Legal Dictionary*.

The suicidal Mackney was appointed a court bureaucrat normally reserved for children or incapacitated elderly people. The appointment of a GAL for the suicidal Mackney effectively meant the removal of the rest of his rights as the GAL was allowed to make nearly all decisions on his behalf. It's even more interesting since the suicidal Mackney repeatedly requested a GAL for his children: those requests were denied.

Bodner was appointed the suicidal Mackney's GAL after he made several suicide threats while incarcerated in 2012. Bodner was released as the suicidal Mackney's GAL in June 2012 and didn't respond to a phone call for comment.

Jennie Melton was in a similar situation when a GAL was appointed for her during her divorce though she was able bodied and in her 40s. "Having less control would make him more that way (more suicidal)," Melton said. "It makes you feel hopeless and now there's really nothing you can do."

From Virginia to Dallas and Back Again: Chris Mackney's Kafkaesque Adventure

"Last, Mr. Bartol again expressed his client's request that you simply disappear following release and not have any contact with her or her family (including the children)." Worster wrote the suicidal Mackney in prison on May 9, 2012. "My understanding (none of this has been submitted to me in writing) is that she will not pursue further sanctions if you do not have any contact with her or her family (including the children)."

The suicidal Mackney was released from jail July 2012. He showed up at Rich Ware's place who described him as, "Very skinny, with long hair, and gaunt."

Ware told me Fairfax County jail, where the suicidal Mackney spent the previous six months, is subsistence living because most people are there for days or weeks, not months like the suicidal Mackney. He also said the suicidal Mackney spent at least a week in solitary confinement after a fight during a volleyball game.

Worster said the suicidal Mackney lost all his prison privileges and was sent to the prison medical/ suicide watch area after his suicide threats.

In January 2013, the suicidal Mackney did as he was told: moved to Texas, cut off all contact with his ex-wife and children, and tried to start over with a job in real estate paying him about $50,000 per year after Terry Hindermann's referral.

"I told him to get healthy, get a girlfriend, and come back and fight when he had the financial resources," Hindermann told me.

The suicidal Mackney was about to start over in his 40s, with no money and no access to his children, but he thought the abuse had ended and the healing had begun- he thought wrong.

About a month after the suicidal Mackney settled in Dallas, Dina Mackney's attorneys called Child Support Enforcement (CSE) to complain about past due child support.

"I left town and moved to Dallas, TX, thinking I would never see my children again, but at least the nightmare would be over. It broke my heart and my spirit, but at least I didn't have to worry about going to jail (or so I thought)." He said in his suicide note. "I got a job and started going to the gym, trying to get healthy again. The first month I was in Dallas working, my ex-wife tracked me down and had Child Support Enforcement come after me. Now that I was in Dallas, I would have no ability to go to Court to change the order."

When the suicidal Mackney asked to have the payments reduced to an affordable level, the offer was ignored. Then the suicidal Mackney threatened to go public about the abuse if his payments weren't reduced; his email was taken to the Fairfax County Prosecutor's Office where unbeknownst to him the prosecutor, Elizabeth Kohut, prepared to charge the suicidal Mackney with attempted extortion.

During the month of July 2013, the suicidal Mackney exchanged numerous curious emails with Kyle Bartol.

In an email from July 19, 2013, Bartol seemed to be setting the suicidal Mackney up for his upcoming attempted extortion arrest.

"Mr. Mackney, Exactly what do you want to stop the publication of this information?" (The resemblance to Dina Mackney's attempt to have Chris charged with blackmail by asking, "What will it take for you to stop talking about my father?" is uncanny and I don't believe coincidental.)

The suicidal Mackney and Bartol then exchanged emails about possibly appointing a guardian ad litem for the children.

"After 5 years of refusing to negotiate or discuss any alternative solutions, can you please confirm that your client still does not wish to appoint a Guardian Ad Litem to protect the children's best interest nor does she wish to voluntarily reduce the child support obligation that I have never been able to afford?" the suicidal Mackney wrote to Bartol on July 26, 2013.

"Assuming that there was an Order appointing a Guardian ad litem and modifying the child support, before drafting such an Order I would need to know the names of people who you would propose to be appointed as the Guardian ad litem," Bartol responded the next day, "as well as what amount of child support that you would agree that you are able to pay. If you give me this information and I draft an order, I would also need to know that if Ms. Mackney agrees to such an order, will these emails and complaints stop?"

This email was a Machiavellian smoke screen; in reality Bartol and his firm knew the suicidal Mackney was about to be arrested again. Wearing only shorts, the suicidal Mackney was visited by a Special Weapons and Tactics (SWAT) team which arrested him inside his apartment on the morning of July 30, 2013. He was extradited back to Virginia flying on Con Air.

The suicidal Mackney couldn't afford his bond and awaited trial in jail, where he begged to plead guilty to a lesser charge.

"I am writing you again to beg you, please, for the sake of my children and all parties involved, to allow me to plead to a misdemeanor or simply to drop the charges against me. Convicting me of a felony will not bring justice and will only lead to tragedy," began a letter the suicidal Mackney wrote to Kohut on September 23, 2013.

Kohut's office ignored the suicidal Mackney pleas; he rotted in jail until his trial date in October 2013.

A Broken Man Reaches His Breaking Point

The suicidal Mackney was represented by two public defenders with no trial experience- Maggie Vaughn and Todd Zincola. His attorneys argued that since child support goes to the children the state couldn't claim the suicidal Mackney was extorting money from his ex-wife because it wasn't her money. The prosecutor told the jury to use their common sense in her closing argument which they did finding him not guilty on October 21, 2013.

The Virginia Attorney General's Office and the Fairfax County Commonwealth Attorney's Office declined to speak to me for this book.

"Something's up here; there's backroom politics at play here." Terry Hindermann remembers Maggie Vaughn telling him.

Zincola and Vaughn are now in private practice and declined to comment for the book.

While the suicidal Mackney was found not guilty, he'd spent months in prison, lost his job, and had even less prospects.

They wanted to "exact their pound of flesh" Worster said of what happened next.

The same people who demanded the suicidal Mackney leave the state to end the abuse from the divorce were about a year ago were now demanding he stay in the state to deal with the divorce.

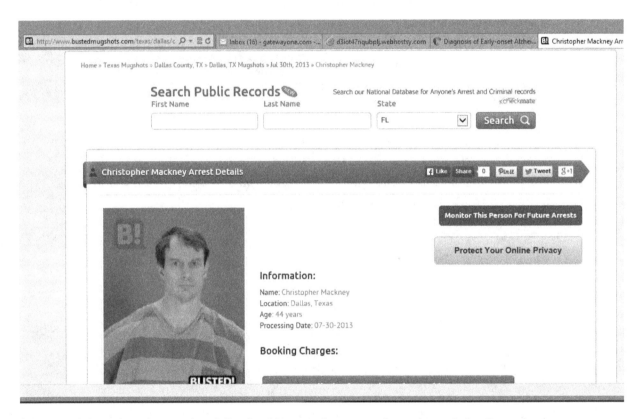

(The suicidal Mackney's mugshot following his extortion arrest from the website *Busted Mugshots*)

Cottrell would only say "not true" repeatedly when I asked him to respond to the charge made by the suicidal Mackney that he was at the center of a legal bullying campaign. After a few questions, Cottrell ended the interview, claiming he needed permission from his client before speaking with me, and hasn't answered more than twenty follow up emails.

Mackney's Last Weeks

Shortly after the suicidal Mackney got out of jail, he moved into the church basement apartment and several of his friends began raising money for the continued divorce battle, but the fundraising was too late, the suicidal Chris Mackney had less than seventy days to live.

Michael Volpe

In a November 21, 2013 email to Bartol, the suicidal Mackney announced his intention to kill himself.

*Either your client can voluntarily agree to a Guardian Ad litem to protect the best interests of our children or **I will take my own life (emphasis mine)**...This is what it is going to come down to. My death or a lawyer to protect the best interests of children, who are being alienated from their father.*

I am in the process of setting up the site (Good Men Did Nothing) and then will announce the site on other parental rights, emotional abuse, domestic violence, psychology organizations. It will contain all of the information as to WHY I BELIEVE my children and I are being abused.

Bartol made the contents of *Good Men Did Nothing* the basis of a show cause hearing scheduled for January 22, 2014. He didn't respond to more than twenty emails including one to explain this cruelty.

Terry Hindermann received several phone calls from authorities concerned about the suicidal Mackney's welfare because of repeated suicide threats. The suicidal Mackney told Hindermann the threat of suicide was for leverage, nothing more.

Beginning on November 20, 2013, the suicidal Mackney started *Good Men Did Nothing*, which was his cyber-defense for everything that happened. In each post the suicidal Mackney pontificated on different aspects of the case and painstakingly provided evidence in the form of hyperlinks to documents he'd created on the internet. Reading the site and checking the hyperlinks would convince most he was getting a shaft. One of his friends was amazed how clear and concise the suicidal Mackney made his case on the site.

The suicidal Chris Mackney spoke calmly and logically to me. Mark Duda said the last time they spoke, about two weeks before his death they joked around and talked sports. A better description of his state of mind comes from Darlene Mansour, part of an on-line parental alienation group with the suicidal Mackney.

"Chris reached out a couple of times in the Group. The first time he was in a good level state of mind. He seemed to grasp the conversation well, seemed optimistic- this was on a post which I was commenting on about parental alienation. This was around March 2013. He seemed optimistic about possibly being able to see his children. The second and last conversation was around December 18, 2013 this was on a post I made to the Group on Shared Parenting. He responded but was distant, lost, disoriented, (and) defeated. He stated that he regretted that he would never be able to see his children and was always great with children especially his own daughter and son. I asked him what changed. He stated that his ex teamed up with his ex in laws. They destroyed him physically, mentally, and financially. He was thrown in jail; had been destroyed completely as a real estate broker. He stated that between his ex and the lies (and) rumors destroyed his business. His ex would talk to potential clients and existing clients about how he was a no good person, husband, or father. (She) Told them he used unsavory business tactics and had been jailed for not paying support payments. He was so destroyed I knew he was about to snap. I have been around suicidal youth via Anti Bullying. I told him he could send me a friend request and even chat with me through my Facebook inbox. I told him do not give up. There are many of us here he could reach out to for moral support. I went to his timeline and knew by his posts that the light was gone. I asked him if he would reach out to his parents as they would be there in person. He said they could not help and he could not leave the area. I gave him a suicide hotline number and told him I worked but was on Facebook a lot after work. He was so depressed at that time. Shortly after this conversation the Group announced his death by suicide. I was floored and have not been able to post much more."

In the same text message exchange with Jill Peterson Mitchell from December 26, 2013, the suicidal Mackney opined on his (lack of) future.

"I found out that I have to be in court on January 22, to show cause." The suicidal Mackney wrote at 7:03 PM ET.

"I told them I would take down the blog if they would just lower my child support. They chose to go to court." The suicidal Mackney wrote in another text message from 7:04 PM ET.

"Talking about Pete, and contacting Kelly Malesardi." The suicidal Mackney wrote at 7:07PM ET, explaining why he was going back to court.

"A parent that Dina manipulated. I was ordered not to talk to them." The suicidal Mackney wrote about Malesardi in a text message at 7:09PM ET.

"Freedom of speech?" Jill Peterson Mitchell responded rhetorically in a text message at 7:10PM ET.

"Exactly." The suicidal Mackney replied at 7:11PM.

"It was determined that it's in the best interest of my children that I not contact people fooled by Dina and Pete." The suicidal Mackney added sarcastically at 7:11 PM ET.

When Jill Peterson Mitchell asked what would happen at this hearing the suicidal Mackney responded at 7:13PM ET, "Fine me. Maybe put me in jail…**I won't be there.**" (Emphasis mine)

My Conversation with Kelly Malesardi: "A Parent that Dina Manipulated"

I spoke briefly with Ms. Malesardi who said she wasn't familiar with details of the court order or why she was referenced, but knew Dina, Chris, and their kids who went to school with her daughter. She called Chris Mackney a "scary guy" who was "mentally ill". She said there was another side of the story, and suggested I was writing a "salacious story."

I said that this was great, and she was the perfect person to speak to me; I was looking for all sides of the story.

"You just called him mentally ill; do you want to expand on that?" I asked.

"Thank you, conversation is over." Malesardi responded as she hung up the phone.

Jim Cottrell, Kyle Bartol, Pete Scamardo, and Dina Mackney's Wickedness

I referred to Mackney as suicidal after he threatened suicide in jail in 2012 because from that moment forward Jim Cottrell and Kyle Bartol knew they were dealing with a suicidal man and their actions should be examined with that in mind. I believe if not legally; ethically and morally from that moment forward they intended for this to happen. I believe it was Pete Scamardo's intent all along, and I believe Dina went along with anything her father decided.

"While I am the one that took my own life, this was a murder conceived and financed by Pete Scamardo who hired Jim Cottrell and Kyle Bartol the day after I discovered he was a murderer, and then paid over $1 Million in legal fees to make it happen. People 'targeted' by psychopaths call it 'murder by suicide'." Mackney said in his suicide note.

Chapter 6: Dr. Samenow and His Bogus Evaluation

"The science of custody evaluation is so in its infancy that our ability to rely on its results should be extremely low."

Dr. Joyanna Silberg, President of the Leadership Council on Child Abuse and Interpersonal Violence

Gas-lighting in Family Court

Gas-lighting comes from the 1944 Oscar winning movie *Gaslight*, starring Charles Boyer as Greg Anton and Ingrid Bergman as his wife Paula and is based on the 1938 play.

In it, Gregory drives Paula crazy by devising a series of devious stunts meant to disorient her and make her question her sanity.

In one scene, Gregory surreptitiously removes a picture from the wall then accuses Paula of removing it. When Paula denies touching the picture, Gregory asks each of the house staff if they removed it. When each of the staff denies removing it, he again accuses Paula of removing the picture.

"If I could only get inside that brain of yours and understand what makes you do these crazy twisted things," Gregory remarks to Paula.

"You're not going out of your mind, you're slowly and systematically being driven out of your mind," said Brian Cameron played by Joseph Cotton to Paula.

A 2011 article by psychologist Charles Pragnell entitled *The Tactics and Ploys of Psychopathic Personalities in the Family Courts* describes why gas-lighting is so easy in family courts.

The grooming of friends, relatives, and professionals is very clear in many cases, and in particular some psychiatrists, psychologists and family evaluators/reporters have been hoodwinked by such tactics and ploys by the psychopathic individual. Their reports, of course favoring the psychopath, have very considerable influence on the Courts and their determinations.

Such professionals now refer to such cases as `high conflict' cases, when it is clear that they are situations of a violent aggressor/tormentor/persecutor and their victims. …They do not recognise the Jekyll and Hyde aspects of the psychopath's ploys and tactics and of those they have effectively groomed in their beliefs.

The high conflict which usually occurs in such cases is most commonly engendered by the respective lawyers, conditioned by operating in an adversarial process and arena, whose own major goal is to 'win', whatever may be the justness and fairness of the result.

The groomed professionals then enable the psychopath to achieve their primary objective, which is to maintain power and control over their victims, their former partner and children. It is an act of vengeance and spite but mostly it is to maintain the power and control and feelings of supremacism and narcissism.

One example of gas-lighting in Samenow's evaluation is when he quoted Dina as suffering "a year of torture" even though in the first year Chris Mackney was forced out his home, drained of funds, and with little access to his children.

Dina Mackney, who hid her father's murder from Chris during their marriage called Chris a "pathological liar", one of many statements which were quoted by Samenow uncritically.

Dina's Side Is the Truth: the Gas-lighting Begins
Example 1

When presented with both sides of the fight from January 19, 2008, Samenow entered Dina's version as the truth.

Ms. Mackney spoke of her husband's explosive nature in citing a particular incident in which Mr. Mackney became upset and scattered her jewelry materials all over the room. This was after an argument which had eventuated in each taking the other's keys.

"He took the drawers out and threw the jewelry – thousands of dollars (sic) worth of jewelry. There were two trays sorted by size. He dumped both of these. I was trying to stop him. I called the police. He was going to delete my work files on the computer."

Example 2

Dr. Samenow quoted Dina accusing Chris of being serial philanderer, saying that Dina "found hundreds of emails from online dating sites. These included photos and schedules of places and times for Chris to meet other women. She grew so disgusted, she told him to leave. However, when Ruby got sick, she forgave him. Later, when she became pregnant with James, she discovered 'another whole round of emails.' Ms. Mackney said that her husband 'texting a 17 year old' was the final straw."

Here's what Chris Mackney stated in notes which never made it into Samenow's report. "This is not true. The marriage was done and in order to begin gathering evidence she went back through phone records and came across a phone number in my text messages. She called the person and the girl that answered said she was 17…During that August, my wife and I were fighting and I told her that I was talking to other people about the troubles we were having in the marriage. The woman I was speaking/texting with was over 40, married, with children and was also having troubles in her marriage. Our discussions (were) entirely about our bad marriages. There was nothing physical or sexual going on whatsoever. In fact, I never met the woman. If the person was the same, I had no idea it was a 17 year old girl. My wife and Dr. Samenow ignored my version of events and painted the incident as something completely different from what it was."

Example 3

"Ms. Mackney has been afraid of her husband at times. An incident occurred when Chris was to move his belongings from the marital residence. It ended up in a confrontation in which Mr. Mackney yelled at Peter Scamardo that he was 'a fucking murderer' like OJ Simpson."

"Complete Lie- I sat in a rented U Haul truck waiting for movers to arrive and when they didn't, I stayed in the truck and beeped the horn. My wife and her father came out of the house and her father says 'what do you want loser.'" Mackney said in notes explaining his side. "The argument escalated from there. My wife was screaming and cursing at me right in my face as I sat in the truck. I also emailed my attorney and Samenow this story right after it occurred."

Example 4

"He lied, cheated, stole. It didn't rise to the level it is now. He could lie like nobody's business. I didn't realize he was such a conman. I guess maybe I was an optimist."

Dina Is the Heroine and Chris the Villain, the Gas-lighting Continues

Example 1

"Ms. Mackney approached this evaluation in a thoughtful, cooperative manner. Under intense stress, she did her utmost to retain her composure while under siege from her husband who indiscriminately attacked her parenting practices, accused her of poor judgment due to an alleged head injury from an auto accident, maliciously defamed her parents in a very public manner, and generally made life difficult for her." Dr. Samenow described the woman who called her husband a liar and conman.

Example 2

"She reported that Mr. Mackney threatened to kidnap the children and 'has terrorized me and my family for money.'" Dr. Samenow said. "She said that Mr. Mackney threatened to reveal information he discovered on the internet, namely that Pete Scamardo had a criminal conviction."

Example 3

"Ms. Mackney has been so emphatic about wanting to spare the children from being harmed by the divorce proceedings that it was the very first subject she raised with this examiner." Samenow remarked of the woman who hired a lawyer who boasts, "He's not the type to settle so have your wallets open."

Example 4

"Ms. Mackney has been at a loss as to how to communicate with her husband. To transmit basic information and obtain a rational response from Mr. Mackney has been a challenge." Dr. Samenow stated. "Instead of succeeding at establishing a constructive dialogue, Ms. Mackney is the recipient of voluminous emails from Chris Mackney in which he attacks, bullies, and threatens her."

Example 5

"Ms. Mackney is very close to family members. Andrea Scamardo said of her daughter, 'Dina was so easy to raise. She always had friends. She was sweet, kind, gentle, and polite.' Pete Scamardo added that his daughter has been 'way too trusting.' Mr. Scamardo is extremely upset with his son-in-law whom he employed, paying him a salary and commission long past the point where it was obvious that Chris was not an asset to the company."

Example 6

"Ms. Mackney believes that, even after the separation, her tendency initially was to be 'nice to a fault.'" Dr. Samenow quoted the woman whose first action was to file for a restraining order.

Samenow Gas-lights the Murder

"I went 41 years without knowing this," Samenow quoted Dina Mackney regarding her father's murder conviction, though she initially said to Chris, "I already know about this and you have no idea about the details and at this point it is none of your business."

"Ms. Mackney and her parents told this examiner that they had nothing to hide. After questioning the Scamardo this examiner found the situation 40 years ago completely irrelevant to the child custody case and informed Mr. Mackney that this was not to be an issue." Samenow quoted the family who hid this murder from Chris Mackney. "Mr. Mackney persisted harping on this subject not just in speaking with this examiner but also in approaching people who are not family members."

While minimizing the murder, Samenow made Chris sound crazy for harping on it, while perpetuating Dina's lie: "Mr. Mackney dwelled on Mr. Scamardo past, or at least his version of it to the point he appeared obsessed. Chris said that he came upon the information because he had 'Googled' it to obtain Mr. Scamardo middle name for a form. When he spoke to his wife about his discovery, he learned that she had known nothing about what allegedly happened 40 years ago in Texas. Mr. Mackney declared that his wife and her family were waging a war to destroy him while trying to bury a family secret that could have a devastating impact on James and Ruby."

Worst of all, Samenow declined to interview Cindy Wallace, one of ten people put on a list to be interviewed by Chris Mackney, determining the murder was irrelevant after interviewing the murderer and those close to him, not anyone victimized by the murder.

Thinking Errors

Samenow's statements are especially egregious considering his philosophy on thinking errors.

"Behavior is the direct result of the way a person thinks. As I have written in this blog before, behind criminal conduct in every case are 'thinking errors.' Thinking provides clues to the personality of the individual. The 'error' is a flaw in a person's thought process that usually results in behavior that injures or, at the very least, inconveniences others. The more extensive the pattern of an error in thinking, the greater the injury. (sic) We all make thinking errors on occasion. My task is to discern whether there is a pattern of thinking errors and how it plays out in the life of the person being evaluated."

If Pete Scamardo had a man killed, that would be a serious thinking error. If the Scamardo family hid the murder from Chris throughout the marriage, that would be a "pattern of an error in thinking". Samenow could only say none of this is relevant to custody if he's ignoring his long-standing philosophy.

This isn't the first time Samenow has inexplicably gone against his long-standing principle. In 2010, he testified on behalf of Evan Gargiulo, a 23 year old military veteran from a wealthy family accused of killing a cab driver giving him a ride in the early morning hours of Sunday

November 2, 2008. According to a videotaped statement Gargiulo made to Fairfax Police, Gargiulo and his cab driver, Mazhar Nazir, got into a verbal argument; Nazir turned around to grab at Gargiulo who was in the back seat. Gargiulo pushed Nazir away, grabbed his 9 millimeter revolver and shot Nazir in the head. Afterwards, Gargiulo grabbed Nazir's cell phone and went into his apartment where he called his father and his college roommate, Francis Roman, telling Roman he'd achieved his "first civilian kill."

Samenow claimed Gargiulo was temporarily insane even though for decades he dismissed insanity in criminals.

"Criminals are not mentally ill or hapless victims of oppressive social conditions." Samenow said in in his book, Inside the Criminal Mind. "Despite a multitude of differences in their backgrounds and crime patterns, criminals are all alike in one way: how they think. All regard the world as a chessboard over which they have total control, and they perceive people as pawns to be pushed around at will."

In other words, criminals are ruthless Machiavellians like Pete Scamardo.

"After spending more than 28 hours with the jailed defendant, Samenow concluded that Gargiulo had led such a sheltered life, and had developed such an exaggerated paranoia," Tom Jackman said in The Washington Post, "that he could not distinguish right from wrong when he shot Nazir in the back of the head."

Samenow even said that because he'd never testified before in favor of temporary insanity this showed he had an open mind. The $25,000 the family paid for Samenow's testimony shows his mind is open for a price; it was money not well spent, the jury found Gargiulo guilty after deliberating six hours.

Dina and Pete's Friends and Admirers Talk about Dina

Tracy Heiden

Tracy Heiden and Dina Mackney have, according to the former, been "each other's confidante and sounding board." Ms. Hayden's daughter has been a close friend of Ruby's since they were three years old. Tracy expressed her apprehensions about Dina's safety.

"I'm afraid for Dina….She hasn't expressed she's frightened. She's more afraid of what he will do – his threat to make it worse. Dina has a lot of friends but people will pass judgment. He sends articles [to people]. He's extremely convincing…Dina's bright but very innocent on a day to day basis." Ms. Heiden said of Mr. Mackey's parents: "We love Andy and Pete. [They're] a part of our family. They've fed my kids, taken care of them…They're like grandparents."

Linda and John Donovan

Linda and John Donovan know Chris and Dina through the preschool where their girls met. Linda characterized Ms. Mackney as "very warm, approachable, very helpful." Apparently, Dina was under such stress that she confided in Ms. Donovan some of the problems she was having, especially with respect to Chris phoning people about her father. Ms. Donovan noted that Mr. Mackney had called a board member from The Potomac School who then approached her. Linda Donovan had nothing but positive comments about Dina as a mother:

'She's a very patient mother. James is a real little boy. She is unendingly patient. She gets down and plays with him. Ms. Donovan clearly admires Ms. Mackney for juggling parenting, volunteering at school, and applying herself to her business. John Donovan described his impression of Dina Mackney as 'a woman with a lot of positive energy, very giving, very focused.'

So when Dina brings someone into the divorce she is under stress and confides, but when Chris did the same he "dragged neighbors, friends, and school staff into the custody dispute. He has gone to them with his reports about Mr. Scamardo and has discussed his difficulties with his wife."

Gail Cavallaro

Gail Cavallaro has known Ms. Mackney since middle school. **Married and living in Richmond with her husband and three children, Ms. Cavallaro seldom spends time with her long-time friend although they maintain contact. (Emphasis mine)** *The importance of citing Ms. Cavallaro's comments is to underscore what it is about Ms. Mackney that leads others to admire her and maintain a relationship that endures for years.*

'[Dina] is loyal and dedicated. I value her advice. She's a very thoughtful person. She always pours herself into whatever she does. She was president of the school...cheerleader....She was a very diligent with lots of friends [and] athletically talented.'

Ms. Cavallaro and Ms. Mackney were roommates for a year after college. Ms. Cavallaro stated, "We never had an issue" and remarked that she still has "fond memories of that year." As enthusiastic as Ms. Cavallaro is about Dina, she is equally fond of Dina's parents whom she came to know quite well (at their home and on a vacation to Hilton Head) and describes as 'lovely people to be around.'

Samenow's report did not indicate whether Ms. Cavallaro knew that one of the "lovely people to be around" was a murderer.

Frederick Spain

Frederick Spain, a colleague of Dina's father, had similarly kind things to say about Dina.

Frederic L. Spain knows Dina Mackney from an entirely different perspective. A commercial real estate broker, he has known Dina's parents, Mr. and Mrs. Scamardo since 1969 and Dina since she was born. Mr. Spain characterized Ms. Mackney as "a perfect lady [who is] neat, fastidious, and incredibly polite." Mr. Spain said that he has been "bombarded" by emails about Mr. Scamardo from Chris Mackney who, at one time, worked for him. He has admired Dina for retaining her "serenity" during all that she is going through.

This so-called business associate actually worked for Scamardo at CDC as a land specialist. Spain, who claimed to have known Scamardo since 1969, should have been aware of the murder, a fact not addressed in the evaluation.

Deborah DeStefano

While Samenow didn't speak to Cindy Wallace, he did to speak to her one time close friend, Debbie DeStefano.

Deborah Destefano is Ms. Mackney's aunt. Recently divorced, Ms. Destefano works as a librarian in Austin, Texas. Spending time with Dina and the children during Christmas holiday periods and on week long summer beach trips, she has had the opportunity to observe her at close hand. As Dina has been under increasing stress, they began speaking almost nightly by phone. Ms. Destefano explained, "We're confidantes; she's like my little sister." Asked to describe Dina's personality, Ms. Destefano replied:

"She's a very sweet, very kind, gentle soul, not aggressive. As a child, she was fairly quiet. She'd measure people before warming up...She is honest, fair, kind and, in terms of the kids, incredibly patient. James has his moments of acting out. She doesn't let it go on forever....She'll sit and play with them, do art projects....Even when she's annoyed and frustrated, she maintains lovingness.

Contrary to Mr. Mackney's repeated assertions that his wife wants to eliminate him from the children's lives, Ms. Destefano volunteered that Dina "has long said they need him and does not want the children to be without a father."

Dina may have told Ms. DeStefano the children needed a father in their lives, but it was lip service; she eliminated him from their lives months later because he didn't fax in a receipt.

The Gas-lighting Crescendos: Samenow Claims Chris Mackney has No Friends

"The facts are that Chris Mackney is 40 years old, unemployed and bankrupt. He listed not one person whom he called a close friend for this examiner to speak with." Samenow said in his evaluation. "He provided various explanations as to why he had reached this point in his life where he has virtually no money, no job, (and) no close friends."

Samenow made this claim despite interviewing two of Mackney's closest friends, Rich Ware and Mike Harris.

Michael Volpe

Richard Ware has known Mr. Mackney since college. After the marital separation, Chris lived with Mr. Ware for brief periods when he had "nowhere else to go". Otherwise, according to Mr. Ware, they saw each other "every week or two at a social or sporting event." Mr. Ware characterized Mr. Mackney as "a nice guy, seems like an honest person, a solid individual." He added that Chris has handled this "ugly" divorce process "quite admirably."

Samenow tried a sleight of hand, claiming a close friend had only known Mackney for a long time.

"I was a close friend of Chris Mackney's and provided him shelter when he was in and out of jail for contempt as I was living in Arlington, Virginia at the time." Ware said in his first email to me.

Samenow did the same thing with Mike Harris.

Mike Harris also knows Chris from college and described him as "confident, extremely social, and a good guy." He has had little contact with Chris in the past two years except for an occasional meal. Mr. Harris was sympathetic to Chris having heard his account of the custody battle. "I like both and I like Chris. Both are capable of being good parents. This is probably more difficult for Chris. He has no safety net in this area. His father-in-law is used to winning."

Why would Samenow say Mike Harris heard Chris Mackney's account of the custody battle? Dina Mackney's friends Tracy Heiden and Gail Cavallaro only heard her "account" of the custody battle, but he didn't use that loaded description when talking about them. Furthermore, Samenow said that Harris didn't have much contact with Chris Mackney the previous two years, a distortion.

"I know that my wife and four kids spent time with Chris, Dina and his kids at our beach house prior to separation/divorce. That we went out to dinner together with our spouses. That we were invited out to Dina's parent's house in Middleburg to watch the horse races." Harris told me in an email. "We even spent New Year's out there. I saw Chris more than any other friend of mine in the area. 2008-2010 was no different. We got together for dinner quite a bit. As much as any busy person with four kids and a growing business could."

Mackney also asked Samenow to speak to Casey Long, another friend from SMU who lived in the area, but Samenow claimed he didn't reach him after four attempts. In fact, Mackney gave Samenow three close friends since college- Ware, Harris, and Long- all living in the area while the only close friend Dina put down from the area was Tracy Heiden. Everyone else- her sister, aunt, Gail Cavarello- lived in other states or Cavarello in a different part of Virginia. Which of the two has a friend deficiency?

"There seems to be no one available who knows Mr. Mackney well enough to discuss in any depth his character and parenting skills." Samenow said.

This too is a distortion. Besides Harris, Ware, and Long, Chris Mackney gave Samenow his neighbors Ed McGinnis and Michael Humphries along with family friends John and Lisa Donovan, all could speak intelligently about his character and parenting skills: none of their thoughts on this subject was in Samenow's evaluation.

Samenow also refused to speak with Terry Hindermann who told me he first met Mackney in 2005 as a business associate and they developed a friendship over time. Through Mackney he's become friends with Harris, Ware, and others from the Fiji fraternity and said he considered Mackney's circle of friends to be bigger than his own. He said his son enjoyed spending time with Mackney and still asks him where he is.

"He was always the gentlest most sincere person," Hindermann said of Mackney.

Samenow failed to interview six of ten witnesses provided by Chris Mackney-Cindy Wallace, John Sobecki, Charles Kehler, Teha Hirsi, Casey Long, and Dr. Colleen Blanchfield.

Kehler is Hindermann's business partner while Sobecki is a business colleague and neither agreed to speak to me for this book. I couldn't reach Hirsi.

Interview Who You Want Victim 1: Page Holdgate

Samenow's behavior, picking and choosing who he interviews, is common in corrupt evaluations.

Page Holdgate, who lives in Massachusetts near Cape Cod, met her husband in 1996, began living with him in 1999, and married in 2002. The troubled marriage included her ex-husband being convicted several times of charges including driving under the influence and domestic violence.

When the divorce proceedings began in 2009, the family court assigned March DuPont to be the Guardian Ad Litem (GAL) in her case; Page never thought that she wouldn't get physical custody of the children because of the history of domestic violence.

DuPont ignored her ex-husband's history of domestic abuse and suggested it was Page Holdgate who was alienating her ex-husband against their children; she was the one with the alcohol problem, and an unfit parent. Page Holdgate recently filed a complaint with the US Department of Justice and explained that like Samenow, DuPont didn't talk to witnesses she was supposed to and witness she did speak with said their statements were misstated.

During her investigation, she interviewed the husband, his father, his sister from Rhode Island (whose input was given a great deal of weight in the GAL's report, even though she and mother barely ever saw each other and hardly knew one another) and other members of father's family.

The GAL failed to interview my two collaterals. She did interview my domestic violence counselor. My counselor read the gal report when it was issued, and she states she was misquoted.

When I emailed Ms. DuPont about her selective interviews, she responded, "I did not conduct a custody evaluation. (I) Suggest you access the probate court file," suggesting that as a GAL she was allowed to be biased.

"I understand that you didn't conduct a custody evaluation. You are a GAL. That is a distinction without a difference and you didn't answer the charges."

She didn't respond to that email.

Like Mackney, Holdgate's ex-husband comes from one of the wealthiest families in the Cape Cod area, whereas she was forced to conduct much of her divorce pro se. Her ex-husband has physical custody of their kids and she's been given a child support payment which she struggles to pay every month.

Interview Who You Want Victim 2: Susan Carrington

Susan Carrington's ex-husband believes she is a drug addict, crazy, and a danger to their children. He's said so in court in Maryland and in New York, but court appointed shrinks aren't simply supposed to take one spouse's word for it. Susan Carrington was deemed mentally ill and a drug addict in a psychological evaluation done by Dr. NG Berrill even though Dr. Berrill didn't even bother to interview her, let alone others she may have provided to counter this assertion. Dr. Berrill's so-called evaluation was a regurgitation of accusations made by her ex-husband.

Chris is Angry, Chris is Crazy

The gas-lighting process is completed when the target is deemed mentally unstable.

Example 1

"The fact is that seldom has this examiner found a litigant in either a criminal or civil case more difficult to interview." Samenow, who's interviewed rapists and serial killers, said of Chris Mackney.

Example 2

"Although Mr. Mackney is the parent behaving erratically and showing questionable judgment, he asserts that his wife demonstrates these very qualities."

Example 3

"As Mr. Mackney told this examiner of his wife's faults, it appeared that he was describing himself."

Example 4

"Clearly, Mr. Mackney has been at his absolute worst when he has contact with Ms. Mackney. He has made simple arrangements difficult. His anger at her permeates nearly all contacts with her. And the children often are not spared the fallout," Samenow said in another portion of the report. "During the first interview, Ms. Mackney said that her husband is angry because she will not capitulate to his attempt to extort a quarter of a million dollars from her." (Dina is referring to Chris's attempts to receive half the $500,000 in equity they had in their home at the time)

Example 5

Here's how Dr. Samenow started the report. "During May, 2008, Ms. Mackney petitioned for a protective order stating that she feared bodily injury if she continued to live with her husband. She also expressed apprehension that Mr. Mackney's 'escalating rage' might cause harm to the children."

Anger Issues- Show Me the Money

Chris is not the only individual- mostly men- who's been accused of being angry during their divorce.

Ronald Pierce is a California father forced out of his home, left destitute by the divorce, and with little access to his kids. Throughout the process court officers wondered why he was so angry: unable or unwilling to understand that taking away his house, job, money, and children might be the source of the anger. He was accused so often of being angry that on one occasion- he hadn't seen his children in about two years- when the judge again accused him again of being angry, Pierce responded, "I'm not angry your honor, I'm apoplectic."

In 2004, Michael Pasierb came home one day to find his wife sitting with several members of her family and told him the marriage was over. Before that day, he thought he had an ideal marriage, a wife, three kids, and a home. He found out later his wife had strayed. When his custody evaluation costing $11,000 was completed, his anger became a central point.

"He is still grieving the loss of his marriage, and his internal cognition regarding these issues continues to cause him much emotional distress and anger most of which he is not aware of. His grief and loss processing timetable is slow." Pasierb's evaluation stated. "In our initial meeting, Michael spent 25 minutes lamenting the end of his marriage and refusing to pay the court ordered 50% of the 50% retainer for the evaluation. He only responded when I threatened to the judge of his refusal to follow the court order. This internal cognitive issue can be very debilitating for him and he would do well to receive some counseling for that."

The evaluation concluded with a list of recommendations for anger management classes for Pasierb.

A man is cheated on, blindsided by a divorce; he is angry about this, and because he doesn't want to pay half of the $11,000 this custody evaluation costs, this is a sign of "internal cognitive issues" which "can be very debilitating for him."

Samenow also used a financial dispute as suggestion of underlying mental instability:

"Mackney said that he would have a check for this examiner which actually was overdue. He then seemed quite agitated, wrote the check, and said it was not cashable, and he did not know when it would be. Then as this examiner and the children with their father left the apartment to take the elevator up to the pool, Mr. Mackney was muttering about his wife taking everything, leaving him virtually destitute."

Think about that the next time you argue about your cable bill, your cell phone bill, or a bill to fix your car. You're not being ripped off; you have deep seated and untreated anger issues.

Who Is the Controller Personality?

In his book, *The Best Interest of the Child*, Dr. Samenow talks about the so-called controller personality.

Many marriages break up when a non-controlling husband or wife stands up to a controller. By refusing to endure any longer the mistreatment dished out for years, the non-controlling spouse precipitates a crisis. The marriage may have gone smoothly in the controller's opinion, largely because he or she went unchallenged. In reality though, the non-controller had walked a tightrope. As a problem solver, he or she has sought to avoid unnecessary and debilitating conflict and picked battles discerningly. Having the welfare of the child uppermost in his or her thoughts, the problem-solving parent let a lot go by rather than subject the household to unpleasantness. When he or she finally becomes fed up with walking on eggshells and decides to do something, the marital equilibrium is disrupted. The non-controlling spouse's sudden assertiveness strikes at the core of the controller's self-concept. At home he or she has been accustomed to having his or her way. Now things are different. The controller reacts by angrily faulting the other spouse for creating the upheaval. If the problem solver fails to back down, the controller becomes more irascible and domineering. In truth, the controller is an abuser. When family members get out of line, he or she becomes harsh and punitive. In extreme cases spouse and offspring know that at any time they may be berated, threatened, or even physically attacked. I have seen a controller psychologically grind down his spouse so severely that she had to seek medical treatment and was placed on tranquilizers or antidepressants. Then the controller alleged that her taking medication confirmed what he'd asserted all along, that she was a disturbed person and an unfit parent. Were he to be asked about his contribution to the marital difficulties, he would portray himself as the victim who had to endure the erratic moods and capricious demands of his unstable partner.

While creating a living hell in the family, the controller may appear to others as a generous individual and a proponent of a strong family. Gregarious and charming, he or she enlists the support and sympathy of neighbors, friends, and even relatives who have not had to live with him or her. During the separation and divorce proceedings, the controller is determined to maintain the upper hand. Now the problem solver is the enemy! The controller is a formidable adversary as he or she enters the legal arena to fight for child custody. Whereas the problem solving spouse wants to resolve differences, the controller is intent on revenge and winning. The spouse desperately wants to reach a settlement and move on with life, but the controller's notion of a settlement is for the problem solver to agree to his or her conditions. If he or she doesn't capitulate, the controller will react angrily and become intent upon destroying the spouse, even threatening financial ruin or tarnishing of reputation. Of course, the most dire threat is to take away what the spouse values most-the child.

Dr. Samenow warned controller personalities abuse sole custody: "A warning about sole custody! It can be a powerful weapon in the hands of the wrong parent, i.e., a controller who would attempt to block the other parent from participating in the child's life. Sole custody does not grant permission for one parent to ignore the other and decides everything unilaterally."

"Your wife is way over controlling. Only she can feed the children, only she knows what's best for the children. Only she can make decisions for the children. She displays a shocking lack of sensitivity of your value to the children." Robert Surovell said to Mackney in an email from January 2, 2009. "More importantly, her flexibility and willingness to accommodate you is shamefully and transparently absent."

Chris moved a mile from her parents, in a house her dad helped pay for, changed his last name because she didn't like it, worked for her dad, went to counseling at her insistence, stopped drinking at her insistence, and was in court 54 times over the course of five years during the divorce at her insistence. Who dictated the marriage, the divorce; which of the two- Dina or Chris Mackney- is the controller personality? All of this is absent in Samenow's evaluation.

Unqualified Evaluators like Samenow and Wong

Dr. Margaret Wong did the psychological evaluation of Hera McLeod's ex-boyfriend for their custody battle. Dr. Wong did this evaluation even though she specializes in treating children not adults and is a school psychologist not a forensic psychologist.

In September 2014, Dr. Wong settled with McLeod for $550,000 largely because as a school psychologist she wasn't qualified to do a psychological evaluation of a potential psychopath. In *The Washington Post's* article from November 6, 2014, by Tom Jackman detailing the settlement, Dr. Samenow defended Wong.

The settlements were "absolutely amazing," said Stanton Samenow, an Alexandria forensic psychologist and a nationally known expert in criminal and custody evaluations. He said psychology is not a "hard science."

"It's not like having a blood test," Samenow said. "There's an awful lot that goes into a judge's decision"...Samenow and Wendy Patrick, a lawyer and mental health expert in San Diego, said subjects of psychological evaluations can fool even the most experienced examiner. "Some of these guys," Patrick said, "are able to manipulate, and they have charisma, and they are able to pull the wool over the eyes of the most practiced psychologist."

Dr. Wong had her license put on probation on September 30, 2014 by the Virginia Board of Psychology because, "Dr. Wong practiced beyond the scope of her license," a fact not mentioned in Jackman's article.

Though Samenow has done custody evaluations for nearly twenty years, he's a forensic psychologist with a specialty in the criminal mind not family dynamics or child psychology. His background and qualifications for custody evaluations are dubious at best and Mackney's is not the only problematic one.

Dr. Stanton Samenow's M.O.

Here is Samenow's modus operandi (M.O.): he broadens the scope of a narrow evaluation, shows clear bias while claiming to be an independent evaluator, does not speak to all appropriate witnesses, fails to provide documents or private records, and turns one side into heroes with the other side is made villainous. He's no independent evaluator; he's for sale.

Tommy Moffett

Tommy Moffett said Dr. Samenow was brought into his divorce as an independent expert to evaluate whether his daughter needed counseling; what should have been a one page report from Samenow was more than thirty pages.

While at one point Dr. Samenow called Moffett's daughter's childhood "idyllic," Samenow also suggested in the report that his daughter would be better off if custody was cut off from one of her parents entirely. Samenow did not name which parent was the problem, but a friend warned Moffett Samenow could try to use the report to end his parental rights.

Moffett willingly participated in Samenow's initial assessment however he clandestinely taped all meetings as insurance against misrepresentation.

On one audio tape, Samenow repeated the most extreme of the charges against Moffett. "Either you are a child molester," Samenow is heard on the audio tape saying, "or we've got a real problem on the mother's end here."

Samenow testified on behalf of Moffett's ex-wife almost a year after the report was written.

During the trial, Moffett questioned Samenow about statements the doctor made during their sessions. Samenow repeatedly denied making statements which Moffett had taped, however after several questions, Samenow angrily asked, "What, did you have me recorded?"

After the exchange, Samenow changed his recommendation from full custody for Moffett's ex-wife and no contact with Moffett to joint custody.

Annette Yunker

Anette Yunker and Chris Mackney got to know each other during the last year and a half of his life. In this email on November 11, 2012, Yunker described to Mackney her experience with Samenow.

He was appointed as an INDEPENDENT court-appointed evaluator for my divorce, with the direction to assess the parents psychologically. My spouse attempted to turn this into a custody evaluation, and was rather successful. My spouse had the full ear of Dr. Samenow. He dismissed anything I said that did not reflect well on the father. He focused ONLY on negative information about me (I could write volumes about this). He accepted close to $20,000 from my spouse, and admitted in court that he did not know that the costs were to be split between *both parents (despite having a copy of the court order). He was paid for by my spouse and worked for my spouse - he even met with my spouse and his attorney for strategy meetings and refused to speak with my attorney about what he would have to say in court (both parties should have been informed).*

He would return my spouse's calls immediately, even allowing my spouse to call him at his residence. He would wait DAYS and weeks to return my attorney's calls. When I returned a call from him to his residence (using caller ID), he immediately told me he could not talk to me at that time, and I would have to wait until he got to his office. I could go on and on. The ONLY thing that save(d) me was 2 things: (1) his testimony was so very slanted that it was obviously biased, and the judge acknowledged it as such. When my attorney asked if he could say ANYTHING nice about me, he said that my kids were well-dressed. (2) My spouse's attorney failed to follow the deadline for submitting Dr. Samenow as an expert witness, so his testimony was weighted just like any other person called to testify, and not as an expert. During this period of time, I asked around and heard other horror stories about how Dr. Samenow took the father's side despite glaring abuse.

During the process, Samenow attempted to forego his written report and simply testify to his findings, saying it would save money. This would have blindsided Yunker and her lawyer, Dorian Hughes, in court, leaving them virtually no time to prepare.

Yunker said the judge in her case, Stanley Klein, treated Samenow's opinion with a great deal of skepticism, remarking during his decision that the only individual who testified with any credibility was an ear and throat specialist.

Yunker's attorney quit the profession after this case.

The bulk of the criticism against Samenow came from Yunker's 23 year old daughter, Caroline, who was 12 at the time she was examined by Samenow.

"He tried to trick me into saying something I didn't want to say." Caroline Yunker said. "I had this feeling that something was not right."

She said she felt as though Samenow steered each interview to get her to speak ill of her mother and worried the things she told him would be used to cut off their contact.

Caroline Yunker said she was traumatized by the experience.

Jeff Wine

Jeff Wine said he and his ex-wife divorced in 2004 and arranged custody on their own which worked without any serious problems until he was jailed for fraud for eighteen months in 2009.

Following his release, his ex-wife attempted to remove all Wine's custody and Samenow was brought in to do a psychological evaluation on both parents.

Samenow treated the psychological evaluation like a custody evaluation, interviewing their three children and making custody recommendations. Samenow recommended supervised visitation for Jeff Wine with his children at locations requiring several hours drive.

In that evaluation, Samenow claimed Wine, who has suffered from bipolar disorder since he was a child, suffered from antisocial personality disorder, another term for a psychopath.

But Wine said that Samenow's report was full of holes: Samenow never performed the proper tests to make his diagnosis, he ignored Wine's bipolar diagnosis from another psychiatrist, and most of the negative feedback about Wine came from his ex-wife.

Wine was saved when his family paid for an alternative evaluation from Dr. Thomas Ryan, another well respected forensic psychiatrist in Virginia. Ryan poked holes in Samenow's evaluation.

With the exception of Stanton Samenow Ph.D., there is a consensus regarding clinicians who have evaluated Mr. Wine that he has bipolar disorder.

...

This examiner is in direct disagreement with Dr. Samenow's psychological evaluation report regarding Mr. Wine on several levels. Although third party sources are important when conducting a forensic examination, Dr. Samenow administered only one psychological measure with no tasks to assess possible diminished effort and/or malingering, yet an eighteen page report was generated. Although providing an excellent history, this examiner finds much of Dr. Samenow's historical information irrelevant to the issue brought before the courts. That is, whether or not Mr. Wine is a safe and emotionally healthy parent, and if so, should the time he spends with his children be increased?

Dr. Ryan's report and subsequent testimony destroyed Samenow's credibility, and Wine said since Samenow has been removed from his custody arrangement he and his ex-wife have joint custody of their children with little to no problems.

This was not the only time Samenow improperly referred to someone as having antisocial personality disorder. Samenow was involved in the landmark case Atkins vs. Virginia in which the Supreme Court determined it would be cruel and unusual punishment to put a mentally retarded person to death.

On August 16, 1996, eighteen year old Daryl Atkins spent the day drinking beer and smoking marijuana along with his friend William Jones; at around midnight they walked into a convenience store and abducted a patron named Eric Nesbitt. After taking $60 from Nesbitt's wallet, they forced him into his car, drove to a nearby automatic teller machine and forced him to withdraw $200. After that, they forced him back into his car, drove to an isolated location, and shot him eight times killing him.

After he was convicted, Atkins' defense attorney called clinical psychologist Dr. Evan Nelson who testified tests performed on Atkins showed his Intelligence Quotient (IQ) was 59, below the minimum of 70 for mental retardation.

The State of Virginia countered with Samenow who said Atkins was not mentally retarded but was of "average intelligence, at least," and diagnosable as having antisocial personality disorder like Wine. The jury gave Atkins the death penalty and this verdict was upheld by the Virginia Supreme Court.

Samenow's evaluation "was based upon two interviews with Atkins, interviews with jail personnel, and a review of school records. Samenow never administered a full intelligence test, instead asking Atkins several questions from an outdated version of an IQ test," according to an analysis of the case by Alexis Krulish Dowling for the *Seton Hall University Law Review*.

The US Supreme Court overturned the ruling of the Virginia Supreme Court, ruling that sentencing a mentally retarded individual to death amounts to cruel and unusual punishment, giving Samenow's evaluation no weight.

All four of the cases mentioned- Mackney, Yunker, Moffet, and Wine- were originally exposed by me on the website *Communities Digital News (CDN)* on May 14, 2015.

Chris Mackney Evaluates Samenow

In a November 28, 2013 blog post entitled *Psychopath or Secret Controller* Mackney evaluated Samenow, a poetic way to end the chapter.

The 'Gold Standard' diagnostic tool used to identify psychopathy is the PCL-R Checklist created by Dr. Robert Hare. This checklist is a simple list of 20 characteristics that one either possess(es) or does not possess, as a pattern of behavior, and can be verified over the life of the individual. It is through people familiar with the individual over time, that it's possible to verify whether or not the behaviors exist. A careful examination of break-ups with old boyfriends and girlfriends is a good place to start. Another location for identifying areas of conflict and people that can verify information is the Court record. Someone who has a lifetime of lying, manipulating, stealing and murdering can easily be recognized by the pattern in which they handle the 'conflict' in Court. This is why the PCL-R is used throughout the criminal justice system. The PCL-R is a reliable predictor of psychopathy, abuse and 'conflict'.

I have read parts of Dr. Samenow's books and he seems to have a complete understanding of psychopathy. He refers to the psychopathic personality in his books as the 'controller personality' in his 2002 Book titled In the Best Interest of the Child: How to Protect Your Child from the Pain of Divorce *or 'secret controllers' as he does in his book* The Myth of the Out of Character Crime. *As I consider Dr. Samenow's books and his clear understanding of psychopathy, I ask why Dr. Samenow does not just refer to them as Psychopaths? If he is describing a different construct, why does he change the name from book to book?*

The psychological construct of Psychopathy is not new. Dr. Hervey Cleckley's book Mask of Sanity, *considered a seminal work and the most influential clinical description of psychopathy in the twentieth century, was published in 1941. From 1970 to 1978, Dr. Samenow worked as clinical research psychologist for the Program for the Investigation of Criminal Behavior at St. Elizabeth's Hospital in Washington, D.C. Dr. Samenow effectively studied psychopaths.*

Even after Dr. Hare published Without Conscience *in 1993, Dr. Samenow attributes the conflict created by psychopaths in divorce, to the 'controller personality' in his 2002 book* In the Best Interest of the Child:

Many marriages break up when a non-controlling husband or wife stands up to a controller. By refusing to endure any longer the mistreatment dished out for years, the noncontrolling spouse precipitates a crisis. The marriage may have gone smoothly in the controller's opinion, largely because he or she went unchallenged. In reality though, the non-controller had walked a tightrope. As a problem solver, he or she has sought to avoid unnecessary and debilitating conflict and picked battles discerningly. Having the welfare of the child uppermost in his or her thoughts, the problem-solving parent let a lot go by rather than subject the household to unpleasantness. When he or she finally becomes fed up with walking on eggshells and decides to do something, the marital equilibrium is disrupted. The noncontrolling spouse's sudden assertiveness strikes at the core of the controller's self-concept. At home he or she has been accustomed to having his or her way. Now things are different. The controller reacts by angrily faulting the other spouse for creating the upheaval. If the problem solver fails to back down, the controller becomes more irascible and domineering.

In truth, the controller is an abuser. When family members get out of line, he or she becomes harsh and punitive.

He begins his 2007 book The Myth of the Out of Character Crime:

The theme of this book is that people always respond in character, that it is impossible for a person to do otherwise. You cannot be other than what you are! The "out of character" crime can be understood only by figuring out what the character of the alleged perpetrator truly is. "Character" as used here is synonymous with the patterns of thinking and behavior that a person demonstrates throughout life. If you do something out of character, you are not being you. That is impossible!

Chapter 4 titled 'Secret Controllers' includes:

I call these individuals "secret controllers" because they are not perceived as controlling. They are successful in attaining what they want. Rarely do others challenge them. These people may not be seen accurately for who they really are until they have done irreparable damage.

Can someone in the Psychological or Legal Community explain why Dr. Stanton Samenow does not just call them by the more widely accepted term 'psychopath'? Does Dr. Samenow have a professional rivalry with Dr. Robert Hare?

Dr. Hare was born in 1934, Samenow in 1941. Dr. Hare worked as the psychologist in the British Columbia maximum security prison in the early sixties. Samenow clearly came into the field after Hare. However, Samenow published The Criminal Personality Volume 1 in 1976; Volume II in 1977; and Volume III in 1986. Dr. Hare's book Without Conscience was published in 1993. From what I read of both men's work, they are describing the same individual.

Dr. Hare's work in defining the Psychopath and in the creation of the PCL-R Checklist does seem to run parallel to Dr. Samenow's work. Does anyone in the psychological community know the history between these two men?

Chapter 7: Techniques for Devious People in Family Court

"It is difficult to get a man to understand something, when his salary depends upon his not understanding it."

Upton Sinclair

...

Introduction

What's Kafkaesque in family court? You've never been violent in your life but on the word of your former spouse you're deemed an abuser and told to leave your home. The massive legal bills leave you broke and forced to represent yourself which the court finds problematic all while saddling you with more costs you can't pay. When you fall behind you're sanctioned leading to more bills you can't pay leading to more sanctions until you get jailed. You speak out and the court tells you to knock it off or go to jail again, calling you the problem. Just when you think your nightmare can't get any worse you're charged with bogus criminal charges. Even if you beat those charges family court says you're behind on their bills. All the while your ex uses all this to tell the court you're an unfit parent so your children are taken away from you by legal procedure which is quite horrible but don't dare complain or the court says you aren't cooperating. Entirely out of their lives, your ex tells your children you are a horrible person and even worse parent and your kids believe you don't want to see them, so you complain and the court says you aren't cooperating.

Because family court is the wicked person's playground, Chris Mackney is far from alone in being destroyed. Family courts foster certain techniques which pervert the process, encourage abuse, and enflame corruption; those techniques are the topic of this chapter.

The Silver Bullet Technique

Using false or dubious allegations of abuse for ill-gotten restraining orders during a divorce is so common it's been branded with the derogatory name- the silver bullet technique- as in accusing your ex of abuse is so effective it's a silver bullet.

"The 'silver bullet' technique is a system of stripping you of your property, your right to own a gun, and your freedom. It can put you out of your own home, with no access to your own money, your children, or your possessions. It can cause you unlimited legal expenses. It can turn your friends and family against you," according to the Family Rights Association, an apt description of Ronald Pierce's ordeal.

Silver Bullet Technique Victim 1: Ronald Pierce

Pierce had three kids, a city job, and lived in a $200,000 home in Dinuba, California, in Tulare County, at the time of his divorce in 2008. He said his story started out similarly to Mackney's; even though his wife started cheating on him about a year prior to the divorce filing, she demanded he move out of their house, accusing him of domestic violence.

"I didn't get accused of domestic violence until I filed for divorce," Pierce said.

Like Mackney, Pierce had no history of domestic violence and his ex-wife could produce no photos, police reports, or any other documentation to back up her claims. Instead, she used the most common tactic in the silver bullet technique: she said she was scared.

"(Pierce's ex-wife) told me (she) and Pierce have been married for several years and during that time she has been in fear of his temper. She told me Pierce has an anger management issue. She told me he has never hit her in the past but he has intimidated her by fear," a Tulare officer wrote on March 4, 2008.

As a result, his ex-wife was granted an emergency protective order (EPO) forcing Pierce out of his home. He was still allowed to see his kids for a while he said, until his ex-wife escalated things one weekday morning.

"As soon as I pulled up to the curb, instead of my kids running out to me as usual, I was surrounded by three police cruisers and a handful of police who looked quite intent on arresting me and beating my ass. I was surrounded where I stood on the sidewalk (I never got near the door to my house that morning). They detained me un-cuffed while some officers went into my house to talk with her and her boyfriend whom she had immediately moved in." Pierce said. "From what I was told by the investigating officer when he came back out is that I was being accused of stalking and harassment. He started to say, 'These two are going to make trouble for you.' (He) Stopped himself from saying anything further, and simply stated that she had the children and the property and that if I was seen anywhere in the area I would be immediately arrested. All of this happened at a time in the morning when nearly all of my surrounding neighbors were exiting their homes to go to work and I found myself surrounded by cops for all of my neighbors to drive by and gawk at."

In a 2011 court filing, Pierce's ex-wife asked the court to extend the protective order because Pierce "had posted comments on Internet Web sites such as the statement that he would like to go on a 'killing spree of global proportions.'"

Pierce said he made those statements while playing the MySpace game *Vampires*, which was not explained in the filing or subsequent hearing. That Pierce's ex-wife was cyber stalking him (how else would she know what he said in a MySpace game) never became an issue in family court.

Pierce said between his child support payments and court mandated domestic abuse therapy at the local battered women's shelter resulting from the protective order, he was broke and living out of his car.

The domestic violence shelter later claimed because Pierce initially refused to move out of his home against his ex-wife's wishes, this was a form of domestic violence.

"I was accused of creating an 'atmosphere of abuse' because I wouldn't leave the home when she demanded it," Pierce said.

The letter Mackney received from Ain & Bank implied the same thing: "The tension in the household can be reduced if you move from (the home)."

Silver Bullet Technique Victim 2: Neil Shelton

Neil Shelton of Mount Airy, North Carolina was a successful entrepreneur with two kids living in a $400,000 home owned free and clear when on May 21, 2012 his wife kicked him out of the house.

Exactly a week later, his wife filed her first restraining order after he purportedly attempted to enter his home without permission.

Shelton's ex-wife has been able to renew the protective order for over three years.

He's since been arrested six times for purported restraining order violations. He's always been acquitted, but those are six of more than two dozen arrests orchestrated by his ex-wife and her divorce lawyer. The damage to his reputation makes him effectively unemployable.

"Boy am I gonna have fun playing with you," Shelton's ex-wife's divorce lawyer Sarah Stevens told him outside court the first day he met her. Stevens initially denied making this threat but had no further comment after I shared a recording proving otherwise.

"It's going to go either one of two ways. First, it's going to go with a restraining order protecting your wife and your children," Stevens told Shelton later that same day. "Or you can agree to a five thousand dollar property settlement and walk out of here today without a restraining order and some supervised visits with your kids."

(The racket run by devious women and men who claim they are "afraid" of their ex-spouses is so common that it's the subject of numerous illustrations like this one from a father's rights group)

"Let me get this straight, I'm dangerous but I'm not dangerous with $5,000 in my pocket." Shelton responded to the threat.

As a result of his divorce, Shelton hasn't seen his three children in more than fifteen hundred days and is destitute. Stevens, who doubles as a North Carolina State Representative, has filed restraining orders against sixty other divorce opponents with no criminal record, Shelton said.

Stevens denied employing the silver bullet technique as a divorce strategy and was dubious as many as sixty people involved in her cases were slapped with restraining orders despite no criminal history; she noted she takes on about 200 cases yearly. As a legislator she's championed legislation which makes it tougher for restraining orders to be granted putting her up against advocates for domestic violence prevention, but she didn't deny that several of her clients filed restraining orders, including against those with no criminal history.

(Neil Shelton's current living arrangements, eerily similar to Mackney's last place of residence)

"That wouldn't surprise me," Stevens told me, "in some cases the domestic abuse is only against the spouse."

Though she's subjected him to repeated restraining orders, Stevens admitted Shelton has never been physically violent toward his ex-wife.

On June 13, 2013, Stevens' law partner, Zach Brinkle, asked Shelton's ex-wife if she felt afraid. She responded, "because I knew at that point he was desperate because he knew I meant it (filing for divorce) this time; instead of taking it and taking it and taking it…the mental issues."

That was enough to approve a restraining order.

"I received a visit from the Chief of (Mount Airy) police yesterday. He is getting questioned by a couple of people who are looking into what they (Mount Airy Police Department) helped do to me." Shelton told me in an email on March 5, 2015. "I'm not in the City Limits so he traveled out of the jurisdiction to ask me what I was planning on saying about him, his office and the DA. I replied just the truth; he patted his gun and said the truth is a dangerous thing, be careful and left."

Shelton plans on writing a book tentatively titled *Growing up Mayberry* on his experiences in family court. Mount Airy is the hometown of Andy Griffith and generally believed to be the inspirational setting for Mayberry of the *Andy Griffith Show*.

Shelton, Pierce, and Mackney's Kafkaesque Nightmare

All three- Mackney, Pierce, and Shelton- 1)had no history of violence (domestic or otherwise) (2) were kicked out of their family homes (3)have seen no equity since (4) have little or no access to their children, and (5) been financially devastated by their divorce. If you think that's a coincidence, I have some swampland in Mogadishu, Somalia I'd like to sell you.

Restraining orders are easily approved because no one is being charged with a crime- burden of proof, rules of evidence, confronting your accuser, and other concepts standard in a criminal trial don't apply. An EPO is usually approved as long as the complainant says the magic words, "I'm afraid."

An EPO is a Kafkaesque nightmare- you're charged with nothing, you're not allowed to present a defense and most often you aren't even allowed at the hearing, but the end result is you can't be in your home or see your children.

The Kafkaesque nightmare continues when an EPO turns into a permanent protective. You are able to present a defense but it's perfunctory- you're presumed guilty- and the hearings are nothing more than a dog and pony show with the outcome being predetermined.

In Pierce's case, an EPO led to a hearing nearly a month later.

"The hearing wasn't a hearing at all." Pierce told me. "A judge had already signed a restraining order," with this hearing being nothing more than a rubber stamp, and for the next two years the order was renewed repeatedly.

In Shelton's case, the charges from a criminal case continue to be the basis for a protective order even though the criminal charges were dropped more than a year ago for lack of evidence.

Though the physical evidence- ripped shirt and bruises- supported his version of the January 19, 2008 fight, Dina made it one of three examples in her initial application for a protective order, arguing she had reason to be afraid of him.

Shelton said a protective order was the basis for holding an ex-parte hearing which restricted his parental rights.

VAWA: Making Restraining Orders Easy

Restraining orders are easy to get because of a little known law called the Violence Against Women Act (VAWA).

"VAWA is always the case in a divorce case where the wife is in any way claiming fear of the husband of any kind. I'm not making this up that all a woman needs to do is say she is afraid of her husband and instantly the court has VAWA jurisdiction." Pierce said.

First passed in 1994 in the Clinton administration reauthorized in the Bush administration in 2006, and strengthened by the Obama administration in 2013, VAWA set up about $1 billion per year in block grants to states, leading to about 600 state level laws and the proliferation of restraining orders. Here's part of a 2007 study by Respecting Accuracy in Domestic Abuse Reporting (RADAR) entitled *VAWA: Threat to Families, Children, Men, and Women.*

In Oregon, restraining orders are euphemistically referred to as "divorce planning." In basketball-crazed Kentucky, divorce attorneys call them "slam-dunks" because of their efficiency and effectiveness. In New Hampshire, people in the business commonly refer to domestic orders as "silver bullets." One Marital Master testified, "Unfortunately, requests for ex-parte relief are based upon many circumstances, some of which are made only for the purpose of obtaining an advantage in litigation."

In Illinois, attorney Thomas Kasper refers to these tactics as "part of the gamesmanship of divorce." Washington state attorney Lisa Scott likewise notes, "Protection orders have become 'weapons of mass destruction' in family courts. Whenever a woman claims to be a victim, she is automatically believed. No proof of abuse is required."

...

Knowledgeable observers have similarly estimated that 40–50% of all restraining orders are requested merely as legal maneuvers. Elaine Epstein, former president of the Massachusetts

Bar Association, further confirms, "Everyone knows that restraining orders and orders to vacate are granted to virtually all who apply."

Based on those numbers, we can conclude that each year about 500,000 persons are evicted from their homes solely on the basis of alleged psychological harm. This represents a serious breach of their civil liberties

A California Bar Association official said, "Protective orders are increasingly being used in family law cases to help one side jockey for an advantage in child custody," noting that protective orders are "almost routinely issued by the court in family law proceedings even when there is relatively meager evidence and usually without notice to the restrained person....it is troubling that they appear to be sought more and more frequently for retaliation and litigation purposes."

"Your job is not to weigh the parties' rights as you might be inclined to do. Your job is not to become concerned about all the constitutional rights of the man that you're violating as you grant a restraining order." Richard Russell a New Jersey Superior Court Judge was quoted as saying in a *New Jersey Law Journal* article from April 24, 1995. "Throw him out on the street, give him the clothes on his back and tell him, 'See ya' around.' … we don't have to worry about their rights."

In a 2014 civil RICO suit, filed by attorney turned litigant, Cole Stuart, Stuart quoted his divorce lawyer stating, "Of course they're unconstitutional—they're illegal as hell, but they know it's expensive to fight it. So they strike first, throw you in the pit and make you pay or work to climb your way out."

"You can either pay her to get out of it or jump through the hoops and pray you make it," another divorce lawyer said.

Silver Bullet Technique Victim 3: Susan Carrington

While restraining orders are usually used by women against men, Susan Carrington's case is an exception. She and her ex-husband finalized a divorce in 2010 in Maryland in which he accused her of being crazy, a drug addict, and violent. All these allegations were dismissed and a final order granted joint custody of their two daughters with Susan getting physical custody. Unhappy with the result, Carrington's ex-husband, John McNelis, moved to Rockland County, New York after falsely claiming to receive a job there, walked into a Rockland County family courtroom and received protective orders using the same allegations which had already been thrown out in Maryland. Though Rockland County had no business wrestling jurisdiction away from Maryland, the Rockland County court refused to acknowledge the rulings from Maryland and the Maryland court refused to get involved even though this is a violation of their jurisdictional rights.

The proceedings turned Kafkaesque when the court demanded Susan Carrington complete a drug rehabilitation program in order to see her children. Carrington was repeatedly denied entry into rehab when her initial drug tests came back clean. Her failure to complete the program was used to continue extending protective orders denying her contact with her children for more than four years. The saga crippled her financially, forcing her to move back in with her mother.

"He promised me three things he would do if I filed for divorce: take the girls from me, bankrupt me and kill me." Carrington said.

Raquel Okyay and I exposed this abuse in a two part article for the *Rockland County Times.* After the first part was published, McNelis showed up at the newspaper's offices acting in a threatening manner before police escorted him out.

Parental Alienation Syndrome Makes Abuse Easy (PAS Victim 1: Wendy Titelman)

Mackney, Shelton and Pierce are part of an epidemic of bullied fathers falsely accused of domestic violence with little or no evidence. The other side of the coin is Wendy Titelman, and millions of bullied protective mothers whose true claims of abuse are ignored and turned against them, with their abusers alleging they are making false claims to alienate the other parent, or because of some unspecified mental disorder. Far too often, courts accept these attacks taking away children from their protective parents and handing them to abusers.

Titelman is author of the book *Let My Children Go*, which describes not only the sexual abuse of her two children at the hands of her ex-husband, Andy Titelman, but the systematic cover-up of this abuse by her home county, Cobb County, Georgia. At the time she wrote the book in 2003, she hadn't seen either of her two daughters in about two years.

When Titelman complained vociferously to the court that her daughters were being sexually molested, rather than investigating the abuse, the court accused Titelman of having Parental Alienation Syndrome (PAS).

Richard Gardner and PAS

PAS is not the same as parental alienation, itself a controversial idea which will be discussed shortly, rather a theory which "could lead children in high-conflict custody cases to falsely accuse a parent of abuse."

Its creator, Dr. Richard Gardner, was an outspoken supporter of Woody Allen telling Newsweek in 1995, "Screaming sex abuse is a very effective way to wreak vengeance on a hated spouse."

The theory is controversial in part due to Gardner's pro-pedophilia proclamations.

Referring to pedophilia, Gardner said, "The determinant as to whether the experience will be traumatic is the social attitude toward these encounters," in his book *True and False*

Accusations of Abuse, "there is a certain amount of pedophilia in all of us" and "pedophilia has been considered the norm by the vast majority of individuals in the history of the world."

Gardner's theory was never tested but based on anecdotal data he collected. PAS is not listed in the International Statistical Classification of Diseases and Related Health Problems produced by the World Health Organization, nor is it in the American Psychiatric Association's Diagnostic and Statistical Manual of Mental Disorders. The District Attorneys Association of the State of New York instructs that "Prosecutors should diligently question any case law or article that is cited as supporting PAS theory."

About the only place where PAS is accepted is in some family courtrooms.

Gardner died in 2003. While ruled a suicide, the death is shrouded in mystery. According to an autopsy done by Bergen County, New Jersey, Gardner was stabbed four times in the chest and three times in the neck. The police investigation into his death done by the Tenafly, New Jersey Police Department found three typewritten suicide notes, no forced entry and no defensive wounds. On the other hand, blood was found in multiple rooms and the knife was found at his side, suggesting he stabbed himself and removed the knife as he lay dying if this was a suicide.

According to Alec Baldwin's book, *A Promise to Ourselves: A Journey through Fatherhood and Divorce* PAS has these seven symptoms: 1) a campaign of denigration, 2) weak, frivolous and absurd rationalizations for the deprecation, 3) lack of ambivalence toward both the alienating and targeted parents, 4) the "independent thinker" phenomenon, 5) reflexive support (by the child) for the alienating parent, 6) absence of guilt over cruelty to and/or exploitation of targeted parent, 7) the spread of animosity to the extended family and friends of the alienated family.

It's the eighth symptom- the presence of borrowed scenarios, where children will level false charges including sexual and physical charges of abuse against the targeted parents- which has drawn a great deal of scrutiny especially from feminist and females.

PAS Victim 2: Sunny Kelley

Journalist Keith Harmon Snow's article entitled *A Life Sentence: U.S. Family Courts Sacrificing Mothers and Children* documented how PAS was falsely used to traffic children to child molesters in more than seventy cases in the New England area including Sunny Kelley's story.

In 2009, Sunny Kelley was an attractive thirty seven year old making six figures working as an audio engineer whose husband worked in internet security. Their combined income afforded them a home, a wing for parents and in-laws to stay, and an acre of land. With their five year old son, she appeared to be living the serene American dream. In private, Kelley was the repeated victim of domestic violence, suffering at least three concussions and multiple rapes. The breaking point came after a police officer called her one evening.

"Will you be safe if your husband comes home tonight?" The officer asked.

After a routine traffic stop, her husband told the police he'd kill her, apparently blaming Sunny for his failure to turn his lights on at night.

On July 3, 2009, she filed for divorce; one nightmare ended but a new Kafkaesque nightmare began.

After her son came home from a visit with his father acting strangely, Sunny took him to the pediatrician where he told the doctor his dad was playing the "tickle the weenie" game.

He came home from another visit with anal tearing. "His butt was shredded," she told me.

Her son told his pediatrician he had feces smeared on his face and in his mouth. Her son also had anal tearing consistent with objects being inserted there. During one doctor visit, her son was suicidal, hitting himself repeatedly.

"I was very, very, very careful never to accuse (my son's) father of anything. With every professional, with every visit to the hospital or therapists or pediatrician, all I did was to repeat what my son had told me." Kelley told Snow. "But no matter what I did, it was always turned around on me that I was the guilty one, that I was making false accusations about my husband."

What should have been a criminal investigation turned into a family court dispute. Child Protective Services (CPS) and the police declined to get involved and instead a near endless stream, more than ten, of court professionals attempted to determine who was telling the truth, Sunny Kelley or her ex-husband.

"You're giving me abundant evidence that your husband abused you and your son physically, emotionally, financially, psychologically." Robert LaMontagne, a family services supervisor assigned to her case told her. "But the more solid evidence you provide of his abuse, the more evidence you provide that you have motive to be vindictive."

"(Sunny Kelley has) taken it upon herself to become the documentarian of record (for what) she believes is a righteous and just cause," the judge said in one court filing. "The downside of that, sincere as her belief may be, is that her conduct towards the child itself is abusive. The taking of that picture (Kelley took a photo of her son's bruises) was abusive."

One court appointed psychologist, Ken Robson, named Gardner along with several other PAS proponents as models for protocols in Kelley's case. During the case, Gardner referred to Kelley as a "French whore" who was "gratified by (her) son's sexualized behavior".

"The details of what happened to Sunny Kelley belie belief. The personal details of Sunny Kelley's relationship, her marriage, her sex life, her personal history with sexual abuse, the toileting of her child- the details of her imperfection as a parent and her emotional response to this judicial abuse - everything has been scrutinized and used against her." Snow added in his article.

Kelley's abusive ex-husband was given physical custody after it was insinuated she was mentally ill and she was forced to pay a local shelter for supervised visits with her son. Having spent more than $1 million on the divorce, Kelley soon couldn't afford the visits, and her contact with her son was severed entirely; she hasn't seen him in more than three years.

PAS in RICO

Karin Wolf's civil Racketeer Influenced Corrupt Organizations (RICO) suit filed in Bergen County, New Jersey alleges that there is a Kafkaesque conspiracy in that county to remove children from protective mothers using PAS; according to her suit, the conspiracy includes: the Bergen County, New Jersey family court, Department of Youth and Family Services (DYFS), and even New Jersey Governor Chris Christie.

Defendants sought to benefit their agenda by promoting Richard Gardner's pro-pedophile, misogynistic, and unscientific theories of Parental Alienation Syndrome, which employs a "witch hunt" to pathologize female victims and marginalize protective mothers in order to subvert, enable, and cover up child abuse; and terrorize, oppress, and humiliate women.

Defendant DYFS n/k/a DCP&P was labeled a systematic failure several years ago and remains as such. Parents dealing with DCP&P often find themselves subject to a Kafkaesque existence where there is no transparency; they don't even know what they're being charged with, nor are they provided pertinent and concrete information per the Freedom of Information Act.

Wolf leads more than forty women in Bergen County and there is a similar suit led by Rachel Alintoff in nearby Monmouth County (New Jersey) making the same allegation. I interviewed about a dozen of these women for an article for *Rebel Pundit*. A New Jersey judge dismissed Wolf's initial complaint but she submitted an amended complaint which was filed in July 2015. Alintoff's suit continues to make its way through the courts.

PAS in Research and Media

A 2008 survey from the Leadership Council on Child Abuse and Interpersonal Violence (LC) found that about 58,000 children yearly are ordered into unsupervised contact with physically or sexually abusive parents following divorce in the United States. Dr. Joy Silberg, President of LC, told me the proliferation of PAS drives that number.

The definitive work on this subject was done by Peter Jamison in the *San Francisco Weekly* on March 2, 2011. The article featured stories from more than a dozen protective mothers from the San Francisco area who lost custody after they were accused of PAS following accusations of child molestation.

One protective mother, Joyce Murphy, suspected in 2003 that her ex-husband, Henry "Bud" Parsons, was molesting their daughter. For the next five years, the court treated Murphy like the perpetrator, referring to her as "crazy" and suggesting she was putting these thoughts in her daughter's head in a campaign of parental alienation.

When the court refused to keep her daughter away from her ex-husband, Murphy fled the state, only to be arrested for kidnapping, resulting in her ex-husband gaining sole custody. Finally in 2008, Parsons was arrested for charges including child molestation, sex with a child, and creating child pornography.

One of Murphy's judges, Deann Salcido, said this as part of her *mea culpa*.

From the moment she arrived in family court as a new judge, she says, she was advised by veterans of the system to disbelieve accusations of child or spousal abuse arising in divorces. "I was basically told to be suspect of anyone claiming abuse," she says. "I had senior judges telling me, 'Be suspect. The dad probably has a new girlfriend, and the mom's upset.'" The concept of parental alienation, she says, arose in private discussions "all the time" among court officials who espoused it.

Salcido says, "In the end, it did turn out that Joyce was right. She was right to be crying, and hysterical, because no one would believe her. I signed a court order handing a kid over to someone who turned out to be a pedophile."

On January 21, 1997, CNN International ran an hour special on PAS interviewing Gardner saying, "We need to jail these moms, gag orders, separate the child from the parent accusing abuse."

One of the stories featured in that special was Maralee McLean, a protective mother accused of PAS by Gardner after a GAL paid for his consultation. Her story is now a book *Prosecuted but Not Silenced*.

PAS and the Father's Rights Movement

Fatherhood initiatives create a perverted financial incentive allowing abusive men to claim their ex-spouses' legitimate concerns about abuse are PAS and other similar schemes. These initiatives were included in the landmark welfare reform bill passed in the Clinton administration, the Personal Responsibility and Work Opportunity Reconciliation Act of 1996 featuring the Temporary Aid for Needy Families (TANF) program. Fatherhood initiatives accompanied TANF largely because fathers rarely get physical custody; only 17% of the time, according to the 2010 census.

Many of these grants work based on raw numbers, meaning it behooves the powers that be to find as many fathers as possible to help. With few responsible fathers available, the only men left are abusers, and fatherhood initiatives far too often become a factory for abusers to turn the tables on protective mothers. While the grants are supposed to go to "responsible fathers" that's a nebulous term; just as women learn to talk the language of VAWA, abusive men- buoyed by a bevy of special interests which always materialize when the government is doling out money- learn to talk the language of fatherhood initiatives. Women who complain about abuse are labeled parental alienators or crazy.

"While major mass media corporations ignore the abuses against protective mothers -- or slam them - they are simultaneously providing platforms for the abusive 'Father's Rights' movement. For example, attorneys with The Father's Rights Foundation - which advertises their ability to 'influence the judge in your case' - have appeared on MSNBC, ABC.com and *The O'Reilly Factor*. Their entire web site spells out the program for fathers to destroy the children and their mothers." Snow said.

VAWA and TANF: The Symbiotic Relationship in the Gender War

It's counterintuitive to think family courts simultaneously target men with false allegations of abuse and women by ignoring legitimate cases of abuse, but that's the state of family courts. It's led to a philosophical war between feminists and MRAs, with both claiming their side happens 99% of the time, while the other side is rare: another manifestation of family court's gender war. Men fight women; dads fight moms; diverting attention from the corruption in the system. In the spring 2014, Mackney's story became a focal point of this ideological debate.

Penny Fisher, a poster on the Facebook page *Parental Alienation World Wide Support Group* saw the dynamic between the domestic violence sector and father's rights group differently, a symbiotic one.

"If supporters of the 'Domestic Violence (DV) sector' (male perpetrators) and supporters of 'Father Rights' (female perpetrators) were to get to together and REALLY LISTEN TO EACH OTHER, they would discover their stories are same--only the details are different. Why? Because the mentality, patterns & tactics of an abuser are the same regardless of gender." Fisher said in the post from December 19, 2014. "Abusers ALL follow the same unwritten script. The saddest part of the gender war is it buys into the abuser's divide & conquer strategies. As long as we fight amongst ourselves, nothing will change. The abusers win. Our children lose."

"I myself was accused of domestic violence but I know many mothers that have reported legitimate cases of abuse and the result is they lose they child; the child gets put with the father. I know one lady she lost her daughter for five years." Ronald Pierce said on October 27, 2014. "Then on the other side you've got a bunch of men being railroaded out of their kids' lives as well. There needs to be a meaningful opportunity to be heard. It's an access issue."

Susan Skipp, who was also featured in Snow's article, summed it up, "If you put an abuser and his victim in an adversarial situation, the abuser will always win," be it physical and sexual as in the case of protective mothers or psychological and legal abuse in Chris Mackney's case.

Was Albert Einstein an Alienated Parent?

"My fine boy has been alienated from me for a few years already by my wife, who has a vengeful disposition." Albert Einstein wrote to his friend and fellow scientist Fritz Haber in 1915. "The boy's soul is being systematically poisoned to make sure that he doesn't trust me."

Einstein's words resonate with the father's rights movement one hundred years later with one site saying, "Some of these letters show Einstein's justifiable anger and distress at the entire thing, illustrating his helplessness in the face of Maric's (Einstein's ex-wife) machinations. Pause a moment and reflect that this was perhaps the greatest mind of the twentieth century here, brought low by one vindictive woman, the mother of his children."

Einstein's ex-wife wouldn't pass on letters to his children and the two got into legal disputes over child support, but the story doesn't end there. As with everything surrounding the nebulous term, parental alienation, nothing is as it seems.

Albert Einstein married Mileva Maric in 1903, shortly after conceiving a daughter out of wedlock. They had their first son in 1904 and their second in 1910. They separated in 1914 and divorced in 1919, largely because Einstein shacked up with his first cousin, Elsa Lowenthal.

At the time he was complaining of being an alienated parent, his first wife demanded he keep his new flame away from his children. Here's from the website, *Duhaime*.

Albert Einstein responded like a typical litigant in family court: he callously canceled or bargained access visits, sometimes directly with his sons, and always infuriating his ex-wife and his sons.

On the day he announced his general theory of relativity to much renown; he penned a letter to his son promising to visit every month, which he then reneged on.

"Dear Papa, You should contact Mama about such things, because I'm not the only one to decide here." His son wrote Einstein after he reneged on a visit.

A biography of Einstein entitled *Annus Mirabilis* by Hans Grossman also revealed he was arrested twice for domestic violence. With parental alienation even geniuses abuse the term.

The Courts Perpetuate and Misdiagnose Parental Alienation

Parental alienation is "a social dynamic when a child expresses unjustified hatred or unreasonably strong dislike of one parent, making access by the rejected parent difficult or impossible," according to psychologist Richard Warshak, though if you ask ten people for parental alienation's definition you'll get eight to ten different answers.

Examples of alienating behavior include not making a child available to speak, bad mouthing the other parent, and saying you won't love them if they see the other parent, but taken too far, litigants, lawyers, and psychiatrists interpret all negative responses by children to their parents as parental alienation.

The courts often perpetuate the alienation.

In Susan Carrington's case, after the court kept her away from her children for about two years, the judge, William Warren, said, "To restart contact with these two little girls who don't know their mother now and are probably pretty terrified of their mother now, is what I would think, and that's not what I would think is a good situation for little children."

The British tabloid *The Daily Mail* featured an unidentified man blocked from seeing his daughter identified as M for years after his ex-wife ignored eighty two court orders for them to spend time together.

"My relationship with my daughter is slipping away," the man told *The Daily Mail*. "Her childhood is disappearing...Parents making applications to establish contact are often left defeated and frustrated by the slowness and lethargy of the court process. Time with your children can never be recaptured – it is lost forever,"

In Mackney's case the January 23, 2009, Pendente lite prohibited parental alienation, "Neither party shall commit any act of parental alienation by words or deeds, by express or implied conduct, by insinuation or otherwise. Both parties shall be required to instill love in the other parent...Neither party shall do anything which may estrange the children from the other party, which would alter the opinion of the children as to either party or which would hamper the natural development of the children's love and respect for either party."

But any action by any parent could be construed as estranging the child, altering their opinion of the other parent, or hampering the natural development of the children's love. Worse yet, despite broad orders forbidding parental alienation, Chris Mackney's children still said it didn't matter that their father was dead "because he's crazy anyway," shortly after his suicide.

On April 30, 2009, James said in front of Dr. Samenow that Dina called Chris "a liar" and said, "I have all the money."

Samenow left that incident out of his evaluation.

"This examiner finds that, despite trying circumstances Ms. Mackney has placed the best interests of Ruby and James ahead of everything," he wrote instead in his evaluation.

Dina took Chris off email lists, interfered with custody time, bad mouthed him to everyone, and demanded termination of his custodial rights because he didn't provide a receipt, but was never accused of parental alienation by anyone but Chris.

Angela Gizzi (nee Hickman) suffered through years of domestic abuse at the hands of her then husband Angelo culminating in him throwing her down the stairs while pregnant. In 2007, Angelo Gizzi was charged with thirteen domestic abuse related crimes including: assault, sexual assault, kidnapping, and child endangerment. He avoided jail time when Angela wouldn't testify due to her abuse related PTSD and plead guilty to lesser charges. Initially, Angelo Gizzi was given supervised visitation with his children while Angela got physical custody.

A series of court professionals were brought into the divorce including Dr. Stephanie Stein Leite who accused Angela of being a parent alienator, "This case sticks out in my mind, in the last ten years, as the clearest case of alienation that I have seen."

In January 2015, in a story I first reported for *Crime Magazine*, Angela Hickman lost all contact with her children when she refused to participate in reunification therapy, a response to her perceived alienation campaign, which would have forced her into counseling with her abuser, a violation of her rights under the Americans with Disabilities Act (ADA), rights eschewed to fix perceived parental alienation.

No court professional suggested there was parental alienation in Mackney's case, while the victim of domestic violence was deemed a parental alienator.

Was Chris Mackney An Alienated Parent?

Chris Mackney became heavily invested in parental alienation, using it repeatedly including in the first sentence of his suicide note and titling a blog post *All It Takes for Evil to Occur in Parental Alienation*, but I don't think he was an alienated parent because I don't believe there's such thing.

Custody litigants like Mackney victimized by this Kafkaesque nightmare don't see the forest through the trees. Their pain is being exploited by individuals and groups with an agenda. Parental alienation is big bucks for many who exploit parents like him. Overcoming Barriers is a five day boot camp for families deemed to have parental alienation. The entire family, including the two divorcing parents, is sent into a campground with no cell phones or other electronics to reconnect. Often this boot camp is compulsory, so if a judge orders it and you want to ever see your kids again, participation is mandatory. The cost of this boot camp is as much as ten thousand dollars. There are all sorts of lesser well-known reunification camps and therapies, all costing families thousands, and most compulsory which court actors have created to combat purported cases of parental alienation.

The courts have a vested financial interest in the proliferation of this term in cases of abuse because that prolongs court battles, provides an excuse for more experts, and for more court programs. The same courts also have a vested financial interest to deny real incidents of alienation because that favors the legal abusers. Of fifty plus hearings in Mackney's divorce, all but a handful were initiated by Dina.

As Upton Sinclair stated, "It is difficult to get a man to understand something, when his salary depends upon his not understanding it."

Parental alienation plays a significant role in the gender war: father's rights groups mostly embrace it while most feminist groups reject it.

"Parental alienation is the language of abusers," both Sunny Kelley and Susan Skipp told me and both believe a better term is paternal/maternal deprivation.

Ironically, the court accused Sunny Kelley and Susan Skipp of being parental alienators keeping their kids away from them as a result, and now neither has seen their kids in about three years making them alienated parents.

Most behaviors associated with so-called parental alienation can be described by other more precise terms- brainwashing, custodial interference, lying, disparaging the other parent, etc. Parental alienation, as it's applied, has no meaning, only each individual's interpretation. It should go away immediately and be replaced with a term which everyone understands and agrees on.

No Free Speech in Family Court (NFSIFC)

Throughout his family court case, Chris Mackney's first amendment rights were assaulted. This climaxed when he was jailed for repeating allegations about Pete Scamardo, but started as early as October 2008 when Mackney was "enjoined and restrained from badmouthing, disparaging, or in any otherwise way denigrating the Plaintiff or her family whether verbally or in writing."

Those whose only experience with the justice system is in their civics class might be wondering how a judge could take away someone's right to free speech so brazenly. In family court, the concept of "in the best interest of the child" trumps all including rights purportedly protected by the Constitution.

Here's part of one such court order which I'll discuss more fully later: "All parties are hereby enjoined and restrained without prejudice from speaking...to any reporters, journalists, newscasters, or other agents/employees of newspapers or other media outlets on the grounds that it is **not in the best interest of the children (emphasis mine)** to have the parties' divorce litigation discussed in a public forum or to have public disparaging statements made about any party by the other party."

If a judge decides your free speech is "not in the best interest of the child" you'll have a choice, parental rights or free speech rights, but not both.

"In the best interest of the child" is an ironic term with roots in the regime of the Third Reich, where Hitler ordered his social welfare agency the Lebensborn to act "In the best interest of the child, we are breeding superior Aryan children" in their quest to combat falling German birth rates. Those claiming to take away free speech, due process, and other rights "in the best interest of the child" have only the best interest of themselves in mind.

"It was determined that it's in the best interest of my children that I not contact people fooled by Dina and Pete." Mackney said referring to Kelly Malesardi and the perverse nature of "in the best interest of the child."

NFSIFC Victim 1: Lou Pelletier

Bullied to Death: Chris Mackney's Kafkaesque Divorce

Justina Pelletier initially went to Boston Children's Hospital to treat the flu in late 2012. Justina had been going to Tufts University Hospital to treat a mitochondrial disease, a rare group of disorders caused by dysfunctional mitochondria. Rather than simply treating the flu, the doctors at Boston Children's Hospital dug into Justina's mitochondrial disease diagnosis. Later in the visit, Boston Children's Hospital concluded not only that Justina did not have mitochondrial disease but that by having Justina's get treated for it her parents were committing "medical child abuse".

(A poster explaining the horrors of in the best interest of the child)

Boston Children's Hospital immediately called the Massachusetts Department of Children and Family (DCF) which made Justina a ward of the state. Over the next year and a half, Justina's health progressively worsened though state authorities insisted it was all in her mind.

In February 2014, her father, Lou Pelletier, went on a media blitz doing interviews with Glenn Beck, Megyn Kelly, Mike Huckabee, and others. By doing so, he risked jail time because there was a gag order in his case. Here's *The Boston Globe* from February 24, 2014.

One issue before the judge in today's hearing was whether Lou Pelletier should be held in contempt of court for violating a gag order. The teen's father has recently given media interviews in which he expressed frustration with the quality of care his daughter is getting while in DCF custody, care that he has asserted has been nearly fatal for her.

The Pelletiers' primary attorney declined comment, citing the gag order.

The media attention from Pelletier's appearances was overwhelming forcing the judge's hand; Pelletier was not jailed. Justina came home weeks later, but most people fighting in family court don't have the benefit of appearing with Glenn Beck and Megyn Kelly. When Chris Mackney started his blog, it was read by hundreds not millions.

NFSIFC Victim 2: Anthony Pappas

Anthony Pappas is an economics professor at St. John's University who went on *Families in Transition (FIT) TV* on Cablevision in eastern Long Island, expressing frustration with decisions in his divorce in Nassau County Supreme Court. On January 19, 2011, Judge Anthony Falanga issued an impromptu gag order, claiming that in his courtroom, Pappas no longer had a first amendment right.

"I am admonishing you right now you are not to communicate with anybody inside the court system, outside the court system, about how you feel you were being treated or anything like that. If you feel I am violating your right to free speech, you have the absolute right to feel that way and do whatever you feel is appropriate. If I decide to hold you in contempt, we'll cross that bridge when we come to it. Do you understand?"

NFSIFC Victim 3: Ron Pierce

On June 19, 2009, Ronald Pierce spoke at a rally sponsored by the group *Fathers 4 Justice*, bringing together fathers wronged by family court.

"I've been in the teeth of the monster for about two years," Pierce started. "I'm one of those classic fathers; I got blindsided by how it really is... Unfortunately, I made the grave error of upsetting my ex-wife who decided she wanted me out of the house unbeknownst to me. As part of the overall plan she called the cops on me....I got into court and I was immediately pegged as having a mental problem, guilty of being angry; that whole set up as I'm sure many people here are familiar with...I've had them (my children) for a week and a half total in the last year and about thirteen hours this year. None of this fits any kind of a visitation order; it's just the way it works."

The sponsor of the event videotaped each speech and downloaded each onto YouTube. Though someone else downloaded it on YouTube and all of it is considered political speech, supposedly protected under the first amendment, his ex-wife's attorney submitted his speech on compact disk at the next court hearing, arguing he was harassing his ex-wife- it currently has less than three hundred views- and asked the judge to extend a previous protective order as a result.

Pierce, acting as his own attorney, argued the speech was protected under the first amendment.

"She (his judge) let me rant," Pierce said but approved the extension of the protective order.

NFSIFC Victim 4: The Connecticut Law Tribune

The *Connecticut Law Tribune* got a hold of a Habeas Corpus filing in a divorce case, Foy versus Foy, where the judge removed the child from custody through a dubious ex-parte order.

Publication of this story would have embarrassed the judge, Stephen Frazzini, so days before the paper planned to release the article he shut it down, issuing an order- one normally reserved only in cases of national security- forbidding the paper from running the story before it was published.

In a ruling from the bench Monday, Nov. 24, (2014) New Britain Superior Court Judge Stephen Frazzini enjoined the Connecticut Law Tribune *from publishing an article based on a court document that had previously been published on the Judicial Branch website.*

Daniel J. Klau, the newspaper's lawyer, said he has already filed an appeal. He and other media law attorneys say this appears to be an extraordinarily rare case of prior restraint on free expression guaranteed by the First Amendment. They say that normally pre-publication court orders have been deemed constitutional only in matters of extreme threats to public safety, on the level of national security.

Frazzini's oral ruling is currently sealed, but Klau said he is working to have it unsealed. "I am actually under a restraining order about what I can tell my own client. There are some things that I can share," said Klau, of the Hartford office of McElroy, Deutsch, Mulvaney & Carpenter. "What the Law Tribune *can say," he said, "is that in a child protection case on the juvenile court docket, the court granted a party's request for an injunction barring the* Connecticut Law Tribune *from publishing information that it lawfully obtained about the case."*

The action before Frazzini was in juvenile court session, where judges have the discretion to limit proceedings to those participants deemed necessary. A writer representing the Law Tribune *was not permitted to remain in the courtroom to witness the proceedings, after his presence was objected to by a lawyer for one of the parents in an underlying custody case and by a guardian ad litem.*

Frazzini reversed himself days later after the story went viral. Frazzini survived a subsequent hearing for his re-nomination even after being grilled about this decision. The *Connecticut Law Tribune* finally released a story on April 27, 2015 entitled *Custody Case Offers Rare View of Usually Secret Proceedings* where a lawyer called this case Kafkaesque.

The Department of Children and Families had obtained an order of temporary custody even though there was no conclusive evidence that either parent had abused the youngsters, according to court documents. Now, more than a year later, the children remain in foster care.

...

Even some members of the Connecticut bar seem exasperated with the status quo. Bethany attorney Norm Pattis, who represented Foy at one point, blogged about the case last fall, though he did not identify the Foys by name and omitted many details. Pattis, who also writes a column for the Law Tribune, *called the matter "Kafkaesque" and referred to secretive proceedings as "surreal."*

What if criminal courts operated on the concept of "the best interest of public safety"? What if basic constitutional rights could be dismissed as long as someone claimed they were doing it in "the best interest of public safety"? What if police could waive getting a warrant before entering your home because they deemed it in "the best interest of public safety"? What if the police could interrogate suspects for days without providing them a lawyer because it was in "the best interest of public safety"? If those things were true, we'd no longer be living in America but a totalitarian country where those excuses are used to eschew basic protections in favor of state tyranny.

Litigating Divorce In Criminal Court (LDICC)

Mackney's last jailing was for a dubious attempted extortion charge, and here the Scamardo's involved the criminal court system to adjudicate their divorce.

I first saw litigating divorce in criminal court in a letter to a judge by criminal defense attorney James Donohue on behalf of his client Jeannie Melton: "I told Judge Mannix (the judge in Melton's criminal trial) that I believe Mr. Melton is attempting to litigate matters pertaining to the divorce in Beaver County (where the criminal proceedings were held); and that his proper forum for addressing these issues is before Judge Folino in Allegheny County (where the divorce was held),"

LDICC Victim 1: Jeannie Melton

Melton is a former gymnast, barely more than five feet tall and one hundred pounds. She certainly doesn't look threatening and never had so much as a parking ticket when her divorce began. Then something happened; by the divorce's end she faced four criminal charges, including stalking and attempted murder.

"For weeks, Scott and Angela Melton (Jeannie' Melton's ex and his new wife) felt events were quickly spiraling out of control with Jeannie Melton reportedly telling people she was going to buy a gun to murder her ex-husband and his new wife," a newspaper reported shortly after Jeannie Melton was arrested for attempted murder.

After a private investigator Melton hired convinced her to buy a gun, imploring her that her life was in danger, he set her up with an undercover police officer. The private investigator proceeded to tell authorities she told him she wanted to kill her ex-husband.

"Hopefully, it's just for decoration," Melton told the officer as the exchange occurred.

But the undercover officer suggested she could use it for something illegal, "don't make me look like a creep," Melton responded, but was arrested on the spot anyway.

The judge tossed out the attempted murder charge, "What do I have? I have a nasty bitter divorce; she also tried to buy a gun," the judge said of the lack of evidence against her.

Melton was cleared of all four charges, but not before the specter of a criminal charge was used as leverage with the entire estate going to her ex-husband.

LDICC Victim 2: Susan Skipp

Like Melton, Susan Skipp was also charged with stalking.

On August 15, 2013, she was "caught" driving in her husband's neighborhood when her friend dropped off presents for Skipp's children while she waited in the car, Skipp told me. Although there was no restraining order, the arresting officer said she was enforcing a civil order, not in the purview of the police. Skipp was arrested for stalking nonetheless.

She was arrested again for violating a restraining order resulting from the August 15 arrest on September 9, 2013, after she sent an email even though Skipp said the restraining order allowed email contact. She accepted a diversionary program to rid herself of the charges because she didn't want them hanging around her neck when she argued for custody.

But her husband's divorce team repeatedly referenced these arrests in pleadings. One of her family court judges, Lloyd Cutsumpas, detailed her arrest in an October 8, 2013 order in which he declared Susan Skipp not of sound mind.

When questioned during a hearing by Democratic State Representative Minnie Gonzalez, a visibly uncomfortable Cutsumpas referred to Skipp's case as "celebrated."

Skipp had no prior criminal record before the divorce and now has no access to her kids from this marriage. I don't think she's celebrating this case.

LDICC Victim 3: Neil Shelton

On April 24, 2013, Neil Shelton's ex-wife, her lawyer, and several other officials received a threatening letter purportedly written by him.

"Sarah Stevens will be dead by Friday," the letter started ominously. "Boston (The Boston Marathon Bombing) was nothing compared to what I am planning."

Eight SWAT team members in a military style Hummer along with two detectives and three deputies executed an arrest warrant for Shelton later that day and charged him with multiple counts of threatening executive judicial officials.

"Someone must have put something in her Jennie Craig because I don't know what you are talking about," a bewildered Shelton said during his arraignment the next day.

In his first meeting with his court appointed lawyer, David Erdmann, Shelton said. "Don't even worry about this letter because as soon as I lose everything in my divorce they will drop these charges."

Erdmann told me he remembers Shelton telling him that but called it Shelton's "conspiracy theory."

Was it really just a conspiracy theory? Shelton was given a $75,000 bond and put in the same cell with a murder suspect, Justin Berry, suspected of killing Shelton's best friend, Don Griffin, during a robbery. He was given this bond even though this was considered the mildest felony, and if found guilty, punishable by probation.

Sarah Stan[illegible] you will be dead by
Friday. I will kill you
and Kim. You both are
done. I want my kids.
No Family. No money. It's
your fault. My nigger lawyer
you are all except
[illegible] Mike, David, Millie, Al, Ginny, Frank,
John, Zack, Rickey, Bowman, Pemberton,
Tim Farrow, Arnder, Hodge, Lowe,
Scott Lowery, Gus Dunne [illegible] Ashley
Jared, Jackman. You are all
dead. Fuck all of you
Y'all need to be committed
not me. To late your
all dead. Boston
was nothing compared
to what I'm planning.

Bullied to Death: Chris Mackney's Kafkaesque Divorce

(Threatening letter purportedly written by Neil Shelton)

He couldn't afford the bond so he spent the next ten months in prison.

Shelton was offered a deal within a month to plead guilty to one felony count of threatening an executive legal judicial official and receive probation.

"Kiss my fucking ass," Shelton said he told the District Attorney, Ricky Bowman.

"I didn't take the deal because I didn't do it." Shelton told me.

Shelton remembers going to five hearings where the prosecutors asked for a continuance because they were awaiting handwriting analysis. Each time Shelton screamed from the back that this was impossible because no one had taken his handwriting to analyze.

In jail, he was only allowed to work on his criminal case. He was allowed to attend his divorce hearings but not allowed to prepare for them. Each divorce hearing, Shelton was in handcuffs, shackles, and a chain connecting both. While in prison, the final divorce decree was granted: his ex-wife got all their assets and sole custody with no visitation for him.

Shelton was finally released In February 2014, two days after the final date to appeal his divorce. Prosecutors said there was a lack of evidence to hold him.

Sarah Stevens said the timing of Shelton's release was merely coincidental but to Ms. Stevens I introduce Leroy Jethro Gibbs of *NCIS* and rule number thirty-nine, "There's no such thing as a coincidence."

Out of jail, Shelton called the FBI who told him they never received any handwriting to analyze and when he took the letter to his own expert the expert concluded with 98% certainty that the handwriting was that of Zach Brintle, Sarah Stevens' law partner.

Though the criminal charges have been dismissed family court continues approving restraining orders suggesting Neil is the writer. Ms. Stevens denied t her law partner wrote said letter, believes Neil Shelton is the author, and considers him dangerous.

On June 6, 2015, Shelton was questioned regarding theft of guns at the Mt. Airy area residence of Dennis Simmons. Shelton said Surry County Sheriff's Officers searched his residence but found no stolen guns or any stolen property.

Security camera footage shows Shelton knocking on Simmons' front door about an hour before the footage shows an individual breaking into the home. Shelton said he visited the home because he was told Simmons had information about his children, but left when no one answered the door.

Shelton said the officer told him on June 6 he would be arrested the following day, but instead, a warrant was issued for his arrest the following week and his name was published in the *Mount Airy News* as a fugitive from justice on June 14, 2015.

He was arrested by Surry County Sheriff's Deputies on June 15, 2015.

Shelton said officers showed him a photo of a man with boots similar to his entering the home. The photo doesn't show the man's face. He's been given no more evidence tying him to this purported crime. The Surry County Police Department provided me with his arrest warrant with his basic identifying information- height, weight, age, crime arrested for, etc. – and nothing else; they said they couldn't provide anything else because "this is an ongoing investigation."

Are arrests usually made while an investigation is ongoing?

Shelton also said when he was initially brought into the station sheriff's officers called Sarah Stevens to inform her of his arrest, even though it was unrelated to the divorce case. Stevens didn't respond to an email for an explanation; she's been hiding under her desk since being caught in a lie. She's declined to respond to more than a dozen emails after doing an initial interview.

The arrest happened three days before a scheduled hearing to extend his restraining order though that hearing was subsequently delayed.

The new case continues to unfold as this book is published.

LDICC Victim 4: Ted Taupier

Edward "Ted" Taupier, who was featured in my article for *Rebel Pundit* on November 12, 2014, also didn't have "so much as a parking ticket" when his divorce began but was soon considered so dangerous a criminal judge in Connecticut wouldn't let him leave his home.

The fifty year old with a shaved head made six figures as a technology consultant to firms on Wall Street when his divorce commenced. In his earlier days, he spent time as a State Department contractor where his four person team was dropped in the jungles of Sumatra in Indonesia for a mission lasting three years.

"Nothing they (family court) do to me will break me," Taupier told me of his past experience, but that's been tested over the last two years.

He divorce began in late 2012. Things first unraveled when his former wife, Tanya Taupier, hired criminal defense attorney Christopher Morano to represent her interests; she hired Morano though she faced no criminal charges. When Morano was Deputy Chief State's Attorney, he was lead prosecutor in the conviction of Kennedy cousin Michael Skakel, since overturned.

On May 22, 2013, Taupier was charged with voyeurism for allegedly videotaping his ex-wife, then still his wife, while giving her a massage. At the time this book is published, more than two years later, prosecutors haven't provided Taupier's criminal defense attorney with discovery and no trial date has been set despite every defendant's right to a speedy trial.

Worse than that, Morano engineered the entire arrest.

"I have the evidence; I've seen the evidence; this guy needs to be arrested." Morano said to the prosecutor, Barbara Hoffman. Based solely on his word, Taupier was arrested. Taupier told me the video in question was made with his wife's consent and she looks into the camera. He said he made the video when he considered becoming a masseuse.

Then, on August 29, 2014, Taupier was arrested again, this time for allegedly threatening his divorce court judge. On August 22, 2014, he sent a group email to six people in which he vented about his family court judge, Elizabeth Bozzuto, with this homage to Charlton Heston, "They can steal my kids from my cold dead bleeding cordite filled fists…as my 60 round mag falls to the floor and I'm dying as I change out of my 30 round mag."

The email also includes this inflammatory portion: "Bozzuto lives in Watertown with her boys…there's 245 yards between her master bedroom and a cemetery which provides cover and concealment…Someone who wants to take my kids better have an F35 and some smart bombs otherwise they will be found and adjusted."

At least one recipient, Jennifer Verraneault, thought the language wasn't just inflammatory but criminal. Verraneult said she was "disturbed" and "scared" by the email and said of Taupier, "It made me really sad and I started to cry because I felt that the email described somebody who's in a lot of pain," during Taupier's trial which started in the spring 2015.

Verraneault was so disturbed, scared, and pained she waited nearly a week to do anything. On August 27, 2014, Taupier filmed police taking his children forcibly out of school at the behest of his ex-wife after an ex-parte order from Bozzuto. Only after Taupier posted this video on You Tube did Verraneault spring into action. She first contacted the other recipients complaining about Taupier, but found no joy. She then forwarded the email to Linda Allard of the Greater Hartford Legal Aid Society who called the Deputy Chief of Judicial Marshal at the Connecticut Judicial Branch, Brian Clemens.

Eventually, a screenshot of the email was forwarded to Bozzuto and the police received a copy. Seventy-five police officers including a SWAT team, detectives and uniformed police officers arrested Taupier serving a "risk warrant" because he had a collection of antique guns.

"They used sixteen Seal members (from Seal Team Six) to kill Usama Bin Laden and they used 75 police to arrest me." Taupier said.

They charged him with threatening in the first degree and harassment in the second degree. His bond was set initially at $30,000 and after his family paid it, the bond was increased to $75,000. His family was able to raise the extra money, but Taupier was still given an ankle monitor and forced to stay in his home while he awaited trial. Bozzuto recused herself from his divorce shortly thereafter.

Verraneault started a divorce mediation business the same month Taupier was arrested. This new business relied on the family court system for much of her clientele though I'm sure that played no calculus in her herculean effort to have him arrested.

She reached out to me after my *Rebel Pundit* story, claiming there was another side to the story but wouldn't go into details because she was going to be a witness in the upcoming criminal trial. When I referred to her rant as gas-lighting, she hung up on me. She's declined further comment even after testifying at trial.

With Taupier's face and name plastered all over the media as a two time suspected felon, he lost his consulting job with CitiBank and, confined to his home, he had almost no ability to make money. With his bail taking most of his savings, Taupier had no money for much of anything else and this man who used to pay about $50,000 in taxes yearly now lives hand to mouth.

During a November 2014 divorce court hearing, his ex-wife's attorney filed a motion for contempt for failure to pay for the mortgage and child support. His ex-wife used the criminal courts to make sure no one would hire him; she followed that with a contempt of court motion to complain about his inability to pay for marriage related bills, while affording Christopher Morano as her defense attorney.

The judge refused to rule on the contempt motion which was heard days after my article. Taupier's harassment trial continues as of the publication of this book.

Shelton, Taupier and Mackney

In all three cases- Shelton, Taupier, and Mackney- the SWAT team executed an arrest warrant over a crime committed with a pen (or keyboard). The pen is mightier than the sword and apparently more threatening. The SWAT team is reserved for murderers, rapists, and three men who allegedly wrote something someone didn't like.

Were all three really so dangerous or was a message being sent? We have the power to turn you into the worst most dangerous criminal, which will be used against you in both family and criminal court. The goal, I believe, is to break their will and less than five months after the SWAT team visited Mackney his will finally broke for good.

Bullying by Involuntary Commitment

On the evening of September 23, 1887, the woman born Elizabeth Jane Cochrane, called Pink or Pinky by friends and family, using the pen name Nellie Bly, and claiming to be Nellie Brown entered the Matron Irene Stanerd Temporary Home for Women, a boarding house for working class women located at No. 84 Second Avenue in New York City. Later that evening, the so-called Brown complained that nearly everyone else looked "sad", "scary", or "crazy." She refused to go to sleep, insisting on sitting on the edge of her bed through the night. Her roommate that evening woke the next morning to "Brown" still sitting in the exact same position on the bed.

Bly, 23, was brown haired with a disarming baby faced beauty, causing many to underestimate her and she always took full advantage especially over the next ten days. She was not crazy, nor was she gas-lighting anyone, but undercover for the *New York World* as a reporter tasked with entering the women's ward of the Bellevue Insane Asylum for an unvarnished report of life among the involuntarily committed. The boarding house called a police officer, who took her to see a judge who ordered her involuntarily committed to Bellevue where she lived for the next ten days until the newspaper sent a lawyer to make sure she came out safely.

(One of the few photos of Bly in her mid-20's)

One doctor made a pass at her during his examination while another doctor hit on his nurse while ostensibly examining Bly. A third doctor presumed her near sightedness was evidence she was under the influence of the drug belladonna.

"Positively demented; I consider it a hopeless case. She needs to be put where someone will take care of her." A fourth doctor remarked of the perfectly sane Bly.

"After this, I began to have a smaller regard for the ability of doctors than I ever had before, and a greater one for myself. I felt sure now that no doctor could tell whether people were insane or not, so long as the case was not violent." Bly remarked after being considered a hopeless case.

The incompetent doctors ruled over these women with an iron fist showing no mercy or humanity. One woman identified as Mrs. Schanze wound up involuntarily committed because she only spoke German; another was involuntarily committed because of a nervous breakdown.

One of her compatriots, Tillie Mayard remarked, "We have been sent here we will have to be quiet until we find some means of escape. They will be few, though, if all the doctors refuse to listen to me or give me a chance to prove my sanity."

The bread was barely more than dry dough, the rooms were freezing, the bed spread consisted of a small blanket and old pillow, many of the nurses beat up patients on a regular basis and the dangerous patients were tied together with a rope.

In her genius, Bly was a Machiavellian puppeteer creating a Kafkaesque nightmare. She created a scenario where in reality the twenty women of the boarding house acted as the judges. By starting there, twenty women, none of whom was sophisticated enough to ever consider they were being played, immediately labeled her crazy. Every other official person- the cop, the judge, and everyone in the mental hospital- was already presuming her guilty. Their own examinations were perfunctory, meaning everyone was really following the lead of twenty women not wealthy enough to stay in any better place than that boarding house.

Joseph Pulitzer, the publisher of the *New York World* directed all newspapers in his media empire to help promote the story; Bly instantaneously became an international sensation. The exposé mainstreamed abuse in insane asylum and of involuntary commitment culminating with her well received book *Ten Days in a Madhouse*.

Because all corrupt entities have certain things in common with each other, there are two parallels to consider between that day's insane asylum corruption and the current dynamic in family courts. First, both Dr. Samenow and the doctors who examined Bly were all given a level of respect they didn't deserve based on faulty professional achievements and credentials. Because of this, the system wasn't providing proper oversight over their work.

Second, power corrupts and absolute power corrupts absolutely, and in both bureaucracies the players- judges, doctors, and lawyers- enjoyed near absolute power.

An insane asylum isn't merely a metaphor of a corrupt entity which strips you of your rights in a Machiavellian and Kafkaesque way; it is a tool of destruction in family court. Susan Skipp told me she knows of seven family court litigants involuntarily committed to psych wards; in four cases the commitments were extorted as stipulations to see their kids. She said she was nearly the subject of a psychological evaluation, a precursor to involuntary commitment.

Involuntary Commitment Victim 1: Christopher Robin

Christopher Robin Sr. hasn't seen his son, Christopher Robin Jr., in more than twenty years. He documented his story in the self-published book, *Christopher Robin's Dad*, in 2013. As with Mackney, Robin had limited resources against big family money and a Machiavellian in-law with secrets to hide.

"Joanne Haverback Hale (his mother-in-law) must have had crime in her genes. When it was time for her mother, Ida Leah Crost, to be housed in a retirement home- even though she owned property and had a $100,000.00 certificate of deposit- Joanne Hale claimed that Ida Leah was indigent. The State of California paid all the bills, while Joanne pocketed her mother's fortune!" Robin said in his book.

Robin became so consumed with family court injustice he transformed his home in Hollywood Hills, California into what he called the *Purple Heart House*, with a purple heart painted on the wall for each family court victim who reached out to him.

After Christopher Robin put up a faux noose in his *Purple Heart House* to signify the destruction of family courts he was visited by members of the Los Angeles Police Department who, purportedly acting on an anonymous tip, took him to the psych ward.

(Robin's *Purple Heart House* from his website)

The destination was the Psychiatric Ward at the LA County USC Medical Center where they photographed me, took blood, X-rayed my chest, and interviewed me at length. They continued to state that I was not under arrest but had been removed for my own safety. Hell, I was just about to pump iron before meeting Colleen (his then girlfriend) and had a late dinner when they abducted me. The head shrink (an older Woody Allen look-alike with (a) thick Hungarian accent) spoke to me...."Haff you effer been in psychiatric hospital before? Haff you ever been under duh care uff a psychiatrist?" I answered truthfully, "No...I haven't...but I've taught singing to 14 psychologists and psychiatrists and they were the nuttiest people I ever knew!"

...

If we hadn't announced we were going to hold a Mock-Hanging, no one would have paid attention to the plight of the destruction of families all over the world by family court judges and lawyers. I added that a noose atop the Purple Heart House *is just a symbol of the death and destruction of all of us as soon as we get in the system of divorce and custody.*

Robin was forced to stay in the psych ward for the next three evenings. He slept on a sofa too small for him and wasn't allowed to shave.

Potential Involuntary Commitment Victim 1: Neil Shelton

On May 28, 2012, Neil Shelton drove to the home he still technically owned to pick up his kids for their scheduled time only the locks had changed and no one was home. He waited in his car. Minutes later, the police showed up due to a break-in report.

"He can't be breaking in," Shelton remembers one officer saying; "this is his house."

But the dispatcher told the officer to hold Shelton while authorities arrived. About a half hour later, Shelton was ushered to the local psychiatric hospital where he was told his sister and wife filed a complaint saying he was bipolar, stopped taking his medication, and was riding around in a limousine threatening people.

"Husband and wife are going through a divorce and wife wants to have husband committed," the commitment form stated.

After a battery of tests, the doctor found Shelton wasn't suffering from bipolar disorder and processed him out. About an hour later, Shelton was picked up again and sent back to the psychiatric hospital with the same complaint recycled.

"What are you doing back here," the doctor proclaimed.

"Beats me," Shelton responded.

The doctor released him shortly thereafter and Shelton was promptly arrested for violating a restraining order also at the behest of his ex-wife.

"How could I have violated a restraining order if I was locked up all day," Shelton proclaimed rhetorically.

Potential Involuntary Commitment Victim 2: Chris Mackney

Was a psych ward Mackney's next stop if he survived multiple prison stops; he had already been deemed suicidal, angry, erratic, and depressed.

"So, today I got an email from Doctors and the County Mental Health Facility. That is so nice of the County to spend valuable resources on the problems created by the Cover-up of abuse, parental alienation and psychopathy, in the Circuit Court." Mackney said in a blog post from December 12, 2013.

In Virginia it is deemed rare but legal and starts with something called a Temporary Detention Order (TDO) and the scheduling of a Commitment Hearing. Once committed, his fate could have been controlled by Dina because commitments can be indefinite. Chris Mackney could have wound up spending the rest of his life under the thumb of his ex-wife, committed to an insane asylum quite possibly a fate worse than death.

Chapter 8: The Child Support Hustle

"If you go to prison, your child support adds up."

Rand Paul

...

Child Support Enforcement: Bureaucratic Bullies

When a non-custodial parent has a problem with child support they are all hounded by the same group: Child Support Enforcement (CSE). Mackney expected CSE to lead the next portion of his torture, telling Jill Peterson Mitchell, "Child support enforcement...Will garnish....Trust me, Virginia will."

Child Support Enforcement: The Grant Money

CSE is governed first and foremost by Title IV D, established in the Social Security Act on January 4, 1975, but Title IV D is merely the top of a complex web of rules, regulations, and grant money.

The grant money incentivizes collection, with both the US Department of Health and Human Services (HHS) and to a lesser extent the US Department of Justice (USDOJ) providing grants for collection of back due child support.

HHS Child Support Division grants are doled out in three areas: the Behavioral Interventions for Child Support Services, the Evaluation of Behavioral Interventions for Child Support Services, and Access and Visitation grants.

"Federal child support enforcement became possible with the passage of the Child Support Recovery Act (CSRA) in 1992. The CSRA aimed to deter non-payment of State ordered support obligations through prosecution of the most egregious offenders." The US Department of Justice Child Support Enforcement Division says on its website. "While federal prosecution efforts were successful under the CSRA, some law enforcement agencies found that the simple misdemeanor penalties provided for under the Act did not have the force to deter the most serious violators. The problem with enforcement under the CSRA was remedied with the passage of the Deadbeat Parents Punishment Act (DPPA) in 1998. This Act created new categories of federal felonies for the most egregious child support violators."

"Finally, the bill authorizes the Department of Justice to make grants to States to develop, implement, and enforce criminal child support legislation and to **coordinate interstate enforcement activities. (emphasis mine)** Up to $10 million could be devoted to these grants for each of fiscal years 1994, 1995, and 1996." President George HW Bush said in his signing statement when he signed CSRA into law on October 25, 1992.

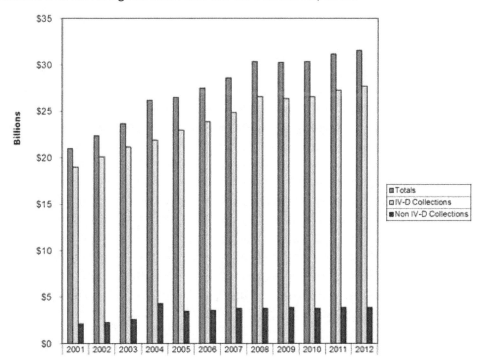

(Data from HHS on total child support collection, which has continued to go up since 2007 even as the economy has gone into a prolonged recession followed by stagnation)

The federal and state governments also run a child support enforcement partnership with terms under the 1998 Child Support Performance Incentive Act (CSPIA) which incentivizes opening and keeping child support enforcement cases, collection of child support, and arrearage- all part of a mix of data points which the federal government uses to award extra grant money.

Federal and state governments are overwhelmingly hounding poor non-custodial parents. Solangel Maldonado, in a study entitled *Deadbeat or Dead Broke: Redefining Child Support for Poor Fathers* found that 70% of what was owed in back child support in 2003 was owed by individuals making $10,000 yearly or less while fathers earning $40,000 and more were responsible for 4% of the arrearages.

In other words, people like Chris Mackney are a cash cow used by states to grab federal dollars and justify their own existence.

Total arrearage had grown to $116,149,340,011 by 2013, according to statistics compiled in the book *The Child Support Hustle* by NK Clark. Clark's book argues the system is designed solely to build and maintain a burgeoning bureaucracy. Clark argued that the increased number of child support enforcement cases during the recession is evidence of corruption in the system because child support payments held steady while people's incomes and employment went down.

Grant Money: The Mackney Prototype

Chris Mackney is a perfect microcosm of Clark's point. In 2007, he made several hundred thousand and by 2013 he had negligible income. Yet, his child support held steady throughout at $2,816 a month based on his 2007 income, based almost entirely on one deal worth $50 million, and CSE first aggressively went after him in 2013 when logic dictated everyone was trying to squeeze juice from a turnip.

Though she aggressively pursued him in all areas of the divorce, Dina Mackney waited until Chris Mackney was out of state- triggering much grant money for interstate collection- before complaining to CSE.

"The first month after I moved to Dallas and began working, I was contacted by Child Support Enforcement (CSE) for the first time in 4 years. My ex-wife waited until I was relocated and working before sending the State to come after me, even though her attorney told me that if I disappeared, no one would come looking for me." Chris Mackney said in a blog post.

All this can be done because of imputed income. By this, judges are allowed to set child support based on income they deem the non-custodial parent should make, the imputed income, rather than their actual income. As such, even though Chris Mackney was unemployed or underemployed for much of his divorce a judge could use imputed income to set $2,816 in monthly child support and hold it there, arguing that Mackney should be making enough to afford $2,816 a month. In this case, his 2007 income was during the height of the commercial real estate boom while in 2009-2012, the commercial real estate market was in a depression. No matter, judges know best and Mackney's family court judges knew better than real estate markets determining he was capable of making enough to pay $2,816 monthly.

"It's often a pretend system not based on reality," said Michelle MacDonald, a divorce lawyer and family liberties advocate from Minnesota.

Michael Volpe

Terry Hindermann remembers for several months early in Mackney's divorce nearly seventy percent of his monthly income was garnished for child support.

Mackney added to his troubles when for several months in 2008 while unemployed he failed to look for work thinking his lack of income would reduce his child support payments. Courts often require the non-custodial parent apply for a minimum number of jobs in any given month and Mackney applied for almost none. His behavior during that period is why we have imputed income because non-custodial parents have been known to reduce or eliminate work hours in order to reduce their child support payments.

The less a parent sees their child the more the child support is. As such, there's financial incentive for custodial parents to limit the custody time of the non-custodial parent; except in North Carolina, where there's no child support payment if a parent is totally removed from their child's life.

To what end is this done? According to the *Child Support Hustle* once there are child support arrearages there are all sorts of penalties, fees, interest, and other charges which the collecting state extracts and keeps for itself before passing on the payments to the child.

CSE Victim 1: Carnell Alexander

Carnell Alexander made national headlines after a Detroit television station investigation found the state insisted he pay about $30,000 in child support arrearages for a child who isn't his. In the late 1980s, an ex-girlfriend put him down as the father in order to collect on welfare benefits even though paternity tests proved later the father was another man. Because of a flaw in the bureaucracy, Alexander has been hounded for child support for more than two decades. Clark said the $30,000 Alexander owed was for interest, penalty and other fees all going to the state. Alexander owed another $30,000 to the child; that was forgiven. The state had no appetite to collect child support for the child only so-called child support for its coffers.

CSE Victim 2: Christopher Robin

Within a week of his release from the psych ward, Robin received a notice to appear in court for his back due child support. Here's part of his book.

On October 22 (1998), the Child-Support Judge Ronald R. Schoenberg and a very masculine Deputy District Attorney, Name of Debra Lamb, insisted I sell the Purple Heart House *to pay child support. I told Herr Schoenberg I had not seen my son nor heard his wonderful voice in more than 920 days and that his mother, the Princess, has a new Lexus and a $15,000 face lift.*

Schoenberg said that didn't matter. He asked again, "Have you sold the house?" I showed him my bankruptcy papers and pled, if the house were sold, I'd be homeless. We showed county court recorded documentation of several liens on the property and showed notarized documentation from three realtors that proved if sold, there would be nothing left after paying off the all the liens and realtor costs. The clown in a gown did not care that I would be homeless and on the street, in my wheelchair. I then offered to wash dishes or do anything if it would keep me out of jail. Judge said, "You had a chance...it's too late."

Robin was sent to Los Angeles County Prison where he was thrown into a holding cell with rapists and murderers. Before his stay was done, Robin, confined to a wheelchair, was wheeled into solitary confinement, all for child support arrearage.

CSE Victim 3: Dr. Carlos Rivera

Dr. Carlos Rivera, a pediatrician from New York State, was taken into custody on May 21, 2013, because he fell behind on child support payments which totaled more than $13,000 per month, or more than $150,000 yearly. Dr. Rivera fell behind because he'd gone from a partner in a thriving medical practice to starting his own practice.

CSE Victim 4: Gerald Frazee

The *Hartford Courant* in 2011 covered the story of a former CEO Gerald Frazee who was sent to prison for two months for failing to pay about $85,000 in back due child support for a child who was well past eighteen. Frazee had been unemployed since 2008. According to the writer of the article, Rick Green, the judge, Harris G. Lifshitz, was notorious for sending folks like Frazee to jail.

When Lifshitz sent Frazee to jail in December, it was for his failure to come up with $85,000 of the $167,000 he owes stemming from a long dispute with his ex-wife in California. Frazee and his lawyer, Oliver Dickins, say Lifshitz has been unwilling to consider the possibility that Frazee is broke.

"This is such a frustrating thing," Frazee told me. "The problem is how do you prove you don't have something?"

"I paid $124,000 in child support. If I was trying to get out of that, why would I do that? It was up to 2003 that was until my son turned 18."

Frazee and his lawyer are now appealing to Superior Court to intervene and dismiss the entire matter. Frazee hopes to start work soon for a Philadelphia lighting company that still has an executive-level job for him. Although he disputes owing his ex-wife any money, Frazee said he would start making payments to her in order to satisfy the court — and stay out of jail. However, he says he does not have the tens of thousands of dollars in back payments and interest that Lifshitz wants immediately.

CSE Victim 5: Peter Szymonik

When courts can't put one in jail for child support arrears, they find other novel ways to jail parents they don't like, as in the case of Peter Szymonik who was jailed briefly for not paying a GAL bill in his Connecticut divorce. Here's part of an Anne Stevenson story on his case from November 26, 2014.

(A chart popular on father's rights sites showing the vicious cycle of deadbeat dads)

Last Friday, Glastonbury father and healthcare executive Peter Szymonik was picking up his children from school when he received notice that Judge Elizabeth Bozzuto issued a warrant for his arrest; he had failed to pay a family court guardian ad litem's (GAL) $9,600 tab.

The State of Connecticut Judicial Branch's case detail shows that since the Szymonik family filed for divorce in 2006, nearly 300 actions have been filed in the hotly contested case. Due to the hundreds of thousands of dollars in fees the conflict has generated for the dozens of professionals who have fed off the case, it is difficult to determine whether it is the parents or the judges presiding over the case who have lost control of the dispute.

	rate	hours	this period
	15.7500	.77	12.13
	15.7500	13.50	212.63
Gross Pay			**$224.76**

Statutory

Social Security Tax	-13.94
Medicare Tax	-3.26
PA State Income Tax	-6.90
Philadelphia Income Tax	-8.81
PA SUI/SDI Tax	-0.16

Other

Child Support 1	-115.01
Net Pay	**$76.68**
Net Check	**$76.68**

(Here's a pay stub from a noncustodial parent who has more than half their gross (not net) income garnished for child support)

"I believe it is clearly punitive and outside the power of this court to incarcerate any person on any debt other than child support" says Szymonik.

Szymonik was jailed in a holding cell for about six hours a week later. He was released after a film crew from *60 Minutes* asked some questions.

Szymonik made himself a target when he gave well-received testimony in front of the Connecticut legislature on January 9, 2014. "One of the things I struggle with; one of the things we all struggle with. When you look at the people who are engaged in your thing and their experiences, you expect the highest in ethical and professional behavior. Why would you not expect that? You people are experts; you know what's going on. What I think a lot of people are dismayed by and where this destruction happens and the financial devastation occurs is when that experience is the exact opposite. (It's) totally unethical behavior; totally unprofessional behavior and no one to complain to."

Szymonik's judge is Elizabeth Bozzutto, from Ted Taupier's case.

Debtor's prison is the harshest among a series of tools CSE can use to force payment including: wage garnishment, driver's license confiscation, professional license revocation, and passport revocation. On occasion a state will even take away someone's license to fish and hunt to incentivize payment of back due child support.

Access and Visitation Grants: the Abusers' Way In

While in prison on a burglary charge, Josh Komisarjevsky filed appeals trying to increase custodial time with his young daughter which he had out of wedlock with then sixteen year old Jennifer Norton. Komisarjevsky used grant funds available for prisoners and parolees. By early 2007, Komisarjevsky was out of prison and wrestled sole custody from Norton.

"We were not on good terms. He's been fighting ever since [their daughter] was born for her to be with him," Norton told the *Hartford Courant* in 2007. "I did not want him with her at all. I wouldn't take her to prison to visit him. ... I didn't want her with a dangerous criminal."

On July 23, 2007, Komisarjevsky followed Jennifer Hawke-Petit and her eleven year old daughter Michaela Petit home from the grocery story. He and his partner, Steven Hayes, broke into their home, tied up four members of the Petit family and Komisarjevsky raped Michaela. Their brutal crime spree left three members of the Petit family dead, and is among the most gruesome home invasions in history. Komisarjevsky was sentenced to death but is appealing.

Months before John Allen Muhammad went on a murder spree labeled *The Beltway Sniper*, he used an HHS grant from a program called Devoted Dads to try to restore visitation with his children after his estranged wife went into hiding at a domestic violence shelter.

Both these murderers received grant money through Access and Visitation (AV) grants. AV grants are the other sides of the coin of the child support grants which are employed to force non-custodial parents pay their child support. With AV grants non-custodial parents apply for more visitation time. While this sounds like a good idea, these grants have been perverted and used by abusive non-custodial parents- mostly men- to get into their children's lives and eventually gain sole custody.

The common thread is a pile of money encouraging corrupt behavior, or as Susan Skipp said, "If you put an abuser and his victim in an adversarial situation, the abuser will always win."

These grants make the government an equal partner with the abuser.

Chapter 9: The Unheard Epidemic

"We owe respect to the living; to the dead we owe only the truth."

Voltaire

What Caused this Man to Break? (Victim 1: Derek Walker)

At about 4:20PM ET in Durham, North Carolina on September 16, 2013, police were called downtown to the Bronze Bull Statue on Corcoran Street after Derek Walker brandished a gun. After negotiating with Walker for about an hour he pointed the gun at one of the officers who shot back with a fatal blow.

A day earlier Walker left a cryptic Facebook message reminiscent of Mackney's last words on Facebook: "Don't call me and don't talk to me because I'm not responding. I hope I die very soon and a fast death because this world I live in is sorry."

(Derek Walker during happier days)

Michael Volpe

"I can't take what my son's mother is putting me through," Walker wrote in the same Facebook post. "She has filled my son's head up with so much false stuff. He has told me I'm a bad father; I'm not a good dad."

Shortly before his death, Walker's six year custody battle resulted in him losing custody of his son.

"He was a father who had been dealing with a nasty custody battle within the court system. He was extremely and emotionally drained." A friend told the television station WNCN.

(Walker shortly before his death)

The mother of his son was remorseless when interviewed by WNCN after his suicide: "I don't blame myself for this at all. I don't blame myself. I can't blame myself. Why should I blame myself for it? We have a child. We're not the only ones going through family court."

To some he'll be viewed as a mentally unstable person who took his own life; to others like Ronald Pierce he is a martyr.

His last statements to the world were of ending his pain -- a pain I can relate to myself where I nearly suicided for the same reason; the entirety of my society seems to require I lose my life with my children. Regardless of my love for them. My innocence. In both senses of that word.

The family court system induces suicide in a way that only child removal and peonage (forced labor based on debts) can describe. To know you will never have a meaningful life ever again with that child (a grown child in some ephemeral future being someone else); it ends your reason for living. If a man or a woman survives it, the person they were before no longer exists; such is the nature of the court system's mutilation of lives for profit.

"I used to think about suicide nearly every day." Ronald Pierce told me. "I even bought a rope several years ago."

When Pierce mentioned his suicidal thoughts on a father's rights website his ex-wife submitted them to family court as evidence that he was too mentally unstable to see his children.

He told me one reason he hasn't followed through on his suicidal thoughts is because he has some access to his kids. A "pittance" he calls it, but Pierce is given about a day and a half every two weeks to spend with his kids, and refuses to give up as a result; more hope than Chris Mackney had.

The Divorced Male Suicide Epidemic

According to the website Fathers Unite, 300 men and 30 women die from suicides monthly from family court corruption.

"In the U.S. about 300 fathers plus 30 mothers commit suicide every month (over 10 per day) as a result of the effects of the divorce system and the grief from the loss of their children, home, property and future income," said Fathers Unites' website.

That statistic is an interpretation of a 2000 study by Dr. Augustine Kposowa, a Professor in the department of Sociology at University of California at Riverside, entitled *Marital Status and Suicide in National Longitudinal Mortality Study* published in the *Journal of Epidemiology and Community Health*, which found that divorced men are 9.7 times as likely to commit suicide as divorced women.

Father's rights, and other groups with an agenda, have quoted the study as evidence of bias against men in family courts with Mackney's suicide now one of the faces of this epidemic.

Though Dr. Kposowa's study examined suicide in the USA, there are similar stories in Canada, England, Germany, Australia, and many other countries. The stresses which caused Chris Mackney to take his own life are not an anomaly but systemic in family court causing once perfectly healthy people to kill themselves.

Christopher Robin said this to AVFM in March 2013.

It has been several years since I have seen or spoken to any of my activist friends. No matter how hard we fought, we always got defeated. Some of my old friends have turned to booze and drugs. A couple have (sic) taken their lives.

As for me, I have dealt with severe clinical depression for more than 15 years. Naturally, I have considered suicide because depression is incurable but I must not do that because I pray every day that my little 10 year old will send me a card or drop by to say hello.

Victim 2: Derrick K Miller

"In the early morning hours of Jan. 7, (2002) 43-year-old Derrick K. Miller walked up to a security guard at the entrance to the San Diego Courthouse, where a family court had recently ruled against him on overdue child support." Wendy McElroy wrote. "Clutching court papers in one hand, he drew out a gun with the other. Declaring: 'You did this to me,' he fatally shot himself through the skull."

Glenn Sacks, a columnist and father's rights activist, singled out Miller's case in an article on Kposowa's study.

The other most common suicide victims are divorced and/or estranged fathers like Derrick Miller. In fact, a divorced father is ten times more likely to commit suicide than a divorced mother, and three times more likely to commit suicide than a married father. According to Los Angeles divorce consultant Jayne Major:

"Divorced men are often devastated by the loss of their children. It's a little known fact that in the United States men initiate only a small number of the divorces involving children. Most of the men I deal with never saw their divorces coming, and they are often treated very unfairly by the family courts."

According to Sociology Professor Augustine Kposowa, of the University of California at Riverside, "The link between men and their children is often severed because the woman is usually awarded custody. A man may not get to see his children, even with visitation rights. As far as the man is concerned, he has lost his marriage and lost his children and that can lead to depression and suicide."

Victims 3-5: Martin Romanchick, Darrin White, and Steven Cook

In the same Sacks article, three other suicides were examined- Steven Cook, Darrin White, and Martin Romanchick- all three, like Mackney, denied access to their children, jailed, and made destitute as a result of dubious domestic violence allegations and unreasonable child support payments.

There have been a rash of father suicides directly related to divorce and mistreatment by the family courts over the past few years. For example, New York City Police Officer Martin Romanchick, a Medal of Honor recipient, hung himself after being denied access to his children and being arrested 15 times on charges brought by his ex-wife, charges the courts deemed frivolous. Massachusetts father Steven Cook, prevented from seeing his daughter by a protection order based upon unfounded allegations, committed suicide after he was jailed for calling his four-year-old daughter on the wrong day of the week. Darrin White, a Canadian father who was stripped of the right to see his children and was about to be jailed after failing to pay a child support award tantamount to twice his take home pay, hung himself. His 14 year-old daughter Ashlee later wrote to her nation's Prime Minister, saying, "this country's justice system has robbed me of one of the most precious gifts in my life, my father."

Self-Immolation- Victim 6: Tom Ball

On June 15, 2011 at about 5:30PM, Thomas James Ball calmly walked to the front door of the Cheshire County (New Hampshire) Superior Court house. Near the front door, he poured gasoline all over himself, lit a match, and set himself on fire.

"I saw a man standing on fire. He walked around a little bit, walked on to the grass, collapsed on all fours and literally sat there and burned," said witness Dan Koski.

Up to now, his act of self-immolation is the most well-known family court related suicide.

(Tom Ball in his act of self-immolation)

Ball likely chose to set himself on fire because protest by self-immolation is effective. On June 11, 1963, Buddhist Monk Thich Quang Duc sat down in a crowded Saigon thoroughfare and set himself on fire to protest the oppressive regime of the American backed Ngo Dinh Diem, the South Vietnamese leader. Diem, a militant Catholic, oppressed all other religions, especially the Buddhists.

Malcolme Browne, a photojournalist with the *Associated Press*, took a historic photo which *The New York Times* placed on page one the next day seen by millions, including US President John Fitzgerald Kennedy.

This event, which precipitated the full scale entry of the USA into the Vietnam War, was recounted in Bill O'Reilly and Martin Dugard's book *Killing Kennedy*.

"John F. Kennedy will read his morning papers horrified by the photograph. Instantly, the president knows that his Vietnam problem has just escalated." O'Reilly and Dugard said in *Killing Kennedy*. "He can no longer support President Diem. The world will turn on the Vietnamese leader after such a horrific image."

Michael Volpe

On December 17, 2010, Mohammed Bouazizi, a Tunisian market trader, set himself on fire in the middle of a Tunisian street after he was slapped by a female bureaucrat during an argument over the denial of a permit for him to sell fruit in the street. This act of self-immolation set off what is now referred to as the Arab Spring with governments in places like Egypt, Tunisia, and Yemen falling.

The next day Ball's 10,729 word suicide note arrived at the local newspaper, *The Keane Sentinel*. The newspaper published the note in its entirety with no commentary. The story received traction in the Boston area, covered by *The Boston Globe* and several smaller newspapers, but unlike Duc and Bouazizi, his self-immolation did not receive widespread media attention. Fox News, CNN, *The New York Times*, the *Los Angeles Times*, and other mainstream outlets mostly ignored the story with Ball's suicide worthy only of a blurb in the tickers on the bottom of television news channels. A *Business Insider* editorial lamented the absence of coverage.

Rather than sparking an "American spring" and shocking US citizens into taking their country back, though, Mr. Ball's act of self-immolation seems to have been largely ignored. There has been scant coverage (and scant is being extremely generous) of Mr. Ball in the mainstream media, and what little coverage there is generally discredits the man as a troublemaker.

This is how the system's gatekeepers have been so adroit at maintaining the status quo— by suppressing dissent, marginalizing the detractors, and distracting the populace with meaningless, irrelevant drivel.

(Malcolm Browne photo from the Associate Press of Duc setting himself on fire)

Chris Mackney and Tom Ball

Bullied to Death: Chris Mackney's Kafkaesque Divorce

Ball and Mackney are kindred spirits in life and death: 1) both weren't allowed to see their children for years at a time, 2) both barely worked as a result of the custody battle, 3) both navigated most of their divorces pro se, 4) both were victimized by the corrosive effects of VAWA funding, and 5) both were saddled with unmanageable child support payments. Both also ended their suicide notes with chilling messages to their kids.

"I have three things to say to my children. First, Daddy loves you. Second, you are my three most favorite people in the world. And last, that you are to stick together no matter how old you get or how far apart you live. Because it is like Grandma always said. The only thing you really have in this world is your family." Tom Ball said.

"Please teach my children empathy and about emotional invalidation and 'gas-lighting' or they may end up like me." Mackney said in his note. "God have mercy on my soul."

Both felt bulled in court.

"I am due in court the end of the month. The ex-wife's lawyer wants me jailed for back child support. The amount ranges from $2,200 to $3,000, depending on who you ask." Ball said in his suicide note. "Not big money after being separated over ten years and unemployed for the last two. But I do owe it. If I show up for court without the money and the lawyer says jail, then the judge will have the bailiff take me into custody. There really are no surprises on how the system works once you know how it actually works. And it does not work anything like they taught you in high school history or civics class. I could have made a phone call or two and borrowed the money. **But I am done being bullied for being a man. (Emphasis mine)**"

Ball said his story started when he slapped his four year old in frustration.

My story starts with the infamous slapping incident of April 2001. While putting my four year old daughter to bed, she began licking my hand. After giving her three verbal warnings I slapped her. She got a cut lip. My wife asked me to leave to calm things down.

When I returned hours later, my wife said the police were by and said I could not stay there that night. The next day the police came by my work and arrested me, booked me, and then returned me to work. Later on Peter, the parts manager, asked me if I and the old lady would be able to work this out. I told him no. I could not figure out why she had called the police. And bail condition prevented me from asking her.

Mackney also had a domestic incident, though less severe; here's part of Samenow's report.

Ms. Mackney spoke of an incident that demonstrates how quickly and impulsively Chris reacts, not just to her, but to the children. She said that Chris was laying around on the ground. Ruby was pestering him, and Chris asked her to stop.

Michael Volpe

"I heard a blood curdling scream."
Ruby said, "Daddy bit me."
Chris said, "Ruby wouldn't stop."
When Dina asked Chris to apologize, he refused but turned to Ruby (who had a red and swollen mark) and said, "You'll never do that again."
Dina remarked that Chris reacts practically on instinct, "he'll do anything and justify it."

"Ruby and I were playing together on the couch and she bit me. I had read earlier in a parenting magazine that had been given as a subscription by Dina's grandmother that sometimes it's ok to bite younger children back in a way that let's children know that it hurts." Chris Mackney said in notes which never made it into the evaluation. "Not my finest parenting moment but I haven't been hurtful to my children before or since."

(Tom Ball)

Like Walker's baby momma, Ball's ex-wife, Karen, showed no remorse telling *The Boston Globe* that his love for his children "made it impossible for him to accept that some of his actions were harmful to them. He was unable to comply with the court's requirement to meet with the children's counselor because to do so would mean acknowledging that he had done something to warrant the requirement."

"Child support enforcement."…"Will garnish."…"Trust me, Virginia will." "I pissed off too many people."

"I just got a letter from child support enforcement; (his ex-wife's) team is garnishing my wages and literally taking everything I make every week." Michael Pasierb said to me in a frantic voice mail from September 23, 2014. "This is where we go from here, and the only alternative from here is suicide."

Pasierb went to his local CSE office the same day and sent me this email: "I tried to google this building. They do not want you to know where it is. Try it! They told me to go back to court and file, file, file. I tried to take a picture and almost was arrested. I talked to the supervisor who would not come out of his spider hole. Coward. He said 'this is a federal building… no pictures'. He would not give me his number for you to call him. 'I do not talk to the media' call Tallahassee. He would not give me a number. He said, 'look it up.'"

Pasierb told me that of his three children, he only sees his eighteen year old regularly, and hasn't seen his two other children in more than a year. He's been forced to represent himself for much of the divorce and his ex-wife filed contempt of court motions creating arrearage totaling $23,739 according to the latest court document he provided me. He's destitute, with wages garnished.

On October 6, 2014, he received a correspondence from Florida's CSE and was told if he didn't pay $1,898.41 in arrearage in the next fourteen days he'd lose his driver's license. It's never been made clear to him how $1898.41 and $23,739 have been determined. Ultimately, none of it matters because he'll never be able to pay off any of these amounts; Pasierb believes these past due amounts will act as a proverbial rope around his neck the rest of his life.

"Living with the fact that I have been alienated from my children, financially annihilated and mentally distressed based on lies," Pasierb told me in an email. "Maybe there is a pill for that. Losing my license will help me calm down."

"They're going to bully me to death," he concluded in the same voice mail.

One thing keeping Pasierb alive is his girlfriend, Stacy, who he met at church.

"God brought him to me." Stacy said. "He'd be on the street."

She also said Pasierb helps raise her daughter, and she considers him an excellent parent and very involved in her daughter's life.

"It's very sad," Stacy said noting he is allowed to be more of a father to her daughter than his children.

On February 18, 2015, Michael Pasierb left me another desperate voicemail: "I've just completely had it; they were going to Baker Act me. So, I'm going to just drop the car off at my girlfriend's work and I'm leaving. I don't know where I'm going, but I'm leaving."

The Baker Act in Florida allows the state to involuntarily commit an individual for psychiatric treatment. While Pasierb has not been involuntarily committed, he remains penniless, desperate, and suicidal.

Victim 7: Jon Pasierb

While Michael Pasierb continues to live, the same cannot be said of his brother, Jon Pasierb, who drank himself to death on November 04, 2011.

"People claim he was just another alcoholic." Michael Pasierb said. "In fact, he forced himself to continue drinking. He committed suicide by alcohol because it is the only way out!"

Jon Pasierb was left penniless after being saddled with an unaffordable child support payment for a son born out of wedlock; a child family court simultaneously prevented him from seeing.

His son, 22 at the time, said to Jon Pasierb in 2010, "you weren't there for me?"

"Let me tell you something, I couldn't be there for you." Pasierb responded forcefully.

In the beginning of 2011, divorce proceeding began with the mother of his second child, and Michael Pasierb said his brother expected the second custody to be as brutal as the first so he drank himself to death.

Victim 8: Randall Couch

The website *Fathers for Life* documented the 1994 suicide of Randall Couch, explained by his lawyer.

I was the second of a series of four attorneys for Randall Couch, a Phoenix architectural consultant. In his long-ago divorce, he had been poorly advised by his first attorney to stipulate to sole custody to the wife, and to a peculiar stepped-increase child support arrangement. A few years later, his first lawyer (who had been his high school classmate) helped him work out a stipulated order in which he and his wife agreed to stop the child support because of the large percentage of time he had each week with his son. But, unbeknownst to Randy, that first lawyer didn't file the agreement with the court.

Years later (last year) the ex-wife decided to go after him by claiming that he owed a huge child support arrearage ($28,000), and alleging that the never-filed agreement was void. He hired me as his second lawyer, and after a heavily contested trial, a judge ruled against us and found that he owed the $28,000, plus his wife's attorney fees. I withdrew, and Randy hired his third attorney; several months later, he hired his fourth.

With a $28,000 judgment in hand, the wife's lawyer seized all of Randy's money from bank accounts, garnished receivables from his architectural clients, had his car taken from him, and most recently, dragged him and his fourth lawyer into court for contempt proceedings.

Randy was ordered to pay $1,500 by noon today, or go to jail.

Last night, Randy blew his brains out.

Victim 9: Andrew T. Renouf

Andrew T. Renouf committed suicide on October 17, 1995 shortly after he had 99.99% of his wages garnished by the Family Responsibility Office, an agency in the Canadian government. Here's his suicide note.

Last Friday my bank account was garnished, I was left with only a total of $ 0.43 in the bank.

At this time I have rent and bills to pay which would come to somewhere approaching $1500 to $1800.

Since my last pay was also direct deposited on Friday I now have no way of supporting myself. I have no money for food or for gas for my car to enable me to work. My employer also tells me that they will only pay me by direct deposit; I therefore no longer have a job, since the money would not reach me.

I have tried talking to the Family Support people at 1916 Dundas St. E. [Toronto] their answer was "we have a court order", repeated several times.

I have tried talking to the welfare people in Markham, since I earned over $520 in the last month I am not eligible for assistance.

I have had no contact with my daughter in approximately 4 years. I do not even know if she is alive and well. I have tried to keep her informed of my current telephone number but she never bothered to call.

I have no family and no friends, very little food, no viable job and very poor future prospects. I have therefore decided that there is no further point in continuing my life. It is my intention to drive to a secluded area, near my home, feed the car exhaust in the car, take some sleeping pills and use the remaining gas in the car to end my life.

I would have preferred to die with more dignity.

It is my last will and testament that this letter be published for all to see and read.

Signed A.T. RENOUF

Victim 10: Frankie Robertson

Frankie Robertson killed himself after he, like Mackney, fell hopelessly behind on his child support in Toronto in 2010. He left two suicide notes; neither has been released but here's part of a *Toronto Star* story on his suicide.

This is not about the failure of Frankie's marriage; marriages fail all the time; instead, it is about what happened to a lovely man who found himself dragged through the long slow hell of family court, and . . .

Yes, it is a given that there are two sides to every story. But let it also be a given that Frankie was a stand-up guy who was broken by the system.

The money he was required to pay was calculated on his after-tax income, and Frankie was not rich. He was a guy who'd had a home, a family, and a couple of sweet kids. And then he didn't have those things.

He worked two jobs. His credit cards were maxed. He was behind in all his bills and couldn't pay his rent. He feared eviction. He owed his lawyers. Worst of all, the time he had been granted with his kids was limited.

He'd had hope.

He was planning to take the securities course in the fall; he thought maybe he could make a better buck on the big board than he could behind the bar. He'd sent a note to a friend, asking for advice about the course.

And then, a short while later, on a day that had begun with optimism, Frankie learned that a family court judgment for thousands of dollars had gone against him.

How does hope end?

Suddenly.

Nick, who is a lawyer, spoke slowly now. "I'd spent the day in court. I went back to the office and checked my email. There was a note from Frankie. The subject heading was, 'Goodbye.' I called his cell, his home, his work. Then I called the police and the ambulance."

And then he went to Frankie's place and found his friend. Nick also found two letters.

Frankie's last wishes: He wanted the people he loved to set up a trust fund for the education of his girls, and he wanted his friends to take a hard look at the family court system that broke him.

Barry Callaghan, a regular and a friend of Frankie, also spoke. He said, "The letters drive me into a rage . . . I have such disdain for the law I can hardly express it . . . it is clear the justice system ate Frankie alive, and it's got to stop . . . Frankie got swallowed by the flippant judgment of judges . . . what was the purpose?"

Victim 11: Allen Wells

Allen Wells took his own life on February 19, 1991, in New Hampshire; he didn't leave a suicide note but contributed long essays about being bullied on a men's rights group.

Forgive me if I'm in a sour mood - but I just heard the latest in my ongoing (2+ years and counting) divorce.

I was looking forward to picking my son up this weekend - for the first time I haven't seen him in 7 months. I had it all arranged and cleared with my ex (in writing, of course).

It seems that this morning she managed to have a warrant issued for my arrest. If I step foot in the state of NH, I will be put in jail. I have no doubt that she will have the Marshall waiting for me if I show up to see my son on Friday.

The way she did it was rather amusing. They took a matter for which a judge had specifically decided NOT to put me into contempt (mainly because it was a reaction to her violation of court orders which she HAD been in contempt for). They managed to get an expedited hearing in front of a different judge at a time my lawyer could not make it. The court turned down a written plea from my lawyer for a rescheduling, and ordered me jailed in a hearing that my lawyer wasn't even at.

My lawyer assures me that this is so irregular and absurd that he should have no problem overturning it - but not before Friday. So, all my hopes for seeing my son (not to mention the non-refundable plane ticket) are down the drain. I knew it was too good to be true.

Debtor's Prison and Suicide

Several men killed themselves while imprisoned for child support arrearages, including these examples from the Yahoo group, *West Michigan DADS*.

Victims 12-18

Randy Orville Brouse, 33, of Illinois, when jailed for felony failure to pay child support, hung himself (2006)

Robert R Steadman, 33, of Sewickley Township, Pennsylvania, hung himself in April, 2003 during his second imprisonment for failure to pay child support.

Reinaldo Rivera, 25, of New Jersey was jailed for failure to pay child support. He hung himself with a sheet after one week in jail in April. (2006)

Carl Tarzwell, Jr., 37, was arrested on June 20, 2001, for failing to pay child support. Carl hung himself within a few hours of being jailed.

David Guinn, 38, incarcerated for probation violations and was behind on his child support, hung himself on November, (2006)

Kenneth Taylor, 40, of Nebraska, hung himself while jailed for felony child support in November (2006)

Dimitrius Underwood, 22, slashed his throat with a kitchen knife when the Lansing (Michigan) police tried to arrest him for failing to pay child support (2006)

Victim 19: Ian Sandywell

Ian Sandywell's disputes with the Child Support Agency (CSA), the British equivalent of CSE started in 2001 when he first fell behind on child support. The pressure was ratcheted up in 2014 when CSA sent Sandywell a plethora of letters warning of dire consequences if arrearage was not satisfied. A court in England found Ian Sandywell 11,000 pounds behind on child support for his 22 year old son Ben in November 2014 and ordered 520 pounds in monthly back payments.

Sandywell called his wife on November 7, 2014, desperate and distraught fearing he'd be unable to make the payments. He hung himself later that day. His wife slammed CSA to the *Daily Mail*.

It is very hard for absent parents and the CSA don't take people's lives into account.

It has been very inconsistent with Ian all along and very unsupportive. A figure of £520 a month was just thrown at him and it's just unacceptable.

There had been letters going back and forth for two years but the amount they wanted was always changing and they were so rude.

Michael Volpe

"The family court system is broken, but from my experience, it is not the laws, it's the lawyers" (Victim 20: Thomas Alaimo)

On February 6th or 7th, 2001, Thomas Alaimo went into the woods of Suffolk County, New York and hung himself. In his suicide note, Alaimo railed against the corrupt family court system: "the judges and lawyers of the judicial system, particularly in Suffolk County."

"Divorce is ugly business. The dissolving of a marriage is a sad thing. It feels like a death. But the court makes it far worse. The only winners are the lawyers. What right does a person have to take away the life savings of a couple for a couple of weeks work? An order of protection prevents the couple from communication, which is especially important when children are involved. Doesn't it just make sense for a judge to hear both sides at least once early in the divorce proceedings? Or do you think justice is better served by waiting months before the chance to be heard? May God himself help you to make the right decision. Money corrupts absolutely. A person has the right to make a living but holding justice hostage for large amount of money is sinful."

"The family court system is broken, but from my experience, it is not the laws, it's the lawyers. They feed off of the conflict. They are not hired to reduce conflict or protect the best interest of children, which is why third parties need to be involved." Chris Mackney said in his suicide note. "It is absolutely shameful that the Fairfax County Court did nothing to intervene or understand the ongoing conflict. Judge Randy Bellows also used the Children as punishment, by withholding access for failing to fax a receipt. The entire conflict centered around the denial of access to the children, it was inconceivable to me that he would use children like this. This is exactly what my ex-wife was doing and now Judge Bellows was doing it for her."

On March 7, 2001, Alaimo's parents wrote the judge in the case.

Our son got tired of playing the game. He was tired of a court system that would not hear him, tired of a court ordered forensic "expert" who held his children hostage for money. She held up visitation with his children for four (4) months, even though he was never a threat to them. He paid her $3,000.00 dollars and she wanted more after seeing Tom, the children and his wife, for only a few visits. She never sent a report nor appeared in court. He was trying to get full custody of his children and had proof that they were being neglected and abused by his wife (deleted) did not care and did nothing to follow up on this. She also refused to return his phone calls.

...I was there each time my son went to court - more than 20 times in less than a year - and witnessed the injustice my son and many other men like him suffered there. I look back on it now with anguish. It really was not much different than a public lynching with an innocent man begging for a hearing and crying out for mercy.

What bothered him most was the flock of hungry "vultures" standing by including his wife, her family, the lawyers, and the courts to devour what was left of him and his assets.

...It is difficult to understand the humiliation he endured by being wrongfully treated as a criminal, jailed three times unjustly by his wife with the encouragement of her lawyer.

More Legal Bullying and Suicides: Parallels to Chris Mackney Victim 21: Mark Edward Dexel

Mark Edward Dexel, 42, a father of five from British Columbia, Canada, killed himself on January 23, 2003, and like Mackney and Alaimo, Dexel left a suicide note which blamed the broken family court system. His suicide note wasn't released but here's part of a press release from the group, *Parents of Broken Families*.

On Friday, the RCMP (Royal Canadian Mounted Police) found Mark's body with a note in which he blamed the judges and lawyers in particular, and the injustice of the family court system in general. On that Wednesday, Mark had also told to a friend in the group that it was the one-year anniversary since he had last seen his 3-year old son. Mark added that he would again have to appear in court on January the 29th. His series of court appearances had spanned a full year, and in all those appearances Mark had gained no relief at all from his acute pain at being maliciously shut out of his son's life.

The stresses of the adversarial system of justice, the humiliation of his abuse in court, and the helpless longing for his missing son combined to form a lethal depression that led Mark to take his leave of the torture. It's an experience many non-custodial parents are put through at the hands of the divorce industry, but Mark's experience was particularly brutal and relentless.

Victim 22: David Bengert

Like Tom Ball, David Bengert's family court nightmare starts with him being the aggressor in an incident of domestic assault. Here's his mother, Donna Bengert.

My son David was married September of 1998. He was only 20 and she was 19 with a baby on the way. The following year brought us a beautiful granddaughter. Unfortunately the stresses of life come along and things happen with consequences. My son and his wife did drugs; that is how he met her. During their marriage I do not believe they were doing drugs, if they were it was minimal. My son was finally growing up – I could see him standing up tall, goals and dreams and proud of his family.

Then one night after Father's Day they had a fight in the early morning hours. The baby was crying; they exchanged words; my son punched his wife on the mouth for which she received a few stitches. As far as I know he had never hit her before but this one incident cost him everything.

The police took her from the hospital to the Women's Shelter. He never got to speak to her again after that night. He never saw his child again after that night. This was June of 1999.

He came to me at my workplace the next day and told me he just got out of jail. I said for what? He broke into tears and told me he hit her – he cried, and cried and cried. I called her mother but understandably met much hostility. His wife stayed at the Women's Shelter for a whole week and then moved home to her mother's. She had put a restraining order on David and also on the 4-plex apartment they were living in. He could not see her and he could not go home. I spent hours talking with David the next month and a half trying so hard to keep his hopes up.

In July she served him with custody papers and he was told the divorce papers would follow soon. He was crushed. I could see him sinking into a hole; I called her mother again and told her to tell his wife he was suicidal – the mother would not let me speak to my daughter-in-law – no contact was allowed. The mother told me to take him to the hospital. On several occasions we tried to contact her family and asked her to please let David talk to his wife and at least ask for forgiveness. He was never granted a conversation. No one had any feelings for David. His wife's family doctor told him he deserves what he's going to get.

During all this time the appointments with the lawyer, counselors, and psychiatrists were all happening. He was enrolled in Anger Management classes. It was his responsibility to show sufficient remorse which her family didn't believe he was doing. The court days came and kept being pushed off for lack of one document or another. Finally David demanded this charge be settled and told his lawyer to finish it even if it meant he went to jail. Every time we went to the courthouse he eagerly hoped for his wife to come – but she never did. The courts were not fair – they gave him a $1,000 fine, a year he could not contact or speak with his wife and a year's probation. It would be their first anniversary in September, only 1 ½ months away.

David sunk deeper with no hope. I convinced him to go to the hospital and he was admitted into the psychiatric ward. He was there for two nights and one day. He again walked into where I worked and I asked him what he was doing out. He said the doctor said he was not suicidal – go home. (I wonder how many more signs they needed – I saw them all.) My heart sank as I once again knew the danger at hand. I told people he was suicidal – they told me he had an attitude.

We managed to get the restraining order of his apartment so we could pack it up as he did not have the rent money and was living with us. We asked the landlord to contact her and tell her to take all that she wanted out as we were going in to pack it up. She said she wanted nothing. It was very hard and emotional to go there with my son and pack up all their things. We put this all in storage in our garage.

He met with his probation officer. That day, Monday, August 16th, 1999 the officer called me to tell me what a nice young man I had for a son and he was going to do just fine. David came and we went for coffee and he told me he was starting a job the next day and was joining a band – and teased me because I didn't know he could sing. Then out of the store across the street from the coffee shop came his wife and baby in the baby carriage. I told him he could not go talk to her yet – we had to do this the legal way. His eyes filled with tears and we left the coffee shop. I watched him leave in his car and my heart sank.

That day was busy and he called me later and talked to me for a while. I tried to lift him up but I was worried. I told him I would be home at 5 and we would talk some more. Work got very busy so I called my daughter to call and talk to her brother, which she did for quite a lengthy time.

At approximately 4:30 p.m. I stood in my store and I felt my son there. My friend asked me why I was staring into the wall, so I brushed it off. A few minutes later I called home, no answer. I left for home right before 5 and all the way home I knew. I came up to the door of the house and it was locked, first clue. I came into the house and saw a note on the door-jam of the basement. I read only the first line before I raced down the stairs – "To my family, if you are reading this note it means I have taken my own life...."

Victim 23: Juliette Cybelle Gilbert

The only female suicide victim I confirmed is Juliette Cybelle Gilbert who hung herself in her hotel room on June 28, 2007. Gilbert had effectively kidnapped her daughter after a court determined her allegations of abuse were without merit and ordered her ex-husband to share custody. After she was caught in her native New Zealand, she was extradited back to the US and spent several months in prison.

Upon being released Gilbert was not allowed to see her daughter and eventually committed suicide.

"I was stunned by this tragedy." Her friend, Joy Henley, told the *Bay of Plenty Times*. "I did not see Juliette's suicide coming. It will haunt me the rest of my life. She should not have ever reached that point."

While this is the only female suicide I confirmed, I believe there are many more. One reason why female suicides like this aren't well-known is because feminist groups don't emphasize female suicides while the MRM puts an emphasis on male suicide. Chris Mackney, Tom Ball, and Derrick Miller are a *cause célèbre* among men's rights groups while there's no woman's suicide treated the same way by feminists.

I did however speak to a number of women who privately told me they are or had been suicidal. Ted Taupier told me he knows dozens of women who struggle every day just to get up and function because of the abuse they've suffered.

Setting the Record Straight on Dr. Kposowa's Study

For about two years Tom Ball had a Wikipedia page before it was removed creating some controversy. His entry repeated an interpretation of Dr. Kposowa's study: "According to research approximately 330 people commit suicide monthly in the U.S. in response to the way family courts and CPS handle(s) divorce, domestic violence and child support."

The "research" is Dr. Kposowa's study and it is the zenith of the notion that family courts kill 330 people, 300 of them men, per month, but Dr. Kposowa told me groups with an agenda have twisted his study beyond all recognition.

Michael Volpe

"The study you cite has definitely been misrepresented online and by some groups with some agenda to prove. I never mentioned 300 men a month dying from family courts. I did not use family court data, so how could I have come up with such number?" Dr. Kposowa told me in an email. "The family court angle was a project that I was planning to do as follow-up just to find out if settlements in court contribute to the excess suicide risk experienced by men following divorce, but I ran into lots of roadblocks."

Dr. Kposowa found divorced men are far more likely to commit suicide than any other category- 9.7 times as likely as divorced women- but used census data not family court records, making any link between suicide and family court faulty.

In a story for CBS News in 2000, Dr. Kposowa hypothesized on the reasons behind the extraordinarily high rate of suicide in divorced men; all factors in Chris Mackney's story.

First, he (Kposowa) cites "financial obligations," adding that "The courts in the United States are in a position now whereby money is given to the woman, or the man is forced to pay alimony, child support. The man is also asked, in some cases, to vacate the house."

Kposowa also notes familial factors. "If a man loses custody of the children and the woman keeps those children, there are situations whereby she may not allow the man to see the children, and that causes some depression," he says.

And there are the methods used. "Generally the methods that men and women use to commit suicide are different. Men tend to use guns, for the most part, in the United States. In fact, in 60 percent of suicides that are committed are by a firearm, a gun."

The idea that men are discriminated against in family courts is far from a proven fact and Dr. Kposowa agrees.

The family court issue is difficult to determine precisely because of lack of data. What I was proposing in the interview on CBS and at other media outlets were some hypotheses that could be tested in future, and some plausible explanations for the excess of suicides in divorced men relative to their divorced counterparts. A similar finding had been observed in Australia, where the relative risk was even higher than what I found in my US study.

Family court decisions (not corruption) may play a role in some of the male suicides, but this may vary by jurisdiction, given that there are community property issues in some states. The circumstances of the marital breakdown may also contribute, along with the ready availability of firearms in the United States, and male tendency not to see personal and professional help in times of crisis. Clearly, these are issues that I wish to investigate, but there are data problems. One should NEVER draw conclusions in research without solid evidence, and one should back up with some certainty only those variables that have been used in the research at hand.

Dr. Kposowa told me that he hoped his study, now fifteen years old would lead to follow up studies but little work has been done on this unheard epidemic.

"As a society, we are quick to fill the evening news with gun homicides, but cover relatively little about gun suicides. Why the silence, I have my suspicions, but would rather keep them to myself," Dr. Kposowa told me.

That said, family court abuse is real, forcing any parent to give up all parental rights, sticking them with unreasonable child support payment, while sending them to jail repeatedly is a recipe for suicide.

"Being alienated, legally abused, emotionally abused, isolated and financially ruined are all a recipe for suicide. I wish I were stronger to keep going, but the emotional pain and fear of going to court and jail [because of exorbitant child support] became overwhelming." Mackney said in his suicide note.

With that caveat, there is an epidemic of divorced fathers committing suicide, and family court bullying plays some role in that epidemic. A disorder common in victims of family court abuse also plays a role these suicides; that's the topic of the next chapter.

Chapter 10: Legal Abuse Syndrome

"Anyone who has ever worked in a legal aid office or law library has met people whose lives have come unhinged after a bad contact with the legal system. The details vary—they may have lost a business or inheritance or the custody of a child—but the common theme of feeling violated by the legal system does not. Even 20 years after losing a lawsuit, some people who suffer from Legal Abuse Syndrome still carry a suitcase of old legal papers around, desperately hoping someone will help them find justice."

Ralph Warner, quoted in the *San Francisco Chronicle* (1997)

Chris Mackney's Pain

Imagine worry turning to terror so overwhelming that it is never-ending dread churning against eternal, desperate aching despair. Your anxiety is so great that you can't sit still or concentrate; the constant effort to focus on one simple task spins into darting confusion. Overwhelmed with fear you are too afraid to open your mailbox, visit certain streets, or see certain people. You have trouble sleeping but when you do sleep, you wake up in the middle of the night in anguish, outrage and grief. On those rare nights when you get a good night's sleep, you wake up exhausted with adrenaline pumping non-stop.

Your memory is weak and your entire life is darkness. You remember that you were happy once; that you experienced joy, but no matter how hard you try, you can never be who you were. Nothing ever feels right, comfortable or safe.

You cry doing routine things like grocery shopping when you walk by everyday items like milk. Soon enough, it becomes too painful to go to grocery stores or other places that decorate for holidays, because other people's happiness only reminds you of your misery. The world closes into a confined space, beyond which is a world you are convinced is there to kill you or feed on you the moment you try to love normally. Your mind wanders aimlessly but always winds back at the pain; a pain so visceral that you're taunted and threatened with suicidal thoughts; sometimes suicide is fantasized about. On occasion, the pain is so great you follow through on those thoughts.

If you feel like this you have Legal Abuse Syndrome (LAS), the same affliction which stymied Chris Mackney and it was this affliction and not some mysterious mental illness that caused his suicide. LAS is a psychic injury, not a mental illness and Mackney's LAS was the result of the strategy devised by his ex-wife's lawyers. Mackney's reaction was perfectly natural. If anyone were to walk outside today and see someone get shot in the head, they would likely develop PTSD because they've experienced a traumatic event. Being bullied- legally, emotionally, and financially- for more than five years is even more traumatic.

First coined by Dr. Karin Huffer, she's written several books about LAS including *Overcoming the Devastation of Legal Abuse Syndrome*. Dr. Huffer told me she considers LAS a subset of PTSD.

Ongoing Traumatic Stress Disorder (OTSD)

Unlike the sort of PTSD we are familiar with in soldiers who come back from war but feel as though they're still there, with LAS, the source of trauma- the legal abuse- continues. LAS would more aptly be called Ongoing Traumatic Stress Disorder (OTSD) and the ongoing legal process continues to flare up the trauma, much like picking at a scab, which not only stops the sufferer from healing but inflames the disorder.

"I was never going to be allowed to heal or recover." Mackney said in his suicide note.

In divorce cases, it is not merely the process of divorce which causes LAS but rather corrupt courts-a lack of due process, unfair rulings, the inability to challenge the unfairness of those rulings, and with money and power more decisive than truth and justice.

Chris Mackney didn't get LAS because of his divorce, or even his nasty divorce; he got LAS because the court allowed his ex-wife to crush him, blame him for everything, take his kids away for spurious reasons, drain him of his money, jail him when he was unable to pay legal costs, and allowed her to do this indefinitely until he broke.

"It was all done to increase the stress and pressure. Nothing I said mattered. My rights as a parent did not matter. They had the power, control, money and the kids and they were not negotiating." Mackney said in his suicide note.

When that process continued without end, he saw no other option but suicide: "I took my own life because I had come to the conclusion that there was nothing I could do or say to end the abuse. Every time I got up off my knees, I would get knocked back down. They were not going to let me be the father I wanted to be to my children...I became paralyzed with fear. I couldn't flee and I could not fight. I was never going to be allowed to heal or recover."

LAS Victim 1: Christopher Robin

Here's how Robin described his LAS to me in an email recently.

Since I have had PTSD and severe depression for the past 20 years, I am not doing well.

My great doctor friend and fellow fathers (sic) rights activist insists that anyone dealing with the loss of children in divorce court always deals with severe depression which, in truth, is mental illness. Unless you have dealt with the loss of a child in divorce, it may be difficult to understand but there is nothing that can compare with that kind of pain and misery.

There is not a day that I do not cry several times... and I am a very tough old man ... but with a very tender heart. When I even think about the abortion of a baby, it makes me cry but to think about what those six evil people did to my little boy is and always will be unforgivable.

LAS Used Against the Sufferer

For many LAS sufferers, rather than being given treatment and consideration, the disorder is used against them in family court. Dr. Pragnell described why this is so easy: "In blaming others the psychopath will allege the former partner is mentally ill and in some cases the former partner may be suffering a Complex Post Traumatic Disorder after suffering years of physical, mental, and sexual abuse and violence. This is often misinterpreted and misdiagnosed as a Borderline Personality Disorder or similar psychiatric term. In effect it is a classic 'blame the victim' scenario."

LAS Victim 1: Cyd Koehn

Cyd Koehn lives in Iowa. At one time, she had a catering business, home, husband, and child; her picturesque life seemed like a model for an updated Norman Rockwell painting, but outward appearances are deceiving. Here's part of her story by a watchdog group, Protest Iowa DHS (Department of Human Services).

Although her husband was charming toward the community, behind closed doors the marriage was characterized by physical and emotional abuse. After she was lifted and choked until she passed out in the garage in front of their child, she finally went to police. He was convicted and spent time in jail, and Cyd filed for divorce.

When Cyd defended herself in a scuffle with her teenager, her husband called DHS, accusing her of abuse. A social worker who was seeing him after work hours was allowed to weigh in on Cyd's psychological evaluation, to find her to have a personality disorder, although more qualified psychologist diagnosed her with PTSD from domestic abuse. Later she was accused of making a tear in her younger son's pajamas, when putting him in time out, and the children were removed from her custody, although evidence was not shown in court. Cyd was only allowed supervised visitation.

On a fateful court appearance in April 2011, her LAS took over; she became dissociative and sounded like blubbering idiot. Dr. Frank Gersch is a court evaluator hired by Koehn and described what happened that day.

"The Post Traumatic Stress Disorder appears to have caused her significant distress as well as problematic behavior in the courtroom in April, 2011, and avoidance of her children…She apparently said things that were not in her best interest during the April, 2011 court hearing. I have no records of this hearing. Cyd herself does not remember it at all. Apparently, she was faced by her husband and his fiancée, both of whom she alleges have been abusive to her, and her level of anxiety became so high that she dissociated during the hearing. Dissociative amnesia has been linked to overwhelming stress which might be the result of traumatic events. Dissociative episodes involve disruptions or breakdowns of memory, consciousness or awareness, identity and/or perception. They occur when a person blocks out certain information, usually associated with the stressful or traumatic event, leaving him or her unable to remember important personal information."

After this court appearance, sole custody was granted to her ex-husband.

LAS Victim 2: Susan Skipp

Susan Skipp described her debilitating LAS: "I avoid going to mailbox or have someone else go. Sometimes, I don't pick up my mail for weeks at a time. It's (triggers for her PTSD) holidays, school supplies, Halloween candy, kids my children's ages. My kids were my life. Not a day goes by where I don't cry at least three times."

Skipp was treated by Dr. Huffer who assessed her with LAS for family court but, like Koehn, her LAS was turned against her when Judge Lynda Munro claimed her LAS was an unspecified mental disorder.

"The only actions of the parties which occurred immediately prior to that notice was the defendant's repeated challenge to the co-parent counselor regarding the title he was using for the service- this communication was off putting. Any chance then that the parents had of co-parenting was removed." Munro said in making her ruling. "The defendant testified that she looked forward to this counseling. If the court takes her at her word then she cannot help herself in her conduct and **THIS IS AN UNADDRESSED MENTAL HEALTH CONCERN.** (Emphasis mine) If the court does not believe this testimony, then she is manipulative and devious in this process for her own ends."

Using this unqualified opinion, Munro demanded Skipp see a psychiatrist of Munro's choosing in order to see her children. When Skipp refused, Munro took all her custodial rights away and Skipp hasn't seen her two children since the end of 2012. Munro, who retired and is now in private practice, has declined my repeated requests for comments on this case; her legal secretary told me she doesn't comment on her old cases, a convenient rule of her own creation; she was also involved in Sunny Kelley's case.

"You can make me live in father's house but that doesn't mean I'm going to be home." Skipp's daughter said in a Youtube video directed at the family court judge in her mom's case in September 2012, one of the last times the two saw each other. "There's a difference between a house and a home, and my home is at my mom's. I know that you don't care but I do."

LAS Victim 3: Ronald Pierce

"(I) am on disability now as a result. I am diagnosed with anxiety disorders. Severe depression and grief from parent-child bond removal." Ron Pierce told me in an email about his LAS. "It is so severe that I am crippled socially. I don't date. I've given up on being happy ever again. I'm diagnosed with AvPD (Avoidant Personality Disorder) but was still managing to eke out a life. Now I'm permanently disabled from the trauma of family court, which has turned my AvPD into a permanent hell."

"But we who live in prison, in whose lives there is no event but sorrow, have to measure time by throbs of pain and the record of bitter moments," Oscar Wilde said in *DeProfundis*.

Pierce had a psychiatrist diagnose him with depression related to the stress from family court for a worker's compensation claim: "Perhaps, but not for a disruption in his fatherhood role, Mr. Pierce would not be suffering from major depression at this time," the psychiatrist stated in 2011. By then, family court deemed Pierce a vexatious litigant and he was not allowed to use this to file a complaint in family court.

LAS Nightmares- Jeannie Melton, John Arndt, and Debbie Wolf: Victims 4-6

Jeannie Melton, like Pierce, has been deemed by family court a vexatious litigant: someone who files too many frivolous motions.

Melton told me she feels anxious about almost anything which reminds her of her family court experience: courthouses, streets on which she was arrested, and even a condominium which replaced the jail she was housed in during one of her arrests.

"I can't sleep; I always have nightmares and get up in the middle of the night." She told me. "Some of them are just upsetting and you can't remember. Most of them are about being trapped or hunted."

John Arndt, who's been involved in a bitter child custody battle with an ex-girlfriend over their son, said he has recurring nightmares from his LAS set in a "stone walled dungeon".

The only light comes with the constant hum from the shower/lavatory. The stone walls reek of dampness, sweat and urine. Twenty men lay in their cots, some snoring, some masturbating, most just sleeping.

I am awoken by sobs- sobs that I know are coming from the adjoining room, through the arch, opposite the wall next to me. I can hear him saying Daddy in between sobs. I know I can't go to him or the guards will come and make trouble, but if he keeps sobbing the cons will become agitated and put him in more danger.

I try to tell him it's ok in my lowest voice, he doesn't seem to hear me or even know I am here. I am pleading with God himself to comfort my son, until I can't take it anymore and rage overcomes me.

Then I am awake.

Debbie Wolf is a battered woman who lost custody to her abusive ex-husband; here's her recurring nightmare: "I am at the top of a huge 'jungle gym'. My children are clinging to me. I think I have them safe to the ground, and the bottom drops out. They are crying, begging me. I climb back up and start over, I wake up exhausted. I feel lost."

LAS and Pro Se Defendants

One of the easiest ways to get LAS is to be forced to represent yourself in a divorce. Divorce is always overwhelming, but a pro se defendant needs to learn new terms, procedures, rules and stand toe to toe with a seasoned divorce attorney.

"There is a great deal of data which would support Mr. Mackney's contention that he has felt overmatched and stressed, that he is not feeling much in control of the circumstances either in the context of his trying to negotiate with his wife and also in the context of the helplessness he feels in the midst of this litigation." Dr. Zuckerman said of Mackney. "As noted elsewhere, he also feels at the mercy of superior forces (his wife and his wife's family, along with their attorney), and he feels without the funds necessary to prosecute his position. These stresses can cause him to experience some dysphoric and even anxious feelings."

Robert Worster said that as a pro se defendant Mackney was ranting and raving in court rather than making legal arguments.

Sufferers of LAS have a tendency to vent in a meandering and uncontrollable manner, the way Worster described Mackney. They can't help themselves because the injustice against them is so great they need to release some of the bottled up angst and frustration, even if that means hurting themselves in the process. Rather than litigating his case, Mackney's LAS was manifesting itself in his rants.

LAS and Anxiety Victim 7: Hera McLeod

Hera McLeod told me bluntly that family court caused her worst nightmare. "My worst fear was that my ex would kill my son."

She said she experienced anxiety as court dates approached during her custody battle and continues to experience anxiety whenever she enters or is near a courthouse: even an upcoming traffic ticket hearing fills her with all-consuming angst.

"It (going to court) made him miserable - he felt like a condemned man going back again and again to get screwed over - almost every time," Rich Ware said of Mackney's court anxiety.

Here's an email Mackney sent to Bartol on January 24, 2013 describing this anxiety.

I'm very sorry but I'm too stressed out to attend tomorrow (a meeting Bartol proposed to have with him). I'm not playing games or jerking you around. The stress that I have gone through just in this email dialogue is more than I can handle. I thought I could do it, but I can't.

...I am so beaten down by you and this process that I will do anything to get some relief and not have to go back to court. I have lost 50 out of 53 hearings.

Is there NOTHING that we can do to keep us OUT of Court? Dina is not willing to grant me ANY relief on child support without going into Court? I live in fear of being served by you for anything, anytime. Please tell me what I can do to make sure that does not happen and I will do it. I just can't live under the current orders.

Like a Hostage

Victims of LAS feel like hostages to their legal bullies.

"Victims are created in two ways: by violence or by deceit. Either type of assault immediately renders the victim hostage to the perpetrator(s)." Dr. Huffer said in her book. "Victims feel as helpless as small children. Personal control becomes the issue. Adult autonomy is formed by a perception of trust. Psychologist Erik H. Erikson (1963) calls this feeling, 'basic trust.' The child must sense this degree of invulnerability in order to grow. This long, hard battle to adulthood is accomplished when one has the ability to take charge of one's own life. The belief that the world is manageable allows a sense of psychological relationship. It is like a kidnapping of the soul. Equilibrium is lost. Regardless of the individual's ability to accommodate stress, all victims must work out of a hostage relationship with the offender."

"I will keep silent, I will go away, I will do anything to get them to take their foot off the back of my neck. This is a life no longer worth living," Mackney said ending the same email to Bartol.

Mackney and Inappropriate Shaming

"Inappropriate shame results from feeling defenseless in the face of power. If you are wronged and then find yourself suffering shame and guilt, we can be confident that a hostage condition exists which was created by power differential. Control has been lost over some part of life." Dr. Huffer said in her book.

Chris Mackney described the imbalance in power in this blog post.

"In my relationship, I had no power or control. My friends, family, and everyone that knows me or my ex-wife and her family, knows that I had no power or control. Dr. Samenow was given the witnesses that would confirm the imbalance of power, control, and money in the relationship."

"Deshaming means exactly what it implies. Victims inappropriately feel guilty, incompetent, and blameworthy. They suffer sensations of disgrace, dishonor and regret…Defense attorneys and law enforcement officers attack any mental confusion." Dr. Huffer said of deshaming. "Attorneys' adversarial manner and impatience to get at facts over feelings perpetuates the victim's deterioration. Invalidation of the victim's stories add(s) to the victim's feelings of shame and guilt. Suicide is often fantasized."

"Invalidation of the victim's stories" is what Mackney referred to as emotional invalidation.

Emotional Invalidation is how abusers manipulate and control. Emotional Invalidation is debilitating, abusive and among the most emotionally abusive experiences, that leads to PTSD and suicide.

…

I have endured years of emotional invalidation during my marriage and my divorce. I was physically abused, beginning on my honeymoon. My ex-wife abused me in front of our children on January 19th, 2008. The police arrived to find me locked in my son's room with my children, with a ripped shirt and scrapes and marks all over my neck and back. Her father then tried to hide the shirt after the police chose not to arrest her. This can all be verified by the police report of the incident, which should be available to the public. Although it wouldn't surprise me if it was hidden by Fairfax County. Dr. Samenow hid this from his forensic evaluation.

It appears, like Dr. Huffer suggested, Mackney was fantasizing about suicide. Rich Ware said throughout 2012, when Mackney was living with him, Mackney repeatedly talked about committing suicide, and the discussion often led to fights, verbal and otherwise, after which Ware would convince him it was a bad idea.

Ware moved from Virginia to California at about the same time Mackney initially left Virginia for Dallas; after that, Mackney no longer had a constant voice in his head to counteract these fantasies.

"I would say that's accurate," Ronald Pierce responded when I asked him if he fantasized about suicide. "The truth and fairness don't matter and instead the system takes away your kids, your money and your life so suicide seems like a good idea."

For those who don't get treatment, they often fall into what Dr. Huffer referred to as an "oppressive cycle" in which false and misleading information is used to win sanctions against LAS victims, and those fraudulent sanctions are used to get further sanctions.

"Tom, John, James, and Manny (four LAS victims featured in Dr. Huffer's book) were called 'disgruntled litigants', fools, crazy, and 'unable to take no for an answer'. Profoundly influencing each of their cases were numerous documents and presentations containing misinformation. When challenged, official explanations were freely transmitted among those who enjoy titles that allude to 'authorized', 'trustee', or 'official'." Dr. Huffer said. "Even though the misinformation caused a massive destruction to these people, it was always accepted without verification. Submissions from Tom, James, John and Manny were deemed 'unofficial'. Therefore, the truth was dismissed repeatedly and without a second look."

Mackney had most of his legal filings dismissed out of hand in the same manner. He was denied: five motions to appoint a Guardian ad Litem, three motions to sanction his wife for not allowing him to speak to his kids on the phone, two motions to change venue, and a motion to have Judge Bellows recused.

"Within every victim's realm of power is knowledge of the truth. He remains the only party in a protracted legal battle who knows the truth and cares that the truth prevails." Dr. Huffer added. "All others will not prioritize truth over efficiency, funding, expediency, or other common motivations of judicial personnel. The victim's evidence and motivations are wasted during the fact finding process."

Mackney, Ball, LAS and Obsession (LAS Victim 8: Tom Ball)

Both Chris Mackney and Tom Ball became obsessed with the central issue in each of their cases: Mackney with psychopathy and Ball with domestic violence. Here's part of Ball's suicide note.

When then a man is arrested for domestic violence, one of two things can happen. If they are only dating and have separate apartments, then he can head home. But if they are living together, then this fellow has a real problem. Bail conditions and then a possible protective or restraining order prevent him from being with her. So he needs to find a new place to live, at least until the charges are resolved. The King of his Castle is no longer allowed into his castle. A feminist name Pence who wrote that was absolutely giddy at that outcome. So he can get his own place if he has enough money. Or he can move in with his mother, his sister or another relative. He might have a girlfriend who would let him stay with her. And if none of this is possible, well then I guess he is sleeping in his car down by the river.

If he has minor children, money will soon turn into an issue. Most men I know do not mind paying child support. They want their kids to have food on their plates, clothes on their backs, and a roof over their heads. But it does stress that man's finances. Child support is usually 33% of the man's gross income. Withholding for taxes, social security and health insurance can range up to 28% of his gross paycheck. So a man making $500 a week gross has only $825 monthly left over after withholding and child support. That is not enough money for an apartment here in Central Massachusetts. That does not include other expenses like heating, electric, gas, groceries, telephone, cable, car payment and car insurance.

"After I realized that the 'source of conflict' in my life was Psychopathy, I read everything I could on the subject. I read books, research reports, pop psychology articles, Law Journal Articles, (and) Psychology Journal articles." Mackney said of his obsession with psychopathy. "I read all the blog sites, victim forums, healing community groups, father's rights groups, that discussed what to do legally, emotionally, financially in order to protect yourself and your children from the 'chaos' that will come."

Jill Peterson Mitchell described one manifestation of this obsession when Mackney was at a dinner party with a group of friends. As the rest of the party was involved in normal dinner conversation, Mackney received a text message from Jill updating him on her divorce. He immediately called her back, "I can't stand the conversation here when there are so many more important things going on in the world."

Mackney then left the party; he was so consumed with his divorce he could no longer enjoy dinner with friends. Jill Peterson Mitchell expanded on this obsession.

The chronic abuse of Chris by Pete and Dina caused Chris to become unable to tolerate any communication that challenged his version of events, triggering additional feelings of helplessness. This dynamic is how people get trapped in the PTSD mindset and reveals how it is self-sustaining. He turned off potential allies because his brain did not allow him to communicate about any other issue in life, which led to his increasing isolation from everyone. This fact also caused him to present physically, dirty ill -fitting close, gaunt visage, and giving off looks of panic in person. Chris had agreed to drive my belongings up to me and met with a long-time family friend to obtain the rental truck, immediately while backing up in the truck, Chris backed into a parked vehicle, but failed to acknowledge it because he couldn't handle the truth that it was a simple mistake. His response to it was to walk away and not acknowledge that he had anything to do with it. Naturally my friend called me and expressed a high level of concern about his overall stability. Because I knew that his mind was engaged in producing very complex, clear communication and how highly sophisticated his mind was thinking I see this as a manifestation of his PTSD, yet my friend only saw a mentally unstable waif.

The panic disorder also caused Chris to rely on his own protective logic which kept him on the treadmill of mind fear. This would cause him to make choices that also alienated him.

Because he became so detached he was unable to pay attention to or value maintaining a normal physical appearance, if he had the ability to separate his attention for a second from his problem he could have gotten further with people. When we met to do something, he would try to behave in conformance with manners, opening doors, etc....but it was clear that those daily living standards were no longer the norm for him and it was a conscious effort, rather than unconscious as it must have been before.

"In fact, the victim cannot be obsessed. Figuring out what happened and forming a basis for feeling safe again preoccupies the victim's life," Dr. Huffer said in her book which dedicated a chapter to obsession. "What defines a critical traumatic incident is the degree of helplessness or lack of control that was felt at the time it happened. Every LAS survivor has been in jeopardy and absolutely is unable to do anything about something. That something, in the face of his or her impotence, will trigger fear motivating obsession...Obsession presents an emotional hyperbole that exhausts the LAS victim. It is like containing a raging bull in your chest as you attend to the day's demands. The victim has a window of energy early in the day and finds the evenings a time of total wipeout. Sleep may come early, but a troubled twilight sleep will usually greet the victim at dawn. It is a time that leaves the victim asking, 'What's wrong with me?' and saying, 'I've gone completely nuts.'"

LAS, Obsession and Exhaustion Victims 9-10: Ulf Carlsson and Sunny Kelley

"I would be tired in the evening, go to sleep and wake up about two hours later.....then I would lay awake for 4 to 5 hours just tossing and turning." Ulf Carlsson said of the exhaustion. "(I) couldn't lay still....very restless....almost like I was covered with ants....then I would finally fall asleep....for a few hours when it was time to get up.....my whole day was a mess.....so tired by the afternoon that I would have to take a nap or I wouldn't make it through the day."

Here's Sunny Kelley:

I don't think anyone would call it obsession if they truly understood where we are. No one would think that slaves were obsessed with freedom. No one would think about whether still-captive hostages were able to have normal conversations with people on the outside or not. No one would even consider that because the expectation isn't there. Framing ongoing trauma in those ways means that the actual experience is not fully understood. There is a very distinct difference in points of view, inside and outside, which I'm not sure could ever be reconciled.

Everything is exhausting at all times, always. Just drawing a breath with the crushing grief that sits on my chest every moment takes every bit of energy I have. People looking in from the outside do not understand the energy you're expending on incredibly mundane things like breathing, remembering what year it is, what your name is, what other people's names are, that people even have names, what you were just talking about.

Michael Volpe

LAS and Banging Your Head against the Wall

Here's an email, one of many, Mackney sent to powerful people asking for help.

Dear Fairfax Law Foundation, Virginia Law Foundation, Virginia Bar Association, Virginia State Bar Chairman and Vice Chairman, Delegate Plum, Delegate Brink and Senator Howell,

I have reached out to you previously about a travesty and miscarriage of justice. I am terribly sorry for writing to you again, but things have only gotten worse since I gave up all efforts to ever see my children again and moved out of town, as requested twice, by my ex-wife ..There is a cover-up of a severe psychopathology, parental alienation, abuse and fraud by Judge Bellows and others on the Fairfax County Circuit Court. As a result of speaking out, I am now being destroyed and bullied into silence, by Kyle Bartol, Jim Cottrell, and now the Commonwealth's attorney...Will someone please help me and my children obtain a Guardian Ad Litem, as recommended by every single expert in High Conflict divorce? Who in the Commonwealth of Virginia will protect children from the corruption of the Court?

I emailed everyone who received this email after Mackney committed suicide and asked each person and/or office what if any investigation they did. I received one response from Virginia State Delegate Ken Plum's office, a Democrat whose district includes Fairfax County. His legislative assistant Kristy Pullen emailed me this response.

We are distressed to hear that Mr. Mackney committed suicide. As soon as he was first contacted, Delegate Plum referred the case to the Fairfax-Falls Church Community Services Board, and they assigned a caseworker. His main concern was dealing with the immediate mental health needs of Mr. Mackney. Appointment of a Guardian Ad Litem is handled by the court rather than the legislature.

Please keep us informed of any information you discover.

In purportedly trying to help, Delegate Plum's office was gas-lighting. Mackney told them of a complex legal corruption and asked for help fixing the corruption. The Delegate's office referred him to the mental hospital as though he was crazy like his ex-wife suggested. It's no different than the Baker Act request in Pasierb's case. In both cases, society is saying, *the problem isn't the corrupt family court system but your own mental issues.*

Delegate Plum's office stopped responding when I pointed this out.

"Legal abuse syndrome is a natural and normal response to an abnormal, unnatural, cumulative trauma, as with all post trauma stress disorders. Any attempt by any individual to discredit an individual's testimony, character or actions due to their suffering from LAS is to clearly demonstrate the aberrant nature of our system of problem solving." Dr. Huffer said in her book. "An ally of civilization must clearly identify such behavior as abusive, put a halt to destructive actions, and devote their energies to restoration of victims of the 'system'."

Throughout his ordeal Mackney told me he contacted a multitude of people in power- non-profits, trade groups, politicians, the media, and law enforcement- begging for help: ignored every time.

"Fifty-eight efforts have been made to report the crimes to law enforcement agencies, regulators, and those in power. No effective response has been elicited." Dr. Huffer said of a mortgage fraud victim with a similar experience.

Chapter 11: Family Court Corruption and the Media

"In any event, the proper question isn't what a journalist thinks is relevant but what his or her audience thinks is relevant. Denying people information they would find useful because you think they shouldn't find it useful is censorship, not journalism."

Michael Kinsley

...

The Unpublished Story

In the introduction I mentioned that an article about Mackney's suicide was denied at the last minute. With a few changes, Here's that UNPUBLISHED article.

Chris Mackney, who committed suicide Dec. 29, 2013, said before he died he was being bullied to death during a divorce and he laid the blame at the feet of the Virginia Family Court system and Dr. Stanton Samenow, a psychologist made famous by his mention on the popular television show The Sopranos. *Furthermore, Mackney said the bullying was in retaliation for his discovering details of his former father-in-law's involvement in a 1960s murder along with actor Woody Harrelson's father, Charles Harrelson.*

Mackney left a suicide note on his website, called "Good Men Did Nothing," and in it, he described the mental and psychological terror that his ex-wife's legal assault had caused him. The note later was removed from the site, but has been republished online.

"I took my own life because I had come to the conclusion that there was nothing I could do or say to end the abuse. Every time I got up off my knees, I would get knocked back down. They were not going to let me be the father I wanted to be to my children. People may think I am a coward for giving up on my children, but I didn't see how I was going to heal from this. I have no money for an attorney, therapy or medication. I have lost 4 jobs because of this process."

According to the organization Fathers Unite, 300 fathers and 30 mothers take their lives every month in the U.S. as a result of family court abuse. In fact, the circumstances surrounding Mackney's suicide have several uncanny resemblances to the most notorious such suicide, that of Tom Ball in 2011.

Tom Ball set himself on fire just before 5:30 on the evening of June 15, 2011, in front of the Cheshire County Superior Courthouse in Keane, N.H. The next day the local paper, the Keane Sentinel, *received his 10,000-plus word suicide note in which he blamed the family court system as well as Children and Protective Services for his suicide. Ball had contended in his suicide note that a minor case of corporal punishment was turned on its head and used to brand him unfairly as a domestic abuser, and with that branding all his custodial rights were taken away.*

According to a study by Augustine J. Kposowa, entitled "Marital Status and Suicide in National Longitudinal Mortality Study" and published in the Journal of Epidemiology and Community Health in the April 2000 edition, both Ball and Mackney are part of an epidemic of suicide of divorced fathers, a group which is nearly 10 times as likely to commit suicide as divorced women.

Both Mackney and Ball had lost all contact with their children, fallen hopelessly behind on child support, and were repeatedly sanctioned by the court for prior violations leading to prison time.

Each had also shown signs of obsession with a concept central to their case. In the case of Ball, it was the constant misdiagnosis of domestic violence and with Mackney it was psychopathy.

A couple months into his divorce Mackney discovered that his wife's father had orchestrated a murder in the late 1960s.

Dina Mackney's father, Pete Scamardo, is a successful real estate developer in Virginia however in 1968 he hired Charles Harrelson, the father of Woody Harrelson, to kill Sam Degelia, Jr. who was not only Scamardo's business partner but friend since the second grade.

Scamardo allegedly wanted Degelia, Jr. dead in order to collect on life insurance each had on the other because they were business partners.

According to news reports at the time, Harrelson had become indebted to Scamardo after losing some heroin he was tasked by Scamardo to sell, and Scamardo used this as leverage to convince Harrelson to commit the murder. Scamardo was convicted as an accomplice in the murder in 1970 and received seven years' probation.

Mackney said that from the beginning of his divorce in 2008 all he wanted to do was settle in an equitable manner but his wife refused to ever offer any deal. Worse yet, she hired the law firm Cottrell, Fletcher, Schinstock, Bartol & Cottrell, where the lead attorney, Jim Cottrell, advertises by saying, "He's not the type to settle so have your wallets open."

Mackney charged that his ex-wife paid an estimated $1.2 million to have the legal team badger him for $2,816 per month in child support until the day he died.

Cottrell would only say "it's not true, it's not true" to the charges made by Mackney in his suicide note that he legally bullied Mackney to death.

Dr. Karin Huffer is a clinical psychologist who saw so many victims of legal abuse she coined the term, "legal abuse syndrome," which she considers a subset of Post-Traumatic Stress Disorder (PTSD), caused by protracted abuse by the legal system.

Mackney said he believed he had PTSD, and in Huffer's book, Legal Abuse Syndrome: Eight Steps for Avoiding Stress Caused by the Legal System *obsession is the title of Chapter 5.*

In 2010, Mackney saw Dr. William Zuckerman for the purposes of being evaluated during the course of his custody. During the evaluation, Dr. Zuckerman described behavior consistent with someone suffering from legal abuse syndrome.

"There is a great deal of data which would support Mr. Mackney's contention that he has felt overmatched and stressed, that he is not feeling much in control of the circumstances either in the context of his trying to negotiate with his wife, and also in the context of the helplessness he feels in the midst of this litigation. As noted earlier, he also feels at the mercy of superior forces (his wife, his wife's family, and their attorney), and he feels without the funds necessary to prosecute his position. These stresses can lead to experience some dysphoric and even anxious feelings. (Both are also symptoms of PTSD)"

Connie Valentine is the co-founder of the California Protective Parents Association and has documented family court abuse for more than two decades. She said that jailing or threatening to jail a parent by setting persistently high child support payments, as in the case of Ball and Mackney, is a form of debtor's prison, technically outlawed in the U.S.

Valentine said that in both the cases of Ball and Mackney, the divorce fell into a category considered high conflict divorces.

Valentine said family court corruption primarily targets women, while men's rights groups like Father's Unite believe the corruption is directed mostly at males. But observers from multiple viewpoints affirm the abuse starts because there is too much power in the hands of so-called experts, a lack of transparency, and a lack of training.

In Mackney's case, he focused specifically on the behavior of Samenow, who became a cult celebrity when his work was featured in an episode of the television show The Sopranos. *Samenow declined to comment on this case.*

In 2009, Mackney and his ex-wife, agreed to have Samenow do a psychological evaluation after little progress was being made in the divorce. Mackney said the corruption started immediately when he was pressured to change this so-called psychological evaluation into a custody evaluation.

Samenow's evaluation was completed on Aug. 3, 2009, and the evaluation repeatedly cited Dina Mackney's side of the story. Samenow referred to her as "thoughtful" and "cooperative" while diagnosing Mackney as "narcissistic" and warned that he had violent tendencies.

Michael Volpe

Mackney said this evaluation was used as the basis for a series of court rulings which limited and then in October 2009 first took all his custodial rights away. In March 2010, after a psychological evaluation by Dr. William Zuckerman restored some custodial rights, Mackney was cited for contempt of court after he only faxed over a copy of his new apartment lease when a court order directed he fax a lease and a copy of the receipt for first month's payment and again lost all custodial rights.

Mackney was jailed numerous times while acting as his own attorney for a variety of contempt of court violations. Mackney was serving his third stint in jail in May 2012 when he received a letter from his then court appointed attorney, Robert Worster, which ended this way.

"Last, Mr. (Kyle) Bartol again expressed his client's request that you simply disappear following release and not have any contact with her or her family (including the children). My understanding (none of this has been submitted to me in writing) is that she will not pursue further sanctions if you do not have any contact with her or her family (including the children)."

Mackney said that he complied and moved to Dallas to try and begin his life anew. But in the summer of 2013, Mackney was extradited back to Virginia, when his ex-wife through her attorneys and the Office of the Fairfax County Commonwealth's Attorney, and specifically their Prosecutor Elizabeth Kohut, claimed attempted extortion.

They alleged it was a crime when Mackney suggested in emails to his ex-wife's attorney he might go to the media with allegations of abuse in the divorce if she didn't voluntarily reduce his child support to a more reasonable level.

The prosecutors refused to accept any plea, and forced Mackney to languish in jail awaiting trial with a bail he couldn't afford. Despite not having any money and using a court appointed attorney, Mackney was acquitted, all of which he explained in his suicide note.

"So, we went to trial and I was found not guilty. I did not ask for any money from her and the child support I owe is to my children, not my ex-wife. The jury saw that my attempts to reduce my child support were not an effort to obtain money at all, and the law supported the verdict.

"It was a clear effort on the Commonwealth's attorney to silence me for threatening to speak out about the fraud of Dr. Samenow, and the Cover-up by Judge Randy Bellows. Why else wouldn't they accept a plea to my first criminal charge, ever?"

After his acquittal his ex-wife successfully reached out to Child Support Enforcement to force Mackney to stay in Virginia, and he was facing further sanction for being behind on his child support as well as starting his blog, Good Men Did Nothing, *which spoke about Scamardo's murder conviction, something a previous court order forbade Mackney from doing.*

Tommy Moffett said he also had Samenow as a custody evaluator. He said he might have wound up like Mackney, but he surreptitiously taped all their sessions and was able to, acting as his own attorney, frustrating Samenow to the point Samenow blurted out, "What, did you have me recorded?" Moffett briefly documented his experience on a blog he started, "Stop Samenow."

Mackney's story was rejected by every media I went to even after his suicide note went viral and I tried selling it as the exclusive opportunity to tell the real story behind a suicide note read by millions. The reasons why are numerous and they are the subject of this chapter.

Investigative Journalist: My Definition

As keynote speaker at the 2012 *Eugene Katz Award* for immigration reporting sponsored by the Center for Immigration Studies here's how I defined investigative journalists: "They (investigative journalists) insert themselves into a situation someone somewhere wants kept hidden from the public, and report on that."

In Mackney's case, powerful people wanted to hide a murder in Texas in the 1960s from a recent divorce in Fairfax County, Virginia. Forty-five years apart, a murder led to a suicide. Then a probate court in Arlington, Virginia was used to hide all this from the public; I inserted myself into all these situations and reported on them.

Court Reporters versus Investigative Reporters

Sharyl Attkisson's book *Stonewalled: My Fight for Truth Against the Forces of Obstruction, Intimidation, and Harassment in Obama's Washington* starts this way: "There's nothing like an unsolved mystery to keep me at the computer or on the phone until one or two in the morning. Most mysteries can be solved; you just have to find the information. But too often, the keepers of the information don't want to give it up even when the information belongs to the public."

Family court abuse is a three and four dimensional puzzle perfect for the likes of Attkisson. Here's the rub. To provide proper coverage of family court abuse we'd need an army of reporters with her skills, reporters who can cut through the complexity and get to the truth, but investigative reporters rarely touch family courts, instead court reporters cover family courts. Court reporters are used to summing up court activities, usually uncritically, and this style won't uncover abuse and corruption.

Family Courts Are He Said/She Said

"I've found that divorce is inherently he said/she said, and generally, unless one or both parties are celebrities, a private matter." I said to Tom Jackman, *The Washington Post's* court reporter. "So, for this reason, the media in general recoils when presented a story involving custody during a divorce even if one of the parties argues corruption or even criminality."

"When presented with a he said/she said story, we are typically hesitant to dive in much further. (When I say we, I am speaking from the perspective of a mainstream print reporter for the last 30 years, nearly all of which has been spent covering police and courts issues.) **We**

get calls all the time, and I mean all the time, from men and women who have a complaint about the way their divorce or custody case went. (Emphasis mine) I have covered these issues over the years, and I have looked into a number of these complaints." Jackman responded concurring with my analysis. "The problem is that, even in cases alleged to involve corruption or criminality, when you speak to the lawyer on the other side; they provide a completely different perspective. Typically one that makes sense. And you sit there and say, 'Oh. I see.' And you're back to he said/she said. And writing a he said/she said story leaves readers unsatisfied and wondering why they spent all that time reading a story that didn't take them to a clear, definitive resolution."

Jackman speaks for many journalists who instinctively view family court as he said/she said; it's a bogus and hypocritical view, and an anecdote about President Obama will prove it.

Then State Senator Barack Obama was an also ran in the Democratic primary in the 2004 US Senate race in Illinois when details from the nasty divorce of the poll's leader, Blair Hull, were made public. After judge shopping, the *Chicago Tribune* got a judge to unseal Hull's divorce and found an accusation by his now ex-wife that Hull was violent toward her. Hull denied this allegation, but the *Chicago Tribune* still printed the allegation largely as fact.

"Struggling to defuse an explosive controversy that threatens his U.S. Senate campaign, Blair Hull and his ex-wife on Friday allowed the release of their 1998 divorce records revealing that she accused him of being 'a violent man' who caused her to fear for her safety," the *Chicago Tribune* reported.

Hull dropped out of the race days after the revelation; Obama catapulted to the lead and won the Democratic nomination going away.

Following Obama's primary victory, the media in Chicago fought for months to unseal the records of the custody battle from the divorce of his Republican opponent, Jack Ryan, from his ex-wife actress Jeri Ryan. (Their marriage lasted from 1991-1999) After months of legal action those records were unsealed over the objection of both Ryan's revealing embarrassing allegations about their sex life- allegations Jack Ryan denied. The allegations were still printed, and Illinois media was blanketed with discussion and analysis of Ryan's sex life causing him to drop out of the race.

Republicans scrambled initially trying to get former Bears coach Mike Ditka to run before settling on Alan Keyes as a sacrificial lamb; Obama received more than 70% of the vote with his keynote speech at the 2004 Democratic Convention his coming out party.

Both cases involve prototypical he said/she said allegations with no corroboration and yet the media proactively sought out their divorces finding judges to unseal them. Then, they printed these he said/she said allegations largely as fact and did numerous follow-ups. The media only views some divorces as he said/she said.

The Current Ideological Paradigm Has No Place for Family Court

In his 1999 book *Bias*, Bernie Goldberg said this about the takeover of the newsroom by feminist forces and its effect on the gender war in family court.

It's true enough some men really are deadbeats. But the deadbeat dad stories we often do are about these rich doctors and businessmen who would rather spend their money on convertibles and speedboats and young blondes than their own children. That happens, but it's not typical. The real story is that a lot of men who didn't pay support are poor; they hold menial jobs; they're undereducated. Many of them pay when they can.

Journalists and liberals in general should care about poor men like that. But to media elites- being as reliably feminist as they are- the very idea that men in divorce and custody cases might be part of an oppressed group is an alien concept. So, only occasionally do we tip near a story about the millions of divorced dads who want to maintain a strong relationship with their kids but are kept away by angry moms. As long as feminism from the Left define to the issue they will always see men as the bad guy.

This might explain why stories sympathetic to deadbeat dads like Mackney and Ball aren't covered by the mainstream media, but it doesn't explain why the conservative media doesn't sympathize with Mackney and Ball, or why female family court abuse victims are also rarely covered.

To understand the broader biases, let's try a thought experiment. What if Pete Scamardo hired a bunch of illegal aliens and they worked in his buildings for less than minimum wage giving him an unfair advantage? In order to keep the flows of illegals coming, he secretly funded groups like La Raza; Chris Mackney found out, and blew the whistle on it. If the rest of the story is the same, Fox News Channel, talk radio, and websites like *The Daily Caller*, Breitbart, and Townhall.com would be interested.

Now, imagine if Scamardo was dumping waste from his buildings and polluting the ocean; he secretly funded groups which marginalize environmental groups calling them wackos so they wouldn't be taken seriously when they attacked him, Chris Mackney found this out and the rest of the story is the same. Many in the mainstream media- the broadcast networks, CNN, MSNBC, and most urban newspapers- and liberal media- Huffington Post, Salon, Mother Jones, etc. - would be interested.

In other words, someone getting away with murder is less important to the media than hiring illegal aliens and polluting the ocean. We live in a liberal versus conservative media, so the story has to be interesting to one or both and family court abuse doesn't advance the agenda of either group.

An example of what I mean is an article Raquel Okyay wrote for the conservative website Townhall.com on February 3, 2015, entitled *More Gun Owners Disarmed on Word of Bitter Ex-Partners* primarily about the aforementioned Ted Taupier and Dan Brewington, who had their second amendment rights squelched due to dubious allegations in their divorces. Okyay had earlier done a story on Taupier from the same angle for *Guns and Patriot*, Human Events section dedicated to second amendment issues. Townhall.com and *Guns and Patriot* weren't interested strictly in family court abuse but how that abuse led to squelching second amendment rights, and sites like that have an insatiable appetite for stories about second amendment rights being squelched.

Michael Volpe

In June 2014, Lenawee County Circuit Court Judge Margaret Noe ordered Navy sailor Petty Officer Matthew Hindes to make his next court appearance or lose custody of his daughter. The Petty Officer already had a prior commitment that day, serving his country on a ship in the Pacific Ocean.

Initially, the judge still insisted he show up for court or lose his custodial rights. This led to local coverage before ABC picked it up and then the powerful news aggregator website, *Drudge Report* on June 20, 2014. From there, the conservative blogosphere and the Fox News Channel gave it wall to wall coverage getting the attention of Ohio Republican Congressman Mike Turner.

"Our service members should not be penalized for serving their country," Turner said on *Fox & Friends*. "Unfortunately, family law courts use the time away for deployment against our service members."

Within a week of intense media scrutiny the judge reversed her previous order and suspended the case until October 2014, after Hindes' return. Hindes and his ex-wife reached a settlement in October.

This story was tailor made for the conservative media which loves military members and relishes any opportunity to expose anyone wronging them.

What happened to Chris Mackney is no less unfair than Petty Officer Hindes, and his story has a catchy opening, "A Fairfax County Judge forbade a father from seeing his two children after he forgot to fax in a receipt," but Chris Mackney was a salesman not a military man so the media didn't care.

PTSD and Defamation

Most family court victims have LAS, making them horrible sources. They develop an inflated sense of paranoia, which can be directed at the journalist. They are victims of a conspiracy and often believe everything is a conspiracy. There are days when they inundate the journalist with information and other days when they say they feel too traumatized to talk about their story. They send long rambling rants which have no focus or discernible point, besides expressing their frustration with the legal system. They speak in a stream of consciousness and get off on tangents. I once asked Jeannie Melton to sum up her story in ten minutes or less and she freaked out, had to hang up, and needed one of her friends sum it up.

I've interviewed more than one thousand people with LAS, and similar trauma related disorders. I even wrote a book entitled *The Definitive Dossier of PTSD in Whistleblowers*, and I still repeatedly get frustrated trying to interview folks afflicted with it. Now, imagine a journalist with no knowledge of the disorder dealing with someone who goes from inundating them with documents to telling them they're too traumatized to deal with it. How many journalists would continue that relationship?

That said, though Chris Mackney's LAS was debilitating, he explained and wrote his story in a lucid and cogent manner: as evidenced by his suicide note and blog.

Finally, there is a thorny issue few in the media would admit: the threat of lawsuit. Divorce cases are tailor made for a libel or defamation suit, no matter how frivolous. If you're wrong on anything, one minor detail could trigger a lawsuit. Few media people would ever admit out loud they are afraid of being sued because that would be admitting cowardice, but couple this threat with all the other reasons I just listed and the cost/benefit calculus for media leans heavy toward cost.

Local versus National

We also have a media obsessed with national politics. Good and great investigative reporters will be digging for stories relevant to national politics. While Chris Mackney's story has national significance, it is ultimately a local story. It's a local court applying state law; there's no obvious national significance. Sharyl Attkisson, whose credits include the Fast and Furious Scandal, the Benghazi attack, Obamacare, and an expose of faulty Firestone tires, is trying to get as close as possible to the President of the United States, the CEO of a major corporation, and a powerful nonprofit and family courts are far away from that goal.

This leaves stories like Mackney's to local reporters, court reporters, like Tom Jackman. Good court reporters move up to cover national issues, leaving bad court reporters who chalk all this up to a case of he said/she said.

Complexity

Valette Clark's story wound up in a 4,051 word feature on October 23, 2013, in the *Pittsburgh City Paper*. The author, Charlie Deitch, spent about six months researching and writing the piece, and alleged that though each of Clark's three children accused their father of abuse, Val Clark was deemed a "parental alienator" by family courts: PAS.

The leading alternative newspaper in Pittsburgh, the *Pittsburgh City Paper* prints 70,000 copies weekly. That should have been more than enough to pique the interest of the rest of Pittsburgh's media, but the story was ignored; the last time I spoke with Clark before this book went to print, her divorce judge, Kathleen Mulligan, was threatening to kick her out of her home. The only real effect of the story was even more pressure on her.

Why would the rest of the media ignore such an in-depth expose? Part of the reason might be its length; at 4,051 words this is a very complex story.

"And domestic cases are complicated and time-consuming to fully understand. I would expect this is even more of a problem for the electronic media who often don't have the time or resources to devote to complicated stories. Proving that there is a clear and definite wrong being committed, by the courts or the police or any authority figure, is a story most reporters and editors absolutely want to pursue." Tom Jackman said. "I know I do. And you can ask the local police, prosecutors and school district if I've pursued them, fairly and intensively. But proving it must be done fairly, fully and completely. And when both sides air out their stories, clarity is often hard to come by."

"As a general matter, we're going to be unlikely to dive into most of these convoluted sex crime/custody stories," an editor told me echoing that sentiment in rejecting a family court abuse story.

Mackney's story is just as complex as Clark's. It spans four decades, two states, requires the journalist to sum up Samenow's twenty page report in a paragraph or two and forces the journalist to sum up five years of litigation and accusations, a daunting task especially if there's no discernable benefit from getting the story right besides correcting a horrible injustice.

Most family court abuse stories are incredibly complex: years in the making, with numerous court professionals, lawyers, litigants, children, and there are at least two sides to the story. But even this excuse is bogus.

If you want complex, try Watergate, broken by Jackman's newspaper. That story is so complex forty plus years later people still don't understand it. How many people refer to Watergate as a break-in when in fact Watergate is about a series of dirty tricks committed by Nixon's reelection campaign and covered up by the White House including Nixon? The break-in at the Watergate Hotel was merely the original spark for the story. How many people believe that Deep Throat, Mark Felt, was the only source on this story when Felt was the most provocatively titled and well-placed of about one hundred sources both named and anonymous?

For nearly two years, the Nixon White House claimed there was no scandal, *The Washington Post* was obsessed with things the public didn't care about and was spinning harmless facts to appear nefarious: how's that for clarity? *The Washington Post* continued to pursue the story despite these roadblocks, but when the same roadblocks are presented in family court it's an excuse to give up. Sure, proving mass corruption in the White House is more important than proving it in a divorce, but then again the same newspaper which proved a president was so corrupt he resigned can't figure out which side is telling the truth in a divorce. For Watergate, *The Washington Post* had Woodward and Bernstein, on every shortlist for greatest investigative journalists of all time, while this story would be assigned to a court reporter.

An Exception

In June 2015, Oakland (Michigan) Circuit Judge Lisa Gorcyca jailed three youngsters ages 9, 10, and 14 in juvenile detention after they refused to have lunch with their father.

The fourteen year old explained why the three refused, "I do apologize if I didn't understand the rules, but I do not apologize for not talking to (the father) because I have a reason for that and that's because he's violent and I saw him hit my mom and I'm not going to talk to him."

The judge is a parental alienation ideologue remarking in court: "I see kids who have been physically abused, tortured, raped, that still want to talk to their father; that still respect their father. Your kids have none of those things," and this case is "tied for my worst parental alienation case," a la Angela Hickman.

The children have been required to undergo psychiatric therapy while incarcerated and were to "be kept away from each other as much as possible," according to a hand-written order from the court.

The story was broken locally and spread like wildfire covered by much of the media. On Fox News Channel the mother's lawyer said, "I have been doing family law for 20 years and I must say this shocks the conscience."

"If this case shocked the lawyer's conscience they haven't been practicing family law for twenty years," Sunny Kelley told me.

The three children were released from juvenile detention but placed in some sort of a camp to deal with their parental alienation and were sent to further family reunification therapy after that. On July 22, 2015, the judge put in a gag order which only applied to the mother, something almost no one in the media reported, but news continues to pour out of this case. In early August it was reported the father's divorce attorney, Keri Middleditch, sent a subpoena to Twitter for information about one of their accounts #JusticeforTsimhoni.

I can only surmise that jailing three kids for refusing to meet their father because of parental alienation, a topic almost no layman understands, is a bridge too far for the media, but the frustrating part of this story is that it's no more shocking than Angela Hickman, Sunny Kelley, Susan Skipp, Chris Mackney, or any of the other stories featured but the media chose only this one to highlight.

Summary of Stories:

While Chris Mackney approached numerous media, including me, unsuccessfully, all the people covered in this book experienced media frustration. Sunny Kelley's story has received some exposure, being covered not only by Snow but also by Al Jazeera America, where they used pseudonyms. Her story was the subject of a contentious confirmation hearing for Maureen Murphy, a GAL in her case, when she was nominated to be a judge, but names weren't used and the media merely repeated testimony with no digging. I mentioned all this when I exposed Murphy in Hickman's case for *Crime Magazine* in May 2015 and for a larger profile on the group Association of Family and Conciliation Courts (AFCC) for Capital Research Center. That is still only alternative media and it wasn't covered in Connecticut, where it would have the most impact.

Susan Skipp has also had her story covered by numerous media, including being part of a story I did on the proliferation of civil RICO lawsuits in family court and the same AFCC profile, but all those were still alternative and never in Connecticut. Hera McLeod's story became the subject of overwhelming media coverage but almost all focusing on the unusual circumstances of her son's death. Very little space was devoted to the custody decision which led to the death; a piece in *The Washingtonian* entitled *The Wrong One* published on December 13, 2013, was an exception. That piece quoted from testimony given by Rams' ex-girlfriend, who described how they engaged in pornography with his other son in the next room, from a Manassas, Virginia Police Officer, testifying about the other two murders where he was a suspect, and a social worker who said Rams was suspected in 2010 of domestic abuse against a minor (his other son).

Ted Taupier and Neil Shelton were repeatedly frustrated by media which refused to hear them until they spoke with me. Even so, while my stories were part of a wave of media coverage in both their cases, it was alternative media and never locally.

Susan Carrington is one exception; her local newspaper, *Rockland County Times*, published my story about her written with Raquel Okyay. The editor did a follow-up and also published a letter to the editor. Still, no other media in the area has picked up on it and Carrington's custody continues to be in limbo as this book is published.

The Pitfalls of Investigative Journalism

There is another reason why family court stories like Chris Mackney's aren't covered. In his story, all the corrupt individuals have enormous power and influence- Pete Scamardo, Stanton Samenow, Judge Randy Bellows, Jim Cottrell, and the Fairfax County Prosecutor's Office. That's true of almost all investigative pieces. Corrupt powerful people don't like anyone challenging them and don't just sit by while their corruption is exposed. They respond and retaliate, applying pressure.

Sharyl Attkison, who until March 2014 spent over two decades working as an investigative journalist for CBS, described a world in which political, business, and nonprofit interests ally together to squash hard hitting reporting.

"Broadly, there are overarching concerns." Atkisson said on *The O'Reilly Factor* on April 10, 2014. "I would just say fear over original investigative reporting. There is unprecedented, I believe, influence on the media, not just the news, but the images you see everywhere, by well-orchestrated and financed campaigns of special interests, political interests and corporations."

Managers receive voluminous emails and phone calls threatening pay back if hard hitting stories continue to run, advertisers threaten to pull their advertising if their companies continue to be painted in a bad light, and powerful people use their connections to kill stories.

"God Damnit Sharyl! *The Washington Post* is reasonable, the *LA Times* is reasonable, *The New York Times* is reasonable, you're the only one who's not reasonable," White House Deputy Press Secretary Eric Schultz screamed at Attkisson after she asked too many hard hitting questions about the scandal dubbed Fast and Furious.

"At one point, when I'm covering safety concerns about the highly profitable cholesterol drug known as 'statins', whose makers buy advertising from CBS, Murphy (her producer) receives what he views as a harsh threat from one of the CBS sales bosses. The manager leaves Murphy a loud angry voicemail saying that the stories 'could really harm business.'"

Lou Jasikoff is editor of the *Scranton Wilkes-Barre Independent Gazette* and his newspaper broke arguably the biggest family court scandal in history, dubbed "custody for cash" at least one GAL , Danielle Ross, was convicted of not paying taxes on bribes she accepted to steer custody cases. He told me his advertisers are often threatened by agents of the family court suggesting bad things will happen if the advertisers continue supporting the paper.

Bullied to Death: Chris Mackney's Kafkaesque Divorce

Pressure Example 1: Joan Kloth-Zanard

For a family court project, I received an email thread with a provocative quote by Joan Klotz-Zanard who runs a family court consulting business, is a Guardian Ad Litem, and a strong proponent of both equal or shared parenting (where time is split at 50/50 or very close to it) and PAS. In it, Zanard suggests shared parenting is best even in suspected abuse cases.

"Shared parenting would actually reduce the issue of abuse, because both parents would be more involved equally. This would provide a chance for the kids to have a safety net. It would also enable counseling much more effectively for all involved. And believe it or not, someone who physically abuses does so because this is what happened to them as a child and it is all they know." Zanard stated. "They desperately need counseling to heal. While not all abusers can be healed, such as those that are sociopathic, there are many a person who has turned this around with proper counseling and education. As for pedophiles, while this is a harder group to heal, at the very least, with shared parenting, the other parent can teach the children right from wrong and how to say no and go get help if it is physical. While I do not condone this behavior, these pedophiles are damaged from their own childhoods or warped thoughts and ideas. But without shared parenting, you have no way to protect your kids."

I confronted her on this quote; she didn't deny it but expanded and clarified it: "Shared custody would give the kids a safety zone at the other parent's (sic) house where proper role modeling and issues can be discussed. Parents who overly report abuse tend to be viewed as the aggressor and the problem even when the abuse allegations are true but unprovable. So what happens is these parents think that child protective services is going to help them and they keep filing abuse allegation after abuse allegation until finally no one will listen or they loose (sic) custody all together. After the first unsubstantiated reporting, it is best to hope (to) have a mandated reporter do it thereafter to report this abuse. It would be better for the kids to at least be able to get space from their abuser with the other parent via shared parenting. At least that parent can teach them right from wrong and who to report the abuse to."

I responded by saying, "So, in your mind then- a child molester should only see the child half the time. Am I understanding your view correctly? You are a proponent of PAS- isn't PAS the main reason that those who report on abuse don't get custody?"

We went back and forth for a while until she said I was twisting her words and was done debating me. I said that this was not simply a debate but an on the record email conversation.

From the next three days, she and several of her supporters inundated me with emails. Klotz repeatedly emailed my editor for the project, the FBI, the FCC, and even my editor at *The Daily Caller* where I sometimes publish.

Her first supporter, Roger Frez, told me he was an ex-Army Ranger, "That seems to garner a little respect young man!"

"Joan is just trying to help we all need to help each other in this terrible problem our kids face now and in the future , let's please work together and not try to destroy each other. Please help Joan do not hurt her she just wants to help kids and parents!" Frez said in his initial email.

Another friend Bryan Finkel said I was defaming Ms. Zanard.

I understand that you have made an effort to discredit Ms. Kloth-Zanard.

I want to let you know that I personally have benefited from her work in addressing alienation and related child related issues that arise in divorce.

In Connecticut the courts and their delegates do not actively monitor children in a divorce, and there are no mechanisms for enforcement of court orders related to the children. As a result, a malicious parent can use the children as pawns to harm the other parent - and this harms the children in the process.

Continuing the defamation theme, Ms. Zanard sent this email to the FCC and FBI: "Dear FCC and FBI: The email below is part of a long chain of harassing and privacy rights communications issue with a man named Michael Volpe. He contacted me under false pretenses and despite my trying to correct his false information that he was given, he is continuing to insist that he is going to defame and slander me."

The whole thing was reminiscent of an anecdote in Attkisson's book in which she investigated Firestone tires and Ford Explorer rollovers in 2000. Attkisson was about to go live with her story when CBS received a fax from the legal department at Firestone.

"I just got a fucking fax from Firestone," her producer tells her. "They're threatening to sue. They say your story is wrong and unfair."

"Shouldn't they wait and see the report before they sue?" Attkisson replied; I replied similarly.

After three days of relentless emails, phone calls, and other things I'm not aware of, the editors backed off and told Zanard they wouldn't use her quotes.

Roger Frez fired off an email, "Joke! Guess we win."

"Don't bet on it." I responded. "Even if the quotes aren't allowed to be in the profile, I intend to use them in my book and by the way everything you've said has been on the record including your last statement which I definitely intend to use as it shows just exactly who you really are."

Pressure Example 2: Ted Taupier

Keith Harmon Snow said the media in Connecticut is far more likely to be skeptical of litigants than the judiciary and that's exactly what happened to Ted Taupier.

Judge Elizabeth Bozzuto, Ted Taupier's divorce judge, comes from a prominent Connecticut family which own Bozzuto Inc., a private manufacturing company employing several thousand in that state. The family owns a series of real estate companies like the Bozzuto Group, with clients like the Blackrock Realty Advisors, Fannie Mae, Bank of America, JP Morgan Asset Management, Pritzker Realty Group, and Boston Properties.

Michael Bozzuto, the CEO of Bozzuto Inc., gave more than $10,000 since 2000 to various candidates including a donation to Bush in 2000 for $1000 and $2,500 for Romney in 2012.

Several years ago, many of the so-called Valley independent newspapers were sold to the *Hartford Courant* which also owned the local Fox broadcast affiliate and with this sale about 75-80% of the media in Connecticut.

The *Hartford Courant* is influenced in many subtle ways by the judiciary. For instance, their nonprofit arm includes two judges, Nina Elgo and Raheem Mullins.

Another influence is the nefarious Judicial/Media Committee run out of the Connecticut judiciary bringing together some of the most powerful judges and media people to do something, though no one is really sure what that is, besides the members. The agendas for their meetings are as bare as a Playboy model; each is one hundred words or less.

Nancy Schoeffler, Metro Editor for the *Hartford Courant*, along with nine judges, five lawyers, and eight other media people made up this committee the last time I checked in July 2015.

A powerful family, monopolized media, and a judiciary in bed with the media; it's all a recipe for stories slanted to favor Bozzuto and very skeptical of Taupier.

The *Middletown Press*, Taupier's city paper, spent three paragraphs in a story on his voyeurism charge defining voyeurism, trying desperately to make an insignificant story sound significant. Both his voyeurism and intimidation charges were covered by the *Hartford Courant*, the local Fox affiliate as well as the *Middletown Press*, with the *Hartford Courant* and *Middletown Press* dedicating several stories. None made an issue of his unusually high bail or ankle monitor. Worse yet, while they breathlessly covered these arrests, none of the media even called Taupier to get his side.

My *Rebel Pundit* article came out November 12, 2014 and Raquel Okyay did her *Guns and Patriots* follow-up on November 17, 2014.

Connecticut gun owner told Guns and Patriots *that his civil rights were stripped from him by an anti-gun judicial branch and a soon-to-be ex-wife who is uncomfortable with him owning guns.*

"High risk SWAT team rolls in and takes all my guns," said Edward F. Taupier the respondent in a two-year divorce action that has escalated to an all-out war. "It took two armadillo armored vehicles, 75 officers with weapons drawn, and 45 minutes to raid my house."

To top it off, within a week of the *Guns and Patriots* story, several other media, including in Connecticut picked up on Bozzuto jailing Peter Szymonik over a GAL bill. Then I did a follow-up with the most explosive charge; Judge Bozzuto had her own divorce sealed meaning she was making judgments about other people's divorces without being transparent about her own.

Still, the Connecticut media remained silent about Taupier's case until his criminal trial started up in March 2015. Taupier was big news again. The *Hartford Courant* sent David Owens to cover the trial daily for more than a week. The *Middletown Press* did a story on a motion being dismissed, giving them the opportunity to plaster Taupier's mugshot again. The trial was covered akin to a celebrity murder as opposed to a technology consultant sending an email to a group of compatriots. The Connecticut media continues to ignore the corruption occurring in his divorce.

Pressure Example 3: Nick Lulli

Nick Lulli at WFXG in Augusta, Georgia did a series of reports on the family court system which forced one powerful Judge to step down, but his success, rather than leading to greater freedom, led to a crescendo of pressure.

Lulli told me his introduction to family courts was at a rally in front of the courts building in town by aggrieved family court victims. At this rally, he met several women who complained about Doug Nelson, a magistrate judge who doubled as a GAL in family court. The complaints included: inappropriate touching, lewd text messages, and biased evaluations.

This culminated in his report which first ran on April 30, 2014.

"We're walking outside the parking lot," one woman told Lulli. "And he puts his arm around me. And he's rubbing my arm up and down. And then he puts his hand on my back. Starts rubbing my back. All the way down to my bottom. As in, my rear. And I'm like. This is no way for a guardian ad litem to be carrying himself with nobody."

"His specific comment was, 'Well, now that he's gone, you're definitely going to be needing a man in your life, and I know how to take care of that," another woman stated.

Lulli's report first ran on the 10PM evening news; Nelson resigned the next morning.

His investigation evolved organically, eventually focusing on a divorce involving Dr. Jeff Donohoe, a doctor suspected of setting fire to his marital home, granted sole custody of his children over the objection of his ex-wife and two court appointed guardians. The case later escalated when the judge, Daniel Craig, admitted in a court order to secret communications with Dr. Donohoe's attorney to suspend the mom's visitation rights and send the kids out of state.

"The judge never even gave a reason why the mom shouldn't get custody." Lulli told me.

After a series of increasingly hard hitting reports, Lulli was shut down. After he sat in on a custody hearing involving an evaluation done earlier by Nelson, he discovered an alcoholic received sole custody.

"This whole story has very little with Judge Nelson." His boss told him. "I think you get way too deep in the weeds. **Under normal circumstances we don't do custody cases. (Emphasis mine)**"

That editor speaks for most.

The resistance was just beginning. When Lulli focused his reporting on a GAL named Janet Weinberger that was shut down when her family, which owned a furniture company, gave the station a good deal.

We're way ahead on this story and we're working with the furniture company on an important deal for the station.

When you run that story we will burn the bridge with the furniture company. So I'd really like to be "across the river" before the story runs - unless we will be put at a competitive disadvantage in news by waiting. You're so far ahead right now, I think you can actually have a line of several stories ready to go and the competition will be even further behind us if we can wait a little.

This pressure we know about because Lulli saved these emails and shared them with me. If Chris Mackney's story was shut down for similar reasons, we'll never know because I wasn't privy to those discussions. All I heard was, "I did my best, but my managers have declined your story entirely."

Lulli has since moved on to WNEM in Saginaw, Michigan.

Playing it Safe

With pressure coming from all sides, the media plays it safe.

"Playing it safe can mean shying away from stories that include allegations against certain corporations, charities and other chosen powerful entities and people. The image of media as fearless watchdogs poised, if not eager, to pursue stories that authorities wish to block is often a false image. Decisions are routinely made in fear of the response that the story might provoke." Attkisson said in *Stonewalled*. "'The propagandists' heavy handed tactics have worked: they don't even have to pick up the phone and complain- news managers demonstrate a Pavlovian-style avoidance response when presented with a story they fear will bring a negative reaction. We're weak and diffident when we needn't be."

Think back to Ted Taupier. Judge Bozzutto, Chris Morano, and the prosecutors are all part of the power structure in Connecticut which the media would rather not challenge. None of the media in Connecticut has covered his divorce, and Attkisson said the media is only "airing stories which certain other trusted media have reported first, so there's no perceived 'risk' to us if we report them, too."

The same dynamic was in place in Neil Shelton's case. He's taking on a powerful politician, Sarah Stevens, and two police departments- The Mount Airy Police Department and the Surry County Police Department- along with the criminal and family court systems. He's already been branded a suspected criminal and erratic by the media. No wonder no television station or newspaper in his area has done a story on the abuse in his custody case. You'd be asking them to stand up for one discredited individual against the entire system. Since no one in the area has covered that part of his story no one else sees any reason to be the first.

By that token Chris Mackney never had a chance. Pete Scamardo is the prominent builder featured repeatedly in *The Washington Post*. Samenow is the prominent forensic psychiatrist who's been all over television, radio, and newspapers offering expertise. Not only had none of the established "trusted media sources" covered his story but they'd portrayed the villains as heroes.

This dynamic is the antithesis of the tradition of investigative journalists. Muckraker Jacob Riis took his camera into the slums of New York to present an unvarnished look at the way the poor there lived. His project *How the Other Half Lived* became a trendsetter because he dared to do go where no one else would.

(Several of the photos Riis snapped for *How the Other Half Lived*)

Riis wasn't the only one. Samuel Hopkins Adams was the first to expose mass corruption in patent medicine with *The Great American Fraud*, and Lincoln Steffens was the first to nationalize municipal corruption with *Shame of the Cities*. The muckraker era thrived and encouraged investigative journalists to seek out stories which took on powerful interests and tackled topics no one else tackled.

Imagine some editor saying to Riis, "This is compelling but I don't see the *Associated Press* has covered this yet, so let's wait until they do a story and then we'll run your piece."

No more, now news editors play it safe, taking their cues from other news media. Lou Jasikoff said news people call him routinely asking that *The Independent* break a family court related story because that media would like to do a follow-up but is unwilling to go first. Much like the national media takes its cues from the *Associated Press* and *The New York Times,* on family court the media takes it cues from him.

Astroturfing and Gas-lighting

Another topic in Attkisson's book apt for family courts is astroturfing.

The whole point of astroturf is to give the impression there's widespread support for an agenda when there isn't. Businesses may fund fake "consumer campaigns" against competitors. Government may call on its corporate partners to use astroturf methods to discredit reporters who threaten their mutual interests. You will no doubt see astroturf techniques used to attack the opinions and themes of this book for obvious reasons.

Once you begin to know what to look for, you can detect astroturf everywhere. Hallmarks include the use of inflammatory language such as "crank," "paranoid," "quack," "nutty," "lies," "truther," "conspiracy theorist," "shoddy," "witch hunt," and "pseudo" in targeting the political industrial complex's enemies. Astroturfers often claim to "debunk myths" that aren't myths at all. Another astroturf technique is to simply shove so much confusing and conflicting information in the mix, the public is left to throw up its hands and disregard all of it- including the truth.

Bullied to Death: Chris Mackney's Kafkaesque Divorce

Astroturfing is a sophisticated form of gas-lighting; the goal is to create the perception that an article is controversial when it really isn't or there is widespread opposition when there really isn't. In other words, an astroturf campaign challenges your sense of reality and sanity: "is this article I read as good as I think or are all these blogs calling it 'paranoid' right?"

Laviidafam, Balins, and Joanne Ver Ploeg were all engaged in a rudimentary form of astroturfing. With Mackney's story going viral, they tried to convince readers the bullying victim was really a mentally unstable bully.

There was a small astroturf campaign against Wendy Titelman's book. On Amazon, it currently has twenty six reviews, including mine, which I wrote in response to the campaign. Of the twenty six reviews, thirteen reviewers gave it one star. This is unusual because those who hate the book are much less likely to let their feelings known than to simply stop reading midway. One of the reviewers claimed to be one of Titelman's daughters: "this book is full of lies!!!!! She used to be my mom and she made me tell lies 2. but no more!!!!!!!!!! she will always tell lies but i will always tell the truth and that is that it never happened.... only in side her head@!!!!!!!"

"As a person actively involved in psychology, it is most evident to me that this lady is not telling the complete truth. She is dangerous because she very effectively cons those that cannot think independently. Very subversive, very dangerous lady. I believe an adequate psychological profile of this lady would be falsely theatrical, self-absorbed and abnormal lack of remorse. A professional would find this lady mentally ill, a histrionic, paranoid personality," said another commenter using the astroturfing term "paranoid."

A third commenter claimed they once worked with Titelman: "I used to work with her in a dentist's office (remember, Wendy?) and she is a dangerous, pathological liar. She is a desperate, egocentric, lying sick-o, who has affairs with married men and only operates in a 'what's in it for me' world. Enough said."

Others claimed that her story was unbelievable because it's impossible for an entire county family court system to ignore and cover-up overwhelming evidence of child molestation: "Just too hard to believe that an entire town/county could be so biased against one person. There are many things she isn't telling us. I too wonder why she moved from her children's home state. (I wouldn't even give it one star but there was nothing lower)"

(Tell that to Chris Mackney)

The same person appeared to write essentially the same review as the pseudonym A Customer wrote four reviews all claiming it's impossible to believe an entire city and county could be against one person.

Successful gas-lighting is maddening and it was a maddening feeling which gave me the overwhelming urge to leave this review of Ms. Titelman's book.

While there's no doubt that Ms. Titelman will not be confused with Oscar Wilde any time soon, and the book could have used a professional editor, I found many if not all of the negative reviews to fit into one of two categories, 1) they are a form of gas-lighting and largely an attempt by anonymous people to try and undermine her credibility. This is ironic since she documented this very tactic in her book. 2) They are done by people who have little or no understanding of the mass of corruption in family courts, Child Protective Services, and in Georgia. Several years after this book was published Nancy Schaefer documented the very top to bottom corruption in Georgia's Child Protective Services in her landmark white paper entitled, The Corrupt Business of CPS, which was documented in this book. Ms. Schaefer, like others who attempted to expose corruption in Georgia, died in a mysterious way.

I am working on a book about family court corruption as well and I have to agree with the review of Sol Gothard (a judge who wrote a blurb for Titelman's book) who said that whether you believe her or not, the things revealed in this book occur in family courtrooms around the country routinely.

If this book does well enough I expect an astroturf campaign on sites where the book is rated and talked about.

The Media Today

Because of the internet and other technologies, the media landscape is changing rapidly and segmented. There is the mainstream media (MSM), including most urban newspapers, broadcast news stations (the news divisions of CBS, NBC, and ABC), as well as CNN and MSNBC. This group is not likely to do any serious investigating of family court abuse because they perceive these stories as he said/she said and the stories don't advance their ideology.

Conservatives have talk radio, led by Rush Limbaugh. Talk radio likes stories which the MSM doesn't cover, but that's not likely to help with family court. They like stories with an underlying theme that liberals are bad and family court abuse doesn't fit that paradigm.

The internet includes both liberal and conservative sites and neither is likely to do much on family court abuse because they take their cues from their more powerful media leaders - the MSM and Fox News Channel- and those media sources don't cover family court.

Family court abuse winds up on specialty sites, like law blogs, mental health sites, etc. The right internet word search uncovers a plethora of stories on a number of themes. Try *battered women losing custody* or *false allegations child custody* as two examples.

Today, the most powerful name in news is Fox News Channel (FNC). Loathed by most liberals and loved by most conservatives, FNC bills itself as fair and balanced. Its power starts with its primetime lineup of Bill O'Reilly followed by Megyn Kelly. Both have covered family court abuse on the margins. O'Reilly has done many stories on corrupt judges, especially in cases of child abuse, but rarely if ever about an incompetent or corrupt family court judges, even judges who give custody to a child abuser. He also occasionally does a story on child support scofflaws but rarely if ever does stories about unreasonable child support payments or other aspects of family court.

O'Reilly's divorce became the subject of media attention when in May 2015 the website, Gawker, broke news that O'Reilly's ex-wife accused him of domestic violence. In a follow-up article, Gawker suggested O'Reilly choked her in front of their daughter. The story was not picked up many other news sources, died quickly, and his ratings were not affected.

Megyn Kelly, who has been on in primetime since October 7, 2013, has quickly become a ratings juggernaut. She did a series of stories on Justina Pelletier. Though this case involved family court abuse, it wasn't during a divorce.

Mike Huckabee, on his weekend show, picked up the Pelletier family story and expanded into an examination of the Child and Protective Services department in Massachusetts. Huckabee has since left FNC to run for President in 2016.

Family Court and Celebrity

Ms. Kelly also interviewed the actor Jason Patric about his divorce and custody battle. On his website, Patric explains his story.

Almost four years ago, I was blessed with a baby boy named Gus. For the first 3 years of his childhood I was a consistent physical and emotional presence in his life. My world was better in every way with Gus in it...I loved being a father.

But that all changed in an instant. I was stripped of my rights as a parent. An outdated statute meant for sperm donors was applied to me simply because Gus' mother and I were unmarried and used IVF to conceive.

Not being able to see my son for almost a year has been the worst pain that I can imagine. Except, when I think about little Gus, who has no idea what happened to his dada...one day his dada was there and the next he was gone.

The family court system is broken and in my journey I have learned of so many other stories where children have lost their parents. I want to use my story and my name to give a voice to those who do not have one.

Kelly Rutherford's divorce has received enormous media attention. Rutherford, star of shows like *Melrose Place* and *Gossip Girl* divorced European businessman David Giersch in 2006. In 2012, Giersch's Visa was revoked and he was forced to stay in Europe. (Though it's never been clear why his Visa was revoked some Father's Rights groups claimed Rutherford was responsible in an effort to alienate him from their kids) Rutherford then asked a California judge for sole custody. Instead the judge gave Giersch physical custody, arguing Rutherford could visit them in Europe while Giersch couldn't see them in the USA. Her two children were forced to move to Europe and are currently living in Monaco with their father. Rutherford filed for bankruptcy in the summer of 2013, primarily due to legal bills incurred from the custody fight, ironic since one of the arguments made by the judge was that she could afford this as an actress. Ms. Rutherford won a major legal battle after noted family law attorney Wendy Murphy took her case pro bono when a California judge granted her temporary custody in May 2015. While that is a victory for Rutherford, the case continues to unfold without end as this book is published.

David Levy, the founder of the Children's Rights Council (CRC), consulted with Mackney over the last six months of Mackney's life. He said when the media covers the family court system usually there is a celebrity involved. He singled out the custody of David Bremner as an example. The custody case of singer Bob Geldoff, in the 1980s, also received a great deal of media attention. Levy died on December 11, 2014, while this book was still being developed.

Some Hope

All is not lost. The documentary, *Divorce Corp*, came out in January 2014, narrated by Dr. Drew Pinskey. The documentary tracked the money within corrupts family courts. It's available on DVD and other formats; it is the subject of much debate among family court reformers.

Anne Stevenson writes a regular column on family court abuse and other issues for *Communities Digital Network* and *The Huffington Post* which has a section dedicated to family court issues.

Raquel Okyay also does a lot of work on family courts, including a series with me on Susan Carrington's custody nightmare for the *Rockland County Times*.

The Scranton Wilkes-Barre Independent is the top print newspaper on family courts abuse however that newspaper is currently mostly focusing on the Scranton Wilkes Barre area.

Paul Nichols of the Bergen County (New Jersey) Dispatch and Nick Lulli have both distinguished themselves for local coverage of family court issues. Nichols' attempt to interview Surender Malhan, a family court litigant who was stopped from seeing his daughter for more than a year was initially blocked by a Superior Court judge. That turned into a well-known legal battle won by Nichols; one I'll expand on later.

I've had family court related stories published on *WND*, *Crime Magazine*, *Rebel Pundit*, *Communities Digital News*, and the Capital Research Center.

Chapter 12: Would a Guardian Ad Litem Have Saved Chris Mackney?

"The nine most terrifying words in the English language are 'I'm from the government and I'm here to help." Ronald Reagan

Chris Mackney Begs for a GAL

The last year of his life Chris Mackney begged for the appointment of a guardian ad litem for his children; here's part of one blog post.

My ex-wife and her father have spent well over $1 million in legal fees. I currently owe my ex-wife over $200,000 in legal fees and my children over $125,000 in back child support. The Court has ignored every one of my fair and reasonable solutions to keep everyone out of Court... I have literally begged the Judges in the case to bring in a Guardian Ad Litem to protect the children in a 'high-conflict' family matter that involves severe emotional abuse, parental *alienation and psychopathy. 6 times, the Fairfax County Circuit Court has prevented my children from obtaining an attorney to protect their rights, while the mother is spending 4 TIMES the amount in legal fees than I will ever owe my children. Conflict of interest, anyone?*

...

The Fairfax County Circuit Court has prevented my case from reaching the Juvenile and Domestic Relations Court, where Guardian Ad Litems are appointed frequently to identify the source of conflict, at a reduced rate, which is shared by both parties.

Several friends and colleagues counseled Mackney that a GAL was not the magic bullet he thought, including Jill Peterson Mitchell.

I repeatedly told Chris that his vision of a GAL being the solution to his problem was not realistic; based on everything else I saw going on in his case and based on my own experience with a GAL in Michigan. This message was never received by him and he never debated me. He was extremely invested in the GAL being the solution that nothing I could say would change his view.

He believed that a court appointed GAL would act ethically and would bring some balance to the imbalance that existed in his divorce at the hands of the judge and Dina's lawyer. He was devastated that he was repeatedly being denied justice, a situation that was materially significant in speeding up the pace of his demoralization and mental decline that occurs in all victims of chronic abuse.

David Levy also counseled Mackney against the appointment of a GAL.

"A GAL is just another third party. You don't know what their motives or biases are." David Levy said. When a third party becomes a derogatory term there are real problems.

Are GALs Independent?

Here again is the definition of a GAL according to the website *Legal Dictionary*. "A guardian ad litem is a unique type of guardian in a relationship that has been created by a court order only for the duration of a legal action. Courts appoint these special representatives for infants, minors, and mentally incompetent persons, all of whom generally need help protecting their rights in court. Such court-appointed guardians figure in divorces, child neglect and abuse cases, paternity suits, contested inheritances, and so forth, and are usually attorneys."

Because a GAL is supposed to protect the rights of the minors in court, it's easy to see how Mackney might think they'd be acting as an INDEPENDENT third party and in the best interest of the child. It's easy to see how Chris Mackney became convinced this was the magic bullet however for the most part GALs are no more independent than Dr. Samenow, just pretending to be.

GALs were created by family courts in the early 1970s. Courts claim GALs are necessary to help navigate especially sticky situations, like allegations of abuse, but in reality, because judges didn't want the responsibility of having to make decisions in especially tough cases they brought in so-called experts to make recommendations which they would rubber stamp. If something went wrong, the judges pawned the decision on the expert.

GALs and Suicides

My Advocate Center, a child advocacy group out of Atlanta led by Deb Beachem, published Mackney's suicide note but pointed out appointing a GAL was foolish.

Where this father was wrong – besides not getting hanging on a while longer to see if help could be found – was that he believed a Guardian ad litem would equate to having help, to having the truth matter. Read below.

Georgia Obituaries:

There are three fathers in Georgia who have also committed suicide for the same exact reasons. Two of the three had the same custody "expert" on their case making decisions that were not based on the evidence and facts of the case. Dr. Elizabeth "Betty" King.

Gregg Eisenhauer of Alpharetta, Georgia died December 4, 2008.

He took his life shortly after Judge Lane in Fulton County rubber stamped the recommendations of GAL Susan Hurst and Dr. King. This is the same attorney Susan Hurst who said to Judge Goger that child pornography should not be taken into consideration in a case involving substantiated claims of child molestation. Hurst helped to suppress this evidence that should have been used to protect a child and a good mother.

GALs are Nebulous and Confusing and that's the Problem

While most GALs are lawyers by trade, a wide variety of professions are allowed to become GALs including social workers, psychiatrists, therapists, etc. That's because the function of a GAL is nebulous and by extension so are the qualifications. Unlike a custody evaluator or even a psychological evaluator which are at least supposed to have certain qualifications, anyone can be qualified to "protect the rights of minors in court" because that is a broad and difficult to define responsibility.

Worse yet, when a GAL is asked to perform a function they're not qualified for, like if the GAL is a lawyer but a psychological evaluation is ordered, the GAL appoints another professional at the litigants' expense.

Stuart Greenberg: The Worst Court Professional of All Time.

For more than two decades Stuart Greenberg was involved in about 2,000 custody cases serving several functions in the State of Washington. Greenberg killed himself in 2012 as investigations into his career were unfolding. His career was investigated by several local media including this Kafkaesque story in the *Seattle Times*.

In summer 1984, Cathy Graden, a 27-year-old surgical nurse from Woodinville, was summoned to King County Superior Court for an emergency hearing in her child-custody case.

Her lawyer said a psychologist's report was behind the hearing. But Graden wasn't allowed to read the report. Nor was she allowed in the courtroom while the psychologist testified.

The psychologist, Stuart Greenberg, had been hired to help resolve a custody dispute involving Graden's only child, a 4-year-old boy who's bright, goopy finger-paintings Graden taped up all over the house.

...

The report Greenberg filed in court eviscerated Graden. It said she posed a grave danger to her son; that she was "probably" sexually abusing him; that she was psychologically unstable and possibly paranoid. Greenberg's report said he had interviewed the boy's day-care provider — and this provider suspected Graden of abuse and said Graden had encouraged daycare employees to beat her son.

In court, testifying, Greenberg described Graden as "quasi-psychotic," but said the diagnosis was tricky, because Graden might appear "quite normal." She would likely deny doing anything wrong to her son, Greenberg said, or alternatively, she "might genuinely not remember."

By the time Greenberg finished, Graden, out in the hallway, had been stripped of all defenses — and without a clue to what had just happened. If she appeared normal — well, Greenberg said she would. If she denied hurting her son — that was part of her disorder. If she challenged Greenberg's work or motives — she was paranoid.

At the end of the hearing, Judge Donald Haley said: "The doctor has convinced the court." The judge ordered the boy turned immediately over to his father, with Graden allowed to visit only if supervised by a therapist.

Greenberg's Prodigy: Laurie Olsen Gaines

Andrea Chen is from Seattle, Washington, and her and her kids were the victims of physical, sexual, and mental abuse during her marriage.

In the summer of 2010, Laurie Olson Gaines was appointed the GAL for her two kids because allegations of abuse automatically triggered the need for a GAL in that area. Olson has a Masters in Social Work, but is not licensed in therapy, psychology, or psychiatry and as a result she has to farm out all therapy sessions which inevitably occur in conjunction with her court duties.

Until he was removed from his position of power Gaines referred all therapy sessions to Stuart Greenberg, Chen said. Chen also said Gaines told her in 2011 that "Stuart Greenberg did excellent court evaluations," and "he died under tragic circumstances."

Chen said the reason Gaines thought Greenberg did good evaluations was because he delivered the evaluation Gaines wanted.

In December 2011, Gaines recommended for Andrea Chen to take custody of their seventeen year old daughter while her husband took custody of their fourteen year old son.

Chen said her daughter complained that whenever she visited her father when her brother was also there the two of them ganged up on her and verbally abused her.

When Andrea Chen couldn't force her daughter to go to her father's place for the regular visits, Gaines scolded her and demanded Chen apply more discipline and force her daughter to go on the visits.

When Chen was unable to force her daughter to visit her father, Olson made that the basis to recommend all of Chen's custody be removed.

GAL Corruption is everywhere

Example 1: Custody for Cash

For years Danielle Ross was the primary GAL for Lackawanna County, Pennsylvania and for years Ross took bribes to fix cases. Like Al Capone, the government didn't convict Ross for taking bribes or fixing cases but rather for failing to pay taxes on the bribes; she was sentenced to one year in prison in April 2014. While Ross was the only one to go to jail, the *Wilkes-Barre Scranton Independent-Gazette* found systemic problems. On March 8, 2014, *The Independent Gazette* published a video on You Tube of a distraught mother who implicated another GAL from Lackawanna County, Brenda Kobal.

"My children and I left their father in 2003. In 2007, I tried to file an emergency relief hearing on behalf of myself and the children against their father. The following morning I come to find out the Guardian ad Litem filed an emergency relief hearing on behalf of the father and the children against myself. Temporary custody had been transferred and since then I have been paying a supervisor to see my children once a week for three hours or whatever I can afford." The distraught woman said. "My entire family insisted that he could never take my children away from me because I never did anything harmful to my children and then in August of 2007 when they were gone they finally realized it was all about money and power. I can't afford anything; the Guardian ad Litem was charging me $250 and hour. Supervision cost me $200 an hour so they told me to get more jobs if I wanted to see my children more often. The father is much wealthier and he has a little more power in Lackawanna County. And he said I told my children to tell a lie; that's never happened I never told my children to tell a lie. The Guardian ad Litem no matter what I do following her recommendations writes up reports that are just insane."

The woman said the GAL, a lawyer by trade, farmed out a custody evaluation for $3,000 and the custody evaluator "stated that I have a personality disorder that is worse than men who are serving life sentences for some malicious crimes and that I cannot be helped."

"I think I just love my children and I want them to come home," the woman responded breaking down when asked if she thought she had a psychological disorder. Later in the interview, she stated she'd never been arrested or accused of any wrongdoing.

Ms. Kobal tried unsuccessfully to have this video removed from YouTube.

Example 2: Gorcyca Case

William Lansat is the GAL in the Tsimhoni case, where Judge Gorcyca sent three kids to juvenile hall for refusing to see their dad, and he compared the kids to Charles Manson in a report: "The children would not answer any adult; they huddled together as if they were sending messages/vibes to each other in some sort of Manson-like behavior."

"At today's hearing Gorcyca and the children's court-appointed guardian, William Lansat, blasted Eibschitz-Tsimhoni, for alienating the children from their father. Lansat asked Gorcyca to send the kids to the camp," a *Detroit Free Press* story stated.

"You have to give her credit," Lansat told the court in a July 2015 hearing. "Whatever she did, she has been successful. She's been on a campaign and she had damaged the children."

In another case, a litigant accused him of running a racket targeting young boys: "My son's 'lawyer' William Lansat-who apparently has a nice little gig, involving kids like my son suggested a partial psychological evaluation of my son and me-if I would pay," a self-proclaimed protective parent wrote on the website, Ripoff Report.

Example 3: Susan Skipp

In Susan Skipp's case, her problems started after the divorce was supposed to be settled. After Skipp went to court because her ex-husband wasn't paying his child support payments on time, her GAL, Mary Brigham, put in her own appearance, inviting herself to a proceeding the court hadn't invited her to. Brigham then proceeded to file more than thirty motions, almost all adversarial to Skipp: paving the way for the removal of Skipp's custodial rights. When Skipp ran out of money, Brigham filed another motion forcing her to clean out her pension to pay her bill or face jail time.

When I initially confronted Brigham about this she replied, "I suggest you check your facts before you print anything," but has never denied or explained the charge.

She has declined to offer any substantive explanation for her behavior.

Example 4: Jeannie Melton

When Jodene Berry was appointed a GAL for Jeannie Melton, after the court deemed her mentally unstable, Berry promptly forced Melton to sell her home and buy one in a neighboring county, Allegheny County in Pennsylvania.

Months after that, Melton was arrested in Allegheny County, where her ex-husband lived and worked, for his attempted murder. Berry then attempted to testify at Melton's trial for the prosecution before the judge shut that down arguing since she was Melton's GAL she was supposed to be protecting her interests not testifying against her.

Example 5: GALs in Atlanta

Here's part of a local CBS investigation in Atlanta.

In Georgia, guardians ad litem are attorneys appointed by judges to determine the best interest of children during contested custody cases, but some parents, attorneys and child development experts question the guardians' expertise and objectivity.

"The mental anguish for my children and me has been huge," said Gracie Ortiz Terrett.

She had asked for a guardian ad litem after a judge limited her custody of her 8- and 10-year-old children to one day a week and every other weekend. But Terret said guardians ad litem Raina Nadler and Jeanney Kutner were far from objective.

In court documents, Terrett's attorney alleged the women improperly communicated with the judge, dictated changes in Terret's custody, yelled and shouted at and tried to influence Terret's witnesses.

Attorney Lisa West said Nadler and Kutner also refused to accept evidence from her for 90 days while the duo continued to work with Terret's husband and his attorney.

"Guardians ad litem simply cannot do that," said West.

Alex Higdon, a former Atlanta Falcon, has sued the guardian in his case.

Higdon said Dawn Smith wasn't objective and recommended educational and custody changes after only speaking with his ex-wife and her attorneys.

Example 6: Wendy Titelman

The 1992 comedy My Cousin Vinny had the famous voir dire scene, where Vincent Gambini (played by Joe Pesci) calls his fiancé Monalisa Vito (played Marisa Tomei) to the witness stand to act as an expert in tire marks. The District Attorney James Trotter objects, suggesting she has no expertise in tire marks, asking her a series of questions testing her expertise, a "voir dire" of the witness, asking her an esoteric trick question, but Ms. Vito didn't fall for the trick.

"She's acceptable," Trotter finally stated, allowing her opinion as testimony. The movie and the scene especially, have been cited by lawyers for accuracy and attention to detail.

In criminal trials expertise is earned; in family court, expertise is granted with a title.

In Wendy Titelman's case, the GAL Diane Woods is a family law attorney but made determinations about the veracity of the child molestation allegations, using her position as GAL to insinuate herself into the process.

Woods had both parents take a polygraph tests. Polygraph tests are NOT allowed to be entered into evidence in any criminal trial because they are notoriously inaccurate and prejudicial. In the case of child molestation, it's even more unreliable. University of Michigan researcher Dr. Kathleen Faller made this conclusion in a 1997 study of the test in child abuse cases.

In examining 42 child sexual abuse cases in which the accused perpetrator underwent a polygraph test during the course of investigation, Faller found that lie-detector results are unrelated to other signs of sexual abuse, such as the child's statements or demonstrations of abuse, medical evidence, psychological symptoms or indicators of sexual abuse from sources other than the child.

In other words, additional evidence supporting sexual abuse existed in these cases, regardless of whether an alleged offender passed or failed a polygraph test.

Woods not only used the results of the polygraph test in her determination, but as part of her reports and testimony which were entered into evidence.

Woods was buoyed by the reports of Dr. Elizabeth King, implicated in the aforementioned suicide of Greg Eisenhauer, who also determined that Wendy Titelman had been coaching the children. Dr. King is a clinical psychologist with dubious qualifications in determining child molestation allegations.

Wendy Titelman had a number of experts either speak to her daughters or examine the reports of Dr. King and others but were all dismissed with King and Woods arguing that they were "hired guns" and not independent like the two of them, something they were not.

Both were friends and colleagues in family court matters like the Titelman divorce. Meanwhile, Dr. King admitted to being a believer in PAS.

"Dr. King was asked about her experience as an expert in child sexual abuse." Titelman said in her book, recounting a court hearing when Dr. King testified. "She admitted to having read most of Richard Gardner's books and using 'Parental Alienation Syndrome.'"

If this was a political debate, we'd call her an ideologue. Would it be fair to allow Sean Hannity to act as an independent expert to determine the worth of the presidency of Barack Obama? How about if Rachel Maddow was to do the same for the presidency of George W. Bush? No one would think such an examination of either president was fair and balanced. Yet, in family court, it's perfectly acceptable for someone who favors an ideology that is decidedly pro-father to walk into court and claim they are independent.

Corrupt GALs in Guardianship

GALs don't merely corrupt family court but probate court as well. Guardianship, which is decided in probate courts, is for someone deemed not mentally capable of making decisions on their own. In 2013, seventy-nine year old Korean and Vietnam War veteran Norman Hughes, Jr. had saved up over $150,000 and lived in Memphis. Having some memory trouble Hughes, Jr. began living in the home of caretaker Debra McCoy in one of her five bedrooms paying $2,700 per month. When Hughes got into a dispute with his cousin, Mary Ann Philips, over money he removed her as a co-account holder on his main bank account. Philips proceeded to trick Norman into seeing a doctor who ran a battery of tests to see if he was of sound mind at the local VA Hospital. When that doctor's tests suggested Hughes, Jr. wasn't mentally competent, the case was maneuvered into guardianship court and a GAL, James Bingham, was appointed. Bingham, a divorce lawyer, made a medical determination.

"Even in my limited interactions with Hughes it is clear he cannot take care of himself," Bingham said. "He cannot name the medication he takes, much less arrange by himself to take them as prescribed."

Bingham took testimony from Dr. Whitney Shroyer, without identifying Dr. Shroyer as a resident, not a doctor, and not qualified to give opinion on someone's mental capacity. Worst of all, Bingham put hearsay evidence from Dr. Shroyer in his report. "I also spoke with Dr. Whitney Shroyer," Bingham said in the report, recalling a meeting he had with her on July 22, 2013. "She does state that Mr. Hughes memory has gotten worse and she did not think him capable of making medical and financial decisions."

Dr. Shroyer never testified; instead Bingham's recollections of their purported conversation were entered as fact: hearsay anywhere else but critical evidence to force a man into guardianship in this court.

Once in guardianship, Hughes, Jr. was moved from McCoy's home against his wishes into a nursing home and charged $7,200 per month for a room where he was one of the few African-Americans. Bingham charged $250 an hour and he and the other court professionals drained Hughes' $150,000 and turned it into less than $80,000 by August 2014, ironic since individuals go into guardianship supposedly because they are no longer of sound enough mind to handle their own money.

"I need somebody to help me get out of here," a desperate Hughes, Jr. told me from his nursing home for my story in *The Daily Caller*.

Probate courts, like family courts, are governed by their own Orwellian rule: "the best interest of the ward."

In this case, Norman Hughes, Jr. was forced to live where he didn't want to live, paying nearly three times as much, and have his bank account get cut in half for his own best interest; Orwell would be proud.

Seventy-one year old Mildred Willis was forced into guardianship after being diagnosed with everything from dementia, massive depression, congestive heart failure, and renal failure. Willis should have been dead within six months with that diagnosis but was still alive four years later. Here's part of my story for *Rebel Pundit*.

Every lawyer associated with this case has been allowed to charge $250 per hour for their services. This includes the Guardian ad Litem (GAL), Kyra Payne.

…

In repeated court filings, the GAL has stipulated that Mildred Willis should remain a ward of the state and she's been buoyed by the 2010 medical report of Dr. Emerito Natanawan. In that report Dr. Natanawan found a laundry list of physical and mental issues with Mildred Willis which would normally suggest she was near death.

Though Ms. Willis being alive proved the diagnoses were bogus, Payne continued to use them as justification to keep her in guardianship against her will; this from someone appointed to act in Ms. Willis' best interests.

Elaine Renoire is President of the National Association to Stop Guardianship Abuse (NASGA), an organization which fights for guardianship reform.

A popular misconception of guardianship/conservatorship victims and their families is that the court-appointed Guardian ad Litem is an advocate or lawyer for their loved one.

The reality is quite the opposite. The GAL is an official arm of the court with the responsibility of fact finding and reporting information to the judge - not advocating for the alleged incapacitated person ("AIP") or the ward. If a nursing home is the GAL's recommendation even though family is ready, willing and able to take care of their loved one at home, the judge will usually follow the GAL's recommendation rather than the wishes of the ward or family or even the ward's best interest.

Samenow, Mackney and GALs

Corrupt GALs and Samenow share numerous similarities. GALs, like Samenow, routinely come in pretending to be an independent third party while working on behalf of one side at the expense of the other. GALs, like Samenow, overstep their original mandate and many of them provide expert testimony without having the proper expertise. As Bingham mischaracterized Dr. Shroyer's professional credentials in a report which amounted to hearsay, Samenow mischaracterized the relationship between Mackney and friends Rich Ware and Mike Harris in a report which was also mostly hearsay.

As an advocate for children or incapacitated adults GALs have a broader mandate than evaluators, allowing them to do far more damage. As a lawyer and GAL, Mary Brigham could not only put in her appearance but file motion after motion, whereas Samenow, a psychiatrist, could only produce a report and testify when called. Berry could force Jeannie Melton to buy a house, something corrupt evaluators only dream they'd be allowed to do.

Rather than being the answer, Chris Mackney was advocating for a far more dangerous court professional.

GALs and the Alphabet Soup of Court Professionals

Mackney thought the problem was he got Samenow while needing a GAL when the problem is they're all the same: they have broad and poorly defined powers, they come into complicated situations only making them even more complicated, and they have no oversight.

When GALs were first dreamed up in the 1970s the proliferation of court professionals- custody evaluator, psychological evaluator, parental coordinator, etc. - hadn't happened yet. In other words, a GAL was supposed to be the answer not one of the answers.

In Hughes, Jr. case, the GAL was one of a group of court professionals including a VA guardian and a conservator: three bureaucrats which all do basically the same thing.

Ironically, Mackney suggested a laundry list of court professional who he thought could help get him out of this Kafkaesque nightmare.

"If the Court had ordered into the case a Guardian Ad Litem, Special Advocate, Parenting Coordinator, parenting plan, family counselor, or psychological evaluator for my ex-wife, I might (not) find this all a neverending, Kafkaesque nightmare, but the Court has chosen none of these options to reduce or understand the 'conflict'," Mackney said in a blog post.

He didn't understand the con; all these professionals are largely the same with different titles. The first one screws up, another one claims the mess is the reason they need to get involved. They claim to be cleaning up the mess, all the while making it even worse, creating justification for another professional. It's one reason why Sunny Kelley's case had a dozen court professionals, including the GAL Maureen Murphy, who Sunny told me, spent most of her time making sure Sunny was kept in check, using her position to justify taking away decisions normally reserved for the mother.

During testimony describing her son's molestation, Murphy, sitting with her wife, made noises which Sunny told me were akin to the famous scene in the diner when Meg Ryan simulates an orgasm in *When Harry Met Sally*.

The Case for the Abolition of GALs

Richard Ducotte, who represented Titleman for several years though long after the conspiracy had been set in motion, published the article *106 Guardian Ad Litems in Private Custody Litigation: The Case for Abolition*.

The flawed rationale for appointing these GALs in custody cases is that all parents, who are presumed competent to raise their children and beyond the state's heavy hand prior to the commencement of the divorce case, are somehow automatically transformed into mere combatants inherently blind to their children's needs, and whose offspring now need the wisdom and control of some typically young lawyer, needing the fee, to avoid falling into the vortex of the litigation.

...

Guardians ad litem must be abolished in private custody cases for well- established reasons: the role is not subject to definition in any way consistent with appropriate judicial proceedings; 2) there is no documented benefit from their use; 3) they undermine and compromise fact finding by usurping the role of the judge and depriving parents of due process; 4) they undermine parental authority and privacy; 5) the costs and fees resulting from their use ultimately deprives parents and children of resources that would actually benefit the child; 6) in child abuse and domestic violence cases, they routinely advocate against the child's safety and protection and directly contravene the child's interests; and, 7) they are unaccountable for their actions.

Dangling the GAL in Chris Mackney's face: the Machiavellian Torture

If GALs are so corrupt, why didn't the other side acquiesce and allow one? Dina Mackney won her divorce. In sports, teams don't give their opponents an extra quarter, period, or inning, after they won in regulation. There was no reason for Dina Mackney to acquiesce. Sure, most GALs are corrupt and if a GAL confirmed the opinion of Samenow and others it would simply be another nail in Chris Mackney's proverbial coffin, but the coffin was already shut.

Besides, the other side used the specter of agreement to their Machiavellian advantage. Here's Kyle Bartol from July 2013 again: "Assuming that there was an Order appointing a Guardian ad litem and modifying the child support, before drafting such an Order I would need to know the names of people who you would propose to be appointed as the Guardian ad litem, as well as what amount of child support that you would agree that you are able to pay. If you give me this information and I draft an order, I would also need to know that if Ms. Mackney agrees to such an order, will these emails and complaints stop?"

Three days later a SWAT team arrested Mackney.

Mackney sent Bartol an email on November 4, 2013, in which he referenced this earlier email while asking again to appoint a GAL.

In the email below, sent three days before you knew I would be arrested in Dallas and extradited back to Virginia, you seem to indicate that your client would be willing to appoint a Guardian Ad Litem.

It would save my friends and your client thousands of dollars in unnecessary legal fees to simply agree to appoint a Guardian Ad Litem. A Guardian Ad Litem will also be able to determine (and prove to all the Members of the Fairfax Law Foundation, the Virginia Bar Association, and the Virginia State Bar, and the Virginia Law Foundation) if I am lying about the fraud of Dr. Stanton Samenow and the Cover-up of parental alienation and abuse by the Fairfax County Circuit Court.

I don't believe Bartol ever responded to this email, and Mackney was dead fifty-five days later.

Chapter 13: Conclusion

"The longer I live, the more I feel that the individual is not so much to blame - not even the worst individuals, not even the 'best' citizens - as the system of corruption which has grown up about us, and which rewards an honest man with a mere living and a crook with all the magnificence of our magnificent modern life."

Lincoln Steffens author of *Shame of the Cities*

Roots of Corruption

Corruption materializes when a conflict of interest presents an opportunity for someone with a lack of moral fortitude. Corruption thrives in complicated situations.

Michael Volpe

In family courts, any solutions must try and attack one of these elements. Because I am an investigative journalist I don't pretend to have all the answers on policy, however here are my solutions to address the problems in family court.

Cut the Funds

The best way to stop the corruption is to stop making it so profitable, and that's what grants money does. There's plenty of grant money for men and women. Billions in Fatherhood Initiatives for men and VAWA state and federal grants for women only corrupt the system and are a counterproductive waste of government spending. Eliminate them, save several billion yearly and remove a lot of the financial motivation for corruption in family courts.

Get Rid of Restraining Orders

Even if you believe restraining orders are necessary to protect people- mostly women- in danger, they are unconstitutional and encroach on the rights of the target of the restraining order. Restraining orders are an end run around due process allowing an accuser to make their case without the accused present, presenting a defense, leading to a presumption of guilt not innocence.

Removing restraining orders would lead to dangerous people having access to vulnerable adults and children, a reality I understand.

On Sunday July 5, 2015, Tony Moreno threw his baby off East Haddam Bridge in Middletown, Connecticut. On June 17, 2015, the mother of his baby, Adrianne Oyola, received an EPO because she feared Moreno would hurt her and their baby.

On June 29, Judge Barry Pinkus, who's currently overseeing Taupier's divorce, denied a permanent protective order.

Oyola said she was "sometimes" afraid Moreno would beat her and recalled hearing cars stop in front of her house "like he's always there, and it's creepy," according to the transcript.

Pinkus was unconvinced saying the relationship was in turmoil and the two needed to work out differences on their own, seven days later their baby was dead.

These are the sort of stories you will hear if my plan was ever implemented and that's what makes implementation so hard. The media rarely covers a story in which a restraining order is misused or is there much analysis of their abuse of power. A tragedy like this is covered, and these sorts of tragedies will occur if restraining orders are eliminated because there are plenty of women using them properly who will also lose theirs, but this is an issue of due process. Protecting the constitutional rights of all citizens benefits public safety.

The stories cited in this book are stark, the numbers even starker, and the fact remains a restraining order takes away liberty without due process. At the very least, all states should use the Maryland model which requires clear and convincing evidence before granting a restraining order.

The Jury System

Judge Michael Algeo, the judge in Hera McLeod's case made this admission: "I'm in Family Law because I have to be. It's a required 18-month rotation. I don't like it. And if I could choose not to do it, I would not do it,"

Here's what one commenter on *The Washington Post* said about Hera McLeod's case: "Wouldn't it be something if this case could have been put before a jury or any right thinking person on the street, or even just some random 5th grader...parent 1 has good job, solid reputation, responsible and primary caregiver, parent 2 is unemployed, except for a porn venture, in 2008 #2 is Person of Interest in the murder of a previous intimate, subsequently makes a name change to that of his first son, in order to facilitate an attempt to collect on a policy intended for the son (and a bit telling that it wasn't left to #2 as parent), 2003 collects insurance policy on their mother's death which is suspicious and family claims and will testify not a suicide as ruled. No one in their right mind (and not receiving grant money from the Dept. of Health and Human Services for the fathers' rights initiatives) would even have to pause before making the decision to protect that child and leave Prince in the charge of his primary caregiver and let parent 1 do their job use their common sense re visitation with parent 2. (And for the record, the mother may have been fooled for a time by Joaquin Rams, but you can't fault her who believed Rams lies, if you don't hold the courts to the exact same standard and Algeo and Wong KNEW what Rams was and all about his history and they considered him a fit caregiver, heard the evidence and still put an innocent child in his care)."

Judges' roles in family court decisions should be reduced as much as possible, with the bulk of their decisions regarding matters of law rather than judgment. As Judge Algeo admitted, most judges don't want to be in family court and their decisions reflect their reticence.

If the parties aren't able to reach a compromise on custody on their own in a certain period of time, let's say eighteen months after the divorce is filed, the case immediately goes to a jury trial which determines custody.

Do we really want twelve people with no special training deciding custody? It's certainly not ideal, but frankly, I have a lot more confidence in twelve strangers with no tie to the matter than judges, who are often a part of the boy's club which is the cause of corruption. If juries can decide on someone's freedom, they can decide custody.

Currently, only Texas has a jury option but I would favor it an option in all fifty states.

No More Pro Se

When one's freedom is on the line, our justice system makes sure they receive legal representation. Family court is just as frightening, with just as much on the line; why should anyone be forced to navigate a process where they stand to lose their children, their property, and sometimes their freedom for months at a time with no lawyer?

Russell Engler, a professor at the New England School of Law in Boston, is one of the main national drivers of so-called Civil Gideon and in 2009 he published the white paper entitled:

Michael Volpe

Connecting Self-Representation to Civil Gideon: What Existing Data Reveal About When Counsel is Most Needed and reported about 60% of civil litigants were pro se.

Conservative readers may be rolling their eyes, *yet more government spending.*

Maybe, but a large percentage of frivolous lawsuits occur when one party knows the other party doesn't have the wherewithal to defend themselves. A study released in January 2015, by the Boston Bar Association Statewide Task Force to Expand Civil Legal Aid in Massachusetts found for every $1 spent on providing lawyers to indigent defendants, the state would wind up saving $2-$5 in backend legal costs.

Laura Abel, in a 2012 white paper entitled *Economic Benefits of Civil Legal Aid* also concluded: "Civil legal aid 'significantly' reduces repeat incidents of domestic violence by helping victims obtain custody and child support arrangements that make it possible for them to leave an abusive relationship. Thus, when a civil legal aid program expanded its services to help every low income victim of domestic violence throughout its geographic service area, requests for protective orders within the area fell by 35.5%, while requests within the entire state fell by only 16.2%."

Chris Mackney defended himself in about fifty hearings. Do you think the opposition would have been this aggressive if they knew he'd have someone with basic knowledge of the law to defend him? Frivolous lawsuits like Mackney's clog up the court with endless hearings to decide things like if a father should lose overnight visits with his children because he didn't fax in a receipt.

This has already been tried on a small scale. In 2009, California passed the Sargent Shriver Act which set up a pilot program and in 2011 in select California courtrooms pro se litigants received attorneys. In Massachusetts, advocates led by the Boston Bar Association's Task Force on Expanding the Civil Right to Counsel completed a comprehensive eviction pilot program in 2012, and started a second round with money provided by the Massachusetts Attorney General. In Mississippi, four counties began a pilot program to provide counsel to self-represented parents in matters of custody.

"Parents who come into my court with issues face daunting tasks. Not only do they have to work on the issues that brought them there, but they are thrown into the most complex legal environment in our society. They need help navigating the system to accomplish the tasks required to either keep their children at home or be able to return them." Judge Tom Broome said to *Clarion-Ledger* for an article on the program. "These delays cost the state millions of dollars for foster care, but the real hidden cost is the detrimental effect on children. They want to live at home with their parents, but can't."

No More Court Professionals

All court appointed psychologists, therapists, GALs, and other court professionals need to go. Only those making money from the system think they have any worth in the process besides charging tens of thousands in unearned fees.

"Custody evaluators are looking into a crystal ball," Sunny Kelley said pointing out that exactly what makes a good parent is entirely subjective.

The system needs to get simpler and more streamlined and court professionals make it more complicated.

The Lottery System

If family court insists on keep court professionals like evaluators, I would use a lottery system for choosing them. What if the custody evaluator in Chris Mackney's case was picked in an entirely random manner rather than being chosen at the behest of the two parties? How much conflict of interest is created when court professionals are chosen by the parties involved in custody disputes?

More Oversight and a Few Heroes

One of the most effective ways to stop the madness is through legislative oversight, requiring politicians with courage: quite possibly an oxymoron. Three state legislators- Nancy Schaefer, Sherry Jones, and Minnie Gonzalez- are the models.

Schaefer is a former Georgia State Senator, who became Chairman of the Health and Human Services Committee. In that role, she met thousands of victims of Child Protective Services (CPS). In 2007, she published the landmark white paper, *The Corrupt Business of CPS*. It's still considered the best, most concise and effective takedown of the burgeoning bureaucracy known as CPS.

In this report, I am focusing on the Georgia Department of Family and Children Services (DFCS). However, I believe Child Protective Services nationwide has become corrupt and that the entire system is broken almost beyond repair. I am convinced parents and families should be warned of the dangers.

The Department of Child Protective Services, known as the Department of Family and Children Services (DFCS) in Georgia and other titles in other states, has become a "protected empire"built on taking children and separating families. This is not to say that there are not those children who do need to be removed from wretched situations and need protection. This report is concerned with the children and parents caught up in "legal kidnapping," ineffective policies, and DFCS who do does not remove a child or children when a child is enduring torment and abuse.

"Fathers are victims of this unjust system. Child support payments even without having visits with their children are choking the very life out of fathers." Schaefer said at the World Congress of Families V in Amsterdam, Netherlands on August 11, 2009. "Three fathers of whom I am aware and have been in touch with committed suicide in the last twelve months because they lost the opportunity to even visit with their children. These are crimes against humanity for financial gain. Rights are removed from parents; human rights, civil rights, and even religious rights."

In those remarks, Schaefer also noted that her fight against CPS cost her re-election in 2008 "however there are causes worth losing over and this is one."

The cause didn't merely cost Schaefer her state senate seat; Schaefer was murdered in 2010. According to Georgia authorities, she was the victim of a murder/suicide at the hands of her husband of fifty years, purportedly distraught over money. While I don't know exactly who killed Ms. Schaefer, her death was not properly investigated and the only people who believe her husband is her murderer are part of the corrupt political structure in the state.

(Minnie Gonzalez giving her thoughts on family court)

Sherry Jones, a Democrat, has held a variety of positions in the Tennessee legislature- the Domestic Relations Committee, Family Justice Committee, Public Health Committee, along with the aforementioned Children and Family Affairs Committee- and gained nationwide attention for taking on CPS corruption.

In February 2013, Jones was featured in a *Tennessean* article on CPS corruption.

More than a dozen families claiming mistreatment by the Tennessee Department of Children's Services gathered Monday in Nashville to share their stories with Rep. Sherry Jones, a longtime critic of the state's child protection agency.

The families — mostly mothers and grandmothers — spoke of child custody battles, perceived violations of law by DCS caseworkers, and difficulties navigating what they described as a confusing and sometimes combative state system.

I came across Chris Mackney's story while looking for a follow-up article to one I published on the website *WND* on August 20, 2013, entitled *Kids snatched 'without warrants, without evidence'* which documented systemic corruption in CPS in Pennsylvania.

The only similarity between Schaefer, a conservative Republican, and Jones, a moderate Democrat, is their interest in exposing the ills of CPS. On this issue, they've been warriors fighting alone in their respective legislatures against the bureaucracy, and the public is far more aware of the problems as a result.

Minnie Gonzalez, a Democrat State Representative from Connecticut, gained nationwide attention for her oversight of family court. As the Democratic whip and member of the Connecticut House Judiciary Committee Gonzalez is a lone voice in providing oversight over family courts in that state, which are generally out of control. Gonzalez was a driving force in creating the Connecticut Task Force to Study Legal Disputes Involving the Care and Custody of Minor Children which held hearings examining corruption and inefficiencies in that state's GAL system. Gonzalez has used a novel legislative trick to bring these issues forward. Rather than holding oversight hearings, Gonzalez brings bills forward which through the legislative process allow public debate. She then recruits hundreds of parents who have been wronged by family courts to testify about their stories.

Back to the Constitution: No More Gag Orders, "Disparaging" Remarks, and Other First Amendment Violations

So-called gag orders or orders not to disparage other parties are violations of free speech and those judges who issue them must be dealt with harshly. Gag orders are issued with a startling amount of regularity not only in family courts but in courts in general, as if the founding fathers didn't understand that we'd have a judicial system along with free speech. They did, and they believed free speech is sacrosanct, and no family court judge has the power to take it away.

A federal court recently took a giant step toward making my vision a reality. In December 2014, United States District Judge William J. Martini ruled that a gag order from a family court trial in Bergen County, New Jersey was unconstitutional. In that case, Bergen Dispatch Reporter Paul Nichols attempted to interview family court litigant Surender Malhan. Malhan lost all access to his children in 2011 with two hours' notice after the judge held an ex-parte hearing with his ex-wife. Malhan was not given an opportunity to refute the charges or cross-examine his ex-wife. It was almost a year and a half before Malhan saw his children.

When Nichols attempted to interview Malhan, the Superior Court Judge who took away Malhan's custodial rights, Judge Nancy Sivilli, issued a gag order, "All parties are hereby enjoined and restrained without prejudice from speaking with, appearing for an interview, or otherwise discussing, the parties' marriage, their pending divorce, the within litigation, or the parties children or making any derogatory or negative statements about the other parties to any reporters, journalists, newscasters, or other agents/employees of newspapers or other media outlets on the grounds that it is not in the best interest of the children to have the parties' divorce litigation discussed in a public forum or to have public disparaging statements made about any party by the other party."

Judge Martini found Judge Sivilli's absurd logic violated the First Amendment and ruled as such. While Judge Martini's ruling does not take away all family court judges' power to limit free speech- Chris Mackney was barred from "repeating allegations"- it does significantly limit gag orders. All family court litigants should be familiar with this ruling and present it as evidence whenever a judge limits their free speech right.

Neil Shelton, when in court July 17, 2015, cited this case when his criminal court judge attempted to enforce a gag order. The judge told Shelton, "You've done your homework" and dismissed the gag order. This case may have power beyond family courts.

On July 22, 2015, Judge Lisa Gorcyca put a gag order on the Tsimhoni case. I don't believe that order has been lifted as this book is published but is apparently unconstitutional based on the Martini ruling.

More Transparency: Cameras in the Courtroom and Recording Your Own Proceedings

Because corrupt individuals operate in the shadows, courtrooms should be moved out of the shadows and into the sunlight. One way to do this is with cameras in the courtroom. Many people would be shocked by the behavior of judges, lawyers, and psychologists in family courtrooms if there was video evidence, and some of these folks might behave better if they knew everything was taped.

With no cameras in the courtroom, court reporting is big business. Litigants often leave court not knowing exactly what transpired. Getting an official transcript is costly, and takes time. Also what is "off the record" is sometimes more important than what is transcribed. We should be able to record our own proceedings, even if it is not "official" so that we can keep up with what is going on and expose what we don't agree with or our opinions of the court.

Family RICO

Congress should expand the Racketeer Influenced Corrupt Organizations (RICO) Act to family courts. RICO is among the most misunderstood and powerful tools in law enforcement. Originally designed to catch heads of mafia families who insulate themselves from direct involvement in much of the criminal activity of their crime families, in RICO if the prosecutors can prove a crime was done in furtherance of criminal enterprise (there are all sorts of technicalities which go along with this to actually get a conviction) everyone in the enterprise could be charged under RICO. No longer could the head of a family claim to not know about a murder, racket, and act of bribery done in the family's name.

As RICO evolved so too did its use. In my first book: *Prosecutors Gone Wild: The Inside Story of the Trial of Chuck Panici, John Gliottoni, and Louise Marshall*, Panici, the long-time mayor of Chicago Heights was charged under the RICO Act arguing the mayor's office was run as a criminal enterprise. Vincent "Buddy" Cianci, the long-time mayor of Providence, Rhode Island and author of the book, *Politics and Pasta*, was also charged under the RICO Act, when it was argued he too was the head of a criminal enterprise in the Providence mayor's office. In fact, in Cianci's case, he was found not guilty on all but one charge, conspiracy, when the jury decided that though he didn't participate in any of the crimes directly, he was responsible as mayor for the actions of all his employees, more than 3,000, including those taking bribes.

In January 2015, I wrote an article for *Rebel Pundit* on the proliferation of civil RICO lawsuits in family courts. One in San Diego County alleged that in the early 1990s a group of powerful judges along with the Sacramento County Bar Association created something which they called Federal Law Executive Committee (FLEC), a group of divorce lawyers from the San Diego Bar Association who would act as judge pro temp, temporary judges, to hear cases to clear up backlogs. In exchange, these lawyers received favorable rulings on all their divorce cases. This would be the sort of case perfect for an updated family RICO law.

The details of an updated RICO law for family court would be book length and not all that interesting so I'll sum it up. What I'd like to see is the techniques I've described as a criminal conspiracy: litigating divorce in criminal court, silver bullet technique, falsely using PAS, etc. In other words, I'd like to criminalize what Dina, Pete, Cottrell, Samenow, and Bellows did. If it can be proven that parties engaged in a conspiracy to have some arrested and charged with a criminal offense in order to gain leverage in a divorce that would be prosecuted under a new family court RICO. Even a bogus evaluation, if it was done strictly to create leverage for one side, could be prosecuted under family court RICO.

Child Support

Child support is the most complex part of the reform process and there are several reform options. First and foremost, imputed income must be eliminated.

I favor the total elimination of child support because as Ron Pierce told me, "child support monetizes custody."

A marriage is a contract and a divorce ends that contract. Once the assets are split fairly the contract ends. Monetary child support forces the continuation of part of the contract while the rest has ended. That makes no sense. Most responsible non-custodial parents will continue contributing financially and otherwise to the care of their children but being forced with a court order only invites bureaucrats into this process. Real child support is not money; it is love and companionship.

This reform may not be politically feasible so I'll also provide several less ambitious reforms.

If a parent isn't allowed access to the children, they cannot under any circumstances be made to pay any child support. A parent who doesn't have any contact with their children is not a parent but a sperm donor, and sperm donors, if you believe the judges in Jason Patric's case, have no rights. If they have no rights, they should not have any responsibility.

Remember the second pillar in corruption- opportunity, devious people see opportunities in child support. They'll take away all access to your children and stick you with a child support payment you can't afford. It's what happened in Chris Mackney's case. This reform will eliminate the most egregious corruption of child support.

In Scandinavian countries like Sweden child support is a flat rate which has nothing to do with visitation time or income. That's the way it should work in the USA if we continue to implement child support. Folks like Carlos Rivera shouldn't be jailed because they fall behind on exorbitant child support. By doing this, child support is also no longer tied to parenting time, giving devious parents less motivation to eliminate the other parent from the child's life.

Most of all, child support arrearages cannot be punished with jail time, that's debtor's prison and technically not allowed in the USA.

Judicial Immunity

On July 9, 1971, Ora Spitler walked into Judge Harold Stump's courtroom and asked for a petition to forcibly have her fifteen year old daughter, Linda, subjected to a tubal ligation to make her sterile. The older Spitler argued her daughter was slightly retarded and associating with older man.

The request was granted the same day without a hearing and ex-parte, or without Linda Spitler's presence. Two weeks later the fifteen year old was admitted to DeKalb Memorial Hospital and told she would have her appendix removed: in fact she could no longer have children.

Two years later, the seventeen year old married Leo Sparkman. When they failed to conceive after trying for months, they went to a doctor, who informed them of the prior surgery.

This turned into the Supreme Court case Stump V Sparkman and the Supreme Court decided a judge could not be sued even if he removed a woman's ability to conceive without her knowledge, let alone approval. Judicial immunity was now precedent.

"[T]his erroneous matter in which [the court's] jurisdiction was exercised, however it may have affected the validity of the act, did not make it any less a judicial act; nor did it render the defendant liable to answer in damages for it at the suit of the plaintiff, as though the court had proceeded without having any jurisdiction whatever." Justice White wrote for the majority opinion arguing that judges could do just about anything as long as it was blanketed in a judicial act without being sued. Short of accepting bribes there is no way to hold a judge accountable for any act no matter how egregious.

"There were no litigants. There was and could be no appeal. And there was not even the pretext of principled decision-making. The total absence of any of these normal attributes of a judicial proceeding convinces me that the conduct complained of in this case was not a judicial act." Justice Stewart wrote in his dissent.

Many family court victims believe judges act with hubris in part because of the broad and overwhelming power against suit they enjoy because of this case. Doctors perform as important a function as judges but are not immune from lawsuit. Journalists are protected under the first amendment but are not protected from defamation suits. Five Supreme Court Justices decided their colleagues would be given special privileges not afforded any other profession and make them immune from suit in nearly all cases.

Because this is now Supreme Court precedent, overturning it is no easy task and might require a Constitutional amendment. Until then, we'll have callous judges like Judge Bellows who will take away overnight visits for failing to produce a receipt, like Judge Munro who believed she was capable of determining mental illness and Judge Algeo who believed a suspected murderer, abuser, porn maker, with no job was a fit parent.

Co-parenting or Equal/Shared Parenting

This is a concept which suggests that the default position for any custody should be equal custody for each of the two parents. As an idea for parents, this makes sense on a case by case basis. It certainly would have helped Chris Mackney and made it more difficult for his ex-wife to remove all custody (though not impossible). As a legal concept, it's an awful idea. I've already discussed ad nauseam the Orwellian legal concept "in the best interest of the child". Some suggest replacing one Orwellian concept "in the best interest of the child" with another "equal parenting". If this was implemented, judges will justify every action by claiming "equal parenting" just as they now justify every action by claiming "in the best interest of the child". That's the problem, judges giving themselves a mandate bigger than the Constitution. Equal parenting is exactly the sort of thing that allows abusers back into the life of a child. As Hera McLeod told me, "family court can't be cookie cutter" and equal parenting is a cookie cutter idea.

I have no problem with lawyers arguing for co-parenting, and judges accepting effective co-parenting arguments. Co-parenting as legislative or judicial policy is a recipe for disaster.

The Quincy Solution

The Quincy Solution is the feminist answer to co-parenting, with numerous so-called protections for protective mothers. While it would provide protection for protective mothers it would also exacerbate false allegations against innocent fathers accused of abuse. The solutions include making protective orders easier to get and "with practices that made it easier for women to leave their abusers and a coordinated community response when they did," which sounds like future grant funding.

Both the Quincy Solution and Equal-Parenting plans are gender specific solutions which would only benefit one sex at the expense of the other thereby enflaming the gender war, which I believe needs to be diffused.

Is Parental Alienation Child Abuse?

In some cases on a moral or ethical level, it probably is. I think it is child abuse to convince your children that it doesn't matter that their father is dead because "he was crazy anyway," but I don't think that Dina Mackney or anyone else should ever be prosecuted criminally or in family court for parental alienation because then bureaucrats and juries would determine thought and speech crimes.

(A photo which has become popular on parental alienation websites and Facebook pages)

If parental alienation proliferates as a crime or a matter in family court then this scenario will become a reality. A child asks their mom to spend time with their dad this coming weekend. Mom says, "No, you have a big test on Monday and you don't study at your father's."

The father, finding out what happened, accuses the mother of parental alienation and she's jailed. If you think that's impossible just remember Chris Mackney had his overnight visits removed because he didn't fax a receipt: anything is possible in family court.

Almost all so-called parental alienation starts with custodial interference and most times the targeted parent has little or no contact with their children. A parent having little or no contact with their children should be a rarity. It is not, but the best way to counteract so-called parental alienation is to make sure in all but extreme cases the non-custodial parent spends a consistent amount of time each week with the child. If that happens in the overwhelming majority of cases all other behaviors won't work because the targeted parent is spending consistent time with the children.

Parental alienation is nebulous; it's a term which is obsessed by certain groups, and that makes it dangerous. Calling it child abuse will mean every aggrieved parent screams parental alienation in order to gain an advantage in their custody fight, especially abusive parents.

Getting Rid of Family Court

If I could rule the world, I'd get rid of family courts but I don't think that's logistically possible; family law attorney Michelle MacDonald believes it is possible. MacDonald was endorsed by the Republican Party when she ran Minnesota Supreme Court Judge in 2014, losing 53-47, is involved in the most controversial custody case in Minnesota, resulting in her spending time in jail as a result of a bogus custody related ruling where she alleges she was tortured, and is the editor of this book. Here's her vision.

MacDonald and her group developed the Family Innocence Process (FIP), a consent process of agreement which provides family innocence advocates, facilitators, mediators, and a friendly decision-maker upon impasse. The difference is that couples come to binding agreements that do not have to be reflected in court orders, and only go to court for orders that are needed, most often, a simple order to terminate the marriage.

"The idea is to not initiate a lawsuit that gives jurisdiction to the court over everything, to move towards communication, and to teach people that divorce and custody breakups are lawsuits that are not necessary." MacDonald said.

She has also developed a process where, after family members come to agreement, an attorney can ethically represent both of them to get the orders they need in court. The thing is that in the realm of divorce, the courts generate numerous orders, essentially injunctions, setting forth do-this-do-that family regulations, subject to contempt.

Another idea is Cooperative Private Divorce, with binding agreements and administrative certificates of divorce, with no judges needing to sign off. MacDonald says judges became unnecessary with no fault divorce because, before no fault, finding fault, like non-support, adultery and abuse, needed to be determined by a judge in order to terminate the marriage.

Michael Volpe

Good versus Evil

The greatest honor and responsibility of this book is that I confronted evil. I believe the noblest thing any journalist can do is confront evil people, expose them, thereby making them less able to commit evil in the future.

Nellie Bly is my favorite journalist and one reason is because at her best no journalist confronted evil people better, but Bly's story serves as a metaphor for the effects of the abuse highlighted in this book.

Elizabeth Jane Cochran was born on May 5, 1864 in the town of Cochran's Mills, Pennsylvania, named after its most famous resident, her father Michael Cochran. Pinky as she became known immediately due to the plethora of Pink dresses she wore was the third of five children of Michael and his second wife, Mary Jane. He had another ten children with his first wife, Catherine Murphy, who died about a decade earlier. Michael was twenty years senior to his second wife and 54 when Pinky was born.

He'd built a series of successful businesses and was according to Brooke Kroeger's book *Nellie Bly: Daredevil, Reporter, Feminist* worth more than $50,000, the equivalent of about $1,000,000 today, by the time Pinky was six. That's when her world fell apart. Her sixty year old father developed a crippling paralysis and died. He left no will and within weeks his oldest son by his first marriage, Robert, was challenging for a piece of the estate. With fifteen children total, it wasn't long before his estate was being picked apart leaving little for Pinky's mother to raise her five children.

Mary Jane received some personal items and $16 per week. Mary Jane, who had been born and married into wealth, was nearing forty and poor for the first time in her life. Here's Kroeger.

"And yet, it was not unusual in 1870 for a man of Michael Cochran's means, especially in his particular circumstances, to die intestate (without a will like Chris Mackney). The difficulty in making equitable distribution between children of two mothers was pervasive."

About three years later, Mary married the Civil War veteran, John Jack Ford. Ford turned out to be a drunk and an abuser. The abuse became so bad Mary was left with no choice but to file for divorce.

This was no easy task, according to Kroeger's research, only fourteen divorces were granted in 1878 in Armstrong County, where Mary applied. In the entire decade of the 1870s, Armstrong County, with a population of about 40,000 residents, only granted eighty-four divorces: leaving thousands of women forced to stay in abusive marriages.

The website *Nellie Bly On-Line* called the divorce process "tortuous."

Mary Catherine was one of the lucky ones, her divorce was granted but not before Pinky was forced to testify, repeating some of the most traumatic moments of her life. Here's how her testimony appeared in Kroeger's book.

"My age is fourteen years. I live with my mother. I was present when mother married J.J. Ford. I (have) seen them married about six years ago. Ford has been generally drunk since they were married. When drunk, he is very cross, and cross when sober. (I have) heard him scold mother often and heard him use profane language towards her often and call her names: a whore and bitch, (I have) seen mother vexed on account of his swearing and bad names and (I've) seen her cry. Ford threatened to do mother harm. Mother was afraid of him. (I've) seen Ford throw the old clothes after being washed and ironed on the floor and throw water at them and seen him upset the table."

While the divorce was granted, the stigma forced the family to move. By age fourteen, Pinky had seen the courts emasculate her mother twice, an experience not lost on her; Bly's second article as a professional journalist was entitled *Mad Marriages* where she argued for the abolition of divorce laws and to make it a crime to lie to your future spouse about your vices like gambling and alcoholism.

At fifteen, Bly thought she'd caught a break when her court appointed guardian, Colonel Samuel M. Jackson, arranged for her to start at the Indiana State Normal School to learn to be a teacher. Jackson said it would cost $400 for her to attend for three years and signed her registration as guardian.

But as the first semester was about to end, Jackson, who was on the board of the school according to Kroeger's research, suddenly got in touch with Bly and told her she'd run out of money, offering no explanation for where the budgeted funds had gone.

It would take years for the Cochran's to unravel the extent of Jackson's fraud, Kroeger found. Not only had Jackson bought the judge's house with part of the estate's money but Jackson inappropriately gave JJ Ford estate money; Ford spent that money on his own devices. Her dreams of being a teacher were dashed.

At the time, a news story on all this legal abuse was about as difficult to publish as one on family court is today. First, newspapers were almost exclusively run by men, creating a natural bias toward males. Newspapers were also generally for the aristocracy and filled with items wealthy people cared about, not some story about how a poor working girl got aced out of her dream of being a teacher by a corrupt individual given too much power by his status.

Michael Volpe

Bly led the way in telling stories targeting working class females, a nearly brand new niche, during her hey day, with the insane asylum expose being the best example. She also paved the way for working class females to become journalists. The National Football League is known as a copycat league in that if a play works for one team, you'll see a bunch of new teams run that same play. In Bly's case, her insane asylum exposé inspired other newspapers to follow, looking for their own young, pretty, and hungry reporter with a working class background willing to go undercover. The term plucky, to describe Bly and female reporters like her, became popular.

Bly's career was marked by remarkable success and turbulence. At 25, she briefly became the most famous person on the planet. About two years after her insane asylum exposé, at 9:40 AM ET on November 14, 1889 Bly left on the Augusta Victoria, a steamboat headed for Europe, for her trip around. She completed the race in seventy-two days and some change, becoming the fastest person ever to circumnavigate the globe, real or imagined. It was a race, Elizabeth Bisland of *Cosmopolitan* raced around the world with Bly going the other way, starting in California at the same time Bly started on the east coast but arrived days later.

Having achieved fame no other journalist, let alone female journalist, had ever achieved before, Bly inexplicably quit. Following her race, Bly did a six month lecture tour to support her book, *Around the World in Seventy-Two Days*. Soon after that, she quietly retired from journalism to take what she thought was a cushy job paying $200 per week job to write mystery stories. Bly failed miserably writing mysteries and got back into journalism three years later with far less success- though she'd interview Susan B. Anthony, Eugene V. Debs, Emma Goldman, John L. Sullivan, and many others before quitting again soon after she married.

She was fiercely independent but at thirty-one Bly married Robert Seaman, forty years her senior, and a multi-millionaire, about two and a half weeks after first meeting him and stayed married to him until he died nine years later. Seaman changed his will while he and Billy were married and she received much of his fortune. She spent the next two decades one of the wealthiest women on the planet and a leading female industrialist before an embezzlement scheme wiped her out- an embezzlement we could now prosecute under RICO- and she found her way back to journalism when her vacation in Europe coincided with the start of armed hostilities for what would eventually be called World War I. She wound up spending more time on the frontlines than the US military, coming back stateside shortly after the war ended.

Bly died at 57 of pneumonia, nearly penniless and having been hand to mouth and well off twice each in her life.

That Bly developed daddy issues is self-explanatory, but she also developed a co-dependency with her mother. When she travelled to Mexico on assignment for six months at 21, Bly took her mother with her.

"Concerned about appearances, Bly convinced her mom to chaperone," is how Kroeger described it but there was much more.

When Bly became well-known in New York she moved her mother in, moved her next door during some of her marriage, and her mother represented her in the bankruptcy case her company went through after the embezzlement while Bly reported from World War I. This ugly episode caused Bly and her mother to barely speak to each other toward the end of her life.

It's impossible to know the direct and indirect affect all this abuse had on making her life so turbulent or if it also made her tougher and more capable in the process. Would she have had her legendary will if not for the turmoil in her life? We'll never know in any quantifiable way, but Bly also quickly evolved into an evil slayer. She was blessed with an embarrassment of riches in two traits: charm and will, and this drove her success throughout.

At the end of a tough but broad ranging interview with then Illinois Governor John Peter Altgeld in which Bly all but accused the liberal Altgeld of having secret anarchist sympathies, (Altgeld is famous for pardoning four of eight anarchists condemned to die for their alleged role in the Haymarket Riots) Altgeld complimented her smile.

"So it was, but it was your smile that did it," he said. "You come in and smile, and sweep everything before you. It's the smile young lady; it's worth a million dollars to you."

During her insane asylum exposé, she determined the first evening in the boarding house that if she fell asleep her cover could very well be blown so she sat at the edge of her bed all night and continued in character, sitting quietly while her roommate slept and until she awoke.

If you thought this was a brutal or tortuous experience, you'd be wrong: "That was the greatest night of my existence. For a few hours I stood face to face with 'self!'" Bly said in her book.

Ten Days in the Madhouse is her greatest conquest over evil. A grand jury was convened within two weeks of the article's release, all her recommendations were immediately adopted, the worst offenders were fired, and entirely new protocols were put in place transforming not only Bellevue but psych wards all over the world.

She also did numerous less celebrated though no less compelling articles slaying evil including her take down of Edward Phelps. Phelps was a real life version of Edward Arnold's character in *Mr. Smith Goes to Washington*, a power broker who through mass bribery in a Machiavellian way controlled the New York State Legislature. With Bly undercover as the wife of a man who needed a copyright bill to not pass, Phelps accepted $5,000 to sway the legislature and boasted that in this sub-committee he had six of the eleven members in his pocket.

"I have control of the house and can pass or kill any bill," Phelps told an undercover Bly. While a grand jury was convened, Phelps didn't go to jail but lost all his power and disappeared soon after the story ran.

But Bly's best work is her takedown of a prolific con man who called himself Ernest DeBlanc pretending to be a "magnetic doctor", who claimed to be able to transmute magnetic energy from himself to the patient. Bly found him in an advertisement in her competitor's newspaper, itself genius because advertisements are the last place most journalists would look for material for a story. Bly went the extra mile and uncovered a gem.

As soon as she believed he was a fraud, she hatched, planned and executed an undercover sting all within a matter of days posing as someone with a migraine headache. Undercover, Bly discovered the so-called magnetism was actually a not so well hidden electric battery which he slipped underneath his shirt, but her exposure was just getting started. From there, she looked for similar advertisements in other newspapers and found several: six cities total. She even made contact with a man named Charles Lafferrand who identified a sketch of DeBlanc as the man who swindled him in an insurance scheme fourteen years prior. DeBlanc lived as a con man for years. He'd swoop into town with a scheme which could work for a while and he'd have to hightail it, a la Charles Harrelson, to another town with a similar scheme after he was exposed, which happened usually within months.

Bly's exposé of DeBlanc was above the fold page one of the Sunday edition of the *New York World* on November 11, 1888. A couple years earlier, Pulitzer first placed the best long form article of the week as the feature story of the week in all his newspapers on Sunday, page one above the fold. That invention, as simple as it sounds, continues today.

DeBlanc was not merely exposed; he had nowhere to hide. Bly's exposé was even featured in that year's Journal of the American Medical Association (JAMA): *Exposure of a Quack* JAMA titled it. I found no more information on DeBlanc but he certainly could no longer work anywhere in America and was probably through as a conman.

One of the reasons I really like this exposé is that it took Bly about a week to destroy this guy dispatching of him quickly with plenty of time to move onto the next bad guy. Mine took quite a bit longer.

This story is good versus evil at its core. Chris Mackney was by no means perfect, no one is, but he was a good person, and everyone who had a hand in his suicide played a calculating and cold blooded evil role. This was a saga started in the 1960s, then five years in the making in family court, engineered by a Machiavellian puppeteer who had infinite power, infinite cruelty and torture without end or limit.

Knowing all that, everyone went along and didn't try and stop it until Mackney was dead.

Bullied to Death: Chris Mackney's Kafkaesque Divorce

I believe like Tolstoy that laws can't root out evil only good men standing up to it can root it out. That's ultimately what this book is about. There is a lot of evil in the story, and that evil reigned free because good men didn't stand up, until now.

Chris Mackney hoped that there would be better understanding and awareness of psychopathy in family courts. I agree but I don't think that is something we can legislate. Psychopathy in family courts is evil in family court and no law will stop evil.

But I have the power to expose it.

The most satisfying interview I did for this book was with Caroline Yunker because of everyone in this book she was the most innocent and with no axe to grind. She was just a little girl when all this happened to her; she's unimpeachable and that's devastating for Samenow and everyone who used him as leverage by extension. She had first-hand experience with Samenow, and he traumatized her; confronting evil at that age is a traumatizing experience.

Ernest DeBlanc probably never dreamed that someone pretending to have a headache would turn the tables on him and con the conman; Phelps was too blinded by money to see he was being played. That was how Bly slayed evil.

Samenow never thought someone like me would find Caroline Yunker, three other adult victims, including her mom, along with Chris Mackney.

Dina couldn't have imagined that I'd find out her kids said it didn't matter that their dad was dead "because he's crazy anyway."

She didn't expect that I'd find out she warned a police officer to be skeptical of Jill because in Dina's words she "took Mr. Mitchell to court for more child support."

She probably never thought I'd get my hands on the email from Liza Mulaney and connect that to Balins, Ver Ploegg, Bryan Mitchell, and the gas-lighting scheme.

Cottrell couldn't have dreamed that I would discover numerous emails Chris Mackney sent him and his colleague, Kyle Bartol, begging them to end his misery. They couldn't have imagined that along with Mackney, I also found Taupier and Shelton, both also arrested by the SWAT team. They couldn't have imagined that someone like me would continue asking questions of them long after it was clear they had no further comment, over twenty emails to each: they like to ask questions not answer them.

Scamardo, ever the Machiavellian, anticipated someone finding out about the murder- the copyright notice included the Google Drive Chris Mackney created about it- but he couldn't stop me from seeing it, downloading most of it before it disappeared, and creating a rough draft of the chapter right away. As such, he couldn't stop me from releasing a draft of the chapter in July 2014 telling the world who this man really is. For more than a year, this man who sues everyone for everything has done nothing while someone called him a murderer; that's because he is a murder.

This was my moment to confront evil, which I did, and by exposing it I believe good finally triumphed over evil.

As I started this book with a quote from Oscar Wilde, so too will I end it.

"Children begin by loving their parents; after a time they judge them; sometimes they forgive them."

Acknowledgment

There are many people to thank in helping me write this book but first it is my family. To my parents, Alex and Julia Volpe, you have helped me in so many ways and I have rarely properly thanked you. Hopefully, this book does well enough for this to be a proper thank you. To my brother Ben, the 2013 winner of the World Series of Poker bracelet in the $1,500 no limit event, you've achieved far more than I ever will but have always believed in me even when I've given you no reason.

To my friends, namely Brian Crowley, who always read portions of this book and relished the role of giving criticism, constructive and otherwise, your support means the world.

Without many of Chris Mackney's friends this book would not have been possible. Because many requested anonymity, you'll have to sacrifice vanity because that extends to the acknowledgements. First and foremost, Rich Ware and Mike Harris proved in life and in death to be great friends. There's an irony to Dr. Samenow's assertion that Chris Mackney had no friends because not only did he have friends but real friends, the kind who stuck with him during his darkest hours. It's easy to be friends when things are good but it's during times of crisis that you find out who your real friends are and Mike Harris and Rich Ware are real friends. Your friendship couldn't change the outcome of his life, but Chris Mackney died knowing he was not alone. Terry Hindermann started as a colleague and ended a good friend, something Dr. Samenow might have found out if he had taken the time to talk to him and his contributions, including a brutally raw photo from Chris's last days, were invaluable.

Jill Peterson Mitchell relived some of the worst and most painful moments of her life, including a breathtakingly sad text message exchange but she did it because she believed in Chris, this story, and me.

To Mark Duda, I hope you'll remember Chris the way he was when you knew him well not the way he ended.

To Robert Worster, you answered all my questions with a degree of honesty I rarely find in attorneys, especially divorce attorneys.

To the other victims of family court who had the courage to tell their stories- Ronald Pierce, Michael Pasierb, Hera McLeod, Susan Skipp, Lori Handrahan, Sunny Kelley, Neil Shelton, Ted Taupier, Anthony Pappas, John Arndt, Ulf Carlsson, Page Holdgate, Susan Carrington, Debbie Wolfe, Janice Wolk Grenadier, Andrea Chen, Christopher Robin Sr., Cyd Koehn, and Jeannie Melton- family courts have no appetite for the truth but the public does.

To my editor and a unique and courageous divorce attorney- one who was detained, tortured, and forced to represent her client while strapped to a wheelchair- Michelle MacDonald Shimota, my deepest and heartfelt gratitude.

To the many editors- Jeremy Segal at *Rebel Pundit*, Jacqui Kubin and Lisa Ruth at *Communities Digital News*, Dylan Skriloff at *Rockland County Times*, and Pat O'Connor at *Crime Magazine*- who took a chance on my family court stories I hope you consider the risk worth it.

To my mentors throughout the years- Trevor Mathias, Jay Werner, George Johnson, Michael Sullivan, and Matt Vadum- you've helped my progression as a person and professional.

Michael Volpe

To the journalists and activists- Henry Makow, Nick Lulli, Paul Elam, Anne Stevenson, Raquel Okyay, Greg Roberts, Lou Jasikoff, NK Clark, Stephen James, and Deb Beachem- who helped me understand family court and the media landscape I owe a great debt of gratitude.

To all those who caused Chris Mackney's death- Dina Mackney, Pete Scamardo, Jim Cottrell, Kyle Bartol, Stanton Samenow, Elizabeth Kohut, and Randy Bellows- you are all evil and cold blooded and I hope proper punishment is exacted in life but if not, I will enjoy as you rot in hell.

To Chris Mackney: you deserved better in life but I hope you have found peace in death.

Appendix

Good Men Did Nothing (blue underlined portions were originally hyperlinks he created, most are now dead links. Spelling errors and typos are Mackney's)

Michael Volpe

Utilising the Dark Triad – Psychopathy

Posted on December 29, 2013 by goodmendidnothing
Reply

Utilising the Dark Triad – Psychopathy.

Posted in Uncategorized | Leave a reply

No presents from Dad

Posted on December 25, 2013 by goodmendidnothing
Reply

In October 2012, my ex-wife violated the orders of the Circuit Court by filing for a protective order against me in the Juvenile and Domestic Relations Court. The orders were that all filings with the Court were to be heard in the Circuit Court.

In order to obtain a protective order, the law is very clear. There has to be a 'threat' or 'act' of violence. Judge Clayton made that abundantly clear as he read the law at the beginning of the hearing. The only problem was there was no threat or act of violence. None.

When my ex-wife got on the stand to testify, she started with how 'afraid' she is even though she already has an order stating that I can not contact her or go to her house or my own children's schools. The orders of Judge Randy Bellows gave her all the protection she was asking and I had not contacted her or threatened her. She knows that I want nothing to do with her but still portrays herself as the victim.

When I cross examined her she could not state a single threat or act of violence. She then claimed that I pointed a shotgun at her over 7 years ago. This was a complete lie. She had forgotten that she had testified in 2008 that I pointed a "handgun" at her, which was also a total lie. Which I pointed out to the Judge.

Then I completely discredited her on the stand when I had her testify that she had lied in an email to our neighbors and Dr. Van Syckle. In the email she claims that she had sent multiple offers to settle when she had never sent any. In fact, every 'fact' she claims in the email is a lie.

I also told Judge Clayton that she had a traumatic brain injury and that Dr. Samenow failed to conduct a 'psychological evaluation'. To this my ex-wife's attorney responded by saying that a Psychological evaluation and a custody evaluation are the "same thing".

So after a hearing in a Court without jurisdiction; where there were no threats or acts of violence and my ex-wife admitting she lied, Judge Clayton granted the protective order 'based on the history of the case', which had no violence by me. Now the only additional protection granted to my ex-wife was the ability to put me in jail for contacting my children by letter or sending them a birthday present or Christmas present, which violates the orders of Judge Bellows. I the other protections she already had.

Additionally, I told Judge Clayton that my ex-wife was manipulating the Court and alienating my children from their father. I reported abuse and asked him to appoint a Guardian Ad Litem for my children. The appointment of a GAL is mandatory in the J&DR court where abuse is alleged. Judge Clayton refused to appoint a GAL.

When I brought this to the attention of Judge Jane Roush, who is supposed to hear all the filings, she denied my motion.

My ex-wife has not let me see or speak to my children in over 3 years. She has blocked all communication and the court has blocked all access to their teachers and doctors, despite the fact that there has been no abuse.

My children get no presents from Dad this year. Merry Christmas, James and Ruby. It's in your best interest that you get no presents from your father.

#corruption

Posted in Uncategorized | Leave a reply

Emotional Invalidation – My concern for the emotional welfare of my children, that was completely ignored.

Posted on December 24, 2013 by goodmendidnothing
Reply

Constant invalidation may be one of the most significant reasons a person with high innate emotional intelligence suffers from unmet emotional needs later in life. A sensitive child who is repeatedly invalidated becomes confused and begins to distrust his own emotions. He fails to develop confidence in and healthy use of his emotional brain– one of nature's most basic survival tools. To adapt to this unhealthy and dysfunctional environment, the working relationship between his thoughts and feelings becomes twisted. His emotional responses, emotional management, and emotional development will likely be seriously, and perhaps permanently, impaired. The emotional processes which worked for him as a child may begin to work against him as an adult. In fact, one definition of the so-called "borderline personality disorder" is "the normal response of a sensitive person to an invalidating environment"

Psychiatrist R.D. Laing said that when we invalidate people or deny their perceptions and personal experiences, we make mental invalids of them. He found that when one's feelings are denied a person can be made to feel crazy even they are perfectly mentally healthy.

This is what happened to me after 5 years living my my ex-wife and her family.

Posted in Uncategorized | Leave a reply

Bullied to Death

Posted on December 24, 2013 by goodmendidnothing
Reply

The pain from the emotional abuse, psychological abuse, parental alienation and legal abuse has been unbearable. My children and I were abused and when spoke out and no one did anything. No one. Not the attorneys, doctors or Judges. They all recognized the patterns of behavior and the source of conflict and turned a blind eye and then blocked me from bringing in a third party or Guardian Ad Litem to identify the abuse. At any point throughout this case, if the Court had ruled in my favor on any of my motions, the outcome would have been different. At any point, if my ex-wife had shown ANY kind of act of good faith, the outcome would have been different. The facts are that not one of my motions were ever granted by the Court and my ex-wife never once acted in good faith.

Judge Randy Bellows did not like my explanation for the conflict and chose to ignore the evidence contradictory with its views. He did not want to admit that he had been so easily mislead. There is nothing I could do to end the abuse or change the view of the Court. As long as I was the problem, there was no reason to consider an alternate narrative.

I had no power or control in my marriage and I had even less when the divorce began. It was not an accident that I ended up with no visitation with my own children and no ability to monitor their emotional welfare. <u>It was orchestrated by attorneys who were paid not to settle and insisted on litigating every single issue without discussion</u>. It was all done to increase the stress and pressure. Nothing I said mattered. My rights as a parent did not matter. They had the power, control, money and the kids and they were not negotiating. Even after I gave my ex-wife full custody, just to appease her. She insisted on litigating visitation, asking the Judge for "no visitation" <u>even though there was no abuse</u>. She also asked for all the assets in the marriage. I got absolutely nothing and I had to pay her legal bills.

The decision was made to eliminate me from my children's lives the day I discovered that my <u>ex-wife had hidden her father's murder conviction, on June 23, 2008</u>. The very next day, <u>her father hired two attorneys</u> who advertise that they are 'not the type to settle, so have your wallet open'. Their job was to "get orders" as Jim Cottrell described it in Court and keep the legal and financial pressure up as high as possible.

Make no mistake, this case was never about money or the children. My ex-wife's <u>multiple requests that I leave town and give up my children</u> is evidence of that. It was about a <u>pathological need for control and domination</u>. I saw behind the mask and the facade and I needed to be eliminated, just like <u>Sam Degelia</u> needed to be eliminated for discovering <u>Pete Scamardo was trafficking heroin</u>. The plan was to have attorneys negatively interpret anything I say or do and and then litigate every issue. I needed to be portrayed as the source of conflict, so the legal and financial pressure could be applied. With no money, I could not afford an attorney to protect me. By denying access to the Children, they would use any reaction from me to distract from the real problem. My reactions to being abused, controlled, bullied and alienated were not the source of conflict. When I spoke out or asked the Court for help, I was ignored and silenced. The patterns of high conflict behavior exist throughout my ex-wife and her family's past. I only pointed out how the pattern seemed to match the patterns also found in 'high-conflict' divorce.

Refusing to negotiate or resolve differences outside of Court and then paying attorneys over $1 Million in legal fees does not lead to peace. But, that was the point. I never wanted to speak out and cause any embarrassment to my children or my ex-wife. I swear I didn't. I only wanted to be away and free from my ex-wife and be the best father I could be. I made countless offers to settle and asked what they wanted to keep us out of Court. I never received a response to any of my requests or proposals. Actually, I did get one proposal the night before our Division of assets hearing, that was completely in bad faith and unlivable. It was not a 'good faith' effort.

They finally told my attorney in 2011, that <u>if I left town and gave up all efforts to see my children, that would end the conflict</u>. I wanted so much to be free of the litigation and the madness that I did just as they requested. I left town and moved to Dallas, TX, thinking I would never see my children again, but at least the nightmare would be over. it broke my heart and my spirit, but at least I didn't have to worry about going to jail (or so I thought). I got a job and started going to the gym, trying to get healthy again. The first month I was in Dallas working, my ex-wife tracked me down and had Child Support Enforcement come after me. Now that I was in Dallas, I would have no ability to go to Court to change the order. When I appealed to my ex-wife's attorney, requesting that they voluntarily lower my child support, they refused to respond. I had no leverage, so I said that if they do not voluntarily agree to a reduction, I would have no other choice but to speak out about the abuses. They decided that I was trying to extort money from them, even though I left town, as requested, and took my emails to the Commonwealth's attorney to have me arrested for attempted extortion.

The Commonwealth's attorney had me arrested in Dallas and extradited back to Virginia, where I was put on trial for a felony. I begged the Commonwealth's attorney and my ex-wife to plead guilty to a misdemeanor, as I did not wish to risk a felony conviction. They both refused. This was also confirmation that my ex-wife did not care about the money or the children. So, we went to trial and was found not guilty. I did not ask for any money from her and the child support I owe is to my children, not my ex-wife. The Jury saw that my attempts to reduce my child support were not an effort to obtain money at all, and the law supported the verdict. It was a clear effort on the Commonwealth's attorney to silence me for threatening to speak out about the fraud of Dr. Samenow, one of their star witnesses, and the Cover-up by Judge Randy Bellows. Why else wouldn't they accept a plea to my first criminal charge, ever?

When I was released from Jail again, I asked my ex-wife's attorney, again to voluntarily reduce my child support or to appoint a Guardian Ad Litem for the children. Even after they put me in jail and had me tried for a felony, they refused to show any good faith. I got no response from my ex-wife's attorney. My child support was still far beyond my ability to pay and now I was without a job.

It was obvious to me a long time ago, that I would be 'bullied until eternity', as I wrote my attorney in 2008. For them to come after me again after leaving town, refuse to let me plead guilty to a lesser charge and to refuse to voluntarily reduce my child support, it was even more obvious that the only objective was to keep the legal, financial, and emotional pressure on me. I was being bullied to death.

I never wanted to speak out about any of this. All I wanted was a fair and reasonable child support, fair and reasonable visitation with my children and be free to move on with my life. The only reason I chose to write this blog and speak out about the abuse was because I thought it would give me some kind of leverage, as I had none. I made it clear to my ex-wife's attorney that the Court was not allowing me to change the orders, I had no information about my children and my child support was far beyond my ability to pay. I was was hoping for some act of good faith to let me know that they wanted to reduce the conflict. It never came, not in 5 years. I felt that my only recourse was to speak out about the abuse and injustice in order to get the legal and psychological help I needed to manage the conflict, so that we could both parent our children. I reached out to my ex-wife's attorney again to ask for ANY other alternative. They offered none, so I started the blog. Even after I started the Blog, I reached out again to tell them I would take down the blog if a Guardian Ad Litem could be appointed. They never responded. Dina knew this would be the outcome and didn't care. As long as I was gone.

In hindsight, I recognize that my reactions to being bullied, abused and denied access to my children gave my ex-wife's attorney the ammunition they were looking for to bring me into Court, but nothing I said or done would have made a difference. I was powerless. I thought that at some point a third party would be involved that would recognize that my reactions were from the emotional abuse; being denied access to my children and bullied in Court. The Court refused at least 6 requests for third party intervention. All of the research said that a third party was the recommended course of action in these situations. A third party was the only way to truly understand the conflict. I was not the person being portrayed in Court. I had no control over anything. The Court would only listen to my ex-wife's attorney granting all of their motions and agreeing to all their "over-reaching" remedies. When I read online about the patterns of behavior of high conflict divorce and how my ex-wife was the one blocking access to the children and negatively interpreting everything I did, I spoke out and tried to address the source of conflict. No one would tell me I was wrong, but no one would speak out about the abuse on my behalf, not the Doctors or attorneys.

Experts in psychology have called it abuse, but none would make such a 'diagnosis', which I could then take to Court to obtain relief. As long as the pattern of behavior was not called 'abuse', my reactions would not be viewed in its proper context, by the Court.

The way I looked at it was that if I remained silent, the abuse would continue. It did. When I finally decided to speak out, they didn't care. They didn't care about how it would affect Dr. Samenow, Judge Bellows, our children, themselves or anyone else. They were not going to take their foot off the back of my neck. They were fully invested in having me out of my children's lives, permanently.

Bullying and parental alienation are all forms of emotional abuse. Psychopathy is an emotional dysfunction. People with psychopathy are identified by how they handle conflict. It is the disturbing lack of empathy, guilt shame, remorse that give them away. They are completely unaffected by the distress of others. As long as they get what they want, you may never see that side of them. If you are in a position of power or status, you will probably not see that side of them either. However, people that are close to them or are of little value to them, will eventually see the pattern. They will slowly begin to realize they are being controlled manipulated and 'gas lighted'. Without even realizing it, you learn to go along to get along. If you break from this, you will experience their wrath. I remember on Memorial Day 2008, when I went to pick up my children for lunch at their grandparents house, Pete Scamardo came outside to confront me. I looked at him and said "Pete, you are nothing but a bully." He responded "That's right, and I love it!' He said this in front of Dina, he wife and my children. When I got in the car to take my children to lunch, my son asked me "Dad, what's a bully?"

Pete Scamardo and Dina Mackney are the most 'successful' father/daughter psychopaths ever to fool the Court. Pete Scamardo has over 100 lawsuits in Fairfax County alone. The litigants in these cases can confirm the patterns. The entire Scamardo family was accused of fraud by Maryland National Bank for $80 Million. Pete and Dina also circumvented the Thoroughbred Ownership licensing laws of Virginia, Maryland and West Virginia. One of her friends from college now refers to her the 'c' word after seeing the real Dina, after working with her. Most of you will not see that side of her, unless you run into conflict. While I am the one that took my own life, this was a murder conceived and financed by Pete Scamardo who hired Jim Cottrell and Kyle Bartol the day after I discovered he was a murderer, and then paid over $1 Million in legal fees to make it happen. People 'targeted' by psychopaths call it 'murder by suicide'.

I was a good father to my children when I was in their lives. No one can dispute or deny that. Dr. Samenow even admitted under oath that I had a 'palpable' relationship with my kids. I know I was an extremely loving and positive influence on their lives and it kills me that I even feel like I have to defend my parenting. My children were the only source of joy and happiness in my marriage. For the Judge Bellows to deny parents and children a 'palpable relationship' and each other's love is corruption. He did not want it to be known that Dr. Samenow committed fraud or that Judge Terrence Ney had a 'close relationship' with a convicted murderer or a parental alienator.

The love that my daughter and I shared was truly special. She is such a sweet, kind and gentle spirit. I am so sorry that I will not be there to see her grow into a beautiful woman. It absolutely crushed me to not be in her life over the last three years. I worked very hard as a father to build her confidence and self-esteem. She is smart, funny and considerate, but she didn't know it yet. I pray that she realizes her strengths and her confidence in herself will continue to grow. I love you dearly, Ruby.

My son James was just entering Kindergarten, when I lost access to him. He is gregarious, outgoing and a great athlete. He is smart and fearless. He could have just as much fun by himself as he could with other kids. Even the older boys in our neighborhood wanted to play with Jack. It absolutely breaks my heart that I will not be able to help him grow into a man. I love you to, James. I miss you both so much.

My identity was taken from me, as result of this process. When it began, I was a commercial real estate broker with CB Richard Ellis. I lived by the Golden rule and made a living by bringing parties together and finding the common ground. My reputation as a broker was built on my honesty and integrity. When it ended, I was broke, homeless, unemployed and had no visitation with my own children. I had no confidence and was paralyzed with fear that I would be going to jail whenever my ex-wife wanted. Nothing I could say or do would stop it. This is what being to death or 'targeted' by a psychopath looks like. This is the outcome. I didn't somehow change into a 'high-conflict' person or lose my ability to steer clear of the law. I've had never been arrested, depressed, homeless or suicidal before this process. The stress and pressure applied to me was deliberate and nothing I could do or say would get me any relief. Nothing I or my attorneys said to my ex-wife's attorney or to the Court made any difference. Truth, facts, evidence or even the best interest of my children had no effect on the outcome.

The family court system is broken, but from my experience, it is not the laws, it's the lawyers. They feed off of the conflict. They are not hired to reduce conflict or protect the best interest of children, which is why third parties need to be involved. It should be mandatory for children to have a guardian ad litem, with extensive training in abuse and aggression. It is absolutely shameful that the Fairfax County Court did nothing to intervene or understand the ongoing conflict. Judge Randy Bellows also used the Children as punishment, by withholding access for failing to fax a receipt. The entire conflict centered around the denial of access to the children, it was inconceivable to me that he would use children like this. This is exactly what my ex-wife was doing and now Judge Bellows was doing it for her.

To all my family, friends and the people that supported me through this process, I am so sorry. I know my reactions and behavior throughout this process did not always make sense. None of this made sense to me either. I had no help and the only suggestion I got from my attorneys was to remain silent. At first, I did what I was told, remained silent and listened to my attorneys. Then after I had given my ex-wife full custody to try and appease her, I learned about Psychopathy and emailed Dr. Samenow about my concerns and asked him for help. Of course, I was ignored. As the conflict continued, I was forced to defend myself. When that didn't work, I thought I could get the help I needed by speaking out. There is no right or wrong way to defend yourself from abuse. Naively, I thought that abuse was abuse and it would be recognized and something would be done. I thought speaking out would end the abuse or at least get them to back off. It didn't. When no one did anything they were emboldened.

Michael Volpe

I took my own life because I had come to the conclusion that there was nothing I could do or say to end the abuse. Every time I got up off my knees, I would get knocked back down. They were not going to let me be the father I wanted to be to my children. People may think I am a coward for giving up on my children, but I didn't see how I was going to heal from this. I have no money for an attorney, therapy or medication. I have lost 4 jobs because of this process. I was going to be at their mercy for the rest of my life and they had shown me none. Being alienated, legally abused, emotionally abused, isolated and financially ruined are all a recipe for suicide. I wish I were stronger to keep going, but the emotional pain and fear of going to court and jail became overwhelming. I became paralyzed with fear. I couldn't flee and I could not fight. I was never going to be allowed to heal or recover. I wish I were better at articulating the psychological and emotional trauma I experienced. I could fill a book with all the lies and mysterious rulings of the Court. Never have I experienced this kind of pain. I asked for help, but good men did nothing and evil prevailed. All I wanted was a Guardian Ad Litem for my children. Any third party would have been easily been able to confirm or refute all of my allegations, which is why none was ever appointed to protect the children or reduce the conflict.

Abuse is about power and control. Stand up for the abused and speak out. If someone speaks out about abuse, believe them.

Please teach my children empathy and about emotional invalidation and 'gas-lighting' or they may end up like me.

God have mercy on my soul.

Chris Mackney

Posted in Uncategorized | Leave a reply

Child Support – Judge White overrules the Objection of both Parents.

Posted on December 23, 2013 by goodmendidnothing
Reply

I have never been opposed to paying child support or caring for my children. All I wanted was a fair and reasonable payment ranging from 20-30% of my income, typical of most child support payments. However, I knew that my ex-wife was not interested in the money. She wanted my support set beyond my ability to pay, so that she could keep me from the children. She had been refusing to negotiate or discuss any way for the parties to stay out of Court, while paying two attorneys over $1 Million in legal fees to drag me into Court over and over again. At one point she had even requested $6,000 per month in support.

It was decided that they were going to use the Family Court system to destroy me for discovering that my ex-wife's father was convicted of accomplice to murder for hiring Woody Harrellson's father, to murder his friend and business partner Sam Degelia. I discovered the truth on June 23rd. On June 24th, my ex-wife's father fired the attorney they were using and hired Jim Cottrell and Kyle Bartol.

At the pretrial child support hearing in March 2009, my income was determined from my 2007, tax return that showed in income close to $300,000, which was from one real estate deal. All my previous years my income was around $100,000. Nevertheless, my child support payment was set at $2,813 per month.

Our Custody hearing was in October 2009. During that hearing my ex-wife asked that I have NO VISITATION with my children, even though there were no allegations of abuse and she had agreed to normal visitation in January. At that hearing the Judge heard lots of he said/she said testimony. After hearing all the witnesses, Judge Randy Bellows even states that he had not heard any allegations of abuse and how unusual it was to be asked to deny all visitation. Even though he is aware, my ex-wife's father is a murderer; that I discovered they had been lying about it for 8 years; that she had a traumatic brain injury and domestic violence was hidden by Dr. Samenow; that I have alleged legal bullying; he orders me to obtain a 'psychological evaluation'. This is now the second order for a 'psychological evaluation' in the case.

Then in November 2009, we have our Equitable Distribution hearing. At that point, my ex-wife still had not had an evaluation and I was being ordered to obtain one, so both me and my ex-wife's attorney object to having the hearing until the outcome of the Psychological Evaluation. Judge Bruce White, denies both our objections and proceeds with the hearing with no regard for the wishes of the parties. He has no idea as to why the psychological evaluation was ordered, but insists on moving forward.

At this hearing, I am prevented from even producing evidence. To this day, I still do not understand why I was prohibited from providing evidence at my own equitable distribution hearing. My opening statement was filled comments about how my ex-wife has repeatedly acted in bad faith and lied and how her whole case was deceitful and dishonest. During her cross examination, I catch her in lie after lie. She even denied sending me an email, on July 17th 2008, (three weeks after I discovered that her whole family had been lying to me), inviting me to a hotel for sex, during our separation. I then pulled out my computer and read her email to the Court, but was unable to 'submit' as evidence.

During the hearing she testifies that her income is $30,000 per year. The Judge stated that based on her tax returns she under-reported her income. She then went on to testify that her Child care expenses were $55,000 per year. She later testified that her household expenses were $264,000 per year. Her parents were subsidizing her income $234,000, but she testified that it was a 'loan'. My ex-wife also testified that our household expenses over the life of the marriage averaged around $264,000. Since my income was only greater than $264,000 1 year during the marriage, either she lied about the amount of the expenses or her parents were subsidizing her lifestyle. My ex-wife also testified that I was "renting" from her, which was a complete and total lie.

Earlier in the year, in June, 3 months after they had my child support set at $2,813 per month, my ex-wife's attorneys got me fired from my job at CB Richard Ellis. I was fired the day after my ex-wife's attorney asked to have CBRE held in Contempt of Court for not allowing the deposition of my supervisor. The 150 pages of documentation provided by CB Richard Ellis, showing no disciplinary action was apparently not sufficient for my ex-wife's attorneys. Even though there was no reason to depose them, the Judge allowed it.

At the equitable distribution hearing, even though I had no income at the time, my income was set at $80,000.

By the end of the Equitable distribution hearing, my child support payment actually went up even though my income went down from over $250,000 to $80,000! I was now ordered to pay $2,816 per month. I also received no assets from the marriage and was ordered to pay my ex-wife's legal bills.

Now the reality is that none of this is about Child Support or the Children. I had money earlier in the process and I was forced to spend it all on attorneys and Doctors because my ex-wife refused to agree to ANYTHING. This whole charade was orchestrated to place as much financial, emotional and legal pressure on me as possible. Judge Bruce White ignored simple math and I was now being forced to pay for the lifestyle that had been subsidized by my ex-wife's father for her entire life. Furthermore, my ex-wife had me put in jail 4 times in three years. Most recently, she had me arrested and put on trial for attempted extortion, which is a felony. I begged her and the Court to allow me to plead guilty to a misdemeanor, as a felony conviction would greatly reduce my ability to earn income to pay off my child support. My ex-wife and the Commonwealth's attorney refused to accept a plea bargain. When 12 jurors were allowed to hear all the facts, I was acquitted.

My child support payment of $2,816 per month is amount attributed to someone making $489,000 per year according to the Virginia Statute. When I was not able to pay because I had no income and no money, my ex-wife put me in jail. When I got out of Jail, Judge Randy Bellows ordered that I am to pay 65% of my income to my ex-wife.

My ex-wife has refused to voluntarily reduce the payment and the Court has refused to hear my motion to reduce the payment in November.

Posted in Uncategorized | Leave a reply

Great resource on Sociopaths

Posted on December 23, 2013 by goodmendidnothing
Reply

Dating a Sociopath is another fantastic site on what's it's like to be in a relationship with a sociopath.

Posted in Uncategorized | Leave a reply

Patterns of behavior

Posted on December 22, 2013 by goodmendidnothing
Reply

Co-parenting with a Sociopath

What my ex wife and her family did was what the female victims of psychopaths call 'Lovefraud', after Donna Andersen's book. Women who are used by male psychopaths feel tricked into the relationships after realizing the guy they love never really cared. In my case, I was the breeder. My ex wife and her parents wanted children and the murder of Sam Degelia would scare any guy away. I was fooled for my genes. Now they are keeping me from them, because I saw behind the mask.

The patterns of behavior of male and female sociopaths all stem from the absence of empathy, guilt, shame, remorse. They fake it really well around people of value to them. The people of no value to them will see the pattern, because they don't hide it with them.

This article is from the mother's perspective who has custody of the children. It accurately describes the chaos of co-parenting with someone with a pathological need for control.

Read it all.

Posted in Uncategorized | Leave a reply

Parental Alienation -Cover-up of a 'Foreseeable harm'

Posted on December 22, 2013

1

Emotional and Psychological abuse is all about Power and Control. It is the misuse of that power and control where the abuse is defined. The Best Interest of the Child statute of Virginia was written to give Judges 'wide latitude' in determining the presence of abuse in the family. Parental alienation is the abuse of power and control by the custodial parent and can be prevented. Parental alienation is not a mystery, and understanding domestic violence, abuse, and the dynamics of power and control are all that are required to prevent it. Dr. Samenow understood this and accurately refers to abusers as 'controllers'.

High Conflict divorce is also not a mystery. All the research into High Conflict divorce shows that they are defined by the extensive litigation. Janet Johnston is the best known researcher of high conflict divorce and parental alienation. Her work dating back to the the 1990's shows that 80% of divorce cases are settled, either upfront, or as the case moves through the process. Studies have found that only 20% of divorcing or separating families take the case to Court. Only 4-5% ultimately go to trial, with most cases settling at some point earlier in the process.' Janet Johnston also found there to be a 'severe psychopathology' in one or both parties, in high conflict divorces where visitation is litigated. My ex-wife has never even attempted to settle. My case has had over 50 hearings and I have been put in jail 4 times, at the request of my ex-wife. Her father was convicted of accomplice to murder, and the Court still has no psychological information about my ex-wife or her head injury.

Domestic Violence is also almost always present in High Conflict Divorce. Peter Jaffe is one of the World's leading experts on children, domestic violence, and custody. The research used by Jaffe to support the claim that Domestic Violence is present in 75% of that 5% of Couples that actually go to trial. The research into Jaffe's research is supported by multiple studies and very well documented.

Michael Volpe

Children in the Crossfire: Child Custody Determinations Among Couples With a History of Intimate Partner Violence," Violence Against Women, Vol. 11, No. 8, August 2005, – See more at: http://americanmotherspoliticalparty.org/ampp-article-library-family-court-custody-abuse-dv/1-research-articles-family-court-bias-custody-abuse-battered-moms/11-high-conflict-cases-likely-have-history-of-domestic-violence#sthash.5e6VnhXN.dpuf

In 1997, The Virginia Commission on Domestic Violence Prevention conducted a study into Custody Cases. The study found that in custody cases where there was also a domestic abuse case in court, only 25% of the custody files referenced the existence of the domestic abuse case. So, of all the cases in Virginia that are high-conflict, about 50% of the domestic violence is not even considered by the Court in making Custody decisions. This is a systemic failure.

In my relationship, I had no power or control. My friends, family and everyone that knows me or my ex-wife and her family, knows that I had no power or control. Dr. Samenow was given the witnesses that would confirm the imbalance of power, control and money in the relationship. Dr. Samenow never contacted my psychiatrist or 5 other witnesses that were provided to verify the abuse of power in the relationship. I even provided Dr. Samenow with a signed release to speak to my psychiatrist who began treating me for depression and abuse, 2 years after my ex-wife's traumatic brain injury. The head injury was very serious and was also identified as a source of conflict in the relationship, in a deposition for the personal injury lawsuit.

Dr. Samenow was also shown a ripped shirt that I had brought into his office, as evidence of domestic violence. My ex-wife had assaulted me, in front of our children, on January 19, 2008. She attacked me from behind as I tried to escape her anger. It all started when she woke me out of bed to help her find her keys, which were in my pants pocket on the floor. Before she woke me up, she had already taken my car keys. She was also already in a state. When I found her the keys the anger did not dissipate. After 8 years, my conditioned response, at this point, was to flee, not to fight. When I attempted to leave and go to the gym, I found my keys missing. She mockingly claimed she had no idea where the keys were and followed me around the house, as I looked. I wanted out of there, so I picked up a tray of her jewelry beads, and explained very calmly, as my children were right there, that if she gives me the keys, I won't turn over the tray. She didn't give me my keys to leave, so I overturned the tray and calmly grabbed another tray. I asked her a second time to for my keys and calmly turned over the second tray. My ex-wife flew into a rage and began hitting and scratching me from behind, ripping the shirt, I showed Dr. Samenow, from my body. The police found me behind a locked door with our children. When they were taken out, I broke down. This event is a microcosm of the dynamic of our relationship and this entire divorce and Dr. Samenow completely misrepresented it to the Court. My ex-wife would become irrational, use instrumental aggression and prevent me from escaping, I would then respond with an elevated reactive aggression. I am not proud of my reactions, but they were not the source of conflict. Just like our divorce.

Here is what Dr. Samenow included in his report about the incident:

Ms. Mackney spoke of her husband's explosive nature in citing a particular incident in which Mr. Mackney became upset and scattered her jewelry materials all over the room. This was after an argument which had eventuated in each taking the other's keys.

"He took the drawers out and threw the jewelry – thousands of dollars worth of jewelry. There were two trays sorted by size. He dumped both of these. I was trying to stop him. I called the police. He was going to delete my work files on the computer."

Dr. Samenow failed to include the Domestic Violence of my ex-wife. I was the one to call the police on her, and I threatened to delete her work files because her father took the shirt, I brought in to show him as evidence. My nature is also not explosive, as anyone has known me or dated me would tell you. I have no history of violence or aggression in my relationships. None. Dr. Samenow also withheld my reports of my ex-wife attacking me on our honeymoon, while I was driving our rental car.

Judge Bellows became aware that there was evidence of domestic violence, that Dr. Samenow left all of it from his report, in April 2009. Dr. Samenow was paid by my ex-wife as a witness to testify after Dr. Zuckerman had testified that there was 'no reason' why I should not have access to my children. Dr. Samenow got on the stand and I pulled out the shirt and asked him under oath if he had seen the shirt before. He admitted that I brought it into his office to show him, but there is no reference to it in his report.

The legal profession and the psychological profession are failing to protect children from a foreseeable harm, by ignoring the dynamics of power and control and the presence of Domestic Violence. The Courts who are responsible for managing the conflict and are beholden on the Psychological professionals and forensic evaluators to understand the conflict. The law empowers Judges to also obtain information about the conflict through other methods, such as Guardian Ad Litems, Parenting Coordinators, and Court Appointed Special Advocates.

The Law, as written, empowers Judges to protect children from parental alienation. They have the tools at their disposal to determine the presence of abuse. Judge Bellows knew there was domestic violence and that Dr. Samenow failed to report it. Two months later, he held me in contempt of court and took away visitation with my children for not including a receipt, when I faxed a copy of a lease to my ex-wife's attorney.

Judge Bellows covered up for the fraud of Dr. Stanton Samenow and failed to protect children from a foreseeable harm, especially when you read all the motions that were filed with the Court that he denied. Judge Bellows chose to protect the professional reputation of Dr. Samenow and Judge Ney over protecting children from abuse. Judge Bellows was the Judge in another case where Dr. Samenow testified as a witness for the Commonwealth and was also accused of not documenting the facts accurately.

Michael Volpe

Posted in Uncategorized | 1 Reply

Gross Negligence and Willful Misconduct

Posted on December 20, 2013

I encountered the Fairfax County legal system first on January 19th, 2008. This was the day the straw broke the camel's back in my relationship with my ex-wife and her family. I called the police after my ex-wife had assaulted me in front of our children, Jack and Lily. I did nothing to threaten or anger her, as I just woke up and she was already angry and hiding my car keys, preventing me from escaping her wrath. I had seen it before and knew exactly that leaving is the only way to avoid the conflict. She knew that I knew that I would leave and deliberately blocked me from leaving.

When I called the police, they found me locked in my son's room, with my children. I had a shirt ripped from my body and scratches and marks all over my back and neck, where she attacked me from behind. My children witnessed the entire situation. Now, Dina had to talk first, which is how she controls the situation and manages 'impressions'. She tried to justify hitting me from behind, as I tried to escape the situation, she had prevented me from escaping, by saying that I turned over a tray of her beads. Her judgement is in denial of facts or an awareness of how her behavior harms others.

After speaking with my ex-wife, I open the door for the police officers, who witness the evidence of assault. Now, if I had been the one to rip her shirt and leave marks on her neck and back, I would have gone to jail, no questions asked, do not collect $200. In this situation, the Police officer decided to leave both the parties and the children in the house together.

After I called the Police, I also called my ex-wife's parents. I wanted them to see how differently Dina was acting and that I had never harmed her. Her parents were there at the time the police arrived and before they spoke to me. When the police officer left and did nothing, after witnessing domestic violence, I was shocked. As I walked out the door, to the gym, in a replacement shirt, I deliberately left the shirt that Dina ripped off me on the kitchen counter. When I came back 90 minutes later the evidence of an assault had vanished. Of course, I asked her about it. She denied any knowledge of the shirt, having no clue of its whereabouts. My reaction to being lied to and 'gas-lighted' was to respond in kind, in an effort to have the shirt returned. I sat down at the computer and threatened to delete her Jewelry business files from the computer. That seemed to do the trick. She then called her father, who had taken the evidence of the assault, and had him drive it back to the house.

This was not the first assault. My ex-wife first attacked me while I was driving our rental car, on our honeymoon. We were talking, I disagreed and she attacked me. It was the first time in any relationship, had I been attacked by a woman.

I told my psychiatrist all about the abuse and the emotional invalidation, who was treating me for depression, directly related to living with Dina and working with her father. I told Dr. Samenow, who knew the patterns of behavior, as per his own book. I even gave Dr. Samenow a signed release to contact my doctor. He never even called her or put in his custody evaluation that I was being seen for depression related to my marriage. He recognized the abuse and hid from his report evidence, facts, witnesses and Doctors that collectively can be viewed as a 'severe psychopathology'. The patterns exist. I told my attorneys about the source of conflict. They even recognized it themselves, as per Robert Surovell's letter of withdrawal, that was also sent to Dr. Samenow.

Refusing every effort to negotiate and then spending over $1 million in legal fees is the behavior that is the source of conflict. It is the very definition of legal abuse and 'high-conflict' behavior. Not-cooperating, ignoring the rights of others, extensive litigation are all red flags of abuse. My ex-wife's father has over 100 lawsuits in Fairfax County alone. My ex-wife's family was accused of fraud by Maryland National Bank for $80 Million.

The staff at the Woodburn Center, the Fairfax County Mental health facility will not address the emotional abuse, psychological abuse or alienation. They are more than willing to get a court order to lock you up if you are in severe emotional distress, but they will not identify the source of the distress as abuse. They are familiar with the details of the case, which is why they will not address the abuse. Psychological trauma requires treatment. Not addressing the abuse or source of the abuse is gross negligence and willful misconduct as, well as a failure to protect children from a 'foreseeable harm'.

The Commonwealth, as Creigh Deeds knows all too painfully, that the Virginia Mental Health System needs reform. If the Virginia Courts acknowledge Parental Alienation as abuse and grounds for loss of custody and Virginia Child Protective Services recognizes abuse as: **Many people think that child abuse is limited to physical harm. In reality, child abuse includes: physical abuse; physical neglect; sexual abuse; and emotional/mental maltreatment.**
For the Fairfax County Circuit Court and the Commonwealth of Virginia to refuse to report or investigate allegations of abuse or bring in a third party, is gross negligence and willful misconduct.

My allegations have never been investigated. My ex-wife has hidden all information about her traumatic brain injury. The Court has denied all my requests to bring in a third party or to appoint a Guardian Ad Litem. The Court has blocked access all access to my children. I can be put in jail, if I even mail them a Christmas present. The Court has denied me due process and is preventing me from lowering my child support or being heard on the violation of Virginia Code 20-124.6 and my fundamental parental rights as per Virginia Code 1-240.1.

Posted in Uncategorized | Leave a reply

Virginia Mental Health Workers and the Potomac School Fail to report Abuse
Posted on December 20, 2013

In Virginia there is mandatory reporting of abuse for any person in their professional or official capacity, with reason to suspect that a child is abused or neglected, including any Mental Health Professional and any teacher or other person employed in a public or private school, kindergarten or nursery school or law enforcement officer.

Michael Volpe

Any person who suspects that a child is an abused or neglected child may make a complaint concerning such child to the local department of the County of city wherein the Child resides.

I REPORTED ABUSE and parental alienation to Doctors from the Fairfax County Mental Health Facility and the Potomac School. The doctors ignored all of my allegations of abuse and did nothing for more than 72 hours.

Any person required to file a report pursuant to this section who fails to do so within 72 hours of his first suspicion of child abuse or neglect shall be fined not more than $500 for the first failure and for any subsequent failures not less than $100 nor more than 1,000.

Posted in Uncategorized | Leave a reply

The Cover-up of Child Abuse by the Fairfax County Circuit Court

Posted on December 20, 2013

Virginia Code says that the appointment of a GAL by a juvenile and domestic relations district court is mandatory in certain cases and permissive in others. Virginia Code § 16.1-266 provides that a juvenile and domestic relations district court shall appoint a GAL in any case involving a child who is:

alleged to be abused or neglected.

the subject of an entrustment agreement.

the subject of a petition seeking termination of residual parental rights.

the subject of a proceeding where the parent(s) seeks to be relieved of the child's care or custody.

This is why the Fairfax County Circuit Court refuses to involve a GAL or allow the case to be remanded to the Juvenile and Domestic Relations Court. For the Circuit Court the appointment is not mandatory! Judge Roush has denied the appointment of a Guardian Ad Litem in March 2013 and again in October 2013. She also denied a motion to recuse herself from the case.

Once a case is remanded to the Juvenile and Domestic Relations Court allegations of abuse MUST be investigated and a Guardian Ad Litem appointed.

Virginia Courts acknowledge Parental Alienation as abuse and grounds for loss of custody and Virginia Child Protective Services recognizes abuse.

Bullied to Death: Chris Mackney's Kafkaesque Divorce

Many people think that child abuse is limited to physical harm. In reality, child abuse includes: physical abuse; physical neglect; sexual abuse; and emotional/mental maltreatment.

This is a COVER-UP OF ABUSE and PARENTAL ALIENATION. I am being denied the ability to parent my children and protect them from abuse. The Court does not like my legal strategy for ending abuse. This is the denial of due process. The Court has yet to even grant a single one of my motions, so it has yet to look at any evidence of the abuse.

Posted in Uncategorized | Leave a reply

Smear Campaigns, Third Party Abuse & How to Cope

Posted on December 18, 2013

Reblogged from Preyed on by a Narcissistic Psychopath:

-

Just when you thought that you are finally free of the sociopath. You might be hurt, but you

are taking time out to recover, and to try to heal. The ruining and smear campaigns start. What is more hurtful is how effective the sociopath is at doing this.
You might have done absolutely nothing wrong. You are probably the victim in all of this, suffering sometimes colossal losses and damage to your life.
Read more... 2,425 more words
This person has decided to speak out about the abuse as well. Sociopaths always blame the victim and try to discredit you by calling you 'crazy' or saying you are the one with mental health problems , just like my ex-wife did.

Remember that they fear only two things: Fear of exposure Fear of losing control

Posted in Uncategorized | Leave a reply

Judge Ney – The Motive
Posted on December 18, 2013

Judge Terrence Ney has admitted to a 'close relationship' with my ex-wife and her family. He had to admit it. I have had dinner at his home and shared his bourbon in 2007. That is why I emailed him. I wanted to inform him that we were both fooled and that my ex-wife and her father are abusers and they were harming all of us with their judgement, especially our children. Judge Bellows and Dr. Samenow were overlooking huge red flags for 'high-conflict' behavior and nothing was being done to identify the source of conflict.

After reporting abuse, fraud, psychopathy to Judge Ney, the emails were forwarded to Judge Randy Bellows. I assumed he would report the abuse and that a third party would be brought into the case. Judge Bellows read the emails and ordered that I am not to contact Judge Ney any further, completely ignoring the content of the emails and the fact that there was already an order in place prohibiting me from 'ex-parte communication' with the Court. The fact that there was already an order in place is significant because of what Judge Bellows should have done. I should have been held in contempt of court, after a hearing on the matter. That would require Judge Ney to be a witness and testify about the emails. Rather than open up the content of the emails, he simply made a second order to avoid having a hearing and having Judge Ney testify. Why wouldn't Judge Bellows take another opportunity to slap me with contempt of Court? My attorney Robert Surovell, warned me to expect it. I was happy not to be found in contempt of Court again, but I was trying to bring out the abuse, have my concerns for the emotional welfare of my children addressed. Judge Bellows blocked the opportunity to uncover the source of conflict or obtain facts about abuse or bring in a third party. This is the pattern of behavior of all the judges on the Circuit Court in my case.

Now all of this might simply be all a coincidence or cruel twist of fate, if not for the fact that the Court still knows absolutely nothing about the psychology or psychopathology of my ex-wife or my children. Dr. Samenow contacted none of her three neurologists about the status of her traumatic brain injury and 'cognitive issues'. He knew her head injury was a concern and that I expected a 'psychological evaluation' as per my requests for information about her memory testing. I had made it no secret that the memory and cognitive issues still existed.

The other fact that does not reflect well on the Fairfax County Judiciary is that Judge Terrence Ney ruled on a case involving his close friend in 2008, THREE TIMES. My ex-father had a dispute with a property owner/neighbor, before the Circuit Court, dated 11-2-2007. The Case # is CL-2007-013329. Now Judge Ney was not the original judge on the case and was ruling on motions before a trial. However, he knew that Pete Scamardo's company was the defendant in the case and did not recuse himself, nor did Pete Scamardo ask that Judge Ney recuse himself from the case on 1-29-2008, 3-7-2008, and on 3-10-2008. I'm not a lawyer, but there is an 'appearance of impropriety' there, right?

If the Court had ordered into the case a Guardian Ad Litem, Special Advocate, Parenting Coordinator, parenting plan, family counselor, or psychological evaluator for my ex-wife, I might find this all a neverending, Kafkaesque nightmare, but the Court has chosen none of these options to reduce or understand the 'conflict'. The American Bar Association and the National Council of Juvenile and Family Court Judges, both have outstanding 'Bench Guides' for managing child safety and abuse in 'high conflict' cases. Then to add insult to injury, the Court has simply blocked evidence of abuse from entering the Court and it has blocked access to the people in my children's lives that could identify a pattern. The Court simply does not wish for it to be known that Judge Ney has a close relationship with someone convicted of accomplice to murder for hiring, Charles Harrelson, to murder Sam Degelia or someone accused of parental alienation. Judge Ney's Judgement might be questioned.

Parental alienation is recognized in Virginia. In 1998, the Virginia appeals court said

In fact, the child suffered parental alienation syndrome resulting from Davis' attempts to turn the child against her foster parents.

The Commonwealth of Virginia acknowledges alienation as detrimental to the best interest of the child, but is denying due process on this very issue as well as preventing an attorney to represent the children in order to prevent evidence from being seen or heard in the Circuit Court. This is a cover-up of abuse.

Posted in Uncategorized | Leave a reply

Sons of Divorce -School Shooters
Posted on December 18, 2013

Sons of Divorce – School Shooters
Why is fatherlessness such a big deal for our boys (almost all of these incidents involve boys)? Putting the argument positively, sociologist David Popenoe notes that "fathers are important to their sons as role models. They are important for maintaining authority and discipline. And they are important in helping their sons to develop both self-control and feelings of empathy toward others, character traits that are found to be lacking in violent youth." Boys, then, who

did not grow up with an engaged, attentive, and firm father are more vulnerable to getting swept up in the Sturm und Drang of adolescence and young adulthood, and in the worst possible way.

Posted in Uncategorized | Leave a reply

LINK
Using The Family Court System to Abuse a Spouse
Will you be able to settle or will you end up in divorce court? The only reason divorcing couples ends up in divorce court is because one or the other refuses to negotiate, mediate or be flexible and come to an agreement with the other.

Ninety five percent of all divorces are settled outside court. That is an encouraging statistic but it needs to be known that the other 5% are the ones that keep the Family Court System working over time.

It is that 5% that tend to go back to court repeatedly. At times over frivolous issues that could be solved if one of the parties would make the choice to respond to the situation in a rational manner. It has been my experience when working with clients that the underlying issue with people who are continually going back to court is the need to get even with an ex-spouse.

There is either the spouse who refuses to follow through on an agreement in an attempt to get back at their ex-spouse or the spouse who withholds child visitation or child support in an attempt to get back at an ex-spouse. They use the Family Court System to keep from having to deal with each other and to keep from having to accept responsibility for the role they play in the ongoing conflict with their ex-spouse. It is toxic behavior that damages all involved including the one engaging in the behavior.

In other words, they keep a legal system backlogged because they have emotional issues that need to be dealt with. So, here is some advice from me, if your ex pushes your buttons emotionally and you want to get back at her/him by going to court, get thee to a therapist's office, not an attorney's office.

Karin Huffner, a marriage and family counselor in Las Vegas has identified a new disorder for a nation already reeling from chronic fatigue syndrome, Internet addiction disorder and other new-age afflictions.

It's called "legal abuse syndrome", and it can strike crime victims, litigants, attorneys and anyone who has dealt with the Family Court System. According to Dr. Huffer, "legal abuse syndrome (LAS) is a form of post traumatic stress disorder (PTSD). It is a psychic injury, not a mental illness. It is a personal injury that develops in individuals assaulted by ethical violations, legal abuses, betrayals, and fraud. Abuse of power and authority and a profound lack of accountability in our courts have become rampant."

Using the Family Court System to abuse an ex only promotes more conflict. If you are of the belief that going back to court or engaging in behavior that defies a divorce court order you are engaging in legal abuse. A therapist can teach you skills needed to resolve conflict in a healthier manner, skills that will save you not only emotional stress but all the money you give a divorce attorney every time you are angry with your ex.

Posted on December 17, 2013 | Leave a reply

The impact of fathers in Children's lives
Posted on December 17, 2013

Boy Trouble

Family breakdown disproportionately harms young males—and they're falling further behind.

In fact, signs that the nuclear-family meltdown of the past half-century has been particularly toxic to boys' well-being are not new. By the 1970s and eighties, family researchers following the children of the divorce revolution noticed that, while both girls and boys showed distress when their parents split up, they had different ways of showing it. Girls tended to "internalize" their unhappiness: they became depressed and anxious, and many cut themselves, or got into drugs or alcohol. Boys, on the other hand, "externalized" or "acted out": they became more impulsive, aggressive, and "antisocial." Both reactions were worrisome, but boys' behavior had the disadvantage of annoying and even frightening classmates, teachers, and neighbors. Boys from broken homes were more likely than their peers to get suspended and arrested. Girls' unhappiness also seemed to ease within a year or two after their parents' divorce; boys' didn't.
Posted in Uncategorized | Leave a reply

All It Takes for Evil to Occur in Parental Alienation
VIDEO
"Parental Alienation is emotional abuse. "

"It harms a child's development"

"It is wrong to witness and allow physical abuse. It is wrong to witness and allow emotional abuse"

"The rejected parent needs help from others"

"Alienating Parents are manipulative and very convincing."

December 15, 2013

Posted in UncategorizedLeave a reply

My ex-wife lies, her attorney hides the evidence.
Posted on December 15, 2013

Michael Volpe

During our divorce, on 5-13-2009, my ex-wife insisted on a deposition, the purpose was to get me to spend more money I didn't have. As another show of good faith, I agreed to yet another request that would cost me more time and money, even though they had never even responded to the extremely fair and reasonable offer to settle my attorney sent to them on 12-8 2008.
During the deposition my attorney asks :
Are your parents paying your legal expenses?
She rather emphatically responds:

No. I paid for much of the legal expenses. They have helped me recently because I have run out of money
Her attorney then explains that her legal bills have not been provided in discovery:

I'll take the blame for that, Rob. That was inadvertent. She provided it. We have — it's not that she's not paying us.
The legal bills that were inadvertently left out of discovery were then asked for three more times. On August 10th 2009 I ask my ex-wife's attorney:

I have been patiently waiting for your firm to respond to my requests for information that I understood should have already been provided by now, through the disclosure process.
In addition to the total amount of your client's legal bills, I will also need a copy of the court testimony from all our hearings. I would prefer to negotiate a settlement agreement, but since I have heard nothing, I will continue under the belief your client does not wish to settle. When can I arrange to pick up the copies?
I get no response for the actual bills themselves, so I on the August 12th, 2009, I ask my ex-wife's attorney simply to provide me with an amount:
Can you also let me know what my wife's legal fees to date equal?
This time my ex-wife attorney actually responds to tell me:

Those exhibits will be exchanged pursuant to the pre-trial scheduling order entered by the court.
I already knew the legal bills were hiding the truth, so I respond to being dismissed again with:
This information was specifically left off the interrogatories and you said in our deposition that you would provide that information. This is highly questionable behavior as it appears that you are either negotiating in bad faith or you lied to my attorney, Mr. Surovell.
This gets no response.

As they continue to reject my requests for settlement we are moving towards trial, I am becoming even more stressed and frustrated, so I email them again about the legal bills on August 26th, 2009: Read the whole email.
'It certainly appears that your firm is 100% guilty of milking Mrs. Mackney and contributing to the ill will of the parties for its financial benefit. Why settle when you can make more money, by filing motion after motion? Why are you hiding my wife's legal fees after you agreed to provide them at the deposition? Can you name ANY specific action that your firm

has done to expedite settlement negotiations?''Once you provide me with the total amount of legal bills, I can respond to your question forthwith.'

I never received a copy of my ex-wife's legal bills until after I had already given my ex-wife full custody and she had asked that I have no visitation.

Her legal bills show that she lied under oath on May 13th and her attorney hid the evidence. She lied that her parents were not paying her bills, she hadn't 'run out of money' and they had 'helped' since the day her father hired her new attorney, as the bills show 7 checks totaling over $72,000 up from June 2008 through April 2009.

DATE	AMOUNT	CHECK #
June 25th, 2008	$15,000	5976
Nov. 18th, 2008	$4,811	6531
Feb. 4th 2009	$15,000	6136
Feb. 24th 2009	$12,205	6153
March 18th, 2009	$9,719	6167
April 9th, 2009	$909	6180
April 10th, 2009	$15,000	6181

TOTAL $72,643.95

Posted in Uncategorized | Leave a reply

'Court Ordered Child Abuse'

Posted on December 14, 2013

In New Hampshire, there was a process for parents to be heard on their complaints in front of a House Committee on the Redress of Grievances. As the name implies, it's a committee of the state House of Representatives. It hears citizen's complaints about public officials, decides whether they're founded or unfounded and recommends action by the full house. Sometimes it recommends that the official in question be impeached.

In 2012, the Committee heard 5 complaints about the behavior of family court Judges or other family court personnel. Here is a few choice comments from their Committee's findings:

Michael Volpe

'[The Committee finds that the Petitioner was wrongly denied by the Family Division all visitation with his child contrary to N.H. law and his constitutional rights for approximately 13 months.'

'Wrongfully recommended the suspension of Petitioner's visitation and parental rights with no findings of abuse or neglect'

'[The resulting effect generally [has] been court order[ed] child abuse in the denial of her access to a loved parent for the period of two years. *This has become a common report before this committee: that the Family division of the court, established to protect children, actually inflicts the injury on the child itself.'*
'Despite never being adjudicated an unfit parent he has been denied all contact with his children for nearly three years without any order of the court preventing such contact in violation of his fundamental parental rights and contrary to NH RSA 461-A:6, (Best Interests of the Child); NH RSA 633:1-A and 633:3-A and 633:4, (Interference with Custody); and, the 14th Amendment to the U.S. Constitution.'
'Also, even when parents are not agreeable, the state has an obligation to protect the best interest of the child.'

Posted in Uncategorized | Leave a reply

"You're harming my children"

Posted on December 12, 2013

So, a real crucial moment in the course of this case was when I was held in contempt of Court for not sending a copy of a receipt. It was in April 2010. This was over a year and a half after the divorce began. Judge Bellows had heard from my psychological evaluator, Dr. William Zuckerman, that I was telling the truth and that there was "no reason" why I should not see my children, despite my ex-wife's baseless request. Mind you, that Judge Bellows had ordered the Psychological evaluation for me, after Dina had requested something he had never been requested before. and now she was asking that I lose overnight visitation (which her false accusations caused) again, as her solution for not sending a copy of a receipt. My ex-wife had asked the Court to deny me all visitation with our children, with no allegations of abuse. Judge Bellows even decides to give them 'wide latitude'? It is gross negligence for the Judge to give a mother wide latitude to take away visitation without allegations or evidence of abuse. The Virginia Statute declaring Parental Rights requires 'strict scrutiny', as it is a fundamental right:

§ 1-240.1. Rights of parents. A parent has a fundamental right to make decisions concerning the upbringing, education, and care of the parent's child.

So, I got my evaluation and the doctor couldn't find any psychological reason to deny visitation (because there were none). Judge Bellows had no choice but to reinstate visitation to what had been previously agreed before Dina's request that all visitation be denied. So after 6 months of being kept from my children by Judge Bellows, I was to have overnights again with my children for the first time in over a year, over Easter weekend. My ex-wife's attorney asks for a copy of 'the lease' as a precondition before I am able to resume visitation. So, Judge Bellows says in Court "and specifically what's required is a receipt documenting receipt of payment for the deposit and first month's' rent'. He says this on March 17th 2010. Judge Bellows also orders that I am to fax this receipt by April 1st to my ex-wife's attorney. However, Judge Bellows orders that my ex-wife's attorney does not have to send me a written copy of the order requiring the fax until April 2nd, the day after I am to send the fax. So, I was going from memory about what I was supposed to send and when. If I had a written copy of the order, I would have done exactly as instructed. So, on April 1st, I fax over a copy of my lease, documenting receipt of payment and rent. My ex-wife's attorney then informs me that I have violated the Judge's order by not sending a lease **and** a copy of this receipt, despite the fact that the lease contains all the same information on the receipt. Any real estate lawyer would also accept a signed copy of a lease as a 'receipt' for payment. It was a 'gotcha' game and Judge Bellows played the role perfectly.

My ex-wife denied me overnight visitation with my children and then filed to have me held in contempt of Court. At the hearing, my ex-wife testified that she handed me a note informing me that the Children were sick. She then testified that she and her father, who was there because she claims she was so afraid, saw me crumple up the note and throw it out the window onto the lawn. <u>This was a complete and total lie</u>, as I brought the note to Court that day and provided the Court the note in pristine, uncrumpled condition. I never crumpled the note and I never through it out the window. I held onto the note and waited for her to come back or to bring me the children. It was all a ruse, to simply keep me from obtaining visitation. Cash for kids.

My ex-wife's motion states that she also drove to the home where I was living on Easter Sunday (the day after she claims she was so afraid of me) to gather evidence and take pictures for the upcoming hearing. Judge Bellows was told that I was going from memory and that the fax of the lease communicated all the information requested. Nevertheless, Judge Randy Bellows found me in contempt of Court and took away overnight visitation with my children, as per the transcript of the exchange. When I objected to the fact that he was taking away visitation because I failed to send a copy of the receipt, which had nothing to do with my children, I became very frustrated and upset. So then Judge Bellows then took away all visitation, simply because I forgot to send a copy of a receipt in a fax.

When I tried to explain that taking away visitation is harming my children, Judge Bellows just got up and walked out. In June 2010, Judge Bellows made his final orders that I was to have no physical or telephone visitation with my children, not for any abuse, or psychological reason or because I was abusing my ex-wife or our children. My children were used by Judge Bellows as punishment for being held in Contempt of Court, at the request of my ex-wife. Judge Bellows simply chose to believe that my reactions to being bullied and abused by the legal system was

Michael Volpe

the source of conflict and willfully chose to ignore all evidence suggesting that my ex-wife was merely trying to deny all access to my children.

Posted in Uncategorized | Leave a reply

Contacted by Mental Health Professionals

Posted on December 12, 2013

So, today I got an email from Doctors and the County Mental Health Facility. That is so nice of the County to spend valuable resources on the problems created by the Cover-up of abuse, parental alienation and psychopathy, in the Circuit Court. This email exchange would not be necessary if the Court had appointed a Guardian Ad Litem to protect the best interests of children or if my ex-wife would simply agree to one.

Below is my email dialogue with the Doctor.

Doctors,

The emotional and psychological abuse I have endured for 12 years has yet to be identified as an issue in my case. My ex-wife is a liar and abuser. She manipulates and creates chaos, where there need not be any. Her father is spending more money in legal fees than I will ever owe my children in Child Support. The psychological and emotional stress and pressure I am under was not an accident or an unfortunate set of difficult circumstances. It's a pattern of behavior. Pete Scamardo never admiitted any wrongdoing in the murder of Sam Degelia, for which he was given probation. I don't wish to belabor the point, but unless you are willing to stand-up and acknowledge that I am being systematically eliminated from my children's lives and bullied to death then there is not much you can do to help me.

I stood up to a bully and an abuser and was silenced and my concerns for the emotional welfare of my children were ignored because the truth might reflect poorly on the Court. Dr. Samenow committed fraud. He was given the red flags for psychopathy and he describes my relationship and the dynamic, I have been describing non-stop since I learned it was a personality disorder, in his book from 2002.

The Court is locked into the misbelief that my 'reactions' to being bullied to death and targeted by a psychopath are the 'source of conflict', completely disregarding all research and literature on the subject of 'high conflict' divorce. The Court is now denying me due process, access to my children, access to their medical records, access to their schools. The Court has also denied my children an attorney 7 times.

All I have ever asked for or wanted was 'fair and reasonable' and let me be on my way. All they have done was 'over-reach' and then the Court would allow it, based on nothing.

I know that I need help, but the source of my stress, anxiety and pressure is not my reaction to the stress, anxiety and pressure. The source of my psychological and emotional pain is 'bullying' or being the target of a psychopath. It is the only explanation that explains my behavior and my ex-wife's.

The Court is willfully ignoring the obvious. I need an expert to look at the evidence available and tell me I am really crazy or testify in Court that I am telling the truth. That is the help I need, but I can't imagine that is the help you are offering? The first step is to stop the bullying.

Kind Regards,

On Wednesday, December 11, 2013 6:07 PM, wrote:

Dr. _____,

Thank you for following up with me. I appreciate your concern. I am currently homeless and have no address.

As you are aware, I have been seen by Doctors at Woodburn before. I have also been seen by Doctors while incarcerated at the Fairfax Adult detention center. I am being abused and targeted by a very wealthy and severe psychopath, who is using the legal system as their weapon and the Court is letting them. Additionally, the Court is willfully preventing any third parties into the case.

Pete Scamardo and his daughter, have spent over $1.2 Million in legal fees, while at the same time refusing to discuss or settle our issues outside of Court. The Court has rewarded her 'high-conflict' behavior and punished me for my 'reactions' to being bullied to death.

I left town and gave up all effort to see my children ever again, in order to escape the abuse and end the conflict. This was their request, as per these letters from my attorney, May 4th and May 9th. When I left town, as per their request, they had Child Support Enforcement come after me. When I contacted my ex-wife's attorney to modify the orders and lower my child support, my ex-wife had me arrested and extradited for attempted extortion. When I begged my wife and the Commonwealth's attorney to allow me plead guilty to a misdemeanor, instead of a felony, they did not respond and insisted on taking it to trial. Fortunately, 12 Jurors saw through the lies and found me not guilty.

My ex-wife and the Fairfax County Circuit Court is covering up abuse, alienation and psychopathy because of the 'close relationship' of Judge Terrence Ney and my ex-wife's family.

Michael Volpe

Please read my blog http://goodmendidnothing.wordpress.com and it may become clearer that my concerns for the emotional welfare of my children are being ingored. I am being silenced and discredited for speaking out about abuse, fraud and a cover-up.

Further discussion with a psychological professional will not help my situation. The orders of the Court are the source of stress and conflict. My children need an attorney to address the issues of parental alienation and abuse. The resources of Virginia would be better spent on an attorney to protect the best interest of my children. If you have any ideas as to how I can get an attorney for my children, I would love to hear them.

Thank you again for your concern, but an attorney can provide far more relief. Fee free to reach me by phone or email.

Kindest Regards,

On Wednesday, December 11, 2013 5:04 PM, @fairfaxcounty.gov> wrote:

Good evening Mr.,

Please accept this e-mail as a follow-up to our conversation on Monday, 12/09/13. As I have mentioned to you in our previous phone calls, we are available 24/7 and more than happy to provide you with support or resources if you are willing to come to Woodburn. If you would prefer to meet directly with me, then we can certainly try to facilitate that. I am copying my supervisors on this e-mail and they have authorized me to work directly with you, if that is your preference. I will also attempt to call you on the same number you used on Monday. If possible, please also provide me with any updated information about your current address and phone numbers. I look forward to speaking with you further and hope that you will be amenable to this outreach effort.

Regards,

Dr. _____,

Posted in Uncategorized | Leave a reply

Open letter to the The Potomac School

Posted on December 12, 2013

Bullied to Death: Chris Mackney's Kafkaesque Divorce

I apologize for reaching out to you in this manner about this matter. It is all so unnecessary. However, James and Ruby and I are being abused and it needs to end now.

The Potomac School needs to get involved to protect children from parental alienation and prevent me from being bullied to death.

The school needs to know that the orders blocking my involvement in my children's education are in violation of Virginia law. Dina knows this.

Because of the 'appearance of impropriety' by Judge Jane Roush, it has become necessary to make the Potomac School aware that James and Ruby Mackney are being parentally alienated from their father. Parental alienation is abuse. The Circuit Court has repeatedly been asked to appoint a Guardian Ad Litem, to legally protect the best interest of James and Ruby. Dina and her attorney have objected and the Court has denied 6 requests. As a result, the abuse has only increased and nothing has been done to address the issue. It has literally been ignored. I have informed Dina's attorneys that I would be reaching out to you for help and that I would take down this blog if she were to allow the appointment of a guardian ad litem. Her attorneys never responded.

The orders of the Court are in direct violation of two Virginia statues that protect the best interest of children, Virginia Code 20-124.6 (Access to Minors records) and 1-240.1 (Rights of Parents).

I have proposed that a Guardian Ad Litem be appointed to address both these issues because It is the recommended course of action in High conflict divorces. A Guardian Ad Litem is legally obligated to protect children. This suggestion, like all my suggestions have been ignored. Perhaps, the Potomac School can speak with their lawyers, as how to best protect the best interests of James and Ruby Mackney, as well as the best interests of the Potomac School. I can assure you, our interests are aligned. I would also strongly encourage the school to speak with Ms. Mackney and encourage her that it would be in the best interest of all parties, especially the children, to have an attorney appointed to protect their legal interests, going forward. Alternatively, I am open to their suggestions, as to what we can do to make sure that the psychological and mental health and welfare of Jackson and Lily are not being jeopardized by parental alienation.

With the recent revelations of Chris Klohman and the Penn State Abuse scandal, I hope that everyone will agree that the appointment of legal counsel would be the best first step, in handling this unfortuntate situation quickly. The Potomac school's involvement is needed as I am powerless to stop the abuse.

Thank you.

Kindest Regards,
Chris Mackney

Michael Volpe

Posted in Uncategorized | Leave a reply

The Virginia Judicial Inquiry and Review Commission does nothing.

Posted on December 12, 2013

So, as I have mentioned, my ex-wife had me arrested and extradited from Texas for asking her to voluntarily lower my child support. While I was in jail on false charges of attempted extortion, I filed motions, on October 9th, with Judge Jane Roush to have my child support modified, my ex-wife held accountable for failing to provide me with my children's report cards from last spring and Guardian Ad Litem appointed. Judge Roush refused to even allow my motions be heard in Court. Then after I was found not guilty by 12 jurors and released from Jail, I filed again with the Court to have the Orders of the Court changed.
The orders of Judge Randy Bellows are actually in violation of Virginia Code Virginia Code § 20-124.6 (Access to Minors records) and § 1-240.1 (Rights of Parents). For no valid legal reason, I am prohibited from contacting my children's doctors or schools. My ex-wife simply asked for it and the Judge granted it. There was no discussion or debate on the issue. So, if there is an emergency I am not contacted. If my children have a medical issue, I am not advised and can not provide any of my own medical history to the doctors.
So, in my motions to Judge Roush, I specifically cite these laws as one of the reasons for requesting a change of the orders. Again, Judge Roush, refused to even allow the motions be heard.

As I am now being denied access to my children and due process, on November 11th 2013, I filed a complaint with Judicial Inquiry and Review Commission to have Judge Roush recuse herself from the case so that a Guardian Ad Litem can be appointed. Donald Curry at the Commission responded to my complaint on November 14th, 2013. Mr. Curry does not even address any of the issues raised in the complaint. He dismisses the complaint citing
'Nothing in your complaint would substantiate an allegation of undue delay by the Judge or otherwise provide any valid basis for Commission action.'

My complaint does not cite 'undue delay' as the reason for my complaint. Furhermore, I am not an attorney. I am only a father, who has not seen or heard from his children in over 3 years.

Now, if Judge Roush will not recuse herself and she will not hear any of my legitimate motions to hold my ex-wife accountable for violating the orders of the Court or to reduce my child support, this is violating my rights to due process and my fundamental rights to parent my child.

In response to the Commission's failure to address Judge Roush's bias and failing to protect children from parental alienation, I faxed this letter to Mr. Curry at the Commission, asking him to reconsider my complaint and have Judge Roush recused from the case.

Mr. Curry,
I have tried to help my children, by six times requesting a Guardian Ad Litem be appointed, in

a case where the mother refuses to negotiate and then pays two partners over $1.2 million in legal fees to drag me into Court.

My 'reactions' to the lies and abuse are not the source of conflict in this divorce. This can be backed up by facts, evidence, witnesses and the Court record. It is extremely unusual for one party to ask for the denial of all visitation without some allegations of abuse. This is exactly what my ex-wife did and Judge Bellows even said he heard no allegations of abuse.

The 'appearance of impropriety' is that the Judge Jane Roush is preventing two children from having access to an attorney who can determine if a 'severe psychopathology' exists or is a factor in the conflict.

Judge Terrence Ney was told about the abuse of children and responded that he has a 'close relationship' with Dina Mackney and her family. The appearance of impropriety is that the Circuit Court is covering up the abuse and parental alienation of Dina Mackney, in order to protect Judge Terrence Ney and Judge Randy Bellows, who turned a blind eye to abuse and the fraud of Dr. Stanton Samenow.
I will be posting this fax on my blog goodmendidnothing.wordpress.com and will be forwarding a copy to my children's Virginia State Delegates and Senator.

I am asking that you reconsider my previous two complaints against Judge Jane Roush for denying me due process and call for her recusal. I also request that the case be administered by a Guardian Ad litem to protect the best interest of our children.

Kindest Regards,
Chris Mackney

I encourage anyone reading this Blog to contact the Mr. Curry at the Judicial Inquiry and Review Commission to inform Mr. Curry that there is an appearance of impropriety and that Judge Jane Roush should be recused from the case.

Posted in Uncategorized | Leave a reply

4 Lies 1 Email

Posted on December 10, 2013

One email from my ex-wife to friends, neighbors and even Dr. Guy Van Syckle, who was involved in our case as a family Counselor, is particularly revealing.
At the end of August 2009, after Dr. Samenow had completed his 'Custody Evaluation', I began reaching out to people to help resolve the conflict and let them know that my ex-wife was not being honest about our case. I knew that Dr. Samenow had committed fraud and I was hoping that exposing the truth would bring resolution.

In response to one of my emails, my ex-wife wrote to everyone:

Michael Volpe

*Dear Friends, I cannot imagine why Chris is including you on this type of email again, again and again; however, you must realize by now that**Chris has lost touch with reality (emphasis added)**. Fact is that the kids and I were waiting for chris all day today for him to pick up the kids and he never showed. No return call, no return email, nothing. Fact is, I have offered numerous make up days that he has declined. He hasn't even showed for many of his regularly schedule times. Fact is, we have made offers to settle and he just hasn't like them —he wants more money despite the fact that he has paid $0 in child support in almost 2 years. Fact is, our motions are not at all ambiguous, they have all been an effort to stop chris from harassing me, my family and kids —on a daily basis.*
I sincerely hope that Chris gets the mental health help he needs and that he stops involving you soon. Thank you.
Every single 'Fact' my ex-wife claims is a lie.

Lie #1 – ' Fact is that the kids and I were waiting for chris all day today for him to pick up the kids and he never showed.'   I never missed a single visit once, ever. My ex-wife was doing everything possible to deny access to my children for over a year and I was extremely diligent about seeing my children at every given opportunity.   I challenge her to produce any evidence, ever, of me ever missing a visit.

Lie # 2 'Fact is, we have made offers to settle and he just hasn't like them'
My ex-wife never made ANY offers to settle, resolve our differences, or keep us out of Court. I challenge her to provide a copy of any evidence of an offer to settle.

Lie # 3 'he wants more money despite the fact that he has paid $0 in child support in almost 2 years.
My ex-wife accused me of blackmail and extortion when I asked her to settle our differences and divide our assets. She claims that I wanted money not to speak out about the accomplice to murder conviction of her father, which she hid from me the entire marriage. I made it very clear that I only wanted what was mine and none of her or her family's money. I also worked as a Commercial Real Estate broker and was earning commission. When I had money I paid, child support and have copies of checks to prove it. Not only is this a lie, its completely disingenuous. Her decisions to litigate every single issue and make no effort to address any issue outside of court. She has spent approximately $1.2 million in legal fees and complains about child support. She is well aware how attorneys can be used to destroy another party. Her father's public record reflects a talent for that weapon, with over 100 lawsuits throughout the metro area, with lots of litigants to verify a pattern of behavior.

Lie #4 'Fact is, our motions are not at all ambiguous, they have all been an effort to stop chris from harassing me, my family and kids —on a daily basis.'
My ex-wife denied me my first overnight visitation with my children in 6 months, after I did not include a copy of this receipt, when I faxed her attorney copy of my lease. Now the lease has the amount of the deposit and all the other relevant information about my residence, but my ex-wife kept me from seeing my children when I went to pick them up the day before Easter because she said I did not send her a copy of the receipt. The 'harrassment' she claims is me trying to have access to my children and requests for a settlement. If she was not for her denying me access to my children, I would have no reason to contact her or her attorney.

Bullied to Death: Chris Mackney's Kafkaesque Divorce

On October 16th 2012, my ex-wife testified in Court and admitted that the information in that email was a lie.

My ex-wife also was aware that I did not have any mental health problems, as I was ordered (for the second time) to obtain a 'psychological evaluation'. Judge Bellows actually ordered me to obtain a Psychological evaluation after being asked to deny all visitation, which only happens in less than 1% of all divorces, by my ex-wife's attorneys, even though he acknowledges there were NO ALLEGATIONS OF ABUSE. The Doctor testified in Court that there was "no reason" why I should not have visitation with my children and that he thought I was telling the truth.

My ex-wife also been diagnosed with cognitive issues, that were completely ignored by Dr. Samenow. Dr. Samenow was asked three times by email about testing for issues related to her brain injury. Dr. Samenow conducted no tests and contacted no doctors.

Posted in Uncategorized | Leave a reply

LINK

The Impact of Parental Alienation
'The experience of being removed as a loving parent from the life of one's child via a sole custody order strikes at the heart of one's being. Suicide rates are reported to be of "epidemic" proportions among alienated parents struggling to maintain a parenting relationship with their children (Kposowa, 2000); and **legal abuse has been noted as a key factor in these cases.***'*

'As Amy Baker writes, parents who try to alienate their child from the other parent subtly or overtly convey a three-part message to the child: I am the only parent who loves you and you need me to feel good about yourself; the other parent is dangerous and unavailable; and pursuing a relationship with the other parent jeopardizes your relationship with me. Alienating parents are themselves emotionally fragile, often enmeshed with the child, with a "sense of entitlement, needing control, knowing only how to take" (Richardson, 2006).'

Posted on December 10, 2013 | Leave a reply

Examples of Manipulation
Posted on December 9, 2013

Throughout my divorce, my ex-wife was manipulating class mothers in my children's classes to take me off their email distribution lists. My ex-wife successfully manipulated one class mom. I noticed that I was no longer receiving emails about my daughter's class. When I asked the mother if my ex-wife has asked her to take me off the list, she admitted that she had.

Later on, after Dr. Samenow conducted his report, my ex-wife sent this email to the team mother for my son's soccer team. She writes:
Can you make sure you NEVER include my ex on email distribution. Call and we can chat. Xd

This is classic alienation behavior.

Michael Volpe

Posted in Uncategorized | Leave a reply

Psychiatric effects of Bullying

Posted on December 9, 2013

http://www.nimh.nih.gov/news/science-news/2013/bullying-exerts-psychiatric-effects-into-adulthood.shtml.
Their numbers, compared to those never involved in bullying, tell the story: 14 times the risk of panic disorder, 5 times the risk of depressive disorders, and 10 times the risk of suicidal thoughts and behavior.

Posted in Uncategorized | Leave a reply

The Best Interest of the Child and the Fraud of Dr. Samenow

Posted on December 8, 2013

So, another reason that I have called this blog 'Good men did nothing' is because I was speaking out about my ex-wife's abusive behavior for years, throughout this divorce and no one would address the issue.

The first good man to do nothing was Dr. Guy Van Syckle. In October 2008, just a few weeks after reporting to the Juvenile and Domestic Relations Court that my ex-wife was denying me access to my children, I sent an email to Dr. Van Syckle making it clear that my ex-wife was not acting in good faith and lied under oath during our first hearing of the divorce, claiming that I pointed a hand gun at her.
On November 16th 2008, when I finally was able to hire another attorney, Robert Surovell, I emailed him that I would be 'These people are going to bully me until eternity'
My attorney even wrote to Dr. Van Syckle and I in December 2008, 'Your wife is way over controlling. Only she can feed the children, only she knows what's best for the children. Only she can make decisions for the children. She displays a shocking lack of sensitivity of your value to the children.'

On December 24th, 2008, after being denied access to my children for every single holiday that year, I emailed Dr. Van Syckle and my attorney Robert Surovell, to let them know that my ex-wife was still denying me access to my children.
By April 2009, Dr. Stanton Samenow had been appointed to conduct a 'psychological evaluation' and my ex-wife was still acting in bad faith and denying me access to my children. Again, in an email titled 'Fair and Equal Protection', I make it clear to Dr. Van Syckle, Dr. Samenow and my attorney Robert Surovell, that 'They have already shown to be unreasonable and not operate in good faith. If she were to be awarded sole custody, I would be virtually eliminated from my children's lives.'
By June 2009, my ex-wife had refused to negotiate and had bled me dry financially again. My attorney, Mr. Surovell, was forced to withdraw from the case. In his withdrawal letter he expresses his frustration with my ex-wife's and her attorneys refusal to negotiate, cooperate or even acknowledge simple facts, that could easily be proven. It is this willful denial of facts, that allows my ex-wife and her attorneys to believe that their behaviors are not the source of conflict. Mr. Surovell writes 'Why it is necessary to torment Mr. Mackney is mysterious.'

Now without an attorney, I am now faced with defending myself alone. I know that they are not acting in good faith and appeal to my ex-wife' attorney and Dr. Samenow. On July 1, 2009, before Dr. Samenow issues his 'Custody Evaluation, on August 3rd, I write'Everything must be done her way, on her terms, regardless of how unnecessary or expensive....This whole case is about control. My ex-wife and her family seek to control our children, ultimately so that they can control and silence me.'

Now, I had not read any of Dr. Samenow's books and I had yet to learn anything about Psychopathy. It was only later, after Dr. Samenow was no longer involved in the case did I actually get around to reading his his book *In the Best Interest of the Child*. When I read his book, I was chilled to the bone as I read his description of the 'Controller personality' and the 'Problem Solver'. Be sure to read the whole thing. It describes exactly what was happening in my case. Dr. Samenow knew exactly the dynamic of my relationship and even the divorce. It was as if he had predicted my future in his 2002 book.

During the separation and divorce proceedings, the controller is determined to maintain the upper hand. Now the problem solver is the enemy! The controller is a formidable adversary as he or she enters the legal arena to fight for child custody. Whereas the problem solver wants to resolve differences, the controller is intent on revenge and winning. The spouse desperately wants to reach a settlement and move on with life, but the controller will react angrily and become intent on destroying the spouse, even threatening financial ruin or tarnishing of reputation. Of course, the most dire threat is to take away what the spouse values most–the child.

'The problem solver is also aware of the controller's success at charming others and convincing them of the correctness of her position. I have had men and women warn me about this as I began a custody evaluation. They worry that I won't be able to penetrate their spouse's persuasive front. Even more, they fear that a judge might be taken in.'

'A warning about sole custody! It can be a powerful weapon in the hands of the wrong parent, i.e., a controller who would attempt to block the other parent from participating in the child's life. Sole custody does not grant permission for one parent to ignore the the other and decides everything unilaterally. A responsible, conscientious parent with sole custody communicates with the other parent, provides information, seeks advice, and demonstrates an accommodating attitude.'

'In truth, the controller is an abuser. When family members get out of line, he or she becomes harsh and punitive. In extreme cases spouse and offspring know that at any time they may be berated, threatened, or even physically attacked. I have seen a controller psychologically grind down his spouse so severely that she had to seek medical treatment and was placed on tranquilizers or antidepressants.'

A review of the legal bills of my ex-wife, shows that Dr. Samenow was in communication with my ex-wife and her attorneys over 40 times during his evaluation, AFTER MY ATTORNEY WITHDREW from the case.

Dr. Samenow committed fraud, by willfully choosing to ignore facts, evidence, and witnesses that could all corroborate my emails that all complain about the 'controller personality' he describes so articulately in his book.

Even Dr. Van Syckle acknowledges that Dina was the source of conflict, after I asked him why he didn't do more to 'preserve the peace early in the process'. He responded by saying 'Remember how Dina was then.'

This is how Psychopaths are able to get away with their abuse. Good men do nothing.

Michael Volpe

Posted in Uncategorized | Tagged Dr. Stanton Samenow | Leave a reply

LINK
Cappuccino Queen

Back in 2012, I had just gotten out of jail for the third time since my divorce began. I find it hard to even write those words, because I had never been arrested or in jail before meeting my ex-wife or during the marriage. Somehow, all of a sudden, for the first time in 40 years, I had lost all ability to stay out of the way of the law. Now that two lawyers who are 'not the type to settle, so have your wallet open', according to their website, were involved, I kept going to jail. Anyway, in 2012, I had just gotten out of jail for posting facts on wikipedia. Judge Randy Bellows ordered that I could not 'repeat allegations' about Pete Scamardo, so I thought posting facts about the murder of Sam Degelia on the Charles Harrelson Wikipedia page, anonymously, would not be in violation of his order not to 'repeat allegations'. My ex-wife paid her attorney to have me held in contempt of Court for repeating allegations. Naturally, Judge Bellows found me guilty and sentenced me to jail, for contempt of Court, even though everything I posted was a fact,that I got off the internet and reposted on the internet, anonymously, until today. In fact, everything I posted is still there and adheres to the Wikipedia standards for posting 'verifiable' information, from a public source.

When I got out of Jail, I was trying to find information about psychopaths on the internet. I looked at everything, because for me the stakes were so high. They were abusing my children and lying to the Court. They wanted me dead for finding out the truth about the murder of Sam Degelia. They fooled everyone up until now, including Circuit Court Judge Terrence Ney, who admitted to a 'close relationship' with my ex-wife and her father, after I told him about the abuse of me and my children. I was desperately seeking the advice of anyone who had dealt with a Psychopath in Court. In the middle of 2012, I stumbled across the site Cappuccino Queen. When I found her site, she was blogging anonymously about her experience dealing with a psychopath in Court. Even anonymously, her writing was so courageous. She was describing the experience that I was going through. Her story is absolutely amazing and you should read posts. Her post about advice in a custody war ended with the sentence 'Our justice system is broken;however, in order to fix it, we must all end the silence.'

Our justice system is broken; however, in order to fix it we must all end the silence. – See more at: http://cappuccinoqueen.com/?m=201209#sthash.iKLW14QL.dpuf

Our justice system is broken; however, in order to fix it we must all end the silence. – See more at: http://cappuccinoqueen.com/?m=201209#sthash.iKLW14QL.dpuf

Our justice system is broken; however, in order to fix it we must all end the silence. – See more at: http://cappuccinoqueen.com/?m=201209#sthash.iKLW14QL.dpuf

Our justice system is broken; however, in order to fix it we must all end the silence. – See more at: http://cappuccinoqueen.com/?m=201209#sthash.iKLW14QL.dpuf

Now, the behaviors of her ex are different from my ex, but the manipulation, control and complete absence of emotion were what were so eerily similar. Her blog really made it clear that what we were both dealing with was an abusive personality disorder. The behaviors were different, but the reasons behind them were the same and we both ended up abused. She had only been blogging a few months and was very selective and discerning about her posts, so I looked forward to them. Then in October 2012, I read the unthinkable. The

Capppuccino Queen's son, Prince, was murdered by his father. He was only 15 months old. After her son was drowned by her ex-husband, she chose to come forward and speak out publicly about the people responsible for her son's death. The Court knew her ex-husband was a psychopath, as the result of a Court ordered evaluation and it did nothing. For psychopaths its about control and domination. They will use children to hurt the person they are targeting. Yet, the Court took no preventative measures to protect her child.
In both our cases, our children were taken to hurt us, because we knew the truth. Cappuccino Queen's story and her courage gave me the inspiration to create this blog and speak truth to power and speak out about abuse. Thank you for your strength, Hera.

Posted on December 7, 2013 | Tagged Cappuccino Queen | Leave a reply

Another Mom Whose Daughter is Stolen Thru Parental Alienation, Her Situation:

Posted on December 7, 2013

Reblogged from Moms' Hearts Unsilenced:

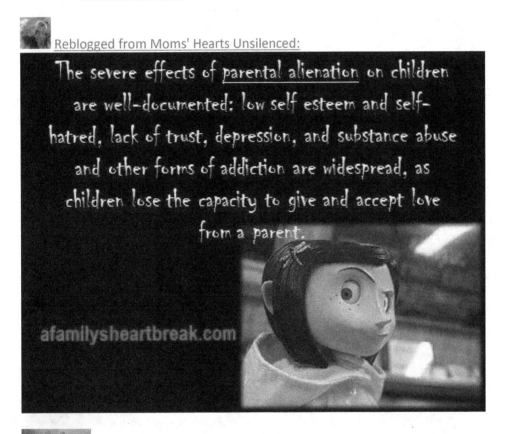

-
  "I am desperately trying to get my 12 year old daughter back home. My ex-husband, who is a police officer, kidnapped her out of school 14 months ago and I have been trying to get her back ever since.

  I have raised her alone as a single mom since she was only 4 weeks old. She was an A student and in girl scouts and dance classes.

Michael Volpe

Read more... 2,546 more words
The Courts are turning a blind eye to abuse. It's a pattern if behavior.

Posted in Uncategorized | Leave a reply

Aftermath of Psychopathy

Posted on December 6, 2013

Now if you find your life spiraling out of control because of the influence of the abuser in y life, this article about the aftermath of psychopathy and how the family members, victims a romantic partners feel after living with someone with a severe emotional dysfunction, may help you understand emotional abuse.

'Psychopathic individuals may even try to convince victims that it is they who are "crazy." This is so common, that victims talking on the internet have adopted the term "gaslighting" to refer to this practice. The term gaslighting comes from the 1944 movie Gaslight, in which a romantic swindler tries to convince his new wife she is insane by lowering the gas fueled lights in their home. She realizes the lighting is different, but he tells her it is fine and that there is no change (as part of his attempt to make her think she is crazy). Due to deception, manipulation and "gaslighting," many victims are left with damage to their sense of basic trust in other people. Some struggle with emotional intimacy for years afterwards. Generally, psychopathic individuals are out to service their own short term agendas. Concern for others in their lives is often non-existent. This lack of concern for others extends even to the immediate family including, children, spouses, parents, and siblings. However, it is not always apparent or clearly understood by those watching it happen or experiencing it.

Dr. Samenow and the Fairfax County Circuit Court had enough to look further into the Psychopathology of Dina Mackney and willfully chose not to protect children from foreseeable harm.

Posted in Uncategorized | Leave a reply

LINK

So, back in July, before I was arrested for attempted extortion, my ex-wife's attorney emailed me and asked me:

What do you want to stop the publication of this information?
I responded:

I want the abuse of James and Ruby to end. The Court is willfully ignoring every red flag for parental alienation and abuse. Dr. Samenow committed fraud when he withheld evidence, facts, witness testimony and completely ignored 4 doctors that could tell him about the mental health of both parties.

This is not about money. It is about control and abuse. Your client is an abuser and 'controller', as Dr. Samenow wrote in his book. You worked with Dr. Samenow and

Michael Volpe

What do children who have been alienated say about Parental Alienation?
VIDEO

This is a 'pattern of behavior' by the Courts, the lawyers, the Judges.

December 5, 2013

Posted in Uncategorized Leave a reply

LINK
Motion to Recuse
This motion to recuse was denied by Judge Jane Roush.

When I filed a complaint with the Judicial Inquiry and Review Commission, they took no action.
Keep in mind my only goal is to obtain an attorney to protect my children from the lawyers and Judges, who appear not acting in their best interest.

Posted on December 5, 2013 | Leave a reply

How Many Psychopaths Do You Know? Far More Than You Think
Posted on December 5, 2013

How Many Psychopaths Do You Know? Far More Than You Think.
Good article about Psychopathy. Its hard to figure out what to do about them when the legal system isn't even looking for them.

Posted in Uncategorized | Leave a reply

What do experts in Psychopathy suggest?
Posted on December 5, 2013

In an effort to seek legal and psychological help for my case, I have spoken to several leading experts in psychopathy. Three experts all suggested that I obtain a guardian ad litem to represent the best interests of my children.

The Fairfax county circuit court has denied 6 petitions to appoint a Guardian Ad Litem.

I have told my ex-wife, her attorney, the Judge and everyone else that I never wanted to speak out about the abuse. I never wanted to make allegations. All I wanted was an attorney, who is legally obligated to protect their best interests.

If the case is in the Juvenile and Domestic relations court, guardian ad litems are granted far more liberally, than the Circuit Court. The benefit for the parents are that the GAL's actually may receive a reduced rate, which is then paid by both parties.

Bullied to Death: Chris Mackney's Kafkaesque Divorce

It is far more challenging procedurally for a pro se litigant in the Circuit Court and expensive. The attorneys in the case will want the case in Circuit Court because this means more fees for them. They can also take advantage of pro se litigants much easier in Circuit Court. The Circuit Court calendar is much busier with criminal proceedings as well, so actually having your case heard will take much longer. The Juvenile and Domestic Relations Court is self explanatory. I think they focus exclusively on the best interests of children.

There is no reason why my children should not have an attorney to protect them from from the lawyers and the Judges. There is a clear effort on the part of my ex-wife and the Court to deny me access to our children by using the Court as a weapon. The Court is willfully enabling the abuse.

Posted in Uncategorized | **Leave a reply**

LINK

The Tactics and Ploys of Psychopath Aggressors in the Family Law System
Tuesday, March 1st, 2011 by Charles Pragnell

In the twenty years I have been advising parents, children, and their legal advisers in several hundred cases in Family Law matters, I have often been asked, "Why is it that children are so often ordered to have contact with, and even into the custody of, parents who have abused them and have perpetrated violence against their partners."

The answer to this question is not simple and involves an examination of the requirements of Family Laws which stress the importance of children having both parents in their lives after parental separation, the dynamics of legal processes, and the often very clear gender biases of the principals involved in judicial processes.

But one of the most outstanding and consistent features of proceedings involving the care of children post-separation are the conduct and behaviours which can be identified as clearly fitting the definitions of psychopathy/sociopathy.

The major personality traits of the psychopath are supremacy and narcissism. The afflicted individual must be in complete control of their environment and all persons who are a part of that environment or can serve the psychopath's purposes in maintaining control.

The psychopath is capable of using both aggressive anger and passive anger with cunning and guile, to achieve their goals of exerting control. Examples of such contrary behaviours are the aggressive violence against intimate partners, with the frequent inherent abuse of children, designed to groom friends, relatives, and professionals into believing they are harmless and indeed very stable and friendly. If thwarted in attaining these goals, however, the passive can quickly turn into the aggressive.

In furtherance of these traits, the major tactics and ploys of the psychopath are:

1. denial of wrongdoings in the face of clear evidence;

2. refusal to take responsibility for behaviours and actions;

3. minimisation of the incident and consequences;

4. blame being placed on others;

5. misrepresentation, fabrication, embellishment and distortion of information and evidence;

6. minimisation of all information and evidence regarding wrongdoing;

7. claims of victim status, alleging the victim was the aggressor;

8. projection of their own actions and behaviour onto the victim; e.g. she abuses/neglects the children/ she is an alcoholic or drug abuser. This is based on the belief by the psychopath that attack is the best form of defence.

The grooming of friends, relatives, and professionals is very clear in many cases, and in particular some psychiatrists, psychologists and family evaluators/reporters have been hoodwinked by such tactics and ploys by the psychopathic individual. Their reports, of course favouring the psychopath, have very considerable influence on the Courts and their determinations. Very often clear evidence of intimate partner violence such as convictions, Domestic Violence Orders, Apprehended Violence Orders and Restraining Orders against the psychopathic aggressor and medical evidence of injuries suffered by the adult and child victims are ignored or dismissed as irrelevant by such professionals.

Such professionals now refer to such cases as 'high conflict' cases, when it is clear that they are situations of a violent aggressor/tormentor/persecutor and their victims. It is easy to see how the cases in Austria and America where young girls were imprisoned for many years by controlling individuals and regularly abused in several ways were undetected, when the aggressors/persecutors/tormentors were able to convince their family members, relatives and associates that they were reasonable, normal people. The same often occurs in other cases of violence and murder where neighbours report that the accused murderer is a nice and friendly neighbour. They do not recognise the Jekyll and Hyde aspects of the psychopath's ploys and tactics and of those they have effectively groomed in their beliefs.

The high conflict which usually occurs in such cases is most commonly engendered by the respective lawyers, conditioned by operating in an adversarial process and arena, whose own major goal is to 'win', whatever may be the justness and fairness of the result.

It is not difficult to see, therefore, how the psychopath is able to readily gain the sympathy and support of some of the professionals engaged in the Family Law system and for them to abandon and forfeit their professional objectivity and impartiality in such circumstances.

In blaming others the psychopath will allege the former partner is mentally ill and in some cases the former partner may be suffering a Complex Post Traumatic Disorder after suffering years of physical, mental, and sexual abuse and violence. This is often misinterpreted and misdiagnosed as a Borderline Personality Disorder or similar psychiatric term. In effect it is a classic 'blame the victim' scenario.

The groomed professionals then enable the psychopath to achieve their primary objective, which is to maintain power and control over their victims, their former partner and children. It is an act of vengeance and spite but mostly it is to maintain the power and control and feelings of supremacism and narcissism. "I am faultless and flawless and in control of my whole environment" are the unvoiced cravings of the psychopath, and "I can continue to inflict my tortures on my victims with impunity" are the psychopath's continuing behaviours.

The Family Law and their shared parenting provisions and its administration by the Family Courts have become ready enablers for the psychopath.

Charles Pragnell is an Independent Advocate for Children and Families.

Posted on December 4, 2013 | Leave a reply

Letter to the Virginia Judicial Inquiry and Review Commission – Donald Curry

Posted on December 4, 2013

Mr. Curry,

I am contacting you again about my case, CL-2008-013013.

I do not know how to make it any clearer to you or to the Fairfax County Circuit Court. There is a cover-up of abuse, parental alienation and psychopathy. There is a manifest injustice. There is an appearance of impropriety.

I am not an attorney but I know when my children and I are being abused.

Judge Jane Roush is preventing children from access to their father and to an attorney in order to prevent a Guardian Ad Litem from protecting them legally.

How many people do you need to hear from in order to acknowledge that it would be in the best interest of Children to have an attorney to represent them, when their mother is spending over $1 Million in legal fees to keep them from their father?

Michael Volpe

This is a conflict of interest.

The Circuit Court is denying children an attorney that can uncover evidence of corruption, abuse and parental alienation. This is a conflict of interest.

Please go to my blog Goodmendidnothing.wordpress.com so that you can read in more detail about the fraud of Dr. Stanton Samenow and how he willfully turned a blind eye to lifetime patterns of high conflict behavior in order to protect Judge Terrence Ney from having a 'close relationship' with a family of a convicted murderer with a severe psychopathology.
Your office needs to take action NOW. This has gone one for 5 years and 2 children are being alienated.

All I am seeking is a Guardian Ad Litem to protect my children. This is not an outrageous request and there is no reason for it to be denied by Judge Roush.

Judge Roush is also denying me and my children Due Process on the issue of Virginia Code 20-124.6.
It is not in the best interest of children that I am forced to speak out about abuse in this manner. Appoint a Guardian Ad Litem immediately, and I will end all communication and take down my blog exposing the truth.

Either there is a severe psychopathology or there is not. So far, this issue has been willfully ignored.

Chris Mackney

Posted in Uncategorized | Leave a reply

Anti-Social Personality Disorder

Posted on December 4, 2013

This is another description of the severe psychopathology that I am facing.

Posted in Uncategorized | Leave a reply

LINK
The High Conflict Couple – A Closer Look
This is another research report into High Conflict Divorce that describes the dynamic of my divorce.

I am fighting to lower my child support to a fair and reasonable level and to have contact with my children and my ex-wife is spending more money on legal fees than all my child support combined, in order to deny me all access to my children. My 'reactions' to being denied all access to my children are viewed as the source of conflict, while my ex-wife's abuse of the legal system is considered normal.

Posted on December 4, 2013 | Leave a reply

LINK
The Empowerment of a Wealthy Abuser in Family Court – A Case Study
When I first read this report on High Conflict Divorce, I didn't think the word 'stalking' was accurate. I thought 'abuse' was a better term. However, I as learned more about Psychopathy, the word stalking took on an entirely different connotation. Psychopaths are predators. Stalking for them is purely to cause harm. That is the only reason they want to know where you are.

This case study is exactly what is happening to me.

Its not that the patterns are hard to detect, nor is it the complexities of the legal system. The patterns of abuse can be determined. The severe psychopathology represented in this report is what is being covered-up and ignored by the Fairfax County Circuit Court.

I was told by my ex-wife's attorney, Kyle Bartol, to leave town and give up all efforts to see my children, as per these letters from May 4th 2012 and May 9th 2012.
When I took them up on the offer to end the conflict and try to move on with my life, this was not enough. They had to remain in control.

Instead of leaving me alone and allowing me to live in peace, in Dallas, TX, my ex-wife sends Virginia Child Support Enforcement after me for the first time in 4 years. This was not an accident or a coincidence. I was contacted by Virginia Child Support enforcement, the month after I began working in Dallas. They were tracking me and waiting until the right moment for an ambush. I immediately contacted my ex-wife's attorney to change the orders of the Court if they were not going to follow through on their request. Rather than discussing the matter or coming up with any solutions or suggestions to keep the parties out of Court, my ex-wife and her attorney went straight to the Commonwealth's attorney to have me arrested for attempted extortion. I was arrested in Dallas, TX by the SWAT team at 7:00 in the morning, in only a pair of shorts. I was extradited back to Virginia by one of the most experienced detectives in Fairfax County.

I had never been arrested or even charged with a criminal offense, so I offered to plead guilty to a misdemeanor, in order to avoid a felony prosecution. The Commonwealth's attorney refused to discuss a plea. They wanted a conviction on the lowest felony, in a high conflict divorce, where the father contacted the ex-wife's attorney asking to lower his child support. I even pointed out that prosecuting me for a felony, would affect my ability to earn, pay child support, pay off legal debts, or pay for an attorney to change the orders.

Michael Volpe

The Commonwealth's attorney was insistent on going to Court. During the trial, my attorney testified on my behalf that Mr. Kyle Bartol and he discussed what would be required to end this conflict. He testified under oath, that Mr. Bartol said that if I 'disappeared', 'no one would come looking for me, as I sat in jail, for posting facts on Wikipedia. This message was also communicated to me in two letters from Mr. Worster.

12 Jurors, who were allowed to hear both sides of the story, were able to recognize that there was no extortion and that Dina Mackney and her attorney are literally using the legal system as their weapon to destroy me and my relationship with our children. The Commonwealth acted way too hastily. There is very little case law on the matter of attempted extortion, as it is a rarely prosecuted offense.

The Commonwealth's attorney, who does not litigate civil, custody related matters, leapt to defense of my ex-wife and her attorneys. She portrayed herself as the victim. According to the Commonwealth, I was attempting to extort money from her, by threatening to damage her character. The reality is that they do not care about the money or the children. The only purpose for the ongoing conflict is domination and control.

That is stalking by way of the Family Court and using the legal system to destroy. That is 'a severe psychopathology.'

Posted on December 2, 2013 | Leave a reply

Email to my ex-wife's attorney

Posted on December 1, 2013

Mr. Bartol,

I think you will agree that my allegations are legitimate and genuine. I remain open to a fair and reasonable solution.

Why don't we agree to a Gal to protect the children from this? The appearance of impropriety is undeniable.

Please let me know if Dina will agree to an attorney for James and Ruby?

Chris

Posted in Uncategorized | Leave a reply

The Cover-up of fraud and abuse

Posted on November 30, 2013

Bullied to Death: Chris Mackney's Kafkaesque Divorce

The patterns of a high conflict divorce are extremely well known to the Judges, Lawyers and Court appointed experts responsible for identifying and reducing conflict in the adversarial process of divorce. Those of us who do not make our living off of conflict can only explain our experience with the expectation that the source of the conflict be reasonably determined.

My story has not changed since the divorce began. Dina Mackney is an abuser and there is a severe psychopathology/traumatic brain injury/emotional dysfunction affecting her ability to make moral, fair, reasonable decisions in this case. She and her attorneys have refused to negotiate or appoint a Guardian Ad litem, and then dragged me into Court for anything they wish. Most recently, they manipulated the Commonwealth's attorney to arrest me and extradite me for 'attempted extortion', after then came after me for child support, when <u>they had told me twice I needed to leave town and give up all effort to see my children, in order to end the conflict</u>.

The legal language that Judges are obligated to follow when they are asked to determine visitation is found under <u>Virginia Code § 20-124.3</u>.Best interests of the child; visitation.
In determining best interests of a child for purposes of determining custody or visitation arrangements including any pendente lite orders pursuant to § <u>20-103</u>, the court shall consider the following:
1. The age and physical and <u>mental condition</u> of the child, giving due consideration to the<u>child's changing developmental needs</u>;
2. The age and physical and <u>mental condition of each parent</u>;
3. The relationship existing between each parent and each child, giving due consideration to the positive involvement with the child's life, <u>the ability to accurately assess and meet the emotional, intellectual and physical needs of the child</u>;
4. The needs of the child, <u>giving due consideration to other important relationships of the child, including but not limited to siblings, peers and extended family members</u>;
5. The <u>role that each parent has played and will play in the future</u>, in the upbringing and care of the child;
6. <u>The propensity of each parent to actively support the child's contact</u> and relationship with the other parent, including <u>whether a parent has unreasonably denied the other parent access to or visitation with the child</u>;
7. The <u>relative willingness and demonstrated ability of each parent to maintain a close and continuing relationship with the child</u>, and the ability of each parent to cooperate in and resolve disputes regarding matters affecting the child;
8. The reasonable preference of the child, if the court deems the child to be of reasonable intelligence, understanding, age and experience to express such a preference;
9. Any <u>history of family abuse</u> as that term is defined in § <u>16.1-228</u> or sexual abuse. If the court finds such a history, the court may disregard the factors in subdivision 6; and
10. <u>Such other factors as the court deems necessary</u> and proper to the determination.
The judge shall communicate to the parties the basis of the decision either orally or in writing. Except in cases of consent orders for custody and visitation, this communication shall set forth the judge's findings regarding the relevant factors set forth in this section.
Everything underlined above has been willfully ignored by Judge Randy Bellows, based on the filings of the Court, alone. Everything underlined above also grants Judge Randy Bellows the authority to determine if there is or is not psychopathy involved in a Custody matter.

Read my filings in this case. Judge Randy Bellows was actively preventing facts, evidence, witnesses from verifying my claims of abuse. He was also using my children as the 'stick' to bully me into silence.

My attorney Robert Surovell, filed two very fair and reasonable motions that would allow Judge Bellows more transparency into the emotional welfare of the children and Judge Bellows simply chooses to deny them.

This Motion for Information and this Motion for a Protective Order were filed in April 2011, two years after the divorce was final. Dina Mackney was withholding information about my children and I was being legally bullied and Judge Bellows chose to do nothing.

Judge Bellows deliberately turned a blind eye to abuse, parental alienation and now Judge Jane Roush is covering up for him by preventing a Guardian Ad litem from being appointed and now denying due process. The orders of Judge Randy Bellows are in violation of Virginia Code 20-124.6 and Judge Roush has refused to hear a motions to modify Judge Bellows orders and appoint a Guardian Ad Litem on this issue.

The last time there was a cover-up of abuse and corruption to this extent, Jerry Sandusky went to jail. I will gladly remain silent about my allegations if my ex-wife would agree to appoint a Guardian Ad Litem to protect the best interests of my children.

Posted in Cover-up, Uncategorized | Tagged abuse, Fraud, Judge Jane Roush, Judge Randy Bellows, parental alienation | Leave a reply

Parental Alienation

VIDEO

The pattern is there for anyone who chooses to see it.

18:23 Listen to the Lawyers answer about the mental health of someone who alienates. "A high rate of psychopathology in a parent who would do this."

November 30, 2013

Posted in Uncategorized Leave a reply

LINK

Is Samenow Corrupt?
Another Blogsite dedicated to stopping Dr. Stanton Samenow? Hmmmmm?

Posted on November 30, 2013 | Leave a reply

Why the two orders, Judge?

VIDEO

Another one of the reasons I named this blog, Good Men Did Nothing was the movie a Few Good Men. Arguably, the best Courtroom scene in movie history was when Tom Cruise's character Daniel Kaffee is questioning Jack Nicholson's, Col. Nathan Jessup. Kaffee knows that Jessup is covering-up a crime, but Col. Nathan Jessup is a highly respected military officer with the enormous responsibility of protecting a marine base in Cuba. The title, obviously refers to those that stood up to power, demanded the truth, and protected the powerless.

This scene is compelling for lots of reasons, but it would be far different if Col. Jessup was a psychopath. Jessup is a man of character, principle and honor. He does not like his authority challenged and uses intimidation and retribution as his defense mechanisms. While his behavior can be viewed as psychopathic, he is not a psychopath.

Col. Nathan Jessup is controlling, abusive, deceptive and a liar. However, it's not just the 'anti-social' behavior that makes someone a psychopath. If you consider the behaviors in the context of instrumental/reactive aggression and whether or not there is an emotional dysfunction, Col. Jessup may not be considered a psychopath.

From my experience in Court, a true psychopath would never admit to anything. Col. Jessup is smart enough to orchestrate the cover-up, but if he was a psychopath he would not have admitted he ordered the 'code-red.' If Col. Jessup were a psychopath, he would have denied everything and Kaffee would have lost the case. Even though there were two orders, that were completely contradictory and made it clear to everyone there was a cover-up, if Jessup would have said that he did not order the code-red, he would have gotten away with it. Kaffee may have even gone on to write a blog about the case.

On January 23rd, 2009, my ex-wife's attorney requested and I agreed to 'psychological evaluation and assessment of the parties and the minor children' 'Each party shall fully cooperate with Dr. Samenow in his conduct of said evaluation, but not limited to, providing Dr. Samenow at his request any medical or mental health information or documentation or releases concerning each party and/or the children.'
This language was specifically changed from 'Custody Evaluation' to 'psychological evaluation', as per my ex-wife's original request sent to my attorney on December 22nd, 2008. I wanted a psychological evaluation because of my ex-wife's head injury; I had just learned that she and had lied to me for 8 years about her father, Pete Scamardo, being convicted of accomplice to murder; and she seems to be unaware of her own 'high conflict' behavior. My ex-wife and her attorneys knew that I was agreeing to a Psychological Evaluation and not a Custody Evaluation.
On August 3rd, 2008, Dr. Samenow completed his 'Report of Independent Custody Evaluation'. My response to Dr. Samenow's report was immediate. 13 minutes after he sent out his fraudulent report, I responded to him in this email 'This report is so completely one-sided it's laughable.'
When my ex-wife's attorney immediately moved to have it included in the case as evidence, I objected and told Judge Bellows that Dr. Samenow did not follow up with 5 witnesses and did not follow the Order of January 23rd.

Judge Bellows did nothing and simply accepted the report into evidence.

After my ex-wife insisted on going to trial over visitation and refusing to negotiate, Judge Bellows is so baffled by the fact that my ex-wife is asking for no visitation, he even comments:

"The only time I can recall being asked to give that kind of relief is in situations where there have been evidence presented to me of abuse, almost always involving physical abuse.

Michael Volpe

> Now, I haven't heard the whole evidence today and maybe there is something that rises to that occasion in this case. I'm not prejudging any issue. But I think that's where we are."

Even though, Judge Bellows has never been asked to deny visitation without evidence of abuse, and knowing about my ex-wife's traumatic brain injury and he knowing that her father is a convicted murderer, he orders me to obtain a 'psychological evaluation'. Now there are two orders that I obtain a 'psychological evaluation'.

On October 16th, 2012, Jim Cottrell, my ex-wife's attorney, called a Psychological Evaluation and a Custody Evaluation "the same thing" in Court before Judge Clayton. Judge Bellows knows that a custody evaluation and psychological evaluation are different, that is why he made the second order. Dr. Samenow did not conduct a 'Psychological Evaluation' as ordered. Judge Bellows knew this and covered-up for Dr. Samenow by accepting the report into the record as evidence over my objection. Judge Bellows could have made Dr. Samenow conduct the proper evaluation, but he didn't. This is the first cover-up. Judge Bellows acknowledges the difference between the 'custody evaluation' and a 'psychological evaluation' by then ordering me to obtain a second 'psychological evaluation' on November 3rd, 2009.

Why the two orders, Judge Bellows?

November 29, 2013

Posted in Uncategorized**Leave a reply**

Psychopath or 'Secret Controller'?

Posted on November 28, 2013

The 'Gold Standard' diagnostic tool used to identify psychopathy is the PCL-R Checklist created by Dr. Robert Hare. This checklist is a simple list of 20 characteristics that one either possesses or does not possess, as a pattern of behavior, and can be verified over the life of the individual. It is through people familiar with the individual over time, that its possible to verify whether or not the behaviors exist. A careful examination of break-ups with old boyfriends and girlfriends is a good place to start. Another location for identifying areas of conflict and people that can verify information is the Court record. Someone who has a lifetime of lying, manipulating, stealing and murdering can easily be recognized by the pattern in which they handle the 'conflict' in Court. This is why the PCL-R is used throughout the criminal justice system. The PCL-R is a reliable predictor of psychopathy, abuse and 'conflict'.
I have read parts of Dr. Samenow's books and he seems to have a complete understanding of psychopathy. He refers to the psychopathic personality in his books as the 'controller personality' in his 2002 Book titled *In the Best Interest of the Child: How to Protect Your Child from the Pain of Divorce* or 'secret controllers' as he does in his book *The Myth of the Out of Character Crime*. As I consider Dr. Samenow's books and his clear understanding of psychopathy, I ask why Dr. Samenow does not just refer to them as Psychopaths? If he is describing a different construct, why does he change the name from book to book?
The psychological construct of Psychopathy is not new. Dr. Hervey Cleckley's book *Mask of Sanity*, considered a seminal work and the most influential clinical description of psychopathy in the twentieth century, was published in 1941. From 1970 to 1978, Dr. Samenow worked as clinical research psychologist for the Program for the Investigation of

Criminal Behavior at St. Elizabeths Hospital in Washington, D.C. Dr. Samenow effectively studied psychopaths.

Even after Dr. Hare published Without Conscience in 1993, Dr. Samenow attributes the conflict created by psychopaths in divorce, to the 'controller personality' in his 2002 Book*In the Best Interest of the Child*:

Many marriages break up when a noncontrolling husband or wife stands up to a controller. By refusing to endure any longer the mistreatment dished out for years, the noncontrolling spouse precipitates a crisis. The marriage may have gone smoothly in the controller's opinion, largely because he or she went unchallenged. In reality though, the non-controller had walked a tightrope. As a problem solver, he or she has sought to avoid unnecessary and debilitating conflict and picked battles discerningly. Having the welfare of the child uppermost in his or her thoughts, the problem-solving parent let a lot go by rather than subject the household to unpleasantness. When he or she finally becomes fed up with walking on eggshells and decides to do something, the marital equilibrium is disrupted. The noncontrolling spouse's sudden assertiveness strikes at the core of the controller's self-concept. At home he or she has been accustomed to having his or her way. Now things are different. The controller reacts by angrily faulting the other spouse for creating the upheaval. If the problem solver fails to back down, the controller becomes more irascible and domineering.

In truth, the controller is an abuser. When family members get out of line, he or she becomes harsh and punitive.

He begins his 2007 book *The Myth of the Out of Character Crime*:

The theme of this book is that people always respond in character, that it is impossible for a person to do otherwise. You cannot be other than what you are! The "out of character" crime can be understood only by figuring out what the character of the alleged perpetrator truly is. "Character" as used here is synonymous with the patterns of thinking and behavior that a person demonstrates throughout life. If you do something out of character, you are not being you. That is impossible!

Chapter 4 titled 'Secret Controllers' includes:

I call these individuals "secret controllers" because they are not perceived as controlling. They are successful in attaining what they want. Rarely do others challenge them. These people may not be seen accurately for who they really are until they have done irreparable damage.

Can someone in the Psychological or Legal Community explain why Dr. Stanton Samenow does not just call them by the more widely accepted term 'psychopath'? Does Dr. Samenow have a professional rivalry with Dr. Robert Hare?

Dr. Hare was born in 1934, Samenow in 1941. Dr. Hare worked as the psychologist in the British Columbia maximum security prison in the early sixties. Samenow clearly cme into the field after Hare. However, Samenow published The Criminal Personality Volume 1 in 1976; Volume II in 1977; and Volume in 1986. Dr. Hare's book Without Conscience was published in 1993. From what I read of both men's work, they are describing the same individual.

Dr. Hare's work in defining the Psychopath and in the creation of the PCL-R Checklist does seem to run parallel to Dr. Samenow's work. Does anyone in the psychological community know the history between these two men?

Michael Volpe

Posted in Uncategorized | Tagged Dr. Robert Hare., Dr. Stanton Samenow | Leave a reply

LINK
Stop Bullying at any Age. Thank you Starbucks.
Anyone that knows me and my 'patterns of behavior' knows that I love coffee. I admit it. My love for Starbucks goes back to the release of their City themed mugs. I was in New York City in 1994 and I bought the first edition New York City themed mug because it was huge. So, this morning as I logged into the Starbucks wi-fi, I was pleased to see that Starbucks was promoting the Stand up to Bullying at Any Age Project.

Bullying is merely a manifestation of psychopathy. Psychopathy is an emotional dysfunction. People with psychopathy do not experience guilt, remorse, shame, or appear to display a conscience. The fMRI neuroimaging shows that there are physical distinctions in the brains and neural communication pathways of the brain. Bullying behavior is the abuse of power, and control for personal gain, with complete disregard for the the rights and feelings of others. People who are bullied display very primitive, but clear signs of fight or flight. They display 'reactive' aggression. The abuse of the power and control over anyone weaker or powerless to prevent it or avoid it is bullying. Psychopath's display 'instrumental' aggression.

The distinction between reactive and instrumental aggression is a critical factor for identifying psychopathy, according to Dr. James Blair, a leading expert on using fMRI technology to identify psychopathy in the brain. In Chapter 1 of his book, The Psychopath-Emotion and the Brain, Dr. Blair make very clear the relationship between bullying and the psychological concepts of aggression.

Bullying is an example of instrumental aggression and, unsurprisingly, individuals who engage in bullying behaviors frequently engage in other forms of instrumental anti-social behavior in other contexts (Roland and Idsoe, 2001).
Dr. Samenow was told the story of Memorial Day 2008. I had just discovered that Pete Scamardo was a murderer on June 23rd. On May 26th, less than a month prior, Pete admits in front of his grandchildren, his daughter and his wife, that he "loves" being a bully. My son even asked me "Dad, what's a bully?" as we drove away to lunch at Panera.

Dr. Blair includes the distinction between instrumental and reactive aggression in the first chapter because these types of aggression are *'mediated by separable neurocognitive systems (Blair, 2001); see chapters 7 and 8. Reactive aggression is the final form of the animals response to threat.'*
Understanding, and identifying bullying and abuse is much easier once you look at the behavior of both the bully and bullied as either instrumental or reactive aggression. The aggression is either instrumental or reactive by the context of the aggression, including the presence of an emotional impairment Dr. Blair writes:

The crucial aspect of psychopathy is not the display of anti-social behavior. Instead, it is the emotional impairment. So, when we consider our four examples (of aggression), we need

not only to assess whether they present anti-social behavior, but also whether they present with emotional impairment.

Posted on November 27, 2013 | Leave a reply

LINK

2012 Presentation on Psychopathy in Family Court

The patterns of behavior of psychopaths in family court is well known. They are known to the judges, lawyers and mostly by importantly by experts. Their job is to not just see the patterns but to rule them out with a few simple questions.

I challenge anyone to peer review Dr. Samenow's work and find no psychopathy.

Posted on November 27, 2013 | Leave a reply

"Its fraud. Its all a scam"

VIDEO

This video is a great example of how psychopaths lie, manipulate and dupe others, and portray themselves as the victim in order to benefit financially.

I am NOT saying that the woman in this video is a psychopath. I know nothing about her or her history. However, her behavior in this situation does resemble the tactics and strategies employed by psychopathy.

This behavior requires a cognitive dissonance. Her behavior does not match the reality. Psychopaths will simply deny facts and the feelings and rights of others in order to justify their actions. Simply verifying the waitresses story with the victim would uncover facts that prove the waitresses story false.

Dr. Stanton Samenow chose not to talk to people who could prove my ex-wife's stories false. He was told where to find the 'reciept' (evidence proving the lie) and he chose not to verify. In many instances, he was actually given the 'receipt', and chose not to report it.

Dr. Samenow's report is as fraudulent as the initial report of the 'hate crime'.

November 26, 2013

Posted in UncategorizedLeave a reply

The Psychopathic Brain: Broken and Free of Blame

Posted on November 25, 2013

Michael Volpe

What is it about a cold-hearted psychopath that intrigues us so?

People who are known psychopathic serial killers like Ted Bundy and John Wayne Gacy instill fear in us, but they also bring us some curiosity. Perhaps the fear stems from our inability to comprehend and identify with their actions and the motives that drive them. This is probably a good thing because it's an indicator that we are not on the same playing field.

Read more... 1,025 more words
Posted in Uncategorized | 1 Reply

Q: Why create Good Men Did Nothing? A: To end the abuse.
Posted on November 24, 2013

Good Men Did Nothing was created for one reason. To end the abuse of me and my children.

This blog is the result of many years of parental alienation and abuse. I never wanted to have to create a blog discussing how my life has been destroyed by the psychopathy of my ex-wife, who spent over $1 million in legal fees to deny all access to my children, after I discovered that her father was a convicted murderer. I never wanted any of this. I only wanted out of the marriage to end the abuse. My plan was to be a good father to my children, regardless of what my ex-wife said or did.

Long before the divorce began, I already knew there was something seriously wrong psychologically in the family and only wanted to get out of the marriage to get away from the abuse. When I discovered on June 23rd 2008, that Pete Scamardo was convicted of accomplice to murder and that my ex-wife her whole family, including my brother in law, Warren Haynes of Gov't Mule and the Allman Brothers, had hidden the murder conviction, it only confirmed that I wanted nothing to do with these people. The very next day, on June 24th 2008, Pete Scamardo fired the attorney already working on the case, Mark Carlin of Ain & Bank, DC's number 1 divorce law firm. Pete Scamardo immediately hired Jim Cottrell, who advertises on his website that 'he's not the type to settle, so have your wallet open'. In 5 years, they have never acted in good faith or engaged in any discussions to keep us out of Court. Instead, they deliberately choose to view anything I say or do as a reason to go back to Court. Jim Cottrell was hired for the same reason Charles Harrelson was hired. It's a pattern of behavior.
In October 2008, after watching my ex-wife and her attorney lie in Court and say that I pointed a "hand gun" at her, I was forced to hire an attorney. I don't even own a hand gun and never pointed any gun at my ex-wife, ever. Never during the marriage was the subject of the pointing a gun ever even a topic of discussion. My ex-wife made it up entirely.
On November 16th, in the first series of emails with my new attorney, I inform him that they would 'bully me til eternity'. One December 4th, 2008, I literally begged my ex-wife and her attorneys not to use the legal system to destroy me. On December 7th, I inform Dr. Guy Van

Bullied to Death: Chris Mackney's Kafkaesque Divorce

Syckle and Dr. Stanton Samenow that my ex-wife was acting in bad faith and that I was concerned about mental health problems. On December 10th 2008, my newly appointed attorney's first action was to propose a settlement. They never bothered to respond. My ex-wife hired two of the most ruthless, aggressive attorneys in the DC Metro area to destroy my life, using the Court as the weapon.

In June 2009, my attorney Robert Surovell is forced to withdraw from the case, I have been bled dry financially again, because my ex-wife refused to negotiate and insisted on going to Court for every issue. His frustration with the case and the bad faith of Jim Cottrell and Kyle Bartol are evident throughout his letter, that was also cc'ed to Dr. Stanton Samenow. The letter of Robert Surovell is consistent with the reaction of people who are 'gaslighted', lied to, manipulated or attempt to work out a fair and reasonable agreement with a psychopath. After Dr. Samenow's fraudulent report, I begged them again not to take me to court. However, they insisted on dragging me into Court even though they had the upperhand. I now had no attorney and they had a bogus report from Samenow recommending full custody for Dina and no overnight visitation for me.

They were so insistent and arrogant about destroying me, they went into Court and asked Judge Bellows to deny all visitation. First of all, parents almost never go into Court to litigate visitation. Research into high conflict divorce shows that couples actually litigate Custody about 5% of the time. Research by Dr. Janet Johnston from 1994 finds that there is a 'severe psychopathology' in one or both parties that litigate visitation. Visitation is actually litigated by a Judge in far less than 1% of all divorces. Yet, my ex-wife went into Court and asked that I have no visitation, despite the fact that there was NO ABUSE reported. Judge Bellows even comments about how unusual it is to deny all visitation. Psychopathy exists in approximately 1% of the population.

5 years later, my ex-wife and her attorneys have yet to put in writing anything that I can agree to end the abuse. In fact, the only thing I have in writing that communicates my ex-wife's suggestion as to how to end the conflict are from the Court appointed attorney, Rob Worster. While in Jail for the third time in May 2012, I asked Mr. Worster to help end the conflict and abuse and to discuss a resolution. Mr. Worster wrote me two letters, on May 4th and May 9th 2012, informing me of my ex-wife's suggestion for ending the conflict is that I 'simply disappear' and give up all contact with my children.

Friends, family and even doctors familiar with the situation, all recognized that I was being bullied to death and strongly encouraged me to get away from the conflict and start over. The Court was ignoring abuse, and parental alienation and preventing any third parties from entering the case, so I chose to leave town and give up all efforts to ever see my children. I moved to Dallas in 2013, just to escape the abuse and not have to go to Court anymore.

The first month after I moved to Dallas and began working, I was contacted by Child Support Enforcement (CSE) for the first time in 4 years. My ex-wife waited until I was relocated and working before sending the State to come after me, even though her attorney told me that if I dissapeared, no one would come looking for me.

Immediately after being contacted by CSE, I began contacting Kyle Bartol, asking them to voluntarily reduce my child support, which is currently $2,816/month. This is the amount someone making $489,000 per year should pay, according to Virginia Statute. I am not opposed to supporting my children, but I am currently owe over $2,000 per month more than my income supports.

I made it very clear to Mr. Bartol and my ex-wife that I DID NOT want to speak out about any of this. The Subject of my first email to Mr. Bartol is titled 'Ending the Abuse'. I only wanted 'fair and reasonable' child support and visitation that was in the best interest of my children. Instead of offering any proposals to keep us out of Court, or telling me that they think my illegals are extortion, Kyle Bartol and my ex-wife went straight to the Commonwealth's attorney to have me arrested and extradited from Dallas for attempted extortion.

I was arrested in Dallas and extradited to Fairfax County Virginia and put on trial. I have no criminal history and or history of legal conflict prior to my relationship with my ex-wife, so I tried to make things easy by offering to plea to a misdemeanor. By pleading to a misdemeanor, I could give them their pound of flesh, get out of jail, and avoid the risk of being convicted for a felony. Strangely, the Commonwealth's attorney Elizabeth Kohut, refused to accept a plea, from a first time offender. She chose to move forward on the rarely prosecuted charges of attempted extortion. It was extremely unusual for the prosecutor to get involved in a domestic relations case, before a detective had determined a crime and then to insisting on going to trial.

When I went to trial, my Court Appointed attorney, Maggy Vaughn, had no trial experience. She had never defended a client in a criminal trial before. She was smart, passionate, ethical and diligent, but she was defending a rarely prosecuted charge against a Commonwealth's attorney that refused to accept a plea. I thought my goose was cooked and that I would be convicted of a felony. I wrote the Commonwealth's attorney three times and told her that it would not be in the best interest of anyone involved for me to be convicted of a felony. I was ignored.

On October 21st, 2013, Maggy Vaughn and Todd Zinicola brilliantly defended me in Court against attempted extortion charges. Elizabeth Kohut's closing arguments were ridiculous. She simply asked the Jury to rely on their 'common sense'. My attorney's relied on the law. They informed that Child Support is not owed to the mother. It is owed to the Children. Child Support is also not 'money'. If child support is not money and it does not belong to the mother, then it cannot be extorted. Not Guilty.

This case has dragged on and the conflict continues because of abuse that continues to be ignored. I will continue to detail exactly how Dr. Samenow committed fraud and how Judge Randy Bellows chose not to investigate allegations of parental alienation in other posts, but I thought it was important to make the point that this blog is the result of years of abuse and doing everything I could to have these concerns addressed by the people responsible for determining the 'best interest' of my children.

I would gladly take down all of this information if my ex-wife would simply agree to appoint a Guardian Ad Litem. She and her attorneys have steadfastly refused to even respond to my requests for a Guardian Ad Litem.

Posted in Uncategorized | Leave a reply

Neurobiological basis for Psychopathy
Posted on November 23, 2013

My ex-wife also suffered a traumatic brain injury during the marriage, so I also began looking into the available information about neurobiological origins of psychopathy. I knew she was not processing emotional information the way I was, but I didn't know if this was a result of her head injury or if this emotional dysfunction was a result of some other brain injury and was it genetic. I wanted to know if my children might also have this condition.

A brain image can be used to determine if there are any structural or functional abnormalities in the way the brain operates. Any lawyer knows that a legal expert will say anything you pay them to say. An fMRI, PET Scan, or MRI of a damaged part of the brain could theoretically identify a marker for severe mental illness or other reasons for cognitive impairment. Custody, visitation, and Support will all need to be reconsidered if one could obtain evidence of psychopathy.

My ex-wife was treated by three neurologists in the Washington D.C. metro area for her memory problems, 'cognitive issues' and 'bleeding on the brain'. She was ultimately referred to Dr. Debra Warden, arguably the leading expert on traumatic brain injury in the Country. So, when Dr. Samenow chose not to contact any of her doctors or hear from them regarding the extent of her injury, I knew he was hiding something.

I went looking for experts and read the work of Dr. James Blair and Dr. Kent Kiehl. Both have independently identified neurobiological markers for psychopathy. Does that mean that a picture of the brain can prove someone a psychopath? Not quite. But it's another piece of evidence that can be considered in context of other evidence available to the evaluator.

These doctors have used functional Magnetic Resonance Imaging to capture brain activity in real time. Apparently, ex-wife had several and Dr. Samenow chose not to to look at any or report them to the Court. If Dr. Samenow had obtained records, they become evidence. Dr. Samenow knew that fMRI neuroimaging of my ex-wife's damaged brain existed, taken by the leading expert in traumatic brain injury, and he chose not to talk to the doctor or have her provide the reason for her fMRI.

The Courts are doing everything they can to keep out fMRI evidence, but are happy to rely on the objective, often biased testimony of experts like Dr. Samenow. Dr. Samenow was accused of 'significant bias' throughout his career, "against the possibility of mitigating evidence based on a defendant's history or background', in a case involving Judge Randy Bellows. A Judge on the US Court of Appeals noted: "Dr. Samenow's professed and public views make him incompetent to aid a defendant in finding and presenting mitigating factors..."

If you are facing a psychopath in Court, you will need to understand the lifelong patterns of behavior first. You will recognize the patterns of behavior long before you will ever need a fMRI. However, an fMRI can go a long way to cross check the behaviors with any identifiable brain differences. If you are ever accused of having mental problems, you may easily prove your accuser wrong by having a positive fMRI. There are two or three tests that need to be conducted to rule someone in or out as a psychopath. I know I would welcome anyone to take an fMRI of my brain. In fact, I even proposed to Dr. Keihl that I send him two fMRI's as a test to see if he could determine the abuser and the abused.

Michael Volpe

Should a Court appointed Psychologist also consult a Neurologist to confirm his findings?

○ Yes, the more 'evidence' the better with psychopaths   ○ No, a neuroimage has no probative value to a evaluator   ○ Maybe, depends on the case.

VoteView ResultsPolldaddy.com

Posted in Uncategorized | Tagged Dina Mackney, Dr. Stanton Samenow Psychopathy, Pete Scamardo |Leave a reply

Best way to deal with a psychopath?

Posted on November 23, 2013

After I realized that the 'source of conflict' in my life was a Psychopathy, I read everything I could on the subject. I read books, research reports, pop psychology articles, Law Journal Articles, Psychology Journal articles. There was no questioning the link between 'high conflict' behavior and psychopathy. I read all the blog sites, victim forums, healing community groups, father's rights groups, that discussed what to do legally, emotionally, financially in order to protect yourself and your children from the 'chaos' that will come.

The discussion comes down to two camps. The 'run away' camp (as I call them) that encourages people to leave immediately and have no further contact. I actually agree with this strategy, but am not in that camp. If you have the ability to recognize these people and proactively avoid those relationships, this strategy wins every time. I am in the 'it's too late to run away camp'. I am like the little girl, chained to the bed, in the basement. It's too late to 'have no further contact'. I need a third party to recognize the abuse and take appropriate action.

Psychopaths do not stop the abuse of their 'target'. If they happen to find you a threat to them or of no further use, you must be eliminated because you know how they operate. You need to be driven away, so you become 'targeted'. A campaign begins to discredit you and make your life so miserable, you have no further choice but to leave. They make false accusations, claim to be afraid of you, call you mentally unstable, undermine you at work, plant drugs, manufacture evidence, hide evidence and anything else they can think of to portray you as the problem and themselves as innocent victims. They need you out of the picture, so they can maintain the facade they meticulously maintain. They do not give up because they got away with it. They hide the abuse at all costs by gaining trust and manipulating people into thinking they are something they are not. The target is portrayed as the problem in order to discredit any attempt to call them on their lies. They see clearly how their actions wreak havoc on their target, but show no mercy and no good faith effort to end the suffering. They are arrogant about it, as they literally destroy people's lives in plain sight. Then when you start to 'react' to being chained in their basement, you must be silenced. You have to consider the thinking of the individual in context to their reaction to the emotional distress of their 'target'. This why people like Lance Armstrong, Bernie Madoff, and Jerry Sandusky are all considered psychopaths. There is a clear underlying emotional dysfunction that affects their judgment. Their inability to experience and process their own emotions as well as perceive the distress of the victims affects their judgment. As a life strategy, they abuse, lie, steal, murder, manipulate because they do not experience shame, remorse, guilt, feelings of empathy or compassion for other people, who do fully feel the effect of normal emotional cognition.

If you can get away, get away. If you can't get away and you know the abuse won't stop, then speak out. The only way to stop the abuse is to speak out until it stops. Jerry Sandusky, Bernie Madoff, Ariel Castro, Lance Armstrong and every other abuser gets away with abuse because Good Men Do Nothing. You can remain chained to the bedpost, accept your fate, and hope one day, everything will be ok or you can speak out until you get the help you need to end the abuse.

Someone in power or authority must stand up on your behalf and recognize the abuse and do something to stop it. In order for that to happen, you will need to speak out to people in authority. People in authority would also need to understand abuse and take appropriate action. Unless there is corruption, a conflict of interest or the person in authority is a 'pawn', being used by the psychopath, your allegations of should be taken seriously.

If you can't get away, and you spoke out and everyone turned a blind eye you might want to consider suicide. I certainly don't suggest suicide as the way to end abuse, but I understand it. That's why I suggest you fight like hell and scream like hell for your life. Someone in the neighborhood will hear you in the basement and do something to free you.

If you screamed for help and you know everyone in the neighborhood heard you and then put cotton in their ears to block out the noise coming from the basement of the creepy guy in the neighborhood, then you may want to think about killing yourself. You are probably not coming out of the basement.

What 's the best way to deal with a Psychopath?

- ○ Get away as fast as possible and have no contact.
- ○ Speak out about the abuse.
- ○ Make no sudden movements, slowly distance yourself.
- ○ Other (Comment added below)

VoteView ResultsPolldaddy.com

Posted in Uncategorized | 1 Reply

God's Gonna cut you down.
VIDEO
November 22, 2013

Posted in UncategorizedLeave a reply

Michael Volpe

Emotional Invalidation, Parental Alienation, Family Law and Psychopathy – Welcome to my world.

Posted on November 21, 2013

5

As many of you already know, I have been reaching out for help for severe emotional abuse, parental alienation and psychopathy in a domestic relations case in Fairfax County Virginia. When I entered the process, I knew my case was different. I just discovered for the first time in 10 years that my children have a convicted murderer for a grandfather. My ex-wife and her father are extremely abusive and controlling and now I discovered they had hidden evidence of this from me in order to have children.

My case has been in the Fairfax County Circuit Court since October 2008. There have been 54 hearings in the case. My ex-wife and her father have spent well over $1 million in legal fees. I currently owe my ex-wife over $200,000 in legal fees and my children over $125,000 in back child support. The Court has ignored every one of my fair and reasonable solutions to keep everyone out of Court. The Court has put me in jail 4 times, at my ex-wife's request. I have literally begged the Judges in the case to bring in a Guardian Ad Litem to protect the children in a 'high-conflict' family matter that involves severe emotional abuse, parental alienation and psychopathy. 6 times, the Fairfax County Circuit Court has prevented my children from obtaining an attorney to protect their rights, while the mother is spending 4 TIMES the amount in legal fees than I will ever owe my children. Conflict of interest, anyone?

Abusers, high-conflict divorces, and psychopaths are all defined by patterns of behavior. Abusers are able to abuse because they have power over their victim and they manipulate, lie, 'gas-light' and create 'chaos' and control. Acts of sexual abuse, domestic violence, and emotional abuse are the fault of the abuser and can be verified or refuted by looking at the misuse of instrumental aggression. The patterns of behavior either exist or they do not. Unless you choose not to see the pattern.

Emotional Invalidation is how abusers manipulate and control. Emotional Invalidation is debilitating, abusive and among the most emotionally abusive experiences, that leads to PTSD and suicide. I am not a legal expert or doctor, so I can only refer to expert opinion on these subjects, but emotional invalidation is always a factor with psychopathy. Psychopathy is an emotional dysfunction that impacts the ability to properly process shame, remorse, guilt, display a 'conscience' and perceive the the rights and feelings of others. They literally generate fear in others and enjoy it.

I have endured years of emotional invalidation during my marriage and my divorce. I was physically abused, beginning on my honeymoon. My ex-wife abused me in front of our children on January 19th, 2008. The police arrived to find me locked in my son's room with my children, with a ripped shirt and scrapes and marks all over my neck and back. Her father then tried to hide the shirt after the police chose not to arrest her. This can all be verified by the police report of the incident, which should be available to the public. Although it wouldn't surprise me if it was hidden by Fairfax County. Dr. Samenow hid this from his forensic evaluation.

Bullied to Death: Chris Mackney's Kafkaesque Divorce

The Fairfax County Circuit Court has prevented my case from reaching the Juvenile and Domestic Relations Court, where Guardian Ad Litems are appointed frequently to identify the source of conflict, at a reduced rate, which is shared by both parties. It has denied every single one of my fair and reasonable solutions to keeping the parties out of Court. It has refused to investigate allegations of severe emotional abuse, parental alienation and psychopathy.

Below is a sample of my filings in this case. The Court has denied EVERY SINGLE one. It is covering up the abuse, parental alienation and psychopathy to protect the reputation of Judge Randy Bellows, Judge Terrence Ney, Judge Jane Roush, Judge Brett Kasabian and Judge Dennis Smith. Each one of these Judges heard about my concerns for the emotional welfare of my children and chose not to grant my petition to appoint an attorney to protect their interests. The Court has willfully chosen to ignore patterns of behavior and the recommended strategy in high-conflict cases, according to the American Bar Association and the sections about 'abuse' in the The National Council of Juvenile and Family Court Judges 'Judicial Guide to Child Safety in Custody Cases.'

The Court is preventing a Guardian Ad Litem from entering the case because according to Judicial System of the Commonwealth of Virginia:

Guardian ad litem (GAL) literally means "guardian for the suit." A guardian ad litem in Virginia is an attorney appointed by a judge to assist the court in determining the circumstances of a matter before the court. It is the fundamental responsibility of the guardian ad litem to provide independent recommendations to the court about the client's best interests, which can be different from advocating for what the client wants, and to bring balance to the decision-making process. The GAL may conduct interviews and investigations, make reports to the court, and participate in court hearings or mediation sessions.

Please read my motions and decide for yourself. Please post in the comments if you think there is severe emotional abuse, parental alienation, psychpoathy, fraud, or a cover-up.

If you want more details or have questions about my case, please post them in the comments. I will provide full disclosure. I will also be addressing specifically the fraud of Dr. Stanton Samenow and how he used his knowledge of Psychopathy to hide Psychopathy from the Court. Then I will go through how Judge Randy Bellows chose to use my children as punishment, which is exactly what alienating parents do to deny access to the other parent. Judge Bellows was not fooled. He was made aware of my concerns and the patterns of behavior before and after I understood psychopathy.

1st Rule to show cause for 6 telephone violations and being called a liar in front of the children 4-20-09 - DENIED

2nd Rule to show cause for 14 telephone violations. 2-10-10 - DENIED

3rd Rule to show cause for 15 telephone violations. 4-29-10 - DENIED

Subpoena for a copy of the emails of Pete Scamardo to Jim Cottrell. – DENIED

Motion to Remand to J&DR Court. 6-22-10 DENIED Includes the patterns of behavior behaviors of psychopaths and wealthy abusers using the Court to destroy a weaker spouse.

Motion to permit Contact 3-24-11 - DENIED

Motion for Information about the Children 4-10-11 - DENIED

Motion to Reconsider Protective Order – 5-12-11 DENIED

Petition for a Guardian Ad Litem 6-30-11 - DENIED

Motion to Unseal File – 7-12-20

Show Cause for failing to Provide Report Cards - 6-20-11 DENIED

Motion to Recuse 7-14-12 - DENIED

Mysteriously, Judge Bellows recused himself, Sua Sponte, from the Case. After he recused himself, without any explanation, I filed 4 more motions to appoint a Guardian Ad Litem.

2nd Petition for a Guardian Ad Litem 3-4-12 - DENIED

3rd Petition for a Guardian Ad Litem 9-7-12 DENIED

4th Emergency Petition for a Guardian Ad Litem 10-9-12 DENIED

5th Petition for a Guardian Ad Litem - 3/1/13 - DENIED

On October 9th, 2013, I filed for a 6th Petition for a Guardian Ad Litem, motion to reinstate visitation, motion to modify child support, and a Rule to Show cause against my ex-wife for failing to provide report cards for the Spring Semester -all were DENIED.

Motion to Recuse and Remand – November 6th – DENIED

A motion for a change of Venue DENIED.

Posted in Uncategorized | 5 Replies

'When men speak...
QUOTE
Posted on November 20, 2013

'When men speak ill of thee, live so that nobody will believe them.' – Plato

Posted in Uncategorized | Leave a reply

'Anybody can be...
QUOTE
Posted on November 20, 2013

Bullied to Death: Chris Mackney's Kafkaesque Divorce

'Anybody can become angry – that is easy, but to be angry with the right person and to the right degree and at the right time and for the right purpose, and in the right way – that is not within everybody's power and is not easy.' – Aristotle

Posted in Uncategorized | Leave a reply

'A man who won'...
QUOTE
Posted on November 20, 2013

'A man who won't die for something is not fit to live.' – Martin Luther King, Jr.

Posted in Uncategorized | Leave a reply

'The world is a...
QUOTE
Posted on November 20, 2013

'The world is a dangerous place to live; not because of the people who are evil, but because of the people who don't do anything about it.' – Albert Einstein

Posted in Uncategorized | Leave a reply

"All that is ne...
QUOTE
Posted on November 20, 2013

Reply ↓

Posted on November 21, 2013

As many of you already know, I have been reaching out for help for severe emotional abuse, parental alienation and psychopathy in a domestic relations case in Fairfax County Virginia. When I entered the process, I knew my case was different. I just discovered for the first time in 10 years that my children have a convicted murderer for a grandfather. My ex-wife and her father are extremely abusive and controlling and now I discovered they had hidden evidence of this from me in order to have children.

My case has been in the Fairfax County Circuit Court since October 2008. There have been 54 hearings in the case. My ex-wife and her father have spent well over $1 million in legal fees. I currently owe my ex-wife over $200,000 in legal fees and my children over $125,000 in back child support. The Court has ignored every one of my fair and reasonable solutions to keep everyone out of Court. The Court has put me in jail 4 times, at my ex-wife's request. I have literally begged the Judges in the case to bring in a Guardian Ad Litem to protect the children in a 'high-conflict' family matter that involves severe emotional abuse, parental alienation and psychopathy. 6 times, the Fairfax County Circuit Court has prevented my children from obtaining an attorney to protect their rights, while the mother is spending 4 TIMES the amount in legal fees than I will ever owe my children. Conflict of interest, anyone?

Abusers, high-conflict divorces, and psychopaths are all defined by patterns of behavior. Abusers are able to abuse because they have power over their victim and they manipulate, lie, 'gas light' and create 'chaos' and control. Acts of sexual abuse, domestic violence, and emotional abuse are the fault of the abuser and can be verified or refuted by looking at the misuse of instrumental aggression. The patterns of behavior either exist or they do not. Unless you choose not to see the pattern.

Emotional Invalidation is how abusers manipulate and control. Emotional Invalidation is debilitating, abusive and among the most emotionally abusive experiences, that leads to PTSD and suicide. I am not a legal expert or doctor, so I can only refer to expert opinion on these subjects, but emotional invalidation is always a factor with psychopathy. Psychopathy is an emotional dysfunction that impacts the ability to properly process shame, remorse, guilt, display a 'conscience' and perceive the the rights and feelings of others. They literally generate fear in others and enjoy it.

I have endured years of emotional invalidation during my marriage and my divorce. I was physically abused, beginning on my honeymoon. My ex-wife abused me in front of our children on January 19th, 2008. The police arrived to find me locked in my son's room with my children, with a ripped shirt and scrapes and marks all over my neck and back. Her father then tried to hide the shirt after the police chose not to arrest her. This can all be verified by the police report of the incident, which should be available to the public. Although it wouldn't surprise me if it was hidden by Fairfax County. Dr. Samenow hid this from his forensic evaluation.

The Fairfax County Circuit Court has prevented my case from reaching the Juvenile and Domestic Relations Court, where Guardian Ad Litems are appointed frequently to identify the source of conflict, at a reduced rate, which is shared by both parties. It has denied every single one of my fair and reasonable solutions to keeping the parties out of Court. It has refused to investigate allegations of severe emotional abuse, parental alienation and psychopathy.

Below is a sample of my filings in this case. The Court has denied EVERY SINGLE one. It is covering up the abuse, parental alienation and psychopathy to protect the reputation of Judge Randy Bellows, Judge Terrence Ney, Judge Jane Roush, Judge Brett Kasabian and Judge Dennis Smith. Each one of these Judges heard about my concerns for the emotional welfare of my children and chose not to grant my petition to appoint an attorney to protect their interests. The Court has willfully chosen to ignore patterns of behavior and the recommended strategy in high-conflict cases, according to the American Bar Association and the sections about 'abuse' in the The National Council of Juvenile and Family Court Judges 'Judicial Guide to Child Safety in Custody Cases.'

The Court is preventing a Guardian Ad Litem from entering the case because according to Judicial System of the Commonwealth of Virginia:

Guardian ad litem (GAL) literally means "guardian for the suit." A guardian ad litem in Virginia is an attorney appointed by a judge to assist the court in determining the circumstances of a matter before the court. It is the fundamental responsibility of the guardian ad litem to provide independent recommendations to the court about the client's best interests, which can be different from advocating for what the client wants, and to bring balance to the decision-making process. The GAL may conduct interviews and investigations, make reports to the court, and participate in court hearings or mediation sessions.

Please read my motions and decide for yourself. Please post in the comments if you think there is severe emotional abuse, parental alienation, psychpoathy, fraud, or a cover-up.

If you want more details or have questions about my case, please post them in the comments. I will provide full disclosure. I will also be addressing specifically the fraud of Dr. Stanton Samenow and how he used his knowledge of Psychopathy to hide Psychopathy from the Court. Then I will go through how Judge Randy Bellows chose to use my children as punishment, which is exactly what alienating parents do to deny access to the other parent. Judge Bellows was not fooled. He was made aware of my concerns and the patterns of behavior before and after I understood psychopathy.

1st Rule to show cause for 6 telephone violations and being called a liar in front of the children 4-20-09 - DENIED

2nd Rule to show cause for 14 telephone violations. 2-10-10 - DENIED

3rd Rule to show cause for 15 telephone violations. 4-29-10 - DENIED

Subpoena for a copy of the emails of Pete Scamardo to Jim Cottrell. – DENIED

Motion to Remand to J&DR Court. 6-22-10 DENIED Includes the patterns of behavior behaviors of psychopaths and wealthy abusers using the Court to destroy a weaker spouse.

Motion to permit Contact 3-24-11 - DENIED

Motion for Information about the Children 4-10-11 - DENIED

Motion to Reconsider Protective Order – 5-12-11 DENIED

Petition for a Guardian Ad Litem 6-30-11 - DENIED

Motion to Unseal File – 7-12-20

Show Cause for failing to Provide Report Cards - 6-20-11 DENIED

Motion to Recuse 7-14-12 - DENIED

Mysteriously, Judge Bellows recused himself, Sua Sponte, from the Case. After he recused himself, without any explanation, I filed 4 more motions to appoint a Guardian Ad Litem.

2nd Petition for a Guardian Ad Litem 3-4-12 - DENIED

3rd Petition for a Guardian Ad Litem 9-7-12 DENIED

Michael Volpe

4th Emergency Petition for a Guardian Ad Litem 10-9-12 DENIED

5th Petition for a Guardian Ad Litem - 3/1/13 - DENIED

On October 9th, 2013, I filed for a 6th Petition for a Guardian Ad Litem, motion to reinstate visitation, motion to modify child support, and a Rule to Show cause against my ex-wife for failing to provide report cards for the Spring Semester -all were DENIED.

Motion to Recuse and Remand – November 6th – DENIED

A motion for a change of Venue DENIED.

Custody Evaluation of Dr. Stanton Samenow (Chris Mackney's notes in red, children's names blacked out)

STANTON E. SAMENOW, PH.D., P.C.

Report of Independent Child Custody Evaluation

Dina M. Mackney v. Christopher H. Mackney
(Case No. CL2008-013103)
Christopher and Dina Mackney married June 3, 2000. They have two children **&^ (DOB: ***** and *&^% (DOB: *****). During May, 2008, Ms. Mackney petitioned for a protective order stating that she feared bodily injury if she continued to live with her husband. (This entirely my wife's side of the story. I have NO history of violence against anyone EVER. On our honeymoon on Maui, she attacked me in the car. I had never been attacked by a woman before, so I stopped the car and explicitly stated to her that I could never do that to her being a 6'5" male. I also told her if she did it again, I would divorce her. It happened at least 6 more times over the nine year marriage, most recently, in January 2008. During that altercation, she ripped a shirt off my body left marks on my shoulders back and neck. All of this was explained to Dr. Samenow. He makes no mention to my version of these events or her physical abuse. Her protective order also comes after her attorney sent me two letters to move out. It is also noteworthy that it was her attorney that sent a settlement offer to mine, the morning the Protective order hearing was to take place.) She also expressed apprehension that Mr. Mackney's "escalating rage" might cause harm to the children. (My wife immediately plays the victim and claims to be afraid, in spite of NO EVIDENCE or WITNESSES to any physical abuse. She has left a hole in our bedroom wall when she threw a book through it, and there is surely a police report from the Jan 2008 incident where the police showed up.) In June 4, 2008, a settlement agreement specified Mr. Mackney would leave the marital home and that Ms. Mackney would dismiss her petition for the protective order. (This was a 2 month temporary agreement signed before I learned about her Father. It was to include an 'informal exchange' of financial information and lead to a 'global settlement') The parties did in fact separate during June, and Dina Mackney was granted exclusive use of the marital residence.

In January, 2009, the Circuit Court of Fairfax County set forth a *pendente lite* visitation order. Mr. Mackney would spend time with the children on alternate weekends from after school on Friday until Sunday at 5 p.m. and every Wednesday from after school until 6:45 p.m. This examiner was named in that order to provide "a psychological evaluation and assessment of the parties and the minor children in order to make recommendations to the Court and the parties regarding what custodial arrangements would best suit the parties and the children."

The following list contains the sources consulted for this evaluation.

Clinical Interviews with Dina M. Mackney

Michael Volpe

January 30, 2009 (1 hour)
February 23, 2009 (1 hour)
- April 29, 2009 (1 hour)
- May 26, 2009 (1 ½ hours)
- June 16, 2009 (1 ½ hours)

Administration of the Minnesota Multiphasic Personality Inventory II: 4/29/09 Home Visit on June 25, 2009

Clinical Interviews with Christopher H. Mackney
February 23, 2009 (1 hour)
March 4, 2009 (1 ½ hours)
- April 10, 2009 (1 hour)
- April 24, 2009 (1 hour)
- May 7, 2009 (1 hour)
- May 22, 2009 (1 hour)
- June 23, 2009 (1 hour)
- June 30, 2009 (1 hour)

Administration of the Minnesota Multiphasic Personality Inventory II: 5/7/09 Observation on playground and in office, 4/30/09
Home Visit on 7/1/09

Clinical Interviews with *&$# Mackney (DOB: &&&&&)
April 9, 2009 (30 minutes)
April 30, 2009, brief interview and administration of the Children's Apperception Test
May 7, 2009, brief interview
June 17, 2009 administration of Bricklin Perceptual Scales

Clinical Interviews with %%*& Mackney (DOB: **(())
April 30, 2009 (15 minutes)
May 7, 2009, brief interview
June 17, 2009, brief interview

Collateral Interviews
Peter and Andrea Scamardo, parents of Dina Mackney, 3/4/09
John and Linda Donovan(requested by me because their daughter is close friends with my daughter and they have seen me with my children on numerous occasions. Samenow does not quote them or reference anything they said positive about me?) **acquaintances of Chris and Dina Mackney, 4/28/09**
Kimberly Gurick, nanny for Dina Mackney, 3/9/09, 5/11/09, 6/17/09
Tracy Heiden, friend of Dina Mackney, 4/23/09
Ronald Salerno, (Ron is the business partner that is the Front man so Pete can invest and hide behind his good name. Ron signs the documents and Pete puts up the majority of the equity in their deals.) **family friend of Mr. and Mrs. Scamardo,**(interesting description- he is Pete's business partner and also invests with Pete in Thoroughbred Horses) **.4/24/09**
Frederic L. Spain, (Fred also has a conflict of interest, as he works with Pete and currently has business dealings with him in West Virginia) **family friend of Mr. and Mrs. Scamardo, 4/27/09**
Cyndi Vasco, (Cindy was high school friends with Dina's rebellious sister, Stefanie, who married to <u>Warren Haynes</u>. Stefanie has a long history of drug abuse including Marijuana and

Bullied to Death: Chris Mackney's Kafkaesque Divorce

Cocaine. Cyndi could testify about if Dina and Stefanie were aware of her Father's past.) **friend of Dina Mackney, 6/10/09**

Collateral Telephone Interviews
Guy Van Syckle, Ph.D., clinical psychologist, 4/13/09, 5/12/09
Andrea Greenwich, &*%%'s first grade teacher, The Potomac School, 5/11/09
Bernie Shea and Destani Leas, **(%'s pre-school teachers, Country Day School, 5/14/09
Stefani Scamardo-Haynes, sister of Dina Mackney, 5/4/09
Deborah DeStefano, aunt of Dina Mackney, 4/24/09, 4/29/09, 5/06/09
Gail Cavallaro, friend of Dina Mackney, 5/14/09
Michael Humphries, (requested by me to provide testimony that I am VERY close to my children and have been VERY active in their care. He can also testify about my care for our home and my marital interest. Samenow includes no testimony from this or any of my witnesses that reflects positively on me.) **neighbor near marital residence, 6/08/09**
Cindy Wallace, (This is the sister of the man that Scamardo had killed. She wanted to talk to Samenow about the murder conviction, Scamardo's character, etc. Samenow's description of her is suspicious) **contacted in Texas by Chris Mackney re Mr. Scamardo's situation, 4/24/09**
Richard Ware, (College friend/fraternity brother from SMU for 20+ years. Also an attorney with <u>Rees Broome Diaz</u>. Samenow later claims I have no 'close friends') **friend with whom Chris Mackney lived, 4/28/09**
Mike Harris, (College friend/fraternity brother from SMU for 20+ years. Mike and his wife have spent weekends with my wife and children. Mike KNOWS EVERYTHING good and bad about me.) **friend of Chris Mackney, 4/29/09**
Edward McGinnis, (requested by me to speak about my involvement with my children and parenting. Suspiciously, McGinnis would only say positive things about me, but is not quoted at all in the report)**neighbor near marital residence, 5/13/09**
Correspondence between Robert Surovell and James Cottrell (and Kyle Bartol), Attorneys at Law, June 12, 14, 2009
Letter from Robert Surovell to Stanton E. Samenow, Ph.D., 3/19/09
Motion to Suspend Visitation, or in the Alternative to Require Supervised Visitation and to Further Enjoin Defendant's Harassing Conduct of Plaintiff (undated)
Affidavit and Petition for Rule to Show Cause, 3/11/09
Amended Complaint for Divorce, 1/26/09
Petition for Protective Order and Exclusive Use and Possession of Residence, (undated)
Petition for Protective Order – Family Abuse (in the Fairfax County Juvenile and Domestics Relations Court), 5/23/08
Affidavit for Preliminary Protective Order (in the Fairfax County Juvenile and Domestic Relations Court), 5/23/08
Temporary Settlement Agreement, 6/4/08
Settlement Agreement Regarding Pendente Lite Exclusive Use and Possession of Marital Residence, 7/15/08
Voluminous e-mails between Dina and Chris Mackney
E-mails between Chris Mackney and Stanton E. Samenow, Ph.D.
E-mails between Chris Mackney and Kyle Bartol, attorney at law
E-mails between Dina Mackney and Stanton E. Samenow, Ph.D.
E-mail to Dina Mackney from Andrea Greenwich, Lily's teacher, 3/11/09
Transcript of hearing before the Honorable Randy I. Bellows, 4/23/09

Michael Volpe

Dina Mackney

Ms. Mackney approached this evaluation in a thoughtful, cooperative manner. Under intense stress, she did her utmost to retain her composure while under siege from her husband who indiscriminately attacked her parenting practices, accused her of poor judgment due to an alleged head injury from an auto accident, maliciously defamed her parents in a very public manner, and generally made life difficult for her. (This is EXACTLY the opposite. I have been the one that was under intense pressure, as I had been accused of blackmail, extortion, libel, slander, and physically abusing my wife. The only thing they have to attack me on is my 'rage', 'anger', etc. I have only wanted to settle and from the first day, I have been accused of being 'angry'. As I told Dr. Samenow, I am not angry. I am FRUSTRATED with my wife's strategy of not negotiating. Samenow continues to run with the 'anger' storyline anyway.) **Throughout her life, Ms. Mackney has formed close relationships, proving herself to be a loyal friend, and remaining devoted to family members who have served as a bulwark of support.** (This is not true. She only has one friend, Gail, talk to Samenow. She has also alienated her two good friends from college, who she worked with on her website business in 2001-2002. One friend, Angelique Finan called her a 'cunt' and no longer speaks to her.) **This examiner finds that, despite extremely trying circumstances, Ms. Mackney has placed the best interests of &*** and #@%* ahead of everything else.** (Not true, she did not allow me to see my children on ANY holidays in 2008, she had the class mom, Kelly Malesardi, take me off my daughter's class email list, and has routinely prevented me from seeing my children. Plenty of evidence to support this.) **Ms. Mackney has been so emphatic about wanting to spare the children from being harmed by the divorce proceedings that it was the very first subject she raised in speaking with this examiner. On January 30, 2009, she stated emphatically:**

"I'd like to settle the custody issue. It's been such a high conflict process. I'm really concerned about my husband's behavior and how it relates to the kids. You can yell at me, but don't bring the kids into it."

The reference in the quote to "you" was to her husband, not this examiner. (COMPLETE LIE- I sent her a formal settlement offer in December. She has not countered that offer or put anything in writing that would allow me to just end the divorce.) **Repeatedly, Mr. Mackney has threatened that, sooner or later, he will let the children know everything.** (I originally said in August 2008, that when the children are older and in therapy wondering what happened to their father, I would let them know the truth. In my mind, it is not a threat, it is a statement of fact. It is a natural consequence. The children can use Google today if they wanted. They have taken this as evidence that I am angry and trying to harm them. Just not true. They are delusional and do not wish to see or be held accountable for their actions. Ironically, I had stated before I found out about the murder conviction, that my wife never accepts responsibility for anything and avoids all accountability, much like her father.) **"They will be able to read for themselves the truth about this divorce and the truth about what YOU have done to them and their father" (e-mail of 10/08/08).**

Repeatedly, Ms. Mackney has implored her husband to spare the children from the details and emotions of their conflicts. (Samenow cherry picks this email. There are far more emails of me imploring my wife to think of the children first.)

"Don't ever – and I mean NEVER drag the kids into this divorce and your issues like you did last night. They are kids and don't need you to say `sorry kids you can't have ice cream because

your mommy won't pay for it' You are ridiculous, selfish and are using the kids for your own personal gain…They are kids and have no place in the middle of OUR issues" (8/29/08)
During the first interview, Ms. Mackney said that her husband is angry because she will not capitulate to his attempt to extort a quarter of a million dollars from her.(Complete LIE- when the divorce began I recognized my wife's family's vast financial resources and have begged for settlement from Day 1. When educating myself of Division of assets, I asked my wife for 'my equity' from the home. At the time, I valued my equity in the home as $250,000 ($50,000 cash to build out the basement+50% of the $400,000 appreciation since 2002 purchase date) I have never asked for anything more or less than 'my equity' in our home. Dina even taped a conversation where she called me to ask "how much do you want to stop talking about my Dad?" I replied "I don't want any money to stop talking about your dad.
I only want what belongs to me." She took the tape to the police to have me arrested for extortion. There was and has never been any attempt to extort money so the Police never took action.) **She reported that Mr. Mackney threatened to kidnap the children and "has terrorized me and my family for money."** (No proof, no evidence, only her orchestrated opinion) **She said that Mr. Mackney threatened to reveal information he discovered on the internet, namely that Peter Scamardo had a criminal conviction** (criminal? How about Felony, accomplice to Murder conviction) **in the 1960s. Ms. Mackney commented, "I went 41 years without knowing about this."** (a COMPLETE LIE- Dina's first email response to my email about learning the truth was "I already know about this and you have no idea about the details and at this point it is none of your business. D"**Ms. Mackney and her parents told this examiner that they had nothing to hide.** (Again a COMPLETE LIE- He has denied the murder for 40+ years, he created a business around hiding his felony conviction, he committed a felony when he and his daughter circumvented Virginia Horse Racing Licensing regulations. He obtained a racing license through Dina circumventing Virginia Code § 59.1-371 - Fingerprints and background investigations; investigations from other states. This is considered a class 4 felony under Virginia Code 59.1-405§ 59.1-405. Conspiracies and attempts to commit violations.Any person who conspires, confederates or combines with another, either within or without this Commonwealth, to commit a felony prohibited by this chapter shall be guilty of a Class 4 felony. Any person who attempts to commit any act prohibited by this article shall be guilty of a criminal offense and punished as provided in either §§ 18.2-26, 18.2-27 or § 18.2-28, as appropriate. (1988, c. 855; 1991, c. 591.) Mr. Ron Salerno is also part of the conspiracy, who was presented as a witness for my wife in meetings with Dr. Samenow.)After questioning the Scamardos, this examiner found the situation 40 years ago completely irrelevant to the child custody case and informed Mr. Mackney that this was not to be an issue. (Sure, because they LIED. Mr. Scamardo was found guilty of perjury and his wife lied under oath at the trial, testifying that the victim and Mr. Harrelson were related. The victim's father testified that was not true) **Mr. Mackney persisted harping on this subject not just in speaking with this examiner but also in approaching people who are not family members.** (I am not harping. I have a genuine and legitimate concern. I would be negligent if I did not express my concern. I find it extremely curious that Dr. Samenow an expert in Criminal Psychology, completely ignores the pattern of 'bad faith', lies and bullying). **On April 23, 2009, Mr. Mackney was ordered by the Honorable Randy Bellows to make no "further communication of any sort" regarding allegations against Mr. Scamardo (this examiner, Dr. Van Syckle, and his attorney being exceptions).** (Isn't this a violation of my First amendment rights? The information is PUBLIC. It's available to anyone with a computer.) **Ms. Mackney has been at a loss as to how to communicate with her husband. To transmit basic information and obtain a rational response from Mr. Mackney has been a challenge.**

(COMPLETE LIE- My wife has not cooperated with ANY of my requests to settle, go to a parenting coordinator, put together a parenting plan, etc. Plenty of documents to refute this.) **Instead of succeeding at establishing a constructive dialogue, Ms. Mackney is the recipient of voluminous e-mails from Chris Mackney in which he attacks, bullies, and threatens her.** (These are cherry picked. There are far more emails begging her, attorney, and her parents for a settlement. I also note his use of the word 'bully'. I shared with Dr. Samenow a story where a former employee of Mr. Scamardo called him a 'bully'. A few weeks after hearing the description, I was at my father in law's house on Memorial Day 2008. He was angry that I showed up at his house to pick up my children for lunch and berated me. After putting the children in the car, I said to Mr. Scamardo with Dina and his wife as witnesses, "You know, you are nothing but a bully." His eyes lit up and said "Your right and I love it." This was said to me BEFORE I ever learned of the murder conviction.)

"Your choices really make me question your decision making and judgment. If its your head injury, I wish you would get help for the kids, if not yourself….**&$ and &&*$, Yes, your grandfather is a murderer and your mother chose to send me to bankruptcy, Dad" (9/24/08)

"Everything you do is duplicitous and misleading…Fortunately for me, I have truth on my side and I will gladly walk into court and tell the truth…It is clear your father taught you well. Just lie, treat people like crap and then hide behind your attorney and avoid all responsibility" (10/08/08)

Ms. Mackney has tried to ignore the taunts and allegations. If she does not respond, Mr. Mackney steps up the pace and intensity. (I became increasingly frustrated and now afraid of what might happen to me. Notice these emails are after I learned of the murder. Dr. Samenow does not recognize the pressure and fear I am now experiencing because he refuses to look at the Scamardo's past) "Throughout this divorce you have show(n) absolutely zero good faith…You routinely do not respond to my email questions and requests. You have notoriously [been] unresponsive to phone calls and voice mails…" (8/23/08)

"Not answering does not make you look good to the judge or your children when they read these e-mails later" (9/24/08). At other times, she has struck back, trying to set the record straight, at least as she sees it. "You care to speak of morality, then you should take a look at yourself before you start casting stones…You have lied, cheated and stolen from me on more occasions that I care to recount. You have committed adultery, given me a sexually transmitted disease, you have physically and emotionally abused your wife, you have emotionally abused your kids, you are not supporting yourself or your family, you do drugs, you buy drugs for you and your friends… you are highly irresponsible in the care of the kids. I suggest you get some help from a mental health professional" (e-mail of 10/08/08) **For more than one year, Ms. Mackney has had to defend herself and her family against charges that her father is a "murderer" and that she suffers from residual effects of a head injury from an auto accident that occurred when she was a passenger in a cab five years ago in New York.** (Defend herself? I would have no reason to say anything if only she would send me a piece of paper I can sign to end the divorce. These are not 'charges' they are facts.) **On July 9, 2008, she told Mr. Mackney:** "And once again you can get off the head injury and memory issue since I have had countless exams by professionals who all say that I am fine and have no permanent damage – but then again I'm sure you know better than the experts. Lastly, like I said before get off mydad. My mom and dad have cared for the kids far better than you ever have and there has never been not one single instance where they put the kids at risk…If you want to sue me over this than go for it -- Otherwise stop harassing me about it." **Mr. Mackney has not stopped harassing her.** (When the divorce began, I had no attorney and only wanted to settle this peacefully. I used my emails as a record of events and to provide full disclosure and

complete transparency. There are far more emails stating that I want to end the divorce. I asked Dr. Samenow to have her memory tested, as she had severe memory issues and continued to show memory problems throughout the marriage. This is not a minor issue, in my mind. She had a severe concussion and my fear is that IF she were to obtain sole custody, what would happen to my children if her memory continued to deteriorate? I asked Dr. Samenow to have her tested so that we can establish a baseline for her memory and can then track it periodically. He completely ignored this request and concern) **Six months later, Mr. Mackney wrote, "Have you told your new boyfriend...that your father is an accomplice to murder yet?...Can you please get your father to admit his crimes" (12/17/08). Ms. Mackney does not have a "boy friend." Mr. Mackney has approached mutual friends, neighbors, even school personnel about Dina's father.** (I have selectively spoken to people close to the Scamardo's and only mentioned it to neighbors in order for them to understand my need to even ask them in the first place. All my neighbors initially did not want to get involved because they like Dina and me and they wanted our children to continue to play together. They simply did not wish to be involved. Since, my family is in California and the only people that could objectively testify as to my parenting and involvement as a father, I NEEDED them to testify and simply gave them facts that would explain my need for them to speak to Samenow about my parenting.) **Ms. Mackney stated that her husband has e-mailed newspapers and magazines about the subject. She reported that her husband showed up at a soccer game "taunting me" about telling mutual friends.** (No proof, no evidence and no witnesses. This is entirely her version of events. I have told no one about the murder at a school event or at any of my children's events. This is a great fear of my wife's and is why she continues to restrict my access to the children and their activities. However, I have done nothing inappropriate in public at any of my children's events.)**"He has been threatening to tell the kids, using it to blackmail me. He is desperate for money." Tracy Heiden and Dina Mackney have, according to the former, been "each other's confidante and sounding board." Ms. Heiden's daughter, &^$$, has been a close friend of &&%$'s since they were three years old. Tracy expressed her apprehensions about Dina's safety. "I'm afraid for Dina....She hasn't expressed she's frightened. She's more afraid of what he will do – his threat to make it worse. Dina has a lot of friends but people will pass judgment. He sends articles [to people]. He's extremely convincing...Dina's bright but very innocent on a day to day basis."**
Ms. Heiden said of Ms. Mackney's parents: **"We love Andy and Pete. [They're] a part of our family. They'vefed my kids, taken care of them...They're like grandparents."**(Yes, I can understand her fear of people learning the truth that she and her family has been hiding, but it is irrational and completely unreasonable for her to think that silencing me will prevent people from learning the truth if they want. I never wanted to learn this truth and I only ever wanted to settle this case peacefully. If the truth somehow gets out, it will be a natural consequence that they nor the judge can ever control. What they refuse to understand is that NO ONE benefits for me to talk about it. My goal is to try and have a functional relationship with them so that I may stay in my children's life and have a positive influence. I gain nothing from discussing the murder.) **Ms. Mackney seldom uses the telephone to communicate with Chris because rational dialogue has been all but impossible. She informed him, in an e-mail written in July of 2008, that he seemed unable to retain "a civil manner." Mr. Mackney has bombarded her with accusatory e-mails. For example, she cited in an e-mail dated 9/30/08 that she had received 36 e-mails in five days. On April 10, 2009, Ms. Mackney commented that dealing with Chris's voluminous e-mails "is a whole separate full-time job."** (This is completely mischaracterized. She has not negotiated or compromised on any issue in our divorce. My emails were meant to act as a record and he cherry picks an email from July 2008 and then on

Michael Volpe

April 2009?) Ms. Mackney has developed a business from what began as a hobby. (No mention of her failed Teen Portal BeautyQ.com or her failed relationships with Angelique Finan and Anne Fowler) As she made jewelry, she found that women admired her creations. She started showing her products at Junior League shows, then was able to exhibit them in January, 2008 at a wholesale show in New York. The New York show was so successful that she picked up an account at Nordstrom's. Now she is shipping to approximately forty stores. "I followed something I was passionate about. My best qualities are my worst – a `can do' attitude. It is a constant juggling act." Dina Mackney has found this business gratifying and an excellent outlet for her talents. However, she emphasized that she has never sought full-time work and values being a mother above all else no matter how Ms. Mackney has tried to respond to her husband, he accuses her of being in the wrong. (Exactly, I have been powerless in my marriage, my job with her father, and in our divorce. On 8/14/2008 I am extremely panicked, I have no more money, no attorney, my wife is not letting me see the children and I only learned of the Murder conviction, less than 2 months earlier. Even Dr. Guy Van Syckle testified that I was 'under tremendous stress')

"Do you really want to destroy me this way. This is my LIFE you are playing with right now. My house is on fire! I am in CRISIS MODE here Dina and you do nothing. In fact you go out of your way to put your foot on my neck" (8/14/08 e-mail)

YOU are the one that is causing this situation. If you don't like it, change it. YOU created this with your unreasonable and unnecessary demands. If you want to stop then stop screwing me over....The power to fix this problem today is entirely in your hands" (8/29/08 e-mail)

Although Mr. Mackney is the parent behaving erratically and showing questionable judgment, he asserts that his wife demonstrates these very qualities (How does one act when they learn that their father in law is a convicted murderer and his wife refuses to discuss it with him. I repeatedly asked Dr. Samenow what is an appropriate way to respond to that. I also asked him how many times he has dealt with parents in that situation No answer was given other than I should not talk about it and that he found it irrelevant.).

"You are truly scaring me with your inability to think clearly. Please I am begging you! For the sake of our children, please have yourself psychologically tested. If we can identify the problem, we can deal with it...You either get yourself tested or I will ask the court to do it" (7/31/08)

Commenting on her husband's persistent charges that she forgets things (attributing it to a brain injury), Ms. Mackney said:

"I can stay on top of [things with] the kids, school, doctors' appointments, extracurricular activities, operating a business. It's convenient for him to say I don't remember things correctly." (Samenow fully accepts her explanation, but there are plenty of email examples during our divorce where she demonstrates memory issues. There is testimony regarding my wife's head injury in a deposition given during our Personal Injury case in the files I provided. She received approximately $400,000 for her injuries) It is noteworthy that, recently, when Mr. Mackney was unemployed, he totally forgot an appointment with this examiner. Told by this examiner about her husband's missed meeting, Ms. Mackney did not attribute this to Chris having a brain dysfunction. (I wonder how many times my wife forgot or needed to reschedule?) The e-mails cited above are not out of context. (why say this?) Torrents of them pour forth, enough to fill numerous binders. Mr. Mackney's communications portray his wife as a merciless destroyer, self-centered, and responsible for the destruction of his life. The only way that Ms. Mackney conceivably could put a stop to Mr. Mackney's battle would have been to capitulate to his demands for money and joint custody. (NOT TRUE- I have begged my wife and her attorney to send me 'a piece of paper I can sign to end this divorce'. I wanted this to end any way I could, just so that I can live to fight another day. I have made my position about this consistent from the beginning.) On April 10, 2009, this examiner had the following interchange with Mr. Mackney. Chris reported: "Dina called me at work one day and asked 'what do you want to stop talking about my dad'?"

Mr. Mackney said that he did not want anything except what he is "entitled to under the law." He specified that this means $250,000 of equity in the marital residence. Chris commented, "She tried to get me for extortion or blackmail." This is in fact just how Ms. Mackney perceives what her husband is doing. (of course she does. She also ignores all the evidence suggesting otherwise.) That Dina Mackney is not the person portrayed by Mr. Mackney is evident from the clinical interviews, from the testing, and from collateral sources. In this examiner's interactions with Ms. Mackney, she was frequently seeking his advice and admittedly at a loss as to how to protect &&%$ and *&#@ while coping with her ex-husband's eccentric, volatile, and irresponsible conduct. (what exactly does this mean?)

Gail Cavallaro has known Ms. Mackney since middle school. Married and living in Richmond with her husband and three children, Ms. Cavallaro seldom spends time with her long time friend although they maintain contact. The importance of citing Ms. Cavallaro's comments is to underscore what it is about Ms. Mackney that leads others to admire her and maintain a relationship that endures for years.

"[Dina] is loyal and dedicated. I value her advice. She's a very thoughtful person. She always pours herself into whatever she does. She was president of the school...cheerleader....She was a very diligent with lots of friends [and] athletically talented."

Ms. Cavallaro and Ms. Mackney were roommates for a year after college. Ms. Cavallaro stated, "We never had an issue" and remarked that she still has "fond memories of that year." As enthusiastic as Ms. Cavallaro is about Dina, she is equally fond of Dina's parents whom she came to know quite well (at their home and on a vacation to Hilton Head) and describes as "lovely people to be around." (Mr. Scamardo has a long storied history in real estate development in Northern Virginia. He has filed for bankruptcy, he has been involved over 50+ civil lawsuits in the DC metro area, a $37 Million satisfied judgment against him in MD, he is well known by real estate professionals for not acting in good faith, being extremely litigious and being "a bully". Mr. Scamardo has a long list of enemies that Samenow ignored. In fact, I had given him the name of one Witness, John Sobecki, who would testify has to his business relationship with Mr. Scamardo. I watched Mr. Scamardo, yell and curse at Mr. Sobecki in his office. Mr. Sobecki claims Mr. Scamardo still owes him thousands of dollars. Dr. Sameow made no effort to contact Mr. Sobecki.)Linda and John Donovan (they were witnesses at my request, to talk about their experience with me as a father)know Chris and Dina through the preschool where their girls met. Linda characterized Ms. Mackney as "very warm, approachable, very helpful." Apparently, Dina was under such stress that she confided in Ms. Donovan some of the problems she was having, especially with respect to Chris phoning people about her father. (MY WIFE IS TALKING to her friends about the Murder) Ms. Donovan noted that Mr. Mackney had called a board member from The Potomac School (the man I called was Enrico Cecchi, who is a real estate developer, who was doing business with my group at CB Richard Ellis. I had no idea he was on the board at the Potomac School.) who then approached her . Linda Donovan had nothing but positive comments about Dina as a mother: "She's a very patient mother. &^#@ is a real little boy. She is unendingly patient. She gets down and plays with him. Ms. Donovan clearly admires Ms. Mackney for juggling parenting, volunteering at school, and applying herself to her business. John Donovan described his impression of Dina Mackney as "a woman with a lot of positive energy, very giving, very focused." (Samenow includes no comments from them about me or their experience with me around my children)

Frederic L. Spain knows Dina Mackney from an entirely different perspective. A commercial real estate broker (who has his real estate license at her father's company and currently has a real estate deal with him), he has known Dina's parents, Mr. and Mrs. Scamardo since 1969 and Dina since she was born. Mr. Spain characterized Ms. Mackney as "a perfect lady [who is] neat, fastidious, and incredibly polite." Mr. Spain said that he has been "bombarded" (I sent him 2) by e-mails about Mr. Scamardo from Chris Mackney who, at one time, worked for him. He has admired Dina for retaining her "serenity" during all that she is going through.

Kimberly Gurick was hired as a part-time nanny four years ago by Chris and Dina Mackney. After the couple separated, Ms. Gurick became a full-time employee of Ms. Mackney in June of 2008. She has worked from 8 a.m. to 6 p.m. Monday through Friday. Ms. Gurick voiced her extremely high opinion of Dina as a parent: "I think she's fabulous, very down to earth. [She has] the patience of a saint..I saw her get hot under the collar only two times. She's a great mother, really attentive to [the children's] needs."

Ms. Gurick mentioned that, although her employer is under constant stress because of the divorce proceedings, Ms. Mackney does not discuss them in front of the children: "We're certain the kids are in another room." Ms. Gurick said that there are times when "the guilt creeps in" about the impending divorce and Ms. Mackney does not use disciplinary measures that might be effective.

"Sometimes ^%@! treats her very badly...Dina doesn't want to be the bad guy, the disciplinarian....One time, I had to put *&&* in 'time out'. Dina couldn't have that battle with him just then." Ms. Gurick noted that, at times, Dina can be "a little bit of a pushover."

"She'll ask them six times to do something. I'll ask once... *&^% listens to me better than to his own mother. If Dina was consistent every day, it would make it easier."

Despite this criticism, Ms. Gurick asserted, "She's a wonderful mother."

Ms. Mackney is very close to family members. Andrea Scamardo said of her daughter, "Dina was so easy to raise. She always had friends. She was sweet, kind, gentle, and polite." Pete Scamardo added that his daughter has been "way too trusting." Mr.Scamardo is extremely upset with his son-in-law whom he employed, paying him a salary and commission long past the point where it was obvious that Chris was not an asset to the company(I was not an asset because Mr. Scamardo could not or would not invest in ANY of the real estate deals that I brought him because of his felony conviction, which restricted his ability to finance the transactions without the help of Ron Salerno). The Scamardos said they wanted the marriage to succeed and did everything they could to help Chris and Dina, financially as well as being devoted grandparents to ^%#@ and &^(*.

Deborah Destefano is Ms. Mackney's aunt. Recently divorced, Ms. Destefano works as a librarian in Austin, Texas. Spending time with Dina and the children during Christmas holiday periods and on week long summer beach trips, she has had the opportunity to observe her at close hand. As Dina has been under increasing stress, they began speaking almost nightly by phone. Ms. Destefano explained, "We're confidantes; she's like my little sister." Asked to describe Dina's personality, Ms. Destefano replied:

"She's a very sweet, very kind, gentle soul, not aggressive. As a child, she was fairly quiet. She'd measure people before warming up...She is honest, fair, kind and, in terms of the kids, incredibly patient. *&@# has his moments of acting out. She doesn't let it go on forever.... She'll sit and play with them, do art projects....Even when she's annoyed and frustrated, she maintains lovingness."

Contrary to Mr. Mackney's repeated assertions that his wife wants to eliminate him from the children's lives, Ms. Destefano volunteered that Dina "has long said they need him and does not want the children to be without a father." (All the statements are contradicted by her actions; keeping me from speaking to them on the phone, not allowing me to see them on ANY holidays in 2008 until July 4th 2009; taking my name off the class email list; etc.)

Stefani Scamardo-Haynes is Dina's sister and, according to her, "^%$* and *&#@ favorite aunt." Married to her musician husband (of The Grateful Dead) (Stefanie is a terrible role model. She smokes cigarettes like a chimney, smokes pot, and is grossly overweight. I even saw cocaine in her purse while she was with our children. She and her husband have been undergoing fertility treatment and have been unable to conceive, primarily because of Stefanie's lifestyle choices. Her Doctor even allowed her to continue to smoke pot to relieve the stress of trying to get pregnant. Stefanie's drug habits are all tolerated and accepted by her parents and sister.) **, she lives in New York. However, she sees her family in Virginia during all holidays, birthdays, and during the week at the beach. Having no children of her own, Ms. Scamardo-Haynes is very attached to &^#@ and *&@#. She admires Dina as a parent and as a business woman.**

"Dina is very engaged with them, very creative with them. She pays attention to details. She is a great Mom. My mom and dad [provide] a great support system [allowing Dina to engage in her business]."

The comments of Ms. Heiden, Ms. Gurick, the Donovans, Mr. Spain, and Dina's family are highlighted above because they present a picture of Dina Mackney starkly different from that portrayed by her husband.

Ms. Mackney knew Chris Mackney for two years before they married. She said that, even though she had doubts, she was "ready to get married and have a family." She reflected,

"I had rose colored glasses on. I made excuses along the way." No matter how bad things got, Ms. Mackney did not want to give up on the marriage. Her parents had enjoyed a long, stable marriage of nearly 50 years. She wanted the same for herself and their children.

"No one has a perfect marriage. I was wrapped up with the kids. Over, time, you get used to it."

Ms. Mackney believes that, even after the separation, her tendency initially was to be "nice to a fault." She said that, in return for being accommodating, she endured "a year of torture." Ms. Mackney reflected, "My kindness has served me not well at all in this process." (Complete LIE- She lied to get two protective orders and then had sex with me the night before we were to go to court for the first order in June. Then, the week after we settled the second protective order, she had sex with me. That week she also invited me to meet her in a hotel room in Tysons. My wife has no reason to fear me at all, as I have never been physical with her or any other woman EVER.) **Ms. Mackney reported enduring years of emotional abuse by her husband.** (I was the one emotionally abused. Not once did she ever send me off to work or greet me at the door with a hug or kiss. I went to therapy and a psychiatrist at her request. I was diagnosed by both as being depressed in the marriage. I was completely powerless in our marriage.Everything was what Dina wanted. The house, the furnishings, the children's schools, etc. I was not earning enough money to pay for her lifestyle and she was unhappy. I would explain that I could not make any money unless her father did a deal that I brought him. My wife did not sympathize and always defended her father, as he was the one with all the money and had always subsidized her lifestyle.) **She said that she finally came to realize he is "a pathological liar."** (This is rich...she hid the fact that her father was a murder. No one in her family EVER mentioned it to me during the marriage.) **She found hundreds of e-mails from on-**

line dating sites. (I repeatedly told my wife that this was a symptom of a problem. The problem was our communication. She never agreed and continued to blame me for the problems in the marriage.) **These included photos and schedules of places and times for Chris to meet other women. She grew so disgusted, she told him to leave. However, when *&#@ got sick, she forgave him. Later, when she became pregnant with *&$#, she discovered "another whole round of e-mails." Ms.Mackney said that her husband "texting a 17 year old" was the final straw.** (this is not true. The marriage was done and in order to begin gathering evidence went back through phone records and came across a phone number in my text messages. She called the person and the girl that answered said she was 17. During that August, my wife and I were fighting and I told her that I was talking to other people about the troubles we were having in the marriage. The woman I was speaking/texting with was over 40, married, with children and was also having troubles in her marriage. Our discussions entirely about our bad marriages. There was nothing physical or sexual going on whatsoever. In fact, I never met the woman. If the person was the same, I had no idea it was a 17 year old girl. My wife and Dr. Samenow ignored my version of events and paint the incident as something completely different from what it was. **Whether every one of the numerous incidents occurred as she says he debates. That they had "horrible issues and fights" was a fact."He lied, cheated, stole. It didn't rise to the level it is now. He could lie like nobody's business. I didn't realize he was such a conman. I guess maybe I was an optimist."** (this is my wife's opinion. She is trying to distract everyone's attention from her and her family's bad behavior by attacking the victim. Which is exactly what her father did in his murder trial and repeatedly employs as a legal tactic. I work in Investment Sales of Commercial Real Estate. I have a stellar reputation for my honesty, showing of good faith, and doing as I say I will do. My livelihood depends on it. I also gave Dr. Samenow 2 people to speak to about me professionally. Charles Kehler and Terry Hindermann. Both were not called and did not refute Mrs. Mackney's claims of dishonesty. I find this extremely suspicious.)

Ms. Mackney spoke of her husband's explosive nature in citing a particular incident in which Mr. Mackney became upset and scattered her jewelry materials all over the room This was after an argument which had eventuated in each taking the other's keys. (this is the event in early January 2008. It was a Saturday morning and my wife had taken my car keys, so I could not leave the house, as HER anger escalated. After searching the house with her following me, I went into her jewelry studio and grabbed a tray of sorted beads and said "please give me my keys or I will turn this over." She did not give me the keys so I calmly turned the tray over. I grabbed another tray and repeated the process. After the second tray she flew into a rage and ripped my shirt and hit and scratched me from behind around the back and shoulders. I grabbed my son and ran into his room and locked the door to get away from her. She called the police who showed up , saw all the evidence and did nothing. I should also note that her parents showed up as well. When I left for the Gym, her father then took the ripped shirt and tried to hide the evidence. It was finally returned after I demanded he give it back.)

"He took the drawers out and threw the jewelry – thousands of dollars worth of jewelry. There were two trays sorted by size. he dumped both of these. I was trying to stop him. I called the police. He was going to delete my work files on the computer."

Christopher Mackney flatly told this examiner, "I was a good father and fine husband until I found out about [Dina's[father's murder." Ms. Mackney provided abundant evidence that Mr. Mackney was abusive during the marriage and even more so after the separation. Mr. Mackney became so unpredictable in his behavior, so irrational, and so explosive that Ms. Mackney began to worry that the children were not safe in his care. In an e-mail written on September 30, 2008, she wrote:

"I have told you that due to your wildly inappropriate behavior and words in front of the children, you are not having visitation until you can abide by the ground rules. I will remind you that you have refused to agree to them and that is why you are not seeing or speaking with the kids." (my wife has orchestrated her entire case of me being angry and violent. I have tried to be very measured in my responses and Dr. Samenow and my wife characterize everything I do as inappropriate and not once has he challenged my wife's **In that same e-mail, Dina Mackney issued a plea to her husband which she repeated in many different ways at different times throughout the divorce proceedings: "If you 'genuinely wish to resolve our differences peacefully and amicably' please stop harassing me, my family and the kids and start acting like a rational adult."** (Every time I cooperate they do nothing. The simply have refused to negotiate anything).**The phrase "genuinely wish to resolve our differences peacefully and amicably" contains words used by Mr. Mackney, in one of many e-mails in which he portrayed himself as the aggrieved party.** (I am the aggrieved party. I have lost my job, my house, my children, my money. My wife's lifestyle has improved. She buys new clothes, goes on trips, bought a new Lexus SUV instead of continuing to drive the vehicle I leased for her. I have been accused of horrible things, called a 'deadbeat dad', all the while my wife spends hundreds of thousands of dollars on a divorce trying to take sole custody of the children and keep all the marital assets. **Despite all the turmoil, Dina Mackney has always granted that the children love their dad.** (I am a great father and everyone that knows me will say so. Including all our neighbors and even casual observers like the concierge at my apartment building. No one can say that I am not a loving and very hands on father. That was always my plan) **She knows that they like being with him, that they have fun. Ms. Mackney said that she could count on Chris to be a good "playmate" for the children even though he seldom was deeply involved in their day to day care** (This is a lie- I was home virtually every night for dinner with the children, I read them books before bed EVERY night, I kept them and cared for them when my wife went out of town for her jewelry business. I was involved in their upbringing on a DAILY basis. That was the whole purpose of moving to DC and changing jobs. I wanted to be there for my children, as my father spent more of his time in the office. For my wife or Dr. Samenow to portray y role any differently is a complete lie. My neighbors will testify to this.). **Ms. Mackney provided numerous examples of how her husband demonstrated that he could not be counted on to be a dependable, stable parent. She recalled his leaving &^#@ at the age of one in a bathtub while he went to watch television** (Lie- no evidence, no witnesses). **Ms. Mackney said that her husband interacted far more with his Blackberry** (I have never owned a blackberry) **than with *&$# and &^(*. She cited his smoking marijuana** (I never smoked marijuana until I met her sister and her brother in law. They are musicians and would ALWAYS have very good marijuana. I no longer use and would be happy to take a drug test if her sister would take one to) **and mentioned that she discovered a bag of the substance near the doll house in the children's play room**(my wife was always taking things from me. I have no idea if this is true or not) . **Ms. Mackney said that, at the age of two, *&#@ fell in her parents' pool. She recalled that Chris "did nothing" and said he wanted to see what would happen.** (This is another HUGE LIE and a often repeated story they like to use to show my 'bad judgment'. I explained to Dr. Samenow, that I was in the pool on the steps talking with the children. I was on the 3rd or 4th step, &^@@ and (*&@ where on the first and second. I was arm's length away from the children, when Jack either fell or walked off the step and his head went below the water. &&^# immediately screamed as I turned my head to watch jack's head go below the surface. *&#@ and I didn't know why it had happened. I thought he was trying to swim. Instantly, it was obvious that he was struggling and needed help. I simply grabbed him and lifted him back to the step. My wife and her family where in the house at the time and came running at the sound of &&^$'s scream. Naturally they were frightened by the scream and blamed me for not watching the children and 'almost letting *&@# drown." It was nothing like that at all. I was in control the entire time and *&#$ and NEVER in any danger. He was scared after I lifted him back on the step, as was &^$$, but I was remained calm and was always in arm's length of both children. Again- No witnesses, and no evidence, and Dr. Samenow wholly relies on Mrs. Mackney's version of events. **Since they have separated, Mr. Mackney has sometimes failed to feed the children and seldom bathes them** (Just a ridiculous claim- no evidence, no witnesses. I have no idea how or why they would even make this claim). **He has not provided adequate sleeping arrangements for them** (my wife violated the March order giving me two beds and I have exhausted all my resources on legal fees and have no idea how long it will go on. Yet Dr. Samenow attributes this to poor parenting). **At times, he did not exercise visitation claiming he lacked money for gas, food, or to do anything with them. (Ms. Mackney told this examiner that when Chris said he had no money she would "plead with him" to take them to the park rather than not see them at all.)** (I have made my financial condition known to all parties. The credit crisis was in full swing and I was completely out of money, borrowing money just to pay for gas to go to work. I thought it would be the mature thing to do to forgo visitation with my children when I did not have the money for entertainment or food, much less gas.) **Despite informing Mr. Mackney about activities on his custodial weekends (e.,g., classmates' birthday parties), the children often missed those events. And, Ms. Mackney reported, Mr. Mackney often did not adhere to the visitation schedule. She wrote in an e-mail dated April 27, 2009** (I asked my wife not to schedule events during my time or to forward me the invitations so that I could plan around them. I would plan a weekend and then be told on the morning of that the kids had events to attend. There was no coordination of these events by my wife.):**"Chris dropped the kids off 35 minutes late on Sunday. When this is a seemingly innocuous occurrence, I note it because Chris has [a] long and sordid history of dropping the kids off extremely early, extremely late and not at appointed drop off locations."** (really??? I have no idea what he is referring to here. My visitation was so restricted, and I knew everything I did would be scrutinized, so I did everything in my power follow the agreements or whatever I had agreed to do. My made no effort to coordinate anything, so there was often confusion. I requested numerous times in Oct/Nov 2008, to put together a parenting plan to avoid such confusion. Dr. Van Syckle and Dina ignored all requests to document a visitation schedule. **Ms. Mackney has been afraid of her husband at times. An incident occurred when Chris was to move his belongings from the marital residence. It ended up in a confrontation in which Mr. Mackney yelled at Peter Scamardo that he was "a fucking murderer" like OJ Simpson.** (Complete Lie- I sat in a rented Uhaul truck waiting for movers to arrive and when they didn't, I stayed in the truck and beeped the horn. My wife and her father came out of the house and her father says "what do you want loser". The argument escalated from there. My wife was screaming and cursing at me right in my face as I sat in the truck. I also emailed my attorney's and Samenow this story right after it occurred. I also emailed my wife's mother about the event The emails are attached at the end of this document. **The conflict escalated to the point of the nanny calling the police. After the police left, Mr. Mackney returned and refused to leave**(I was told by the police that I did not have to leave. I did exactly as the police asked me to do, which was to move the truck out of the driveway and down onto the public street.). **The next day, he yelled at Andrea Scamardo in front of the children, calling Mr. Scamardo "a fucking murderer."** (LIE- NEVER happened. What is interesting is that there are never any witnesses and it's always someone in the Scamardo family that claims I did these things. All

the worst things are only supported by testimony from my wife.) **Ms. Mackney reported that her husband was "obsessed about getting his shotgun."** (I was not obsessed. I was afraid of Mr. Scamardo and did not want it in his possession. I gladly agreed to have it kept in Mr.Cottrell's office where it is now. **"He cocked the gun once at me in a fight and aimed it. He pulled it out from the mattress. I hid it. He's been crazy for the shotgun."** (This is lie and is not supported by anything. I have emails asking politely for it and my wife never responding. If I ask about something more than once when they do not respond to my request, it is categorized as an 'obsession' **In her motion to suspend visitation or to have it supervised, Ms. Mackney pointed out that her husband "demanded that he be given his shotgun...which in emails he claimed to need for protection from his father-in-law". Dina noted that Chris is neither a hunter nor a person who shoots recreationally. An agreement was reached that the shotgun be kept at her attorney's office. Ms. Mackney expressed concern about her husband's judgment when he recently took the children to a gun show.** (Truth be told, I did this because I knew it would get under my wife's skin. Meanwhile, her father is a convicted murderer and she objects to me taking my children to a completely legal gun show, which was attended by dozens of children. My son &^&& also LOVES guns and swords and lightsabres, so he loved going to the gun show.) **Dina Mackney has had to contend with her husband's denigrating her in the foulest of language to the children.** (This is a lie- it is my wife that is always the one to escalate the discussion. My wife has also cursed at me in front of the children and I have referenced those events in emails. My wife has cursed at me in front of the children and hit me in front of the children and Dr. Samenow, makes no reference to any events.)**She pointed out that she and her husband have entirely different roles in the children's lives.**
"I have a lot more to enforce – all the responsibility, Chris is a play date, and they see it as such. During the week, it's schedules. He has no responsibility. He rarely gives the kids a bath. He hasn't paid child support in 1 ½ years. He will buy them a toy. I bear the brunt." (This is of her own creation. She has not tried to negotiate with me and has taken extraordinary steps to reduce my role and my involvement. I WANT to see the children more. She acts like the victim here, as if this was my fault.)**Ms. Mackney spoke of an incident that demonstrates how quickly and impulsively Chris reacts, not just to her, but to the children. She said that Chris was lazing around on the ground. **&$ was pestering him, and Chris asked her to stop. "I heard a blood curdling scream. *&#@ said, `Daddy bit me'. Chris said, `**&& wouldn't stop.'" When Dina asked Chris to apologize, he refused but turned to Lily (who had a red and swollen mark) and said, "You'll never do that again." Dina pointed out that Chris reacts practically upon instinct: "He'll do anything and justify it."** ((*%$ and I were playing together on the couch and she bit me. I had read earlier in a Parenting magazine, that had been given as a subscription by Dina's grandmother, that sometimes it's ok to bite younger children back in a way that lets children know that it hurts. Not my finest parenting moment, but I have never been hurtful to my children before or since. This is a onetime event and there is not a pattern of any 'bad parenting'.**On the MMPI-2, Ms. Mackney "did not show any significant amount of conscious defensiveness."** (strange that he wrote this first) **According to the "custody" profile report, Ms. Mackney was "reasonably straightforward." Among the observations on that report are the following:**
"In general, she should show generally positive and cheerful moods";
"She would be seen as wanting to avoid antagonistic confrontations";
"Her awareness of the ways in which she upsets or provokes others appears somewhat uneven";
"Her scores indicate an adequate to relatively good level of immediate personal organization and efficiency";

"The intensity of a child's emotionality per se should not be problematic for her:'
"Her scores indicate a mixed general balance between some of her problems as external to herself and caused by other people versus an awareness of other problems as being due to her own misjudgments or mistakes";
"Her thinking may be seen as usually `well-grounded'"
"Her level of control needs is…slightly below the average for child custody litigants";
"Her temper should be generally well controlled and not a serious risk;'
"Essentially stable bonding should protect the interests of the children over time and her love and caring should be dependable";
"Her scores do not suggest any particular tendency to dichotomize people as being for her or against her".(All I can say is he is that she has lived a lifetime developing skills of denial and hiding a terrible secret. She is very charming when you meet her but she is very adept and keeping the focus and accountability off herself.)
Dina Mackney has made it clear repeatedly that she did not ask for the intensely difficult situation in which she finds herself.
"It could have been so civilized. I would have been happy with joint custody. I need the help. I could regroup and get stuff done. You miss your kids when they're not there. I don't need to control every aspect….I don't think his judgment is good at all…I don't know the right thing. I want them to see their father but in a healthier state….I'm trying to focus on thepositive. It's difficult." (LIE-After I learned about the Murder, she switched form Ain and Bank to Jim Cottrell. It turned into a passive aggressive campaign to paint Mr. Mackney declared that his wife and her family were waging a war to destroy him while trying to bury a family secret that could have a devastating impact on *&^& and *&#$. (look at the results of their actions)
"They're accusing me of being unfit and unstable. I've waved the white flag and given up. I'm basically bankrupt, owe everyone…. I have nothing to hide – full disclosure."
The fact is that seldom has this examiner found a litigant in either a criminal or civil case more difficult to interview. Throughout the evaluation, Mr. Mackney did precisely what he accused his wife of doing. He presented himself as a victim and repeated endlessly what others had done to him. He said that he saw no reason for this evaluation and stated that the whole idea "is my wife's decision." (I knew from the first day that Samenow was not going to be objective and I wrote an email to Cindy Wallace telling her so. My position going in was that I had never done anything violent to my wife or children and the only thing they could accuse me of was 'bad judgment'. If they wish to attack my character by claiming I have 'bad judgment' then that would be ok with me. Mrs.Scamardo and her family have a long documented history of bad judgment and should not have been concerned if the Dr. were to look objectively at both parties.)The facts are that Chris Mackney is 40 years old, unemployed and bankrupt. (I was out of cash, but not bankrupt. Isn't that libel for him to say this? He provides no evidence.) **He listed not one person whom he called a close friend for this examiner to speak with.**
(COMPLETE LIE- I gave Sameow 3 college friends, who live in the DC area. Samenow did not ever speak to one of my college friends, Casey Long. Casey is getting his cell phone records to refute Samenow's claims that Casey Long never returned his calls.
Casey will testify that he did to coordinate with Samenow, who made it very difficult.) **Nor did he list a single member of his family.** (I did not list a family member because my family lives in Los Angeles and has had very little interaction with me as a father to my children. He was getting paid by the hour and I did not think my family could provide as compelling testimony as my neighbors or even Linda and John Donovan.) **Even when asked by this examiner about gaining access to family members, Chris agreed to do it but never provided the information**
(Lie- I sat in his office and he asked for contact information for my family and I explained that I

didn't think they could give him and relevant information about my parenting skills. I finally said, fine if you want them I will give them to you. Then he said 'well if you don't want to, then you don't have to." I then replied "ok, fine". He provided various explanations as to why he had reached this point in his life where he has virtually no money, no job, no close friends, and estrangement or at least a lack of closeness with family members. (This is my wife's version of events. Not mine. I have many very close and supportive lifelong friends, all of whom would willingly testify about me, my character, and my love for my children. I provided more lifelong friends for Samenow to speak to than Dina provided.)Mr. Mackney depicted himself as virtually a lackey of his wife and a pawn of her parents. (his words, not mine. I was indeed powerless in the marriage as I have been powerless in this divorce.) Mr. Scamardo hired Chris in his commercial real estate business and paid him a salary and commission. He said he was a patient teacher of his son in law trying to equip him to function as a broker. Mr. Scamardo said that Chris was disorganized and functioned poorly. (Samenow does not mention that Scamardo did not invest in 1 single me as angry, dangerous, and trying to embarrass and

blackmail her family. I have literally begged my wife to settle from January 28th. I did not wish to learn about the murder. It was an accident. After I quietly pointed out their credibility issue, they refused to address it and only increased the legal pressure on me.

Christopher Mackney

This examiner was initially contacted by Mr. Mackney on October 20, 2008. He said that he had been referred by a "father's rights organization" and was "in the middle of a divorce." He mentioned immediately that his father-in-law had been involved in a murder for hire plot approximately 40 years ago. He said that his wife's family was trying to "destroy" him, and added that he was "concerned about my own life" as well as the welfare of his two children. (Absolutely true. I was very afraid of what he might do. I wanted an independent Doctor to evaluate him and his character to tell me if my children would be safe with him. I had known him to be a bully and not very well liked
 in the real estate business. I thought Samenow's background in Criminal Psychology was exactly what was needed to look into how Mr. Scamardo's character would affect my children. Little did I know that Samenow was 'good friends' with Cottrell, according to my wife. This is another reason I was so disheartened after his report. His expertise in Criminal Psychology qualified him to look carefully at Mr. Scamardo's character and he completely avoided doing so.)
This examiner heard nothing more about this case until February 3, 2009 when Mr. Mackney called again. Before the first meeting, Mr. Mackney wrote an e-mail to this examiner reminding him of the earlier (October) conversation and how troubled he was to learn about his father-in-law and the impact that Mr. Scamardo might have on &^#$ and *&^^.
"As the father of *&*&** and (*$%, I am extremely concerned about their character development being poisoned, growing up in a house of lies and denial and with a unrepentant murder as their primary role (sic), should my wife be awarded sole custody."
Mr. Mackney dwelled on Mr. Scamardo's past, or at least his version of it(my version? Why does he say it this way? I only provided facts most of which were backed up by evidence, such as the Texas Department of Public Safety file, the shirt ripped off my back, newspaper articles, testimony by Cindy Wallace), **to the point that he appeared obsessed.** (I was not obsessed. I kept repeating I was concerned, because I just learned, after 9 years of marriage, that my father in law was convicted of accomplice to murder, but never went to jail and never admitted the crime. They I find out irrefutably that he was involved, and I have evidence proving that the motive was not the Insurance money, but Heroin. I extremely concerned as I

state in the email above. Dr. Samenow refuses to look at the evidence and condemns me for being concerned about it?)Chris said that he came upon the information because he had "Googled" to obtain Mr. Scamardo's middle name for a form. When he spoke to his wife about his discovery, he learned that she had known nothing about what allegedly happened 40 years ago in Texas. deal that I brought to him, even though I was able to sell the deals to other people. I brought Mr. Scamardo, large and small, residential and office deals of every shape and size from 2000 until 2005. This was a time of explosive growth in the commercial real estate industry and in Washington D.C. In all his wisdom, Pete Scamardo did not invest in any deals I brought to him during this time. This caused friction at home and work, which I explained to Samenow.

"He knows more trivia than anyone. He focuses on the wrong stuff. I encouraged him to get another job with a bigger company, to getmore exposure." (he knew he could not help me, but didn't want to tell me why.) Ronald Salerno, a business associate of Mr. Scamardo's, got to know Chris. Mr. Salerno commented:"The issue I had was he was a know it all guy – bull in a china shop. He didn't want to take direction. Pete took him in and taught him the basics of the business and helped him get his broker's license... If you said something, he'd blurt out something you told him not to discuss." (I was honest and dealt in good faith. AS a business practice they operated in the shadows and were always hiding the truth. My honesty desire to make a deal was looked at by them as a liability.)

Frederic Spain, a business associate of Mr. Scamardo told this examiner that he has been the recipient of e-mails with "vicious" allegations leveled against Pete. (Vicious allegations are actually facts given to him in a very matter of fact, just thought you should know manner. I have the 2 emails that I sent to Fred Spain as evidence.)

"He's gone quite far with his knowing I'm a friend of Pete's. I consider him dangerous....These are people who helped him....You don't just try to destroy someone as he has." (Fred has business dealings with Pete Scamardo and had his real estate license with Pete Scamardo's company, at the time of the divorce.) On February 23, 2009, Mr. Mackney told this examiner, "I won't rock the boat about this murder thing [unless] they pursue sole custody…" He then sounded a theme that he reiterated many times. Chris asserted that his children "will be much different without me as a father": "I don't want to give up my parental rights." This examiner explained to Mr. Mackney that, whatever the custodial arrangement might be, he would not be relinquishing his parental rights. However, on at least two occasions, Mr. Mackney acknowledged that, in essence, he would be the one choosing to abandon his parental rights by leaving the area if the custody arrangement is not satisfactory to him. In fact, as recently as July 29, 2009, Mr. Mackney wrote Kyle Bartol, attorney for Ms. Mackney:

"If my wife receives sole custody, then I search for work elsewhere. They will only continue to make my life even more miserable if that happens." (I have had no attorney and have been bullied by my wife and her attorney for months. Moving away was seriously an option. However, I love my children too much to abandon them, ever. I will accept whatever custody arrangement I can get and then play by the rules for a few years and then petition the court for more time. My goal is to get as much time with my children as possible. My fear is that if my wife had sole custody, she would abuse that right and use it to further keep me out of the children's lives. She has clearly shown that she does not want me around. In fact, on August 5th, she stated on the phone "because I don't want to deal with you" when I asked her why it was SO important for her to have sole custody. I am a constant reminder of who they really are, and they want to eliminate me from the picture as much as possible.Mr. Mackney said that his "formative" years were spent moving around a great deal since his father was in the hotel business. Beginning in fifth grade there was some stability, and Chris remained in St. Louis until he finished high school. After high school, Mr.Mackney attended Southern Methodist University where he received a B.S. in economics. Mr. Mackney's father died nine years ago when he was struck by a car that a neighbor lost control of. His mother, formerly a house wife and then in retail sales, lives in Los Angeles. He had not seen her in four years. He is estranged from an older brother whom he describes as a teller of "outrageous lies." He has contact with Jeffrey, a younger brother, whose wedding he, &&^^, and Jack recently attended. After experience in the securities industry, he moved to New York City where he met Dina. (what this has to do with anything escapes me. He does not provide any background information about Dina's childhood) Mr. Mackney regrets leaving a good position with Bloomberg in New York to "chase money" working for a software company. At the end of 2000, the startup (internet) company for which he worked failed. He then went to work for Mr. Scamardo. (I told Dr. Samenow, I had an offer from BEA Systems for $125,000 salary and was going to accept it before working for my wife's father. He leaves this out.) To the present, Mr. Mackney does not understand why his father-in-law rejected consummating the deals that Chris brought to him. (I understand clearly and told Samenow so. He could not sign any loan documents and every deal had to be worked through Ron Salerno. He was a convicted Felon, which is why he could not do more deals.) He eventually went to work for Trammell-Crow and "felt vindicated" especially as he earned a $600,000 commission for his first deal. That company was purchased by another, and Chris was retained. He said that this was because "my reputation is fantastic." (I gave him Terry Hindermann, who hired me at Trammell Crow and Charles Kehler, a client that knows me well, but we have never actually done a deal together. Samenow did not call either.)Chris Mackney pointed out that he and Dina participated in couple's therapy even before marrying. As he sees it, marriage became like a prison sentence.(His words, not mine- I said that our communication was always terrible and that it did not improve after we went to therapy before our marriage and it never improved after. My wife has never taken any responsibility or accountability for the communication issues in our marriage. I was lonely, frustrated at work and home, and didn't have enough money to support my wife's lifestyle.

"After being married, it was what she wanted to do. I neglected my own passions....My wife will say it was about porn , internet and girls. I'd say that was a symptom."

Mr. Mackney said that as he and Dina grew apart, he began "looking for an emotional attachment." In their third year of marriage, Dina found out about his internet searches. is the one who was found in contempt of court. On April 9, 2009, the Honorable Randy Bellows found:

"That the Father is in contempt for violating the terms of [a previous order] due to his threatening and harassing behavior towards the mother."

"That the Father is in contempt for violating the terms of [a previous order] due to his use of disparaging words against the Mother in the presence of the parties' minor child *&^%." (I never disparaged my wife in front of my daughter. This goes back to my wife's contention that my daughter over heard a heated cell phone exchange. My wife claims that after hearing the exchange my daughter was distraught and cut her own hair with my permission. *($# did not hear the exchange. The day before the exchange, on Saturday, she asked if she could cut her own bangs. I advised her not to, but said ok, if she really wanted to. On Sunday night, when she was home with her mother, she had taken out the pony tails and realized her hair cut was not exactly as she expected. My daughter, much like her mother cares deeply about her appearance, was very unhappy with the results. My wife insisted that I had 'done something to &&*&' and took her to see Dr. Van Syckle. My wife told Dr. Van Syckle that something was very wrong because 'a mother knows'. Dr. Samenow was aware that she had cut her hair but still claimed that she was upset about hearing me talking to her mother. I rejected this claim because as I had told Dr. Van Syckle, my daughter has heard my wife and I fight dozens of times and was never visibly upset by it. On the other hand, she had never cut her own hair before and was only unhappy about her appearance.)

According to Mr. Mackney, his wife rejects joint custody because she does not want to have to deal with him in making decisions about *&%$ and (*#@. The e-mail correspondence will show convincingly that Dina Mackney is usually unsuccessful in resolving the most minor matters having to do with basic logistics of custodial time, much less matters of greater importance. (where? I'd like to see this. The email record shows that I am the one trying to seek resolution. I proposed a parenting plan and forwarded several versions to my wife and Dr. Van Syckle. I received no response to any of my requests. The email record shows that my wife has dictated how our visitation schedule and had routinely made changes to the schedule for her convenience. She took two weekends from me and has ignored all requests from me to reschedule them. And then Mr. Mackney will make a unilateral decision such as buying a skateboard for their three year old. When his wife questioned his judgment about the purchase, Mr. Mackney retorted that Dina was overly cautious in not wanting to let the children fail or fall. He noted that "it is like a hot stove" in that "the learning is greater" when the individual benefits directly from experience. Mr. Mackney discounts, it seems, even a possibility that his wife has anything positive to contribute to the children's development. In an e-mail to her dated March 11, 2009, he proclaims, "*&%% and *&^^ have grown into the people they are today because of my influence." (This is just a lie. I have a copy of the email where I respectfully address my wife's concerns about the skateboard and acquiesce to her feelings. See email attached at the bottom. I gave this email to Samenow and he just misrepresents the events. Mr. Mackney spoke in the 3/11/09 e-mail of his wife's sense of entitlement but wrote in that very e-mail that he is "only asking to leave with what is entitled to me under the law." He buttresses his arguments by blaming his wife for the destitute situation in which he finds himself: "You and your family have millions and you want all of it." He adds, "The logical consequence is that I will have no place for the children to call home when they are with me." The March 11, 2009 e-mail concludes:"I plan to share these emails with *&&* and *((* when they are old enough. They should know how our actions shaped their life and which one of us to talk about in therapy." (I believe in being honest with my children at an age appropriate level. I am not trying to harm their relationship with their mother or grandparents. However, I do not want to lie to them if or when they approach me about the subject when they are older.

Chris Mackney has dragged neighbors, friends, and school staff into the custody dispute. (This is a COMPETE LIE- I never wanted to include them. My wife has refused to negotiate and called me a bad father with bad judgment, and has been using her Daddy's money to take away my parental rights. I have been forced to go to these people to try and defend myself from my wife's allegations. If my wife did not continue her unnecessary litigation, then I would not have needed to talk to anyone.) He has gone to them with his reports about Mr. Scamardo and has discussed his difficulties with his wife. He told this examiner on April 10, 2009 that he intends to "protect my parental rights."

"I'm going to neighbors. I never wanted to call my neighbors. When I'm faced with having to provide witnesses for you, they don't want to get involved. I'm speaking to the only people who know me and have seen me with my children. I have to let them know the consequences of them not speaking." (exactly. I had to get them involved otherwise, I would have no witnesses. No one wanted to say anything negative about me or my wife. We have had good relations with all our friends and neighbors. My wife simply does not want them or anyone else to know the truth. I don't blame them. However, with my back against the wall, I needed someone that knew me to stand up for me and my children and speak truthfully about me as a father.) This examiner asked about the purpose of communicating to school staff members' allegations about Dina's father. Mr. Mackney conceded, "Should I have done this? probably not." Having said this, he qualified his statement:"It may be objectionable. It's public information, like me saying you're a doctor."

Mr. Mackney then did what he has habitually done throughout this evaluation – blame his wife and her family: "I never wanted any of these things to happen. I don't want this to go on….I was a good father and fine husband until I found out about her father's murder." (This is true. Dina claims that she only started seeking sole custody after I "started acting crazy" .Basically meaning after I found out about the murder. **This examiner spoke with people who have seen Mr. Mackney with the children and have superficial knowledge of his parenting skills and involvement.** (superficial??? All my neighbors have the best knowledge of my parenting skills outside of my wife and her **Chris acknowledged, he was "caught" by Dina three times. In the first instance, he had a sexual encounter with the woman.** (this was a onetime event. There was no affair or multiple women.)However, the marriage continued. Mr. Mackney said that he saw a therapist and provided the name, but this examiner was unsuccessful at contacting this person for an interview. Sandra Laeser, another therapist, informed Mr. Mackney that she did not want to be involved. (As I explained to Samenow, my wife was upset and angry. I was to. I didn't want to be unhappy so I voluntarily went to therapy and even saw a psychiatrist named Dr. Colleen Blanchfield. Dr. Blanchfield said 'you are depressed' after our first meeting and put me on anti depressants. Dr. Blanchfield also told me that I either needed to get into couple's therapy or I would need to get divorced. I told Dr.Blanchfield all the details about the marriage and signed a release for Dr. Samenow to review her materials. I wanted him to hear what Dr. Blanchfield had to say about me. He leaves that part of his report and provides no information from her.)Mr. Mackney asserted that Dina is all about money and image. He said that he and his wife outspent their earnings, but Dina's father "basically supplemented our income." He said that by November of 2007, "we'd burned through $300,000" which included half the savings from an award received from injuries sustained in a car accident. (it was closer to $400,000.$50,000 of this money went to finishing off our basement which included a jewelry studio for Dina. She now claims that I have 'no equity' in the marital home and has spent more in legal fees than my equity in our home.) Almost no matter what issue was being discussed, the topic came back to Mr. Scamardo. "If Dina told me her father was a murderer, I wouldn't want my children to have a grandfather who was a murderer."

Mr. Mackney told this examiner that he did not feel safe, that he wanted his shotgun. "I only asked for it after I learned my father-in-law was a murderer, after they changed attorneys. I'm trying to get it away from them as much as for my protection. I don't want to end up dead…He had all the reason to want me dead." (If Samenow looked at what Scamardo has done in his life, it is not so farfetched. I was really scared of what they can do to me. When I found out about the murder I told no one. Then when they started accusing me of Blackmail and extortion, I felt I had to tell someone so they could no longer accuse me of trying to get money. Then when I told someone about it wanted me held in contempt of court.**As Mr. Mackney told this examiner of his wife's faults, it appeared that he was describing himself. He said that she is not accountable and has a sense of entitlement. Actually, Mr. Mackney in a lengthy series of e-mails, spanning many months, blames his wife for almost every difficulty that the two of them or their children have** (This is a LIE- I do not blame my wife for almost every difficulty, but as I told Samenow, I think she is 49% responsible. I would be more than willing to accept 51% of the responsibility. **He demands that she settle the case on terms acceptable to him.**(I demand nothing. I have no power. I have made a generous offer to my wife and even included a confidentiality agreement in December of 2008) **Mr. Mackney said that his wife is above the law, but he** family and Samenow did not quote any of them on the subject.) **It is clear to them as it is to this examiner that both &*^% and ^$#@ enjoy being with their Dad. He does things that they enjoy. However, Michael Humphries, a neighbor not involved in the Mackney's domestic turmoil, noted that "as things began to deteriorate, [Chris] was using *&%% as a sort of foil to get to Dina."** (Dina has been using the kids as a weapon against me for a year and 8 months and I provided Samenow with email evidence to prove it.) **And, on the day that Chris came to move his possessions, he spoke to Mr. Humphries about Dina's father's involvement in a "murder-drug" case**(this is a lie. It NEVER happened). **Mr. Humphries said that, later, he learned from Dina that her husband had actually gone on- line and composed part of the article in Wikepedia about what allegedly happened 40 years ago** (what proof does she have? Again no witnesses and based entirely on my wife's testimony). **People available to this examiner who have been around Chris Mackney for any significant amount of time are mostly Dina's friends and family** (In this area that is true. We spent most of our time with her family and her friends. I knew no one when we moved to this area in 2000. It was a conscious decision to move here. Her parents and friends were here.). **They have little positive to say about Chris as a parent. Stefani Scamardo-Haynes, Dina's sister** (Knew about the murder and is extremely dependent on her parents) **Ms. Scamardo-Haynes spoke of Chris's trip to New York City with the children. When Mr. Mackney arrived at her office, he had no money** (this is a lie. I had money and bank records to prove it.) **said he had plans for the next night and would obtain a sitter. Stefani replied that she and her husband would gladly take the children to their home. Ms. Scamardo-Haynes noted that *&#@ and *&^^ were unbathed, hadn't eaten, that *&## lacked a coat** (a lie- we had been out all day and it was spring break in New York City. The weather was warm during the day and cooled off at night.). ***&^% had no clean clothes and one shoe without a match to it.**(Just a lie- I have never taken my children out like this. Again there is no witnesses and no evidence to support this statement other than her testimony.) **En route in the car to the hotel, Stefani heard Chris ask *&%$, "If you get killed, (*&&, would you rather be frozen or buried in the ground?" Five minutes later, (*@# made a comment about his dad one day buying him a motorcycle.** (there was an advertisement on the radio for a cryogenics business. *&^^ asked what it was, and I explained it to her.) **According to Stefani, Chris replied, 'I'll cut your arm off now" making the point that motorcycles are not safe. "Mainly, he's inappropriate around them," she commented.** (This was said in a totally joking manner, to make the point that I didn't think he should ride a motorcycle. These are the worst things she can accuse me of in Nine years???

Deborah DeStefano, Dina's aunt "[Chris] let Dina manage the children because he wants to be on the computer.

We spend a lot of time hanging out at the beach or at Christmas. At the beach, he'll read his book while Dina builds sandcastles. Not to say he's never done this. He's more passive – watches TV with them. In day to day organization of the children, Dina's more the one."
Ms. DeStefano observed an incident at the beach in 2006. Chris wanted &^%% to ride a bike that was too big for her, her feet did not reach the pedals. "It scared her and was uncomfortable. Chris started riding his bike. She was terrified. I'm holding her running along, asking Chris to stop. Chris talked sharply, `Deborah, let her go'." (I have no idea what the this is supposed to mean, but this is the worst thing she can come up with in Nine years???)

Kimberly Gurick, nanny Asked to describe Mr. Mackney's personality, Ms. Gurick replied, "The first word is unstable. Excuse me if I get angry or emotional. He's been inappropriate with me….He approached me and leaned over and [and asked] `what's up with this murder thing'?"….I'm scared to death. I'm dropping these kids with a man who can change at the drop of a dime." Mr. Gurick said that, when she was at a CVS drug store with the children, *&^^ reached up to touch a lighter and mentioned how his dad showed him how to use it. Jack then retracted the statement but said, "I couldn't do it; (**& could." Ms. Gurick immediately informed Dina. Ms. Gurick acknowledged that she phoned the police three times the day that Chris came to pick up his belongings. "I thought he'd shoot her," she commented. Ms. Gurick remains concerned that Chris Mackney might physically harm his wife. In an e-mail dated May 21, 2009, Ms. Gurick wrote to this examiner about a conversation she had with Mr. Mackney: "He made comments about there being a `media event' if he is `pushed into a corner and his parental rights are taken away'. He brought up Dina's father at least twice alluding to `the case' against him, claiming that `the law failed that family and the law is failing him'." (this is just a lie. I do not have the temper or have I ever been angry with the Nanny. The nanny has told me many times that I am a good father to the kids. I always greet them and say good bye with big hugs and kisses. Strangely, Dina has made sure that I cannot talk to the nanny. The nanny's and my wife's fears are completely unjustified. I have no history of violence whatsoever, and the nanny has never seen me do anything inappropriate around the children. Having a irrational and unjustified fear does not mean that I am a threat. I am not. **Several individuals told this examiner that they did not like Mr. Mackney drawing them into matters that should remain private. John Donovan (neighbor) said that Chris had asked him to speak with this examiner, then "went into depth about Dina's father" conveying the impression that the Scamardos were "not to be trusted." Mr. Donovan told this examiner, "I was very uncomfortable to be in the middle of this."**
"Part of the discomfort was I felt I was being manipulated. This goes to my view of Chris as a shallow person. I felt I was being pushed" (I was very apologetic to the Donovon's and explained that I needed people to speak to Samenow that knew me, my parenting and my children. John Donovan has been through divorce and was sympathetic to me. It is also interesting to note that Samenow never uses and positive quotes about me from my own witnesses. **On April 24, 2009, after the judge had found him in contempt of court, Mr. Mackney declared to this examiner, "I can control myself and my behavior."** (I explained to Dr. Samenow, that I was not the problem. I was on the defensive and that my wife was lying and could not abide by the Judge's order to keep me involved with the children. I made the statement that I have and would control myself. It is not a problem for me. **As for the court outcome, he told this examiner he was hiring a new attorney because Mr. Surovell was "unprepared and…offered no evidence."** (this is not true- it was initially Mr. Surovell's idea to withdraw from the case because he "could not get a settlement" for me and would only continue to cost me more money that I did not have.) **As it turned out, Mr. Mackney eventually stopped paying his attorney who withdrew from the case.** (compete mischaracterization. I made my financial condition very clear to Mr. Surovell and Dr. Samenow. It was a mutual decision for Surovell to withdraw. **Mr. Mackney sounded a theme of desperation which grew only stronger in the following months: "I have no weapons to use, no friends, no family, no witnesses. I'm getting hammered and steamrolled by these people….Let's end this. They're destroying my character."**
Mr. Mackney said that, if his wife gains sole custody, "I lose everything." After this examiner again explained what sole custody is, Mr. Mackney stated: "I'll just move away. I'm not going to live my life like this….I have two beautiful children…I don't have anyone on this side of the

fence....I'm scared of losing my parental rights." (partially true- Samenow tried to downplay sole custody for my wife. I asked Samenow if it is true that I would have no legal rights to my own children. He said yes, and I told him, this is exactly why I want joint custody. I did not trust my wife to include me in their lives and I believed would only be empowered to do even more if awarded sole custody. She does not want sole custody because we cannot agree on parenting issues. The facts show that we rarely disagree about the children. It is everything else on which we disagree. I want joint custody so my wife cannot call the police on me when I show up for a soccer game or an after school event. After numerous e-mails, letters, and statements begging to end this case, Mr. Mackney told this examiner on April 24, 2009, "I hope this case goes on for a long time; I can control myself." (I was referring to the fact that I am not resisting the process. I was asked to control myself and I have. The longer this goes on the more my wife's true motives become apparent. Dr. Samenow tries to make it sound like I want this divorce to continue like this. He knows this is not true and all the evidence shows that all I have ever wanted was to end the divorce and move on with my life. Mr. Mackney planned to take &^%% and (*#$ to Los Angeles so they could participate in his brother's wedding in July. He feared that his wife would interpose numerous objections. The correspondence between them about this is exemplary of the ongoing difficulty communicating. Ms. Mackney does not trust her husband's judgment. (this is an irrational and unjustified fear to make discredit my parenting. There is no evidence to show that my parenting or judgment is any worse than hers or any other parent.) Mr. Mackney told &^&^ and *&## about the wedding before discussing it with his wife.(I made Dina aware of the trip over a month in advance) (Dina asked to have the airline schedule, where they would be staying and the phone number. She also inquired as to who would care for them if there were late night or other events perhaps not appropriate for young children. Ms. Mackney wrote (6/29/09), "If you are not able to discuss this potential trip with the kids then I will not allow them to go." Mr. Mackney was infuriated (infuriated? No. I completely expected her reaction and I used this occasion to point out to the Dr. that my wife has irrational and unreasonable fears and wants me to give her information about the trip that she have never provided me. and when he met with this examiner on June 30, he declared, "There's a double standard. I'm comfortable giving her anything. She doesn't give me anything." It is true that, on a very rare occasion, the children have stayed with the Scamardo's, an example being Dina's business trip to Denver. Mr. Mackney commented, "She trusts her parents more than me." This is definitely an accurate assessment. The Scamardo's have a record of providing attentive care and providing recreation and fun for &*%% and **&&. Mr. Mackney never denied that the children enjoy spending time with their grandparents. In any event, this examiner urged Mr. Mackney to "take the high road" and provide all information his wife requested about the impending trip to California. (I told Dr. Samenow that of course I would provide the information, but I wanted to point out my wife's unreasonable and unreciprocated demands.) Later that day, Mr. Mackney wrote that he would give Dina his cell phone number and nothing more (e-mail of 6/29/09 at 4:20 p.m.). On July 1, this examiner intervened in the stalemate. In an e-mail, he urged Chris to "please send Dina the details she requests. Her request is reasonable." On July 7, Mr. Mackney sent Dina the following e-mail: "I am uncomfortable giving you the event details. I do not want you or anyone showing up and ruining the wedding or killing me and my entire family. My insurance policy for $1 Million dollars only has my brother as beneficiary. If he and I died, then you would benefit if we are not divorced....I will be happy to give you the hotel and flight information."

Bullied to Death: Chris Mackney's Kafkaesque Divorce

This matter was resolved. The children went to the wedding in Los Angeles with their father and returned in satisfactory condition. But it took days of hassling until Chris, under pressure, provided the information that should have been offered initially (a complete mischaracterization. I made her aware of the trip, she wanted the itinerary of all the events; the names and phone numbers of any baby sitters; and name address and phone number of where I was staying. My point being was that NEVER had my wife ever volunteered that information to me. In fact, when she took the children on Spring Break during my designated weekend, gave me no information and made no attempt to reschedule my weekend.

On the MMPI-2, Mr. Mackney "showed an extensive amount of conscious defensiveness." The computer generated report stated, "His profile appears to be of questionable validity." The child custody profile report contains the following observation: "He may be described…as poised, persuasive, or as otherwise having proficient social skills";

"In general, he should show generally positive and cheerful moods";

"He would be seen as not wanting to engage antagonistic confrontations";

"At times he would fail to appreciate how his reactions bother or annoy [others] or why they see him negatively when they feel offended by him";

"He is likely to see things in terms of his own agenda and personal interests";

"His scores indicate a quite positive and well above average level of immediate personal organization";

"The intensity of a child's emotionality per se should not be problematic for him:'

"When stressed or threatened, he could pursue his self-interests in urgent or even forceful ways."

"He tends to see his problems as external to himself";

"His scores indicate a potential for some peculiarities or unusual shifts in his stream of thought. When he feels threatened, his ideas may be oddly connected and possibly difficult to follow:;

"His scores suggest serious difficulties in being able to forgive and forget";

"Others are likely to find him more controlling of them than they want or feel necessary";

"The potential for antisocial behavior appears somewhat above average";

"His scores indicate a serious and well above average risk of loss of control over his temper";

"The depth of his parent-to-children bonding appears likely to be mostly adequate but sometimes uneven";

"He tests as disposed to dichotomize someone or various others as either for him or as against him."

There seems to be no one available who knows Mr. Mackney well enough to discuss in any depth his character and parenting skills (he chose not to quote my neighbors or friends, all of whom would say wonderful things about me as a father.). Richard Ware has known Mr. Mackney since college. After the marital separation, Chris lived with Mr. Ware for brief periods when he had "no where else to go". Otherwise, according to Mr.Ware, they saw each other "every week or two at a social or sporting event." Mr. Ware characterized Mr. Mackney as "a nice guy, seems like an honest person, a solid individual." He added that Chris has handled this "ugly" divorce process "quite admirably." Mike Harris also knows Chris from college and described him as "confident, extremely social, and a good guy." He has had little contact with Chris in the past two years except for an occasional meal. Mr. Harris was sympathetic to Chris having heard his account of the custody battle.

"I like both and I like Chris. Both are capable of being good parents. This is probably more difficult for Chris. He has no safety net in this area. His father-in-law is used towinning." (Mike told me he raved about me and this is the quote he chose to use? Curious) On July 25, 2009, in

an e-mail, Mr. Mackney voiced dissatisfaction that this examiner had not spoken with Casey Long who has known him for twenty years. Mr. Mackney said that Mr. Long would "provide you a objective and knowledgeable opinion." This examiner left messages for Mr. Long on 4/16 at 11:42 a.m, 4/21 at 8 p.m., 4/28 at 3:55 p.m., and May 13 at 7:40 a.m. He did not receive a call back and was not able to schedule an interview. (this is a lie. Casey told me about the phone calls he had with Samenow and how difficult Samenow was to get in touch with. Casey is getting cell phone records to refute Dr. Samenow's claims. **Between May and July, Mr. Mackney's situation worsened as he lost his job. On May 7, 2009, he told this examiner, "I don't want blood money, just what's mine." And, he added, "I want 50% of the time with my children." On May 22, 2009, Mr. Mackney asked this examiner what his chief concern is. The reply was, "Your judgment and stability." Greatly displeased by this answer, Mr. Mackney did what he customarily does, become accusatory: "It's a miscarriage of justice. I'd like to open this up to peer review of you and Cottrell." On May 25, 2009, he wrote his attorney, "I have questions about Dr. Samenow's objectivity." Months before, he had been displeased with Dr. Guy Van Syckle, a psychologist who recommended in court that Mr. Mackney's time with the children be supervised.** (Not true-I had no problem with Van Syckle's recommendation because any supervisor would see that I am a great and loving father to my children. I want more objective people to see for themselves that I am a capable and competent father.) **On June 22, 2009, Mr. Mackney reported that he was bankrupt** (I never used the word bankrupt to describe my condition. I always said 'broke'.) **and considering seeking employment in New York as well as in the "government sector." When this examiner visited Mr. Mackney's apartment in Arlington, Chris seemed ill at ease.** (he does not state that it is an extremely nice, safe, clean, well located, building near the metro, 66, an ice skating rink, a park, movie theater, library, an indoor pool and countless shops and restaurants.) **Clearly, there was an insufficient number of beds.** (yes, because my wife did not give me the two beds that were specified in the order. She gave me three bed frames and one queen size mattress. I have since filed a show cause petition to hold her in contempt for not giving me the bed and other items owned by Casey Long. **He was displeased at this examiner's asking *&#$ about who slept where.** (he must have asked them three times how and where they slept.) **He was even more irritated when &*%% said that she did not have many of her belongings at the apartment.** (I was irritated watching him interrogate my daughter and watching her trying very hard to provide the right answers. He was very pushy with his questioning, but I remained silent and said nothing for him to characterize as irritated. **He walked to a bureau and began taking out items and saying to **(, "What is this? What is this?" Whether he overheard **&& say that she didn't have much to do inside the apartment "except walk around" is unclear. Mr.Mackney said that he would have a check for this examiner which actually was overdue. He then seemed quite agitated, wrote the check, and said it was not cashable, and he did not know when it would be.** (I was very clear with Samenow about my financial condition from the beginning and told him that I was now out of money. He pressed me to write a check and post date it. I was irritated because I told him that there was none left.) **Then as this examiner and the children with their father left the apartment to take the elevator up to the pool, Mr. Mackney was muttering about his wife taking everything, leaving him virtually destitute. On July 27, 2009, Chris Mackney wrote the following bitter e-mail to his wife: "I assume you will be dropping my last name and going back to Scamardo? You seem to hate me and love and respect your father so much, you should honor him by taking his name back."**
As she sometimes did, Ms. Mackney did not use restraint and responded on that same date, "That's rich – mental health advice from chris mackney." (he is making apologies for her?)

Twelve days earlier (7/15/09), in an e-mail to this examiner, Mr. Mackney described his current situation as follows: "No, the funds are not good. I am now unemployed in the middle of an unnecessary legal battle with my wife's family who refuses to negotiate but would rather spend over $100,000 to destroy me. I have nothing left. I am broke. Everything I have left is being held hostage by my wife. Please encourage my wife to try and work this out with me. She has refused to send me a piece of paper to sign that would end this for me. I cannot continue to live like this."

As August approached, the e-mails between Chris and Dina Mackney were continuing to fly back and forth. In addition, on July 31, Mr. Mackney wrote Tracy Heiden an e-mail about Dina with the subject heading "Your wonderful friend."

"[Dina] is a real sweetheart. Just pray that you do not cross her or her family. You might end up dead or worse, like me. Those people are truly EVIL." (this is a fact, there are countless people that will testify to this. Why would they continue the strategy and tactics when they do not benefit the children or themselves. They are entire motivation is to remove me from the children's lives. A Note on Dr. Guy Van Syckle's Involvement in this Case Dr. Guy Van Syckle, a clinical psychologist, became involved in this case essentially in the role of a treatment provider for **((and ****. The Mackney family was referred to him by Mr. Mackney's attorney, Mr. Surovell. The psychologist began meeting with the parents and the children in September, 2008. In testimony before Judge Bellows on April 23, 2009, Dr. Van Syckle said that he found Ms. Mackney to be "a warm attentive mother, very patient, very nurturing". He also said that she was "very honest in asking for my assistance." In speaking with the psychologist, Mr. Mackney emphasized his concerns about Mr. Scamardo, a degree of focus that Dr. Van Syckle termed "an obsession." (I have been totally frustrated because both Van Syckle and Samenow elected not to consider any of my wife's family's past. It is exactly this past that concerns me. As the father of those two children I deserve to have my concerns addressed. (What was far more serious in an immediate sense to Dr. Van Syckle was Lily's telling him that she heard her dad swearing over the phone at her mother "and saying things where he was going to hurt mommy and hurt her grandfather" [p. 47 of hearing transcript] (my daughter did not and could not have heard the conversation, as I was outside on the balcony and my daughter and son where inside in a bedroom. My wife implied that this was the reason for my daughter being upset after cutting her own hair.Dr. Van Syckle was so concerned that he sent an e-mail on March 11, 2009 to Mr. Mackney, attorney Surovell, and this examiner.

"*&$# told me she overheard a very loud phone call that Chris was having with Dina at his house this past weekend. *&^^ told me that she had heard her father yell at her mom, use profanity, especially the `f' word and say mean things `about people' she loved. I told Chris last night that he had to stop having these angry calls especially if the kids were in the house. He agreed. I had never seen &^%% so distressed." (as I have stated, this was just not true. My daughter was upset about her hair, and I am sure she was upset about being grilled by Van Syckle pressing her to tell him what she heard. If you read the transcript of Van Syckle's testimony, he does say what **&^ says she heard. I think she was upset about her hair and Van Syckle was trying to get her to say she was upset about what she heard. **&& has seen and heard Dina and I fight numerous occasions and has never remained visibly distressed. I am 100% certain that she was upset about her haircut.

Based on his experience with the Mackney family, Dr. Van Syckle recommended that Mr. Mackney's visitation be supervised [p. 54]. Judge Bellows did not think at that time that supervision was warranted. Ten days before the hearing, Dr. Van Syckle told this examiner that he found Ms. Mackney to be "a good parent". He said that the children were "attached" to their father and "glad to see him." He added that &&*% "adores his Dad." Dr. Van Syckle told this examiner that he had been very direct with Chris Mackney about his "obsession" with Mr. Scamardo: "I've counseled [Mr. Mackney] this is something not be spread in the neighborhood and talked about in front of the children." Dr. Van Syckle said that he was "very concerned about Chris's judgment and emotional outbursts." He was concerned that on November 22, Chris took *&### to a gun show because the child likes guns. They were not admitted onto the premises. The psychologist said, "I pleaded with Chris to get help, to do something about his rage." (I have no rage. I only want to be free. I am exasperated and frustrated. It is extremely frustrating when the other party continues to make outrageous accusations and refuses to negotiate. Neither Samenow or VanSyckle acknowledge this fact.)

On May 12, 2009, Dr. Van Syckle told this examiner that Chris is "so erratic that I'm not sure about his judgment and being emotionally appropriate around the children."

"He couldn't keep his emotional outrage separate from the children. Unreliable isn't the right word. He's relentless." (to this day I remain concerned about the welfare of my children with the Scamardo family. I have every right to be. I have been told by Samenow and Van Syckle to ignore it. My parental concern outweighs their professional advice, especially considering they are my wife's witnesses. I will follow your recommendations on what to say and not say regarding my wife's father. To be honest, I really don't care about him. I only want to be free from them, and I have absolutely been picking this issue because, he showed extremely 'bad judgment' and never lost custody of his children. I only want the same treatment.)

^%$^ Mackney*&%# is a lively, active, curious engaging child. Ms. Birnie Shea at Country Day School said that he is "one of the more social children" to whom others are drawn. She characterized the boy as having "that leader quality, a charismatic quality." Ms. Shea indicated he is a child who needs firm boundaries. "*%@! does better with clear limits and consequences to his actions and follow through....He will test the limits, then will follow through....He will be impulsive at times, agitated by loud noises."

The teacher mentioned that early in May, a child bumped into *&@!. His response was to push the youngster back forcefully enough so that the child suffered an injury.

Academically, there are no problems. Ms. Shea said that *&%$ has a good attention span, picks up concepts, and recognizes numbers and letters. She described him as "articulate and aware."

Ms. Shea said that Ms. Mackney attended conferences, organized class parties, and has served as head of the auction committee. Asked if she is easy to deal with, Ms. Shea responded, "Absolutely." With respect to Mr. Mackney, he attended the second teacher conference, not the first. "We didn't have much communication in the beginning of the year," she noted but, more recently, he has asked questions and offered to be of help.

Although Ms. Mackney has referred to marital difficulties while discussing *&&^ with Ms. Shea, Chris sent an e-mail having nothing to do with *&$#. The issue was Dina's father, and Mr. Mackney asked to schedule a conference. Because school was closing at year's end, that did not occur.

On April 30, 2009, &^#@ told this examiner that when he is with his dad, they go to the mall, eat at McDonalds. He mentioned enjoying his spring break trip to Florida with his mother, going to the beach and the pool. He said he enjoys visiting his grandparents.

Asked if anyone reads to him, he mentioned "Mommy, Granny, and Pop Pop". Asked who Pop Pop is, *&@# replied, "Not the dad that's here – that's Pete" meaning it is Mr. Scamardo who reads to him.

On June 17, 2009, this examiner was interviewing *&#@ who was brought by the nanny. (*%$ was with them. When *&$# completed her time speaking with this examiner, &*** actually asked to come in and talk. He said that he had some Father's Day cards but his mother would not let him give them to his dad. "She said I had to make them," *((* commented. Asked if anyone had instructed him to report this, the boy replied, "No, I just wanted to." However, before this had occurred, Ms. Gurick, the nanny told this examiner that Ms. Mackney was irritated with her for spending money on cards without her permission when the children could as well make them. When this examiner discussed this matter by phone with Ms. Mackney, Dina denied telling Jack he could not give his father the cards. She did think it preferable to make cards as the children have before.

She said she would immediately clarify this with Jack and did not want him to be unhappy about it.

During the home visit to Ms. Mackney's on June 25, 2009, *&^% immediately took over. He rushed to the door and offered this examiner lemonade he said he had made. He then showed this examiner around the house discussing each room and his favorite toys.

When it came to showing the master bedroom, *&^%$ demeanor changed from being boisterous and cheerful to a bit more somber as he pointed to an item that his father had left behind. He also showed this examiner which closet had been his dad's. (My son especially misses me terribly.)

*&@# Mackney

&# just completed first grade at The Potomac School in McLean, Va. Andrea Greenwich said that she has performed academically at grade level. She was meeting with a math specialist for special help. Ms. Greenwich said that (*^% was shy and reserved at the beginning of the year. When she broke her leg early in the academic year, the other girls helped her: "She came out of her shell and formed great friendships." There are absolutely no behavioral or interpersonal difficulties that this child has experienced. Ms. Greenwich noted that the week of March 9, *&#$ seemed quieter than usual, this being after the episode in which she overheard her father swearing on the phone at her mother. (She had also been supplied by her father with scissors to cut her own hair at her father's residence and, apparently, did not like the result.) Apparently, after Ms. Mackney raised a question about *&@#, Ms. Greenwich was concerned enough to respond to her in an e-mail (dated 3/11/09) as follows: "I was actually wondering if something was up with &^%$. She has just seemed a little quieter and more reserved than usual this week….Nothing about her behavior is overtly different or obvious; she just seems to be in her own thoughts. Today for our Dialogue Journals she wrote to her dad which I noticed because I don't think she's addressed her letters to him in the past. I'll make sure to keep an eye on her to see if I notice any changes."

Ms. Mackney has helped with field trips and with costumes for the first grade play. She attended both parent-teacher conferences. Ms. Greenwich said that Mr. Mackney came to the Fall part-teacher conference and has e-mailed asking about *&^& progress. However, he also wrote about "the custody situation."

An incident occurred around the end of October, 2008 when no one knew where *&%$ was. The child was not on the bus as she was supposed to be. Apparently, her father had come to the bus stop and picked her up. Because the school had not been advised of the change, there was for a time some consternation. (at this time, my wife was keeping the children from me and the only way to see my own children was to go to school to pick them up.)

When this examiner met with *&& for the first time on April 9, 2009, she was very reserved. Asked what she likes to do at her father's apartment, she said they play outside or play computer games. At first she said, "We didn't do anything" which sounded very much like her telling this examiner at the home visit that she just walks around inside the apartment. *&#@ said that her father is a good cook and mentioned his preparing pasta with tomato sauce and macaroni and cheese. (I had very little money for anything and was stretching all my money, as I had no idea how long the divorce would go on.)

In general, this is a poised, intelligent but reserved child. She expressed no dissatisfaction. She said she'd like to be a veterinarian or perhaps an artist, indicating she might want to be "a jewelry designer like my Mom." She enjoys school and likes to play soccer. She takes jazz and tap dancing. *&$# enjoys spending time at her grandparents and was looking forward to dying Easter eggs at their house. She said that she likes spending time with her Aunt Stefani from New York ("she's really nice and lets me do a lot of things").

The second time that this examiner met with *&&&, she seemed more withdrawn and less inclined to talk. On April 30, she said that she had enjoyed spending spring break with her mother, *&@! and friends of her mother and her friend Hope. Asked what she had done at her father's place the preceding weekend, she said, "I forgot" but then recalled they went out to eat Saturday, then he cooked pasta on Sunday. (my time with the children was continually changing and not consistent. It's been almost a year since I had moved out and I did not have my own apartment until January 2009.)

On the Children's Apperception Test (telling stories to pictures), *&$# depicted the nurturing person as the mother. On Card #1, it is the mother who is feeding the children, even though no parental figure is present.

Card #19 (a card that also showed no female figure)

"There was a room and there was a baby in the room – a teeny, tiny baby. The baby was sick, and the mother gave her whatever she wanted, and she got better and went back to school and she played."

Card #15

"There was a storm and two twin boys, baby boys in the crib all alone. And there was no one else. It was pitch black and they went out to find the mom...."

There is little mention of a male figure except for a rather unsympathetic depiction on Card #3, when **** says that a king is trying to find help to "run the kingdom." He had great difficulty in this quest because "no one wanted to help him."

((*&'s approach on the Bricklin Perceptual Scales was in keeping with her overall demeanor during this evaluation. She seemed to do her utmost to disclose as little as possible. Of 31 items that she answered, she scored her parents within three points of each other on 21 items. By the way she responded to the task, it appeared that she basically checked off the top rating or close to it on each item, regardless of content. Thus no conclusions can be drawn from the use of this instrument.

Is There a Need for Supervised Visitation?

On page 255 of the April 23, 2009 hearing transcript, Judge Randy Bellows said regarding supervised visitation, "I believe we're not there yet and I also believe that the children will be adversely affected if Mr. Mackney is either deprived of visitation or that visitation is supervised." (Judge Bellows felt that nothing informative was to learned from supervised visitation.) **This examiner finds that a very strong case can be made for Mr. Mackney's time spent with the children to be under supervision. Mr. Mackney has not shown himself to be a consistent and competent caretaker.** (I have been in a divorce and under tremendous financial and legal pressure. He has no actual evidence other than my wife and her family's testimony to support this claim.) **His failure, after months, to provide separate beds for the children is noteworthy**(I have a queen size bed and I purchased an inflatable mattress that lies next to my bed and we all sleep on it together.). **He has exposed them to unnecessary stress by denigrating their mother** (my wife has actually done this more that I have. It is usually my wife that initiates the communication. She has a very hard time controlling herself and separating her feelings from the children, yet Dr. Samenow makes it sound like I am the only one responsible.. And, at times, he has refused to exercise visitation claiming that he has no money to do anything despite the fact that in the Washington, D.C. area, there are numerous free activities. (I would forgo visitation if I did not have enough money to suitably care for my children. I thought I was being responsible.) Clearly, Mr. Mackney has been at his absolute worst when he has contact with Ms. Mackney. He has made simple arrangements difficult. His anger at her permeates nearly all contacts with her. And the children often are not spared the fallout. (this is laughable. It is my wife that is angry and spending hundreds of thousands of dollars on legal fees to remove me from the children's lives despite no actual evidence that I am or have ever been a bad father. However, as Judge Bellows found, imposing a third party will not help this situation. Instead, it will likely to lead to more resentment, conflict and, most certainly, to expense that the father cannot at this time afford. Furthermore, there is no evidence that the children have suffered physically or emotionally to such an extent that supervision is called for.

Recommendations

Ms. Mackney shall have sole legal and physical custody of the children.

Ms. Mackney will keep Mr. Mackney informed regarding the children's health, mental health, education, athletic and other activities.

Ms. Mackney will not schedule activities on Mr. Mackney's limited time with the children.

Ms. Mackney will consult with Mr. Mackney regarding major health and education decisions, although it is she who has decision-making authority.

Mr. Mackney's visitation with the children will occur as follows:
Every other weekend on Saturday from 10 a.m. to 7:30 p.m.
On Wednesdays after the weekends when Ms. Mackney has the children from after school dismissal until 7 p.m. (through dinner).
Either Christmas Day or December 24 between 2 and 6 p.m.
Father's Day between 10 a.m. and 7:30 p.m.

Mr. Mackney will do all driving for the visitations.

Mr. Mackney will take a parenting class.

When Mr. Mackney has the funds, he will participate in individual psychotherapy or he will seek psychological services at a community clinic.

Neither parent will denigrate the other to the children nor will they discuss with the children any matters related to custody/visitation.

Mr. Mackney will not disparage Mr. Scamardo in any public forum or to the children.

Mr. Mackney may attend school, athletic, and other public functions in which the children participate.

Michael Volpe

Mr. Mackney may speak with the children by telephone at any hour that Ms. Mackney deems reasonable. Unless there is an emergency, there will be no more than one call per day. And the children are free to call their father as they wish.

Stanton E. Samenow, Ph.D. August 3, 2009

Chris Mackney's Complaint to AFCEI

October 20, 2011

American College of Forensic Examiners International
2750 E Sunshine
Springfield, MO 65804

Dear Ms. Sickman,

    I would like to file a formal complaint against Dr. Stanton Samenow and request an investigation into violations of the Ethical Principles of your organization for which he is a member.

    On January 23rd 2009, pursuant to §Virginia 20-124.2(D), Dr. Samenow was appointed by the Honorable Leslie Alden "to conduct a psychological evaluation and assessment of the parties and the minor children in order to make recommendations to the Court and the parties regarding what custodial arrangements would best suit the parties and the children.", as per the parties Pendente Lite Visitation Order (Exhibit 1).

    Both the order and the Virginia Code specify that he was to perform a psychological evaluation. Dr. Samenow failed to conduct the proper evaluation. As I am sure your organization is aware a psychological evaluation is very different from a custody evaluation. Had a psychological evaluation been conducted as ordered, the truth about the mother's psychological condition would no longer be in question. Dr. Samenows failure to conduct the proper evaluation is a violation of your organizations Principles: 'Members are to be forever vigilant of the importance of their role and to conduct themselves only in the most ethical and professional manner at all times.'

    In addition to conducting the wrong evaluation, Dr. Samenow's report was misleading and did not 'serve justice by making an accurate determination of the facts involved.'

1.   Dr. Samenow was made aware that I was being treated by a psychiatrist for the previous 4 years and was voluntarily on medication for depression related directly to the marriage and my employment with my ex-father in law. Dr. Samenow was given a signed release in order to speak with the psychiatrist Dr. Colleen Blanchfield (Exhibit 2), in order to confirm and verify allegations of emotional and physical abuse. Dr. Samenow was asked to verify the reasons for his treatment and the Mother's refusal to meet with Dr. Blanchfield and participate in the treatment. Dr. Samenow did not serve Justice by withholding the information provided to him

regarding my treatment for depression and the reasons for the treatment.

2. Dr. Samenow was made aware of Domestic violence committed by the mother on me, on January 19th 2008, in the presence of the children and witnessed by Fairfax County Police. After custody had already been determined, Dr. Samenow admitted that he had been shown a shirt that the Mother had ripped from my body during the assault. Dr. Samenow left this incident out of his report. Dr. Samenow was also told how the mother's father, Pete Scamardo, tried to hide evidence of the mother's physical abuse when he took the ripped shirt after the altercation.

I also reported to Dr. Samenow a hole in the Mother's bedroom wall, created when the Mother threw a book in anger. Dr. Samenow could have verified this allegation during his home visit and reported accordingly.

3. Dr. Samenow left out of his report emotional abuse and manipulation of our son. On April 30th, 2009, my son repeated in front of Dr. Samenow that my ex-wife had called me 'a liar' and that I "have all the money". I was concerned about Dr. Samenow's impartiality and emailed details of the incident (Exhibit 3) to my attorney and Dr. Samenow as a record.

4. Dr. Samenow did not accurately report the facts of the Traumatic Brain Injury of the mother. I informed Dr. Samenow of the Mother's Traumatic Brain Injury, suffered from a cab accident, during the marriage, on January 1, 2003. The Mother's Brain Injury was specifically identified, as a source of conflict in marriage to Dr. Samenow in his office and in sworn testimony in 2004 (Exhibit 4; Exhibit 5).

Dr. Samenow was also specifically empowered by the Order to obtain 'any medical or mental health information or documentation or releases'. Dr. Samenow's report does not indicate that any information was obtained from Dr. Spector, Dr. Deborah Warden (a leading expert in TBI) or Dr. Cooney.
Dr. Samenow only refers to an 'alleged head injury' in his report (page 3).

5. Dr. Samenow was made aware of the concerns that I had about my father in law and the fact that I had discovered that he was, in fact, guilty of the murder he had denied all involvement for over 40 years and was concerned for my safety. Dr. Samenow does not accurately

communicate my concerns for my children's character or my safety, as he was given numerous 'acts of bad faith', lying and manipulation:

a. The Mother's father admitted to trafficking heroin across the Mexican border (Exhibit 6, 7, 8).
b. The Mother's Father had his business partner murdered and was convicted of accomplice to murder. After exclaiming in Court "But, I didn't do it. I didn't", he was sentenced to Probation instead of the death penalty sought by the prosecutor. (Exhibit 9)

6.   c. The Grandfather attempted to forge a polygraph examination (Exhibit 10)
7.   d. The Mother's father committed perjury (Exhibit 11)
8.   e. The Mother's mother committed perjury (Exhibit 12)
9.   f. The Mother's father has over 108 lawsuits in Fairfax County alone (Exhibit 13).
10.   g. The Father in law had a $56 Million judgment against him in Maryland
11.   h. The Mother and her father conspired to circumvent Thoroughbred Racing Licensing laws, a class 4 felony (Exhibit 14).
12.   i. The Mother manipulated the daughter's class mother, Kelly Malesardi, to remove me from his daughter's Class email list (Exhibit 15).
13.   j. The Mother manipulated the son's Soccer 'team mother', Karla Brown, to not send information to the father (Exhibit 16).
14.   k. The mother lied under oath on May 13th, 2009, (Exhibit 17) during the time of Dr. Samenow's evaluation that her parents were paying her legal fees. Her attorney's own legal bills prove that her father wrote 7 checks, totaling $72,643.95, from his Business account to pay legal fees prior to her statement on May 13th. Both of these issues were brought to Dr. Samenow's attention.
15.   l. The Mother's father has a well known reputation for bullying and abusive behavior throughout the real estate community. A witness and victim of Pete Scamardo's wrath and abuse, John Sobecki, was not contacted by Dr. Samenow, as requested by the Father. Two other witnesses, Charles Kehler and Terry Hindermann, that could testify to my character and the abusive character of Pete Scamardo were not contacted by Dr. Samenow.
16.
17.   Dr. Samenow's report prejudicially refers to the felony accomplice to murder conviction of the Mother's father and his subsequent denials as a 'criminal conviction' and 'the situation 40 years ago'. The truth and details of the 'situation' glossed over and withheld from the Court by Dr. Samenow are extremely disturbing for the callousness, remorselessness and manipulation exhibited by Pete Scamardo. This is a pattern consistent with his reputation, well known in the business community, as reported to Dr. Samenow by the Father. In his report Dr. Samenow knowingly mischaracterizes the Father's legitimate "concern" for the emotional welfare of as being "obsessed" (page 13 of his report).
18.

19. In addition to withholding material facts that reflect extremely poorly on the mother, Dr. Samenow reports the mother's statements and makes conclusions, in his report, that evidence, witnesses and emails prove to be untrue. Here are examples of emails that prove that I was attempting to act in good faith and repeatedly offered to settle our differences out of Court and <u>completely contradict Dr. Samenow's conclusions</u>. (<u>Exhibit 18</u>)

20.

21. Dr. Samenow also repeats the mother's allegations that I was in communication with a 17 year old girl and gave her a venereal disease without ever reporting my side of the story. I had communicated to Dr. Samenow that I had made my wife aware that I was communicating with other men and women who were also going through a similar experience. The person that my ex-wife claimed was a 17 year old girl was in fact a married 40+ year old woman, whom I had met publicly and even told my wife about. Her accusation that she was 17 or that I was in communication with her is baseless, as I explained to Dr. Samenow. Furthermore, I informed Dr. Samenow when my wife accused me of giving her a venereal disease, I vehemently denied it and even offered to go get tested before she even told me the specific disease. For three hours, my ex-wife berated me and yelled at me to admit that I had given her a disease, before even telling me the actual disease. For three hours, I remained calm and simply told her that the disease, trichomoniasis, did not come from me. Dr. Samenow did not accurately report my side of the story.

22.

23. Dr. Samenow also did not attempt to contact 5 character witnesses that I had given to him (Casey Long, Terry Hindermann, Charlie Kehler, Teha Hirsi, and John Sobecki) that would refute many of the accusations of my ex-wife and prove the reason for my concerns. Dr. Samenow also makes no reference to these witnesses in his report. A sixth witness I gave to Dr. Samenow, our across the street neighbor, Mr. Ed McGinnis, was identified in the report, but none of his positive comments are included in the narrative. Ed McGinnis works for the Federal Government very high in the Department of Energy and is an extremely credible witness, who had given Dr. Samenow a very favorable report of me as a father and a person.

24.

25. Dr. Samenow also reports that I have 'no close friends', yet his report contains three friends of over 20 years, all of whom live in the area, that were willing to speak with Dr. Samenow about my character, Rich Ware, Casey Long and Mike Harris. My ex-wife, on the other hand, provides only one friend from high school with whom she rarely saw, Gail Cavallaro, and Cyndi Vasco, who was a friend of her sisters, with whom she only socialized when her sister was in town.

26.
27. After the completion of his report, Dr. Samenow was given a subpoena (Exhibit 19) to provide all documentation regarding his forensic evaluation. Dr. Samenow simply ignored the subpoena without explanation.
28.
29. Dr. Samenow was also told and provided documentation that I have never tried to Blackmail her or her family. I have never asked for any of their money. When the Mother and her attorney falsely claimed that I was blackmailing them I sent this email, which was later forwarded to Dr. Samenow. Dr. Samenow was very aware that I felt that I was being bullied and yet distorted the facts in his report. There is an enormous disparity of power and wealth in the family that is completely ignored and disregarded. It is this the pattern of using a position of power and wealth to abuse, bully, control and manipulate others, that exists in my ex-wife and her family that is being ignored by Dr. Samenow.
30.
31. After the completion of his evaluation, Dr. Samenow forwarded emails, sent directly to him from me, to my ex-wife's attorney that he then used in motions in Court against me. Dr. Samenow never forwarded me or my attorney any emails from my ex-wife.
32. After our Custody hearing, where my ex-wife asked that I have no visitation with my own children, the Judge in the case ordered that I obtain a second psychological evaluation from a list of evaluators to be provided by Dr. Samenow. When Dr. Samenow only provided one name, my ex-wife's attorney filed a motion attempting to force me to using the only Doctor provided Dr. Samenow, despite the Judge's order that Dr. Samenow provide 'a list' and that 'the Father shall choose the evaluation professional from the list prepared by Dr. Samenow.' Their motion included 15 emails that I sent only to Dr. Samenow.
33. Here is my motion, and the emails referenced on page 5 section c. of my motion.
34.
35.
36. Most egregiously, Dr. Samenow perpetuates my ex-wife's attorney's case-long narrative that I wanted to prolong the proceedings and was somehow dragging out the case. Dr. Samenow knows this is completely untrue as per the numerous emails I sent to him and Dr. Guy Van Syckle stating the contrary. On page 18 of his report he writes "I hope this case goes on for a long time; I can control myself." This statement was taken completely out of context. This statement was made in reference to the point that every time, my wife would accuse me of anything; I would take steps to prevent her from being able to make that same allegation. This statement was made to communicate to Dr. Samenow that the

37.
38. The family history of the mother and the Divorce itself, all reflect behaviors that can best be explained by a very severe psychopathy. Psychopathy is identified by looking at patterns of behavior and personality that exist. Dr. Samenow willfully chose to ignore the pattern. Only after I was accused by Dr. Samenow of having a personality disorder did I learn of psychopathy and how well it explained my relationship with my ex-wife and her family. Dr. Samenow is an expert in criminal psychology and is well aware of the patterns of behavior that define psychopathy. His report clearly attempts to obfuscate the patterns of behavior and personality of the mother and her father that are closely resemble those identified by the PCL-R checklist for psychopathy.
39.
40. I ask that the ACFEI carefully consider this complaint and find that Dr. Stanton Samenow violated the Principles of Professional Practice and hold him accountable for what appear to be willful misconduct and or gross negligence.
41.
42. Kindest Regards,
43. Chris Mackney

Email from Chris Mackney to Kyle Bartol, November 20, 2013 (Mackney's children's names changed Ruby and James)

From: Christopher Mackney
Date: November 20, 2013 at 11:02:17 AM EST
To: Kyle Bartol
Reply-To: Christopher Mackney

Mr. Bartol,

I understand that your firm has been paid over $1 million in legal fees to pretend that my reactions to, helplessly, being severely emotionally abused and watching my children being emotionally abused and alienated, as the Fairfax County Circuit Court turns a blind eye, but from where I sit its horror that
I can not escape. You refuse to negotiate or agree to anything I suggest to keep us out of Court. There have been 54 hearings in the case, over 5 years.

You have been well paid to use the legal system to destroy me and keep me from my children since June 24th, when <u>Pete hired you</u>, <u>the day after I learned for the first</u> time that Dina and her family had hidden her father's murder conviction. Dina admitted she 'already knew'. Dina then lied to Dr. Samenow telling him that she never knew. Dr. Samenow knew that Andrea Scamardo brought Dina and Stefani to the trial of their father and sat in the front row. <u>Andrea also lied under oath at that trial</u>. These are just facts and I am just the messenger. You can not prosecute the messenger for reporting abuse.

As I have said repeatedly, I do not wish to harm Dina or my children. Dina's behavior, judgement and 'cognitive' ability is the source of conflict and it is emotionally abusive. There is a history and pattern of high conflict behavior that has resulted in abnormal amounts of litigation, including being accused of <u>fraud by Maryland National Bank</u>.

For example, to tell my attorney <u>twice</u> that if I left town and gave up all efforts to communicate with my children ever again is not normal.
For example, to follow me through my employment and then contact child support enforcement for the first time in 5 years, the first month after I agree and move to Dallas, TX simply to escape the abuse is not normal.
For example, for you and her to go to the commonwealth's attorney and have me arrested and extradited for 'attempted extortion' because I wanted my $2,816 per month child support payment reduced after doing exactly what you wanted in order to end the conflict is not normal.
For example, for <u>Dina Mackney and the Commonwealth to refuse to agree to allow me to plead guilty to misdemeanor</u>, rather than the class 6 felony, and then being found NOT GUILTY at trial is not normal.
For example, to refuse to then make some kind of good faith effort to avoid

further conflict, embarrassment, legal fees, all in the name of the 'best interest of the Child', is not normal.

Speaking out abuse, bullying, lying, fraud, alienation, corruption is normal. Being completely ignored is cover-up.

The severe emotional and psychological abuse that I am experiencing is directly attributable to the patterns of behavior of Dina Mackney and Pete Scamardo. The abuse is so severe that I plan to commit suicide and detail the abuse on a blog site. I will not be quiet and silently go off and end my life
to escape the abuse. I plan to make everyone aware that I plan to commit suicide if a Guardian Ad Litem is not appointed to protect my children. I have no date picked out yet, but it will happen before Christmas. It will be as soon as I am done linking all the content to the website.

Either your client can voluntarily agree to a Guardian Ad litem to protect the best interests of our children or I will take my own life. In my mind,I believe that appointing a third party with the obligation to legally protect the best interest of Ruby and James, would be in their best interests. I am giving Dina the power to prevent the suicide of her children's father, by simply choosing to voluntarily appoint a Guardian Ad Litem to make sure that her children's rights are not being violated by the Court.

This is what it is going to come down to. My death or a lawyer to protect the best interests of children, who are being alienated from their father.

I am in the process of setting up the site and then will announce the site on other parental rights, emotional abuse, domestic violence, psychology organizations. It will contain all of the information as to WHY I BELIEVE my children and I are being abused.

Feel free to contact me any day up until my suicide to agree to a Guardian Ad Litem. The power to end the abuse is in your clients hands.

Kind Regards,

Bullied to Death: Chris Mackney's Kafkaesque Divorce

Chris Mackney

Email Exchange between Chris Mackney and "Mitch Jefferson" July 2013

----- Forwarded Message -----
From: Chris Mackney <cmach@yahoo.com>
To: MitchJefferson <backatu@yahoo.com>
Sent: Wednesday, July 10, 2013 9:28 PM
Subject: Re: Re: null

Brian,

Please talk to Dina. You are a father. I just want to see my children.

I'd she lets me see my children, i can't complain about alienation. It's that simple. I don't care about her or her family. Those kids are going to realize that she could have allowed it and resent her.

Think about it. Denying access is just not worth whatever she gets from keeping them from their father.

Chris

Mitch Jefferson <backatu@yahoo.com> wrote:

True or not, none of that justifies or refutes the fact that you are a deadbeat Dad using blackmail and extortion to try run away from your minimal financial obligations to your kids.

At this moment, it all comes down to one thing - you have promised silence if you are relieved from any obligation and you have promised unending damage to all involved but most significantly to your own children if you are to be held accountable.

You fail to see that society cannot and will not accept extortion and blackmail as a way for deadbeat Dad's to succeed in remaining deadbeat Dads. The cost to society is too high. Your misguided effort to be the Rosa Parks of parental alienation will make you the poster child for the prosecuting deadbeat Dads.

You are severely miscalculating what the world finds distasteful - there are few catagories of offenders that are held in more disdain and contempt than deadbeat Dads. Until you get yourself out of that category you are howling at the moon and you will likely be doing that through the bars of a jail cell.

From: Christopher Mackney <cmach@yahoo.com>
To: Mitch Jefferson <backatu@yahoo.com>
Sent: Wednesday, July 10, 2013 11:12 AM
Subject: Re: null

Brian,

What is despicable is a parent denying children access to their father.

This case is not about money, its about Psychopathy and parental alienation.

Look into the history of Pete Scamardo and Dina Mackney and you will see a lifetime filled with conflict and abuse. Dina has never held a job at a company not subsidized by her father for more than a year. She slept with her boss. Her good friend from college, who she started a business with, now refers to her as 'a cunt'. Her father is referred to as 'a bully' by people that used to work with him. He has over 120 lawsuits in the DC Metro area. Her entire family was accused of fraud by Maryland National Bank.

She is a liar and a psychopath and will be exposed.

Chris

Michael Volpe

From: Mitch Jefferson <backatu@yahoo.com>
To: Chris Mackney <cmach@yahoo.com>
Sent: Wednesday, July 10, 2013 9:13 AM
Subject: Re: null

While I don't know much about the case, I do know this ... you are a deadbeat Dad. You are in breach of State and now Federal Law and your actions, in the eyes of the law and of society, are an assault on your children of the most despicable sort and if it persists you will be going back to jail.

18 USC § 228 - Failure to pay legal child support obligations

*(a) **Offense.**— Any person who—*

(1) willfully fails to pay a support obligation with respect to a child who resides in another State, if such obligation has remained unpaid for a period longer than 1 year, or is greater than $5,000;

(2) travels in interstate or foreign commerce with the intent to evade a support obligation, if such obligation has remained unpaid for a period longer than 1 year, or is greater than $5,000; or

(3) willfully fails to pay a support obligation with respect to a child who resides in another State, if such obligation has remained unpaid for a period longer than 2 years, or is greater than $10,000;

shall be punished as provided in subsection (c).

*(b) **Presumption.**— The existence of a support obligation that was in effect for the time period charged in the indictment or information creates a rebuttable presumption that the obligor has the ability to pay the support obligation for that time period.*

*(c) **Punishment.**— The punishment for an offense under this section is—*

(1) in the case of a first offense under subsection (a)(1), a fine under this title, imprisonment for not more than 6 months, or both; and

(2) in the case of an offense under paragraph (2) or (3) of subsection (a), or a second or subsequent offense under subsection (a)(1), a fine under this title, imprisonment for not more than 2 years, or both.

*(d) **Mandatory Restitution.**— Upon a conviction under this section, the court shall order restitution under section 3663A in an amount equal to the total unpaid support obligation as it exists at the time of sentencing.*

*(e) **Venue.**— With respect to an offense under this section, an action may be inquired of and prosecuted in a district court of the United States for—*

(1) the district in which the child who is the subject of the support obligation involved resided during a period during which a person described in subsection (a) (referred to in this subsection as an "obliger") failed to meet that support obligation;

(2) the district in which the obliger resided during a period described in paragraph (1); or

(3) any other district with jurisdiction otherwise provided for by law.

*(f) **Definitions.**— As used in this section—*

(1) the term "Indian tribe" has the meaning given that term in section 102 of the Federally Recognized Indian Tribe List Act of 1994 (25 U.S.C. 479a);

(2) the term "State" includes any State of the United States, the District of Columbia, and any commonwealth, territory, or possession of the United States; and

(3) the term "support obligation" means any amount determined under a court order or an order of an administrative process pursuant to the law of a State or of an Indian tribe to be due from a person for the support and maintenance of a child or of a child and the parent with whom the child is living.

You are a deadbeat Dad because you continue to refuse to pay $47 per day for each of your kids. You are a deadbeat Dad because you haven't paid anything - not a single penny - in years to support your kids. Not one example of paying what you can. Not one example of a partial payment. Not any demonstration of any effort whatsoever to support your kids. Your intent is clear - pay nothing at all cost.

You are a deadbeat Dad because you are using blackmail and extortion against the very people that are paying your bills. You are a deadbeat Dad because when the system finally caught up with you, you attacked your children and their support network to make it stop. It is the system, both State and Federal, that is pursuing you under the Deadbeat Dad Laws. You are a deadbeat Dad because you are willing to undermine your kids and there relationships with friends, neighbors and teachers for the want of $47 a day per child. You are a deadbeat Dad because you are willing to walk away from your kids, trading them for $47 a day in relief for you. Society won't make that trade even if your ex would.

You are a deadbeat Dad because your willingness to lie to justify your inexcusable criminal actions. Child support calculations for VA support $47 a day or $33,792 per year based on a $180,000 a year job, not $489,000. The people at BMC expect you to perform in a manner that generates at least that level of pay. If not, pay something - anything. You are a deadbeat Dad because you can afford to pay something, anything, yet you never pay anything. You are a deadbeat Dad because you use your time and effort to avoid State and Federally mandated payment instead of trying to make payments. If you put half the effort into financially supporting your kids that you put into trying to destroy them and those that do support them, $47 per day would be easy. You could emerge from the world of the terrorist and criminal and return to the world of the responsible. Your choice - but I know this - these are the facts and whatever facts you think you know - nothing you can say refutes the fact that you are the definition of a deadbeat Dad.

From: Chris Mackney <cmach@yahoo.com>
To: MitchJefferson <backatu@yahoo.com>
Sent: Tuesday, July 9, 2013 1:35 PM
Subject: Re: null

Michael Volpe

I'm not sure who you are, as i have never emailed you. However, visitation is separate from child support.

You know nothing about the case, but if you want facts, I'll be happy to share them with you, as i intend to post them all on the internet.

Dina Mackney is a liar and her attorney is a liar. She has mental problems and has always had her way paid for by her father.

The reason i am a 'deadbeat dad' is because my child support is to high. $2,816 per month is the equivalent of a $489,000/year salary. If my child support was set at a reasonable level i could pay it.

I also was physically and emotionally abused by Dina throughout the marriage.

You are clearly duped by whatever Dina had told you.

Mitch Jefferson <backatu@yahoo.com> wrote:

>You demonstrate your instability with every flailing e-mail. The people you are e-mailing know that you are a deadbeat Dad who is lawless and mentally unstable. You prove it with every ridiculous outbound e-mail you send. The system treats you the way it does because of your lawlessness - your reckless actions are a threat to society and that is why society is pursuing you. The state has a clear interest in making sure deadbeat Dads like you are made to pay their financial obligations.

True or not, none of that justifies or refutes the fact that you are a deadbeat Dad using blackmail and extortion to try run away from your minimal financial obligations to your kids.

At this moment, it all comes down to one thing - you have promised silence if you are relieved from any obligation and you have promised unending damage to all involved but most significantly to your own children if you are to be held accountable.

You fail to see that socicty cannot and will not accept extortion and blackmail as a way for deadbeat Dad's to succeed in remaining deadbeat Dads. The cost to society is too high. Your misguided effort to be the Rosa Parks of parental alienation will make you the poster child for the prosecuting deadbeat Dads.

You are severely miscalculating what the world finds distasteful - there are few catagories of offenders that are held in more disdain and contempt than deadbeat Dads. Until you get yourself out of that category you are howling at the moon and you will likely be doing that through the bars of a jail cell.

From: Christopher Mackney <cmach@yahoo.com>
To: Mitch Jefferson <backatu@yahoo.com>
Sent: Wednesday, July 10, 2013 11:12 AM
Subject: Re: null

Brian,

What is despicable is a parent denying children access to their father.
This case is not about money, its about Psychopathy and parental alienation.

Look into the history of Pete Scamardo and Dina Mackney and you will see a lifetime filled with conflict and abuse. Dina has never held a job at a company not subsidized by her father for more than a year. She slept with her boss. Her good friend from college, who she started a business with, now refers to her as 'a cunt'. Her father is referred to as 'a bully' by people that used to work with him. He has over 120 lawsuits in the DC Metro area. Her entire family was accused of fraud by Maryland National Bank.

She is a liar and a psychopath and will be exposed.

Chris

From: Mitch Jefferson <backatu@yahoo.com>

Michael Volpe

To: Chris Mackney <cmach@yahoo.com>
Sent: Wednesday, July 10, 2013 9:13 AM
Subject: Re: null

While I don't know much about the case, I do know this ... you are a deadbeat Dad. You are in breach of State and now Federal Law and your actions, in the eyes of the law and of society, are an assault on your children of the most despicable sort and if it persists you will be going back to jail.

18 USC § 228 - Failure to pay legal child support obligations(a) Offense.— Any person who—
(1) willfully fails to pay a support
obligation with respect to a child who resides in another State, if such obligation has remained unpaid for a period longer than 1 year, or is
greater than $5,000;
(2) travels in interstate or foreign
commerce with the intent to evade a support obligation, if such
obligation has remained unpaid for a period longer than 1 year, or is
greater than $5,000; or
(3) willfully fails to pay a support
obligation with respect to a child who resides in another State, if such obligation has remained unpaid for a period longer than 2 years, or is
greater than $10,000;
shall be punished as provided in subsection (c).
(b) Presumption.— The existence of a support obligation that
was in effect for the time period charged in the indictment or
information creates a rebuttable presumption that the obligor has the
ability to pay the support obligation for that time period.
(c) Punishment.— The punishment for an offense under this section is—
(1) in the case of a first offense under
subsection (a)(1), a fine under this title, imprisonment for not more
than 6 months, or both; and
(2) in the case of an offense under
paragraph (2) or (3) of subsection (a), or a second or subsequent
offense under subsection (a)(1), a fine under this title, imprisonment
for not more than 2 years, or both.
(d) Mandatory Restitution.— Upon a conviction under this section, the court shall order restitution under section 3663A in an amount equal to the total

unpaid support obligation as it exists at the time of sentencing.
(e) Venue.— With respect to an offense under this
section, an action may be inquired of and prosecuted in a district court of the United States for—
(1) the district in which the child who is
the subject of the support obligation involved resided during a period during which a person described in subsection (a) (referred to in this subsection as an "obliger") failed to meet that support obligation;
(2) the district in which the obliger resided during a period described in paragraph (1); or
(3) any other district with jurisdiction otherwise provided for by law.
(f) Definitions.— As used in this section—
(1) the term "Indian tribe" has the meaning given that term in section 102 of the Federally Recognized Indian Tribe List Act of 1994 (25 U.S.C. 479a);
(2) the term "State" includes any State of
the United States, the District of Columbia, and any commonwealth, territory, or possession of the United States; and
(3) the term "support obligation" means any amount determined under a court order or an order of an administrative
process pursuant to the law of a State or of an Indian tribe to be due from a person for the support and maintenance of a child or of a child and the parent with whom the child is living.

You are a deadbeat Dad because you continue to refuse to pay $47 per day for each of your kids. You are a deadbeat Dad because you haven't paid anything - not a single penny - in years to support your kids. Not one example of paying what you can. Not one example of a partial payment. Not any demonstration of any effort whatsoever to support your kids. Your intent is clear - pay nothing at all cost.

You are a deadbeat Dad because you are using blackmail and extortion against the very people that are paying your bills. You are a deadbeat Dad because when the system finally caught up with you, you attacked your children and their support network to make it stop. It is the system, both State and Federal, that is pursuing you under the Deadbeat Dad Laws. You are a deadbeat Dad because you are willing to undermine your kids and there relationships with friends, neighbors and teachers for the want of $47 a day per child. You are a deadbeat Dad because you are willing to walk away from your kids, trading them for $47 a day in relief for you. Society won't make that trade even if your ex would.

Michael Volpe

You are a deadbeat Dad because your willingness to lie to justify your inexcusable criminal actions. Child support calculations for VA support $47 a day or $33,792 per year based on a $180,000 a year job, not $489,000. The people at BMC expect you to perform in a manner that generates at least that level of pay. If not, pay something - anything. You are a deadbeat Dad because you can afford to pay something, anything, yet you never pay anything. You are a deadbeat Dad because you use your time and effort to avoid State and Federally mandated payment instead of trying to make payments. If you put half the effort into financially supporting your kids that you put into trying to destroy them and

those that do support them, $47 per day would be easy. You could emerge from the world of the terrorist and criminal and return to the world of the responsible. Your choice - but I know this - these are the facts and whatever facts you think you know - nothing you can say refutes the fact that you are the definition of a deadbeat Dad.

From: Chris Mackney <cmach@yahoo.com>
To: MitchJefferson <backatu@yahoo.com>
Sent: Tuesday, July 9, 2013 1:35 PM
Subject: Re: null

I'm not sure who you are, as i have never emailed you. However, visitation is separate from child support.

You know nothing about the case, but if you want facts, I'll be happy to share them with you, as i intend to post them all on the internet.

Dina Mackney is a liar and her attorney is a liar. She has mental problems and has always had her way paid for by her father.

The reason i am a 'deadbeat dad' is because my child support is to high. $2,816 per month is the equivalent of a $489,000/year salary. If my child support was set at a reasonable level i could pay it.

I also was physically and emotionally abused by Dina throughout the marriage.

You are clearly duped by whatever Dina had told you.

Mitch Jefferson <backatu@yahoo.com> wrote:

>You demonstrate your instability with every flailing e-mail. The people you are e-mailing know that you are a deadbeat Dad who is lawless and mentally unstable. You prove it with every ridiculous outbound e-mail you send. The system treats you the way it does because of your lawlessness - your reckless actions are a threat to society and that is why society is pursuing you. The state has a clear interest in making sure deadbeat Dads like you are made to pay their financial obligations.

Dr. William Zuckerman's Psychological Evaluation of Chris Mackney

Bullied to Death: Chris Mackney's Kafkaesque Divorce

William B. Zuckerman, Ph.D., P.C.

LICENSED CLINICAL PSYCHOLOGIST

The Evaluation of Christopher Mackney

2/16/10

Re: Case No. CL2008-013103

Reason for Referral:

Mr. Mackney was self referred pursuant to an Arlington County Circuit Court Order by Judge Kendrick that he be evaluated as part of the proceedings involved with his family's custody evaluation. A neutral, court ordered psychological evaluation had been performed by Dr. Stanton Samenow, and Mr. Mackney chose this office to perform this individual psychological evaluation from a list of potential evaluators offered by Dr. Samenow.

Michael Volpe

Procedure:

In carrying out this evaluation, Mr. Mackney was interviewed individually on two occasions. A battery of psychological tests was administered, some relevant collateral documents were reviewed, and some relevant collateral parties were interviewed.

The schedule of my face to face contacts is as follows:

Mr. Mackney

Individual Interview

Date Hours

2/04/10 1.0

2/09/10 2.0

2/11/10 .50

Testing Sessions

Date Hours

2/04/10 1.50

2/11/10 2.00

Collateral Contacts:

1. Telephone Interview with Dr. Stanton Samenow (2/15/10)

2. Telephone Interview with Dr. Colleen Blanchfield (2/15/10)

3. Telephone Interview with Dr. Guy Van Syckle (2/16/10)

Documents Reviewed:

1. Custody Order signed by Judge Bellows (11/20/09)

2. Dr. Samenow's "Report of Independent Child Custody Evaluation" dated 8/3/09

3. Mr. Mackney's annotated copy of Dr. Samenow's report

4. Petition for Protective Order- Family Abuse filed by Dina Mackney dated 5/23/08

5. Motions Day- Praecipe/Notice filed by Mr. Mackney 10/7/08

6. Contempt Order signed by Judge Randy Bellows dated 11/03/09

Background Information

This section represents my transcription of relevant historical data provided to me by Mr. Mackney. As such, it may contain some factual inaccuracies, either expressed by them or misreported by me. This section does not necessarily reflect my beliefs or interpretation about the material described.

Early Development

Christopher Mackney (DOB: 11/17/68) is the middle of three boys born to Greg and Caroline Machnij. He remarked that he changed the spelling of his last name when he married at his then wife's request. He was born in Boston, after which he lived for a period in North Carolina, after which he lived in New Mexico where he went to kindergarten. His early elementary years were spent in St. Louis, and he attended, he remembers, fourth and fifth grade in Hawaii. Following that, the family, following Mr. Mackney's father who was in the hotel business, settled in St. Louis where he completed school, going from about sixth grade through his high school graduation.

Mr. Mackney's father died in 1998 at the age of 56, some two years before Chris and the former Ms. Dina Scamardo, married. Following his work in the hotel business, Mr. Machnij had also been a portfolio manager for a real estate company. Mr. Mackney's mother died in September of 2009 at the age of 63. During his growing up years she had worked off and on, usually in retail, but she had also worked as a flight attendant. His parents remained married to one another until his father's death.

Mr. Mackney's older sibling is 44 year old Greg, Jr. Greg has never married and has had no children. He lives in Los Angeles where he works in the retail area. Mr. Mackney stated that his brother had struggled in school and had not attended college. Mr. Mackney's younger brother, 37 year old Jeffrey, also lives in Los Angeles where he recently married for the first time. He works in the security industry and has a college degree. He and his wife do not have children as of yet.

Describing his developmental years, Mr. Mackney recalled that his father had been a hard worker, one who aimed to provide for his family, but one that was not around a lot on a day-to-day basis due to his work schedule. By contrast, his mother was very much involved in his upbringing, and Mr. Mackney remembers having been involved in a variety of sports, activities such as Cub Scouts, etc. He remembers having played, more specifically, baseball and basketball, along with football and baseball while in high school. He remembers feeling quite close to both of his brothers and his mother while growing up.

There was considerable difficulty for his mother to adjust to the death of his father, a death that took place when the elder Mr. Machnij was hit by a car. Mr. Mackney remembers having had difficulties himself dealing with the loss, though, at the time, he was already nearly 30. His mother, however, had been quite dependent on his father, and she had difficulty putting her life in order after he died. Indeed, she ultimately, he went on, lost hope and became quite depressed. He remembers that in order to help herself, she saw a therapist, and she may have taken some medications, but he is not sure which ones. She had no such depression prior to the death.

Mr. Mackney described himself as a good, generally average student, earning C's and B's, not really putting much effort into the academic studies. Nevertheless, he attended college in Dallas at Southern Methodist University, where, again, he was an average student, ultimately graduating in 1990 with a Bachelor's degree in economics.

He denied that he got in any serious trouble while in school, and was never, for example, suspended. Rather, he feels he got along with others, was involved in a lot of normal and age appropriate activities such as sports. Further, his ability to get along with others was enhanced by the fact that he had, along with his family, moved a great deal, allowing him to become more skilled at getting to know people easily.

He denied having any criminal history whatsoever, and while he drank some in college, he denied that anyone would make the case that alcohol or drugs has been an area of difficulty for him. He noted that his wife might claim that he smoked pot during the marriage, but, he went on, it is really, in this situation, a non issue. Similarly, he remembers his wife having become angry at his getting drunk on one occasion, an occasion after which he stopped drinking altogether. He did, earlier in the marriage, drink socially but rarely at home. He has no DWI's, no black outs, and he has never been treated for alcohol related difficulties. After having stopped drinking he began using alcohol again after a couple of years, but, again, his drinking had remained social, never having more than 2 drinks. Mr. Mackney also denied any history of physical or sexual abuse, and, with the exception of his mother's depression following his father's death, he denied any family psychiatric history. He noted that his younger brother, while in high school, had become depressed over the loss of a high school girl friend, and while this led to a suicide attempt, Jeff has gotten over the problem and does not struggle with any depression at this point.

Mr. Mackney stated that prior to his marriage he and his wife had done some marital counseling as a result of the fact that they did not communicate well. Indeed, he remembers that they fought and found it difficult to compromise. They had, he asserted, "poor conflict resolution" skills. That period of marital counseling lasted for a couple of months. They continued to do some couples' therapy, however, when they moved to the Washington, DC area to be near his wife's family. That work dealt with the result of the stresses within their marriage and the stresses they experienced at work. He remembers having been in psychotherapy between 2003 and 2004.

In 2005 he began seeing a psychiatrist, Dr. Colleen Blanchfield, and he continues to see her, primarily for the administration of medicines, including both Welbutrin and Effexor. He remembers having considered going off those medications in 2008, but was convinced to remain on them because of the stress of the marital situation.

He also raised the discussion of a feeling of personal inadequacy that led him to become involved in internet chat rooms with women, an effort, he explained, to reach out, trying to validate himself. It was when his wife found out that she insisted that he see a therapist.

Mr. Mackney remembers having met his wife, the former Dina Scamardo (DOB: 4/12/67), in New York City in1998. He remembers having been attracted to her physical looks, the fact that she had a sweet personality, and that she had a MBA degree. As noted earlier, he remembered that a few months later, perhaps around Thanksgiving, his father had been killed, and he was impressed, too, with the fact that his wife responded in a sympathetic way. The couple married in 2000, a first marriage for each, with the marriage ending in separation in 2008 and divorce in 2009.

In retrospect, he sees problems having developed early in the relationship. He recalled, for example, his wife berating a waitress while in a restaurant. At that point, however, he rationalized that she was a strong person, but it became clear to him, as time went on, that she becomes angry too easily. Indeed, anger became a problem in her relationship with others from then on.

He noted, as also earlier described, that he and his wife did not "fight well". He described her as a person who is not a terribly deep thinker, but one who can be materialistic. He feels she gets upset if she does not get her way, and, in fact, he remembers her having become very angry with him while on her honeymoon. On that occasion she became so angry that she struck out at him, hitting him with her hands and fists, ultimately scratching him. She, however, will deny, he stated, that such occurred.

Despite his concern that Dina was quite emotionally volatile, despite his perspective that he has never been physically violent in his life, that he has never hit a woman, he noted that Dina would make the case that he was physically violent with her in a variety of situations, that he is unable to manage his impulses. One such event took place prior to the divorce, in January of 2008. Mr. Mackney remembers his wife having locked up her laptop, but, without her knowing it and without her permission, he used it. She became angry that he had gone into her study, that he had used her laptop without permission. He remembers her "ranting and raving", demanding that he return the key (to the studio) and he, before long, gave it to her.

Planning to leave the house to avoid the conflict, Mr. Mackney remembers thinking about going to the gym, but being unable to find his own car keys. It became clear that she had them, but she would not give them to him. In his frustration, he demanded that she give him the keys or, he threatened, he would turn over a tray of her jewelry. He noted that she creates jewelry and that what he would have been turning over would have been a tray of her creations. In the end, he stated, Dina refused to give him the keys, and, as a result, he turned over her jewelry tray, spreading her jewelry on the floor, but destroying none of it. She still refused to give him the keys, and, in reaction, he turned over a second tray. Mr. Mackney stated that throughout this activity he was calm, and he rejected the adjective "angry", preferring to see himself as both frustrated and upset. He offered that her recollection would be that he "trashed" the jewelry studio, but it is his sense that her complaint would be a considerable exaggeration. He noted that the children were there at the time and witnessed this altercation. Subsequently, Dina is remembered to have hit Chris, to have ripped off his tee shirt and scratched his neck.

Chris is not sure whether it was she or he who called the police, but 911 was called, as were, by him, her parents. Both her parents and the police arrived, to find, Chris stated, himself and his son locked in his son's room, a move he had taken to avoid the conflict. The police were presented with the ripped shirt, but they did not arrest her. Mr. Mackney stated that he has been unable to obtain a copy of the police report. While Dina was not arrested, Chris did get his keys back. Having received them, he remembers having walked past Dina's parents, planning as he had been earlier, to go to the gym. They had taken the tee shirt he was using as evidence of his wife's violence, and, though he requested it back from them, they refused to return the shirt. At that point, frustrated, Chris said something to the effect of, "give me the shirt or I'll delete all of your work files".

Once again, Mr. Mackney was questioned by this examiner regarding his anger reaction. Once again, he denied being angry, describing himself as a "laid back guy", but adding that Dina would say that he was angry, that he berates her, and that he can be violent. Indeed, she would make the case that she is afraid of him, that he has cursed at her, that he is unable to control himself. Nevertheless, it is Chris's view that it is she who is the angry one; it is she who has hit him on four or five occasions. Ultimately, Chris got the shirt back. (Indeed, he showed me the shirt).

In discussing some of the other issues of conflict, Mr. Mackney stated that none of these battles occurred before the couple began discussing divorce between themselves, sometimes in January of 2008. Nevertheless, once the conflict began to manifest, he received a letter from Dina's attorneys, from the law firm of Ain and Bank. That letter requested that he move out of the house, something he did not want to do, fearful that he would be seen as abandoning the children. Further, he could not afford such a move, and, as a result, he did not comply with their request. As a result, they sent another letter, and when he still did not move out, Dina filed to obtain a Protective Order. In her complaint she noted that she was "afraid", and she referenced some of the battles that had taken place such as the altercation that had taken place regarding the jewelry. At that point, Chris agreed to move out of the house.

Another episode occurred wherein each would present the history differently. He recalled an argument during which she threw his cell phone, along with a stack of his work files. She then "stomped on" a wireless USB adaptor of his. At one point he began running toward the cell phone in order to retrieve it, so that she could not further injure it. She, he explained, interpreted his running as chasing her, and she began to run away, screaming, making an effort to alert the neighbors. As a result of these complaints she was awarded the Protective Order. At that point Chris agreed to move out of the house, and it was further agreed that they would negotiate in good faith a "global settlement". Not having much money, Mr. Mackney moved in with a friend.

Subsequent to the separation (sometime in the middle of 2008), Chris remembers having read an article he found on the internet regarding Dina's father, Mr. Pete Scamardo having been connected with and convicted of being an accomplice to murder in 1970. Further explaining the circumstance, the court had reached the position that Mr. Scamardo had paid a man (identified as Woody Harrelson's father, Charles Harrelson) to kill his business partner, a childhood friend. The murder is said to have taken place in

1968. When Chris asked Dina about this piece of history, she responded that it was none of his business. As a result, Chris became upset that this had been hidden from him, that she wouldn't discuss it with him. His initial reaction was to not make too much out of it, given the fact that they were already involved in what seemed like a hostile divorce.

However, in a phone call that Dina is said to have recorded, she encouraged him to speak about demanding money to not speak of her father's past. The conversation involved comments from Dina, Chris recalled, wherein she said something along the lines of "what will it take for you to stop talking about my father?" Chris remembers having said that he did not want money that he simply wanted his equity in the house. That recorded conversation was taken to the police as evidence of black mail but the police did not see it that way.

Mr. Mackney presented a picture wherein he felt progressively more and more over matched, more and more overwhelmed by a combination of factors. Among these factors was the fact, he explained, that he did not have much money, and he felt himself up against his wife who was backed by a substantial amount of money that her parents had. His sense of being disadvantaged grew in the face of his perception that she hired the strongest lawyers she could (with her considerable financial advantage), and he always felt that he was unable to discuss the issues with her, as she would be unwilling to communicate with him. He remembers having sent an email requesting that the conflict be settled, and, between January and February of 2008 he had sent some emails requesting the end of the conflict. However, because he felt stone-walled, the nature of the emails began to change by October of 2008, when it became clear to him that his wife would not negotiate with him. His frustration grew when he learned about Mr. Scamardo's criminal history, a finding that he uncovered on June 23, 2008. Further creating tension for him was the fact that in that month (June of 2008) his wife began restricting his visits with the children, a plan that he sees as deliberately aiming to create frustration for him. Thus, by November of 2008, further frustrated, without much in the way of funds, he filed a petition in the Fairfax County Juvenile and Domestic Relations Court to complain about Dina's restricting the children from him. In that proceeding he was pro se. At that point, too, perhaps related to the concerns they had about the exposure of Mr. Scamardo's past, Mrs. Mackney changed attorney's, leaving Ain and Bank and hiring Mr. James Cottrell on June 24, 2008. Mr. Mackney remembers becoming more frustrated when Mr. Cottrell made an effort to frustrate his processing of the problem in the J&DR Court, preferring, rather, to move it to Circuit Court, a move that Mr. Mackney interpreted as a delaying tactic.

Mr. Mackney remembers the court proceeding as one in which, when it finally did take place, Mr. Cottrell accused him of sending improper, "harassing" and "blackmailing" emails which Mr. Cottrell described as "subtle threats". In those emails he feels that they had some "alarmist qualities" wherein he would be complaining about Dina's father being a murderer. Nevertheless, his aim was not to harass or threaten; rather it was to move her to settle with him, to remove the pressure he was feeling in the midst of this great conflict.

Mr. Cottrell was successful in getting the court to require him to stop sending his "harassing and disparaging" email. He remembers Mr. Cottrell having chosen just those aspects of the emails that were, in fact, harassing and disparaging. However, explaining that his frustration about not moving ahead had reached very high levels, feeling again over matched and overwhelmed, he remembers not having ceased, not having stopped sending the emails. He explained that in his marriage his wife was the controlling party in most decisions, and in his reaction to his frustration he did, in some of the emails, threaten to send some of the material regarding Mr. Scamardo to the Washington Post. He remembers feeling that "no one was listening". Also relevant to what he described as his frustrated state of mind, in October of 2008 he received a file from the state of Texas regarding Mr. Scamardo's criminal history. He learned that there had been other charges against Mr. Scamardo, including the fact that the murder had to do with some aspects of the heroin distribution business. Mr. Mackney's frustration increased by learning of this material, in addition to not being able to see his children, and not being able to make any headway in his efforts to get her to work with him on the divorce. In an effort to move things ahead, he hired a new attorney, Mr. Robert Surovell, with the express aim of seeking a settlement with Dina and her attorney, Mr. Cottrell. Mr. Surovell offered a settlement agreement, one that requested less money than he earlier had requested due to his having more accurately understood the amount of money he really would have been entitled to in the equity of the marital home. That amount came to about $120,000. He also requested "standard visitation" with the children, which would include every other weekend visits, in addition to a midweek dinner visit.

With Mr. Surovell as his attorney, a court proceeding took place in January of 2009 in Fairfax Circuit Court. There, a Pendente Lite visitation agreement was reached wherein he would, in fact, see his children every other weekend from Friday to Sunday and every Wednesday for dinner. In order to accommodate the visits he also took a 2 bedroom apartment, and, he felt things were moving along reasonably well. He remembers having agreed to participate in a "parental evaluation" also part of that January 2009 proceeding, and he agreed to make use of Dr. Samenow as the neutral evaluator. Mr. Mackney remembers having first found Dr. Samenow on his own, but Dina liked the idea. Nevertheless, he began to feel that Dr. Samenow did not behave in an independent manner, making him even more frustrated. Dr. Samenow's report was issued in June of 2009, at a time when Mr. Mackney was once again running out of money. Making things more difficult was the fact that Mr. Surovell, his then-attorney, quit because he felt that he wasn't being effective in moving the parties toward resolution. In his frustration, Mr. Mackney stated, he continued to send what he described as "inflammatory emails", between January and June of 2009, emails that were sent on occasion.

Making things more difficult was the fact that he was fired from his commercial real estate job with EB Richard Ellis because the economy had become seriously problematic. Indeed, he has not really worked since June of 2009.

Mr. Mackney repeated his position that he is frightened of his wife and her attorneys, that he feels extremely overwhelmed. He noted that in the proceeding which took place in court of November of 2009, with the impact to Dr. Samenow's findings, she was given sole custody and all of the marital assets. In order to prepare him for that proceeding he hired Mr. James Watson as his attorney. Making things even more difficult was the fact that his mother died in September of 2009, in California, a loss that, from a positive perspective, left him with about $156,000 in inheritance, money he would be able to use to continue his battle.

Nevertheless, knowing that the facts were against him, having been apprised as much by Mr. Watson, Mr. Mackney voluntarily gave up custody. However, the other side wanted him to have no custody whatsoever, they wanted him, in fact, to only have supervised visitation. As a result of the case they made, the judge made the judgment that Mr. Mackney had violated the judge's orders to cease the harassing emails, and on that basis, he lost all visitation for a 3 month period.

Returning to Dr. Samenow's report, Mr. Mackney stated that many of the positive aspects of his presentation were not included in Dr. Samenow's report. In fact, Dr. Samenow recommended supervised visits due to the emails, making the case that Mr. Mackney is not in sufficient control of his impulses to see the children in an unsupervised manner. Mr. Mackney stated that Dina's case was strengthened by the fact that after the separation, but before there had been a visitation order in place, he would sometimes come to see the children after Dina had told him he could not. On those occasions he would come to the house without her permission. Again, they are making the case that he is unable to manage his behavior. Mr. Mackney stated that the emails were sent consciously and not as a result of any lack of control. It was his sense that he was hoping to use them to promote settlement and, in fact, he thought that the situation would never wind up in court. He also spoke of the "all consuming" nature of the litigation which made it impossible for him to focus on looking for new work. Currently, he has some potentials for reasonable employment.

Evaluation of Tests Administered Evaluative Interviews Rorschach House-Tree-Person Test (H-T-P) Kinetic Family Drawing (KFD) Thematic Apperception Test (TAT) Behavioral Observations and Test Results

Behavioral Observations

Mr. Mackney was fully cooperative with all test procedures and requirements. He was always appropriately dressed and groomed, and he demonstrated good social skills, making, for example, good eye contact, responding to all questions asked, etc. His manner was friendly, and he seemed to enjoy the interpersonal interaction, as he tended, from time to time, to interject socially appropriate conversation (i.e., discussion of the weather, etc.) However his presentation of the history had a slightly pressured or obsessive quality, emanating, perhaps, from his need to have his position heard, his sense that others had not been listening or had discounted his perceptions. Nevertheless, he acceded to the pace and structure of the procedure I set forth, thereby demonstrating some flexibility, and he presented material in a clear and organized fashion, reflecting no serious cognitive psychopathology. In general, his manner suggested confidence in his positions, confidence in the interpersonal interaction. At the same time, his narrative was consistent with the sense of him feeling overwhelmed, overmatched, not in control, and frustrated, along with some suggestions of depressive qualities. He did not appear inordinately anxious, nor was there any indication of difficulties maintaining focus or concentration. Indeed, he appears quite focused on the ongoing litigation and the upcoming hearing, quite focused on having his position understood and accepted.

Mr. Mackney's description of some of the relevant events that had taken play between him and his wife suggested that in response to the frustrations and lack of control he felt he had had to endure, he experienced considerable anger. These stressors included his perception that his wife wouldn't discuss things with him, she wouldn't compromise, and she'd never apologize. He feels that he was in her setting, away from his friends and family, and in a place where she was supported by friends and family. She has, he went on, the advantage of having the support of her parents' money, while he is unable to compete financially, and he was not able to see his children. The issue of Mr. Scamardo's past was not one his wife would discuss with him, and she would not negotiate with him about the divorce, etc. However, he rejected the reflection that his reactions could involve anger, explaining, rather that he is a "laid back guy", a man with no history of violence, someone who has never hit a woman. He did not see, for example, his dumping his wife's jewelry as an act of anger, explaining that he had not remained calm during this altercation, and he similarly did not see his threat to delete his father-in-law's work files as a manifestation of anger. In the same vein, while he described some of his emails (between January and June of 2009) as harassing, even subtly threatening, he did not see this response as a reflection of anger. These findings suggest an inconsistency between the experience of anger and how he sees himself, an inconsistency that leads him to deny angry feelings so as to diminish his insight into his feelings and, at times, effectively manage them.

Mr. Mackney offered fairly common disclaimers regarding his artistic ability in response to the request to do projective drawings. Nevertheless, his drawings, while generally small of stature, were well organized and of reasonable proportion. They tended to be drawn in such a way as to suggest a relatively stable sense of self, and while they were done with a normal level of confidence, certainly within a normal amount of time, they tended to be under-detailed. The models for his drawings (House, Tree, and People) tended to be self-focused, with self, family members, with his own house, etc, being the primary subjects. Human figures tended to, also, be somewhat under-detailed, and it is interesting that while he spoke on occasion during the interview process of his large physical size (he reports being 6' 5"), his figures were on the small side, reflecting some inconsistency between his physical sense of self as large, on the one hand, and, perhaps, an inner sense of being somewhat smaller. His human figures suggested a responsible level of energy tending to project physical strength, a sense of self as responsible, and while none of the themes expressed were out of the ordinary, there were some indicators on his Human Figure Drawings of both the experience of inner tension, and, perhaps, some aggressiveness in his approach to others.

His Kinetic Family Drawing involved himself and his two children. In this setting he placed himself somewhat distant from his children but engaged with them in recreation (playing Frisbee). His comments on the first drawing (i.e., the House) suggested some discomfort with being alone, as he imagined, sometime in the future, the possibility of marrying again as, he explained, "I'd want to be with someone".

Validity Consideration

Mr. Mackney provided a useful and valid Rorschach protocol, giving sufficient response and sufficient detail to yield useful information. On the MMPI-2, Mr. Mackney was highly consistent throughout the inventory, suggesting that he was able to read and comprehend all test items. Further, the findings suggest that he was attentive in considering his responses. He was quite guarded and self-favorable in his approach to the inventory, tending more than most takers of this test, and, in fact, more than most custody litigants, to intentionally underreport emotional and interpersonal concerns. This result would suggest a tendency, perhaps a relatively sophisticated one, to understate his personal discomforts and perhaps under emphasize the severity of his current emotional state. As is the case with many custody litigants, his responses demonstrated a major amount of conscious defensiveness, a tendency to reactively set aside concerns that other may have about him. While these results would provide a questionable validity outside of the custody setting, the findings are within acceptable validity limits, though a more accurate measure of his functioning could possibly be elucidated with greater cooperation. These findings do not suggest that he necessarily is prone to lying. Rather, they reflect deficits in self knowledge, along with a high potential to be defensive, reactive to criticism.

On the MCMI III Mr. Mackney's responses suggest an effort to present himself as socially acceptable, along with a resistance to admitting personal shortcomings. This orientation to the test is not uncommon amongst custody litigants.

Collective Results of Projective Self Report Tests

The results of the self report tests in conjunction with the projective tests suggest a profile with a range of strengths and weaknesses that bear on his ability to parent and which relate to the questions under consideration. On the positive side there would appear to be no cognitive psychopathology and no serious affective psychopathology. His ability to judge reality is generally well within the norm, and his thinking is likely to be organized and coherent. The difficulties he might have in judgment would seem more likely to occur in difficult emotional circumstances, perhaps especially those involving his relationships with other people. It is also noted that Mr. Mackney's focus can become impeded at times, a difficulty which makes it harder for him to synthesize the various aspects of his experience. As a result, he could, at times, "lose the forest for the trees" and, results suggest, it is more possible for him than most to focus on one detail without appreciating the essence of the "big picture". Nevertheless, for the most part, findings suggest, he is able to interpret the actions and motives of others with reasonable acuity. His level of motivation is an area of strength, and findings suggest that others would see him as quite well organized, quite able to plan for both the short and long term.

There are some mixed findings in terms of his social interactional abilities, but for the most part, the data would suggest good social skills. He would tend to be extroverted, to be seen by others as self confident, poised, and persuasive. His responses suggest a normal interest in people and it is likely that most people will find him good company.

The findings suggest that Mr. Mackney understands what is expected of him, what is conventional in terms of his behavior, but the data also suggest that he can, at times, set that aside and follow a path that is more idiosyncratic, one that he feels is right.

Nevertheless, while Mr. Mackney reports having a normal variety of friends and while test results support the potential for him to be able to make relationships, some data suggest that these relationships will be somewhat more superficial than is typical, perhaps a bi product of all the moving around he experienced as a youngster. He may, then, be somewhat more isolated than he reports, and it is consistent with these findings that he would be uncomfortable by himself, that he would seek, as he explained during the projective drawings, sometime in the future, to find another mate. The quality of his interpersonal relationships is likely to be influenced by a relative discomfort in dealing with emotion, a characteristic that protects him from unwanted emotions of his own, but which also keep him more at arms' length from those with whom he does have relationships. Consistent with this finding is the suggestion that his bonding with his children, while not way outside the norm, may be less reliable than is typical for custody litigants. Though it is likely, as he states, that he enjoys a positive and loving relationship with his children, it is also more likely for him than for the average person to set aside those connections in the face of great stress or discomfort. Indeed, he spoke of the possibility of leaving the area if his goals are not realized.

There is a great deal of data which would support Mr. Mackney's contention that he has felt overmatched and stressed, that he is not feeling much in control of the circumstance either in the context of his trying to negotiate with his wife, and also in the context of the helplessness he feels in the midst of this litigation. As noted elsewhere, he also feels at the mercy of superior forces (his wife and his wife's family, along with their attorney), and he feels without the funds necessary to prosecute his position. These stresses can lead to experience some dysphoric and even anxious feelings. It is also to be noted, however, that the test data reflect that others would see him as more likely than most to be controlling in relationships, more likely to need things his own way, and the degree to which he feels helpless, then, is probably exacerbated by those control needs.

A major focus of this litigation involves concerns regarding Mr. Mackney's propensity for violence. On the positive side, results across the test protocol do not reflect deep wells of anger or resentment, they do not portray him, indeed, as an especially angry person, and the risk for him to lose his temper, to endanger the safety of a child, is not elevated. Indeed, he manifests a relatively elevated threshold for allowing his emotional feelings to surface.

On the other hand, test results suggest that while he can at times demonstrate a moderate level of self- awareness, a characteristic that allows him to meet his own needs, there is a greater than average tendency for him to deny uncomfortable feelings, to look the other way rather than face stressful emotion. It is to his credit that he has sought, in the past, psychotherapy, and it is to his credit that he has been, voluntarily, under the treatment of Dr. Blanchfield for the past several years. Nevertheless, there are also findings which would diminish his potential to seek help. More specifically, Mr. Mackney's tendency is to internalize his feelings, to be reluctant to express them, and, in fact, he will tend to blunt or deny those uncomfortable feelings. Depression, for example, tends to be blunted through intellectualization, and the considerable anger that has been evoked in him as a result of the conflicts he has had with his wife and with the courts, has been subjected, to a large degree, to rationalization. This process for him, makes him, then, less aware of his negative feelings. On the one hand, from a positive perspective, it helps him greatly in managing stress, in moderating the internal stressors with which he has to deal. On the negative side, he is less aware of these feelings and therefore considerably less likely than most to appreciate his impact on others, especially when those feelings are being manifest. It is not surprising, too, that not being fully attuned to his level of anger and depression, he would find it somewhat more difficult that most to put angry feelings behind him, to forgive and forget (though his level in this regard is similar to most others in the midst of custody litigation).

The issue of his ability to cope with stress is also an area which Mr. Mackney demonstrates both adaptive and maladaptive characteristics. Despite a somewhat lower reservoir of that sort of intraphysic energy that is necessary to deal effectively with internal and external stressors, Mr. Mackney does not, on self report instruments, acknowledge much in the way of depression and anxiety. Similarly, on projective tests (i.e., the Rorschach, TAT) he tests as generally being able to manage stress reasonably effectively. This ability derives from the combination of his tendency to, as earlier discussed, set aside, minimize, or distance himself from internal discomforts such as anger and depression, and it is probably helpful to him, too, that he will tend to remain in situations in which he feels comfortable and accepted, situations that help him manage the amount of new and different things he has to deal with. The balance he brings to bear, then, promotes a low level of anxiety, generally, along with a low level of irritability, and it is supportive of his sense of self as a "laid back" individual. Individuals with this profile also tend to have a relatively stable sense of identity, a comfort with themselves that can sometimes make change more difficult for them when it becomes necessary. Indeed, other findings support the view that he will be more likely than most to consider beliefs, even in the light of new information, that he will present to others as somewhat more close-minded.

This situation, however, findings would predict, would have stretched his resources, lowering his tolerance for frustration and increasing his risk of impulsive behavior, and increasing the risk of demonstrating some difficulties with impulse control. Further, some self-report data (on the MMPI) suggest a somewhat higher potential for "anti-social" behavior than the typical custody litigant. Though given his history which is relatively devoid of antisocial behavior, it is probably helpful to see this behavior as a result of what he experiences as a "narcissistic injury" and his self-centeredness. More clearly, this finding would suggest that his potential for such behavior is "somewhat above average", if he were "strongly provoked", to behave in a way wherein the control of his behavior is less than desirable. However this behavior is not aimed at procuring personal gain, rather, it is to shore himself up in the face of perceived injury. It is this finding that could be seen as consistent with the episodes where he overturned his wife's jewelry, where he threatened to destroy records, where he threatened to expose his wife's family, etc. While his tendency to rationalize makes it more difficult to appreciate the impact on others of these actions for him, there are also data to support the view that such behaviors are considerably less likely when the circumstance that create his upset and stress have been resolved. Indeed, there is no history known to this examiner of anti-social behavior in the past, and one would predict that resolution here would bring him back to a pre conflict situation.

MMPI Results

From a social perspective, the scores suggest a tendency to present positive and cheerful moods to others, along with a generally positive belief in himself and a tendency to demonstrate poise, persuasiveness, and generally proficient social skills. The test results, too, suggest that others would see him, typically, as generally productive and self confidant.

Mr. Mackney tests as a somewhat repressive and denying individual, one who would tend to avoid antagonistic confrontations when possible, one who would be quite uncomfortable in the face of others anger focused toward him. Indeed, the findings suggest the potential for him to "look the other way" in order, at times, to avoid facing uncomfortable problems. This sort of defensive structure would create the likelihood of a general lack of awareness in the ways in which he could provoke or upset others. Thus he might fail to appreciate how his reactions bother or annoy others, fail to appreciate why others might feel offended by him.

Despite the aforementioned good social skills, a tendency to be mildly extroverted, and, in fact, a person who would be somewhat uncomfortable spending extended periods of time alone, his pattern, nevertheless, reflects a greater than average degree of distrust in others and an uneven level of empathy. Not surprisingly, then, he also tests as tending, even more than most custody litigants, to be oriented toward his own needs and interests, a finding which, along with unevenness in empathy, could, at times, make his children's needs secondary to his, and it could function to lessen to some degree his ability to manage his own behavior. Nevertheless, the findings suggest a high degree of personal organization, an ability to function independently and competently in many situations, an ability to plan effectively for the short term and long term.

While the stresses of a tense divorce context could, findings suggest, elicit some intense and dramatic emotional outbursts, over the longer term his score anticipate a somewhat higher than average threshold for allowing his emotional feelings to surface. That is, his emotions would be seen by others as relatively constricted and carefully modulated while there is a somewhat greater than average potential for problematic, even inappropriate reactions, to take place if he felt strongly provoked he did not obtain a pattern that would suggest difficulties with temper control. That is, his temper, in most situations, would be well within the norm, reasonably well controlled and not a serious risk. These results suggest that past outbursts that have taken place would have required a "substantial provocation to be triggered".

The difficulties that Mr. Mackney demonstrates with empathy can effect his, as noted, focus on others, and, as a result, his potential for safe and secure bonding is somewhat less than the average custody litigant. This does not mean that his relationship with his children is necessarily more; rather, it suggests that his potential to provide unconditional parental love may be somewhat more questionable than average. However, his scores do not suggest any particular tendency to dichotomize people as being for him or against him, and he is not therefore likely to promote any alienation against a former spouse.

Mr. Mackney, findings suggest, may be seen by others as somewhat more controlling of them than they feel is needed, though it is only slightly higher than is average for child custody litigants. He would clearly want to be seen as dependable and ethical, as a person with stable moral values, though others may tend to see him as somewhat restrictive or inflexible. While there is some suggestion of findings that would limit his ability to manage his behavior, there are also findings that suggest an effort to maintain strong self-controls. He will mostly present as respectful, i.e. such as toward authority, considerate and fair to others while his negative feelings may be restrained, if not at times hidden. There are some findings that suggest a tendency to externalize blame, to rationalize his own behavior, and he might be seen as tending to project angry feelings onto others. Despite his wish to present a controlled front some problems with impulse control are indicated, and he would be more prone than most to hold onto past anger, being less likely than most to forgive and forget. Nevertheless, his thinking is likely to be seen as logical, linear, and coherent.

Results of the MCMI III

The profile suggests a generally easygoing and non-conformist social style with a tendency toward an interest in risk taking activities and a tendency toward some impulsive and exhibitionistic behavior. Despite reasonable social skills, findings suggest that his interpersonal relationships may be somewhat shallow, that he may be perceived as being less tuned into the welfare of others than is average. He can be self-focused in his activities, and because of difficulties with empathy, he may behave with a lesser degree of strong conscious than most.

Mr. Mackney is likely to appear productive, clever, charming to others, but in closer relationships he might be seen as testy or flippant, prone to occasional outbursts of temper. His disregard for the feelings of others would seem to occur more than is typical, but it does not necessarily represent hostile or malicious motives. Rather, it is more likely to be tied to difficulties with empathy, along with a high level of self-assurance, and some difficulties in having his conscious manage his behavior. Interestingly, the results suggest that he could tend to be more manipulative than most, a tendency that would be diminished in the face of serious conflict, such as the sort of conflict he is currently facing.

Summary

The complaints against Mr. Mackney involve concerns of violent behavior, along with charges that he has become obsessed with details that are not of primary relevance to his custody situation, and that he has "blackmailed" his wife, threatening to "expose" what he sees as her father's unsavory history. It is alleged, further, that he has expressed some of his concerns not only repeatedly, but also in the presence and to the detriment of the children, and that he has failed, on more than one occasion, to follow orders set forth by the court. The collected data support the likelihood of some of these contentions being true, while others are not supported. Mr. Mackney's profile suggests fairly even-tempered functioning in most situations, a tendency to be the "laid back" individual. Dr. Samenow adds that he feels Mr.

Mackney has been "emotionally abusive" in "defiling" Ms. Mackney, often in front of the children, or to other people (i.e., school personnel), that he has threatened to tell the children the "truth" of his concerns about their mother, and that, in so doing, he has put unnecessary harmful doubts in the children's minds. Dr. Samenow went on to express concerns about Mr. Mackney's inability to appreciate conventional boundaries, his tendency to blame others, to fail to take responsibility for his contribution to the problem.

His profile suggests that intense emotion will be expressed only when he feels strongly provoked. Indeed, the likelihood of losing his temper is within the norm for custody litigants, suggesting that he is not an out of the ordinary risk to physically harm the children. It is of interest to note that the earlier MMPI, taken for Dr. Samenow, yielded many of the same interpretations, but a greater likelihood of having difficulty managing his temper. The change on this test administration, in a positive direction, may indicate a greater level of self-control than existed earlier. He describes himself as "laid back" when his situation is uncomplicated and when stresses are reasonably managed, and this is probably a reasonable self-assessment. There is no record of violence in the history presented to me, no criminal history, and no indication of such histories in the material reviewed (Dr. Samenow's report, the transcript of the judge's ruling).

On the other hand some of the other allegations are supported, at least to some degree.Certainly, Mr. Mackney makes a strong case for feeling overmatched and overwhelmed Indeed, while his defensive structure is such that he minimizes negative feelings in order to help himself cope, while his sense of self and this defensive structure will combine to help present him positively to others in a variety of contexts, characteristics that will also be valuable to his ability to parent (interest in fun, relaxed attitude, poise, self-confidence, leadership qualities, etc,) he, nevertheless, is probably honestly describing his feelings of frustration and personal pain regarding his marriage and his relationship with Ms. Mackney. As noted, he is able to make friends, but his relationships may be more superficial than most, and he would likely not have experienced a sufficient amount of support from them. Concerns about feeling shut out of communication would have frustrated him, and he would have felt further frustrated by the support his wife got (from her parents), by his precarious financial situation, by not feeling listened to and understood, etc.

In such a setting results would predict, when stressed beyond his coping capacities, the likelihood increases for him to feel overwhelmed, to have difficulty tolerating frustration, to be considerably more irritable. At such times, the data suggest, he would have been more prone toward impulsive behavior, and the possibility of him behaving outside the realm of conventional and acceptable behavior would have increased. Also at such times, his own interests can come to the fore, causing him to have difficulty balancing his needs with those of the children, and, the findings predict, his otherwise normal good judgment can become considerably less effective. Some deficits in his ability to empathize diminishes his ability to appreciate the impact of his behavior, and he would seem more likely than most, at such times, to behave in a way that could be seen as detrimental to the interests of the children.

It is within such a context that many of the behaviors of which he is accused would have occurred, without his effectively appreciating their impact on others. It bears repeating that his profile does not predict violent behavior, but there was several behaviors of which he is accused that reflect a high degree of anger expressed in the context of feeling helpless and without a sufficient and tolerable level of control. Verbal outbursts would be consistent with the findings in this context, as are the threats of which he is accused, threats that are inappropriate and hurtful, but threats aimed primarily at having others see his position, at vindicating himself and having others support him.

Thus, he can have become obsessed on the issue of Mr. Scamardo's past, and even, potentially mis-assess the likely danger that Mr. Scamardo might pose (though I don't know anything about the objectivity of his concerns). Further, he can have had difficulty balancing the relative importance of these factors.

It is of great importance to note that Dr. Blanchfield, (who offers a diagnosis of Major Depression and ADHD) spoke of the fact that she has known Mr. Mackney for several years. During most of that time he has been a willing and compliant patient, making all appointments, responding positively to advice, paying his bills. Indeed, she recalled his wife's unwillingness to meet with her around Mr. Mackney's treatment. However, she also related that he had been quite reluctant to enter into therapy with a person to whom she referred him (Dr. Horowitz, at her clinic), and she feels that the stresses associated with the divorce and litigation, stresses that derive, at least in part, from his sense of injury at the way he feels he's been treated, have compromised his judgment, and promoted some obsessive thinking. Her view is consistent with the collected test and interview material in predicting that the problems will, indeed, settle down when Mr. Mackney feels supported and listened to, when the stresses associated with the litigation have ended.

Diagnosis

Axis I- 300.40 (I feel he remains affected by depression though I do not feel, at this time that the depression reaches a "severe" level.

Axis II- 301.9 with narcissistic, obsessive-compulsive features

William B. Zuckerman, Ph.D.

Licensed Clinical Psychologist

Exit Letter from Robert Surovell to Jim Cottrell and Kyle Bartol

Michael Volpe

SUROVELL MARKLE ISAACS & LEVY PLC

ROBERT J. SUROVELL

by facsimile and first class mail

Kyle F. Bartol, Esq.

James R. Cottrell, Esq.

Cottrell Fletcher Schinstock

Bartol & Cottrell

re: Mackney v. Mackney

Gentlemen:

This tragic case isn't getting any better. When I got into this case I sent you a proposal. It was a reasonable proposal. I've never received a response to it. Instead I have had motion after motion after motion trying to drag whatever you can out of Chris Mackney - his gun, his participation in a second experience with a mental health professional, money which he doesn't have, cessation of his drumbeat about his fatherin-law's criminal background.

Now you are trying to get him fired. That is exactly what is going to happen if you keep screwing around with his employer. You know what his income is. You do not need to bother his employer. It certainly won't help his career, and certainly won't help support the children.

You even asked for alimony for a wife who has been supported by her parents all the way through the age of forty-two. I mean no disrespect toward Dina. She is actually an interesting and industrious woman who has had remarkable success with her creativity designing and selling jewelry, but we all know that Chris has never supported her. He has contributed to his own support and has worked hard, and he has made some contribution to his family's welfare. We all know that the lifestyle comes from Dina's parents' great wealth. It is the same place that all the fees you are collecting in this case come from. I don't mean to cast any aspersions at the Scamardo wealth, nor at your fees, but rather to say the obvious. It has been obvious since I got in the case.

Why it is necessary to torment Mr. Mackney is mysterious. It surely has not helped Dina at all. It hasn't seemed to have helped their kids.

Now, my casual discovery that Mr. Scamardo's company seems to have had his daughter on the payroll in earlier years at a time when she wasn't rendering any services for them, appearing to deduct what would have otherwise been gifts and not deductible, raises some interesting questions which depositions and further discovery might elaborate.

As observed, Dina's great success in the jewelry business raises some other interesting opportunities regarding that marital asset, which is her business. Chris has never been interested in Dina's business, as you know. Nor has he been interested in conducting any legal war. And, as you should know, he did pay off $50,000 on that credit line to the Bank of America. Why it is necessary for him to jump through hoops in order to prove that is a mystery to me.

You have finally succeeded in pushing me out of the case. I will be withdrawing. You may deal with Chris on your own. You may "poke him in the ribs, tickle his feet, make sure that he can't pay any of his bill, and run him out of town. Tar and feather him." Have all the fun you like. I'm getting out of the case.

Whatever you do, do not offer him a reasonable deal. Don't trade the arrears of child support for the money he has invested in Dina's home, and don't trade the arrears of child support and the attorneys fees issues for a waiver of his interest in Dina's business.

Sincerely,

Robert J. Surovell

RJS/dle

cc:

Christopher Mackney

Dr. Stanton Samenow

Michael Volpe

Marc Randazza letter to Rachelle Hill

Re: Notice of Copyright Infringement and Privacy Violation

Dear Ms. Hill:

This law firm has the privilege of serving as counsel to Mr. Paul Elam and the blog, "AVoiceForMen." We are in receipt of your demand letter of April 15, 2014 and we have been asked to respond.

1. Introduction and Background

The genesis of this dispute appears to be that Mr. Christopher Hines Machnij a/k/a Christopher Hines Mackney and his estranged wife were in an acrimonious relationship. Due to the strains of that relationship, Mr. Mackney started a blog in order to express his thoughts about his treatment in the family law system. This culminated in a suicide note, which he published to his blog from Washington, D.C. on December 29, 2013, and then he committed suicide on December 29, 2013. His writing and his suicide note were admittedly unflattering to your client. Your client then petitioned a Virginia state court to grant her some ambiguous (and questionable) intellectual property rights to the blog's contents, which she is using to attempt to purge Mr. Mackney's expression from every corner possible. One of those corners is my client's blog.

2. Copyright Issue – Fair Use

It is our position that A Voice for Men's republication of the suicide note is not copyright infringement, pursuant to 17 U.S.C. § 107. Accordingly, even if Mr. Mackney were to rise from the dead and insist upon the depublication of the suicide note, it is my client's position that it has a right to continue publication of the letter.

3. Copyright Issue – Implied License

Mr. Mackney intended for his suicide note to be published. He did not intend for it to be a private matter, and clearly wished for it to be distributed as widely as possible. While we cannot divine what his actual thoughts were before he took his own life, we can certainly review how he published it, where he published it, and infer that prior to his death, he granted an implied license to my client and any other party who wished to excerpt or republish the note in its entirety. Once that license was granted, it could not be revoked. Even if it could be revoked, someone who was not the copyright owner at the time cannot revoke it after the fact.[1]

4. Copyright Issue – 17 U.S.C. § 512(f)

Under 17 U.S.C. § 512(f), any party who uses a DMCA takedown notice improperly may be held liable for that misuse of the DMCA. The U.S. Court of Appeals for the Ninth Circuit recently held in Garcia v. Google that copyrights can be quite expansive. Even under the broad re-definition of copyrights in that case, I do not believe your client would have any possible justification to claim a copyright in any part of the suicide note prior to her dubious "acquisition" of the rights in the Virginia state court. In fact, if you were to claim a Garcia v. Google copyright, it would seem that her only part in the creation of the note would be her purported behavior in driving Mr. Mackney to his unfortunate end. We would find it to be a quite creative use of Title 17 for a person to drive another person to suicide, and then to claim a copyright in any story about that, because she was in instrumental actor in the underlying story. I presume that you would not be so brash as to rely upon this as a theory, but I wish to at least address it and caution you from doing so. Courts have been willing to hear 17 U.S.C. § 512(f) claims in the face of rights much less ambiguous than those your client claims here. In Lenz v. Universal Music Corp., 572 F. Supp. 2d 1150 (N.D. Cal. 2008), the seminal case on 512(f) claims, defendant Universal Music Corporation sent Youtube.com a takedown notice after the plaintiff posted a video of her children dancing to the song "Let's Go Crazy," a song to which Universal actually owned the rights. After YouTube took down the video, the plaintiff sued Universal for sending a DMCA takedown notice containing knowing, material misrepresentations under 17 U.S.C. § 512(f).

Based on Lenz's claim of fair use, the court denied Universal's motion to dismiss, stating that the purpose of 17 U.S.C. § 512(f) is to prevent abuse through the sending of unnecessary takedown notices. The court found that "the unnecessary removal of non-infringing material causes significant injury to the public where time-sensitive or controversial subjects are involved and the counter-notification remedy does not sufficiently address the harms. A good faith consideration of whether a particular use is fair use is consistent with the purpose of the statute." Lenz, 572 F. Supp. 2d at 1156. The court even concluded that Lenz had successfully shown damages in the form of her attorneys' fees resulting from Universal's misrepresentation of infringement.

1 We do not concede that Mrs. Mackney is actually the proper copyright holder. However, even if she were, her acquisition of the copyright after publication and republication would not be a valid basis on which to revoke the license.

It is my client's right (as well as the right of every other service provider or blog that you have bullied into taking down this note) to bring suit against your client under 17 U.S.C. § 512(f). We can assure you that if your client insists upon pressing forward with her attempts to censor this material, my client will file a counterclaim under 17 U.S.C. § 512(f). [2]

5. First Amendment Issue

Fair Use is found at the confluence of free speech. However we feel there is an additional First Amendment element to this case. Mr. Mackney clearly intended for his expression to be published and disseminated far and wide. He published information that was critical of your client, which (if he were still alive) she would never be able to suppress, as she would never have a claim to any ownership of the copyright. Now that he has passed on, it may appear to you that my client should not have such a feeling of having a dog in this fight. Nevertheless, there is a manifest injustice in your client seeking to do something procedurally, which she could never do substantively. She is attempting to take the dying words of this man as her own property, despite no intention by him to grant her any such right. Then, she is attempting to use that right in order to erase his expression from any further public existence.

I personally take no position on whether what Mr. Mackney had to say is true, or just. I am certain Mrs. Mackney has a side of the story as well. I do not wish to be uncompassionate toward her or her family. She certainly has the ability to rebut everything he had to say in that letter, if she wishes to do so. In fact, I find it difficult to believe that she would not be granted an interview with almost any journalist with whom she sought an audience. Further, she could seemingly express herself continuously, and without being challenged by Mr. Mackney, by virtue of the fact that he is no longer with us. Accordingly, it seems there is equal opportunity for her to promote her side of the story, without engaging in the somewhat horrific act of attempting to turn this dead man into a non-person, and squelching everything he had to say while he was in this world, including his dying words.

6. Conclusion

We are not insensitive to some of the more heart-wrenching elements of this case. In fact, prior to engaging you, my client and I engaged in the exercise of considering the effect of this case upon Mr. Mackney's family, including his minor children. With our compassion sensors deployed, it was our determination that not only does Mr. Mackney have a right to continue to speak from beyond the grave, not only does society have an interest in hearing what he had to say, but his children have an interest in maintaining that their father not be wiped from the

Michael Volpe

slate of existence, simply because their mother was creative enough to attempt to use intellectual property law to smother his voice after his death.

If she believes that what she is doing is in her children's best interest, we would suggest that at some point during this dispute, not only should the intellectual property issues be questioned, but there

2 We do not wish to mislead you into thinking that we could only bring this as a counterclaim. My client reserves the right to bring this as an independent claim, and is considering doing so should also be representation ad litem for both the children and Mr. Mackney's continuing First Amendment rights.

We would also like to note that any republication of Mr. Mackney's letter was fading well into obscurity before your client attempted to suppress it from publication. At this point, the matter has taken on a life of its own, beyond anything it might have had before this ill-considered attempt at censorship. You may wish to consider this, prior to following through on any actual or implied threats to attempt to litigate this matter. We can assure you we are prepared to litigate the matter, and we will not rest for as long these efforts to silence Mr. Mackney remain intact.

Best regards,

Marc J. Randazza

cc: Mark Bennett